CONTENTS

2 The Basics 15

3 URLs and Links 57

HTML 3.0 CD with JavaScript

For the Mac and Power Mac

VIVIAN NEOU

•

MIMI RECKER

For book and bookstore information
http://www.prenhall.com

Prentice Hall PTR
Upper Saddle River, New Jersey 07458

Library of Congress Cataloging-in-Publication Data

Neou, Vivian.
HTML 3.0 CD with JavaScript for the Mac / Vivian Neou, Mimi Recker.
p. cm.
Includes index.
ISBN 0-13-439399-6
1. HTML (Document markup language) 2. Java (Computer program language)
I. Recker, Mimi. II. Title
QA76.76.H94N43 1996 96-2835
005.75--dc20 CIP

Editorial/Production Supervision: Lisa Iarkowski
Interior Design: Gail Cocker-Bogusz
Acquisitions Editor: Mary Franz
Manufacturing Manager: Alexis R. Heydt
Cover Design Director: Jerry Votta
Cover Design: Anthony Gemmellaro

Prentice-Hall, Inc.
A Simon & Schuster Company
Upper Saddle River, NJ 07458

The publisher offers discounts on this book when ordered in bulk quantities.
For more information, contact:

Corporate Sales Department
PTR Prentice Hall
One Lake Street
Upper Saddle River, NJ 07458
Phone: 800-382-3419
FAX: 201-236-7141
e-mail: corpsales@prenhall.com

Printed in the United States of America

10 9 8 7 6 5 4 3 2 1

ISBN 0-13-439399-6

Prentice-Hall International (UK) Limited, London
Prentice-Hall of Australia Pty. Limited, Sydney
Prentice-Hall of Canada, Inc., Toronto
Prentice-Hall Hispanoamericana S.A., Mexico
Prentice-Hall of India Private Limited, New Delhi
Prentice-Hall of Japan, Inc., Tokyo
Simon & Schuster Asia Pte. Ltd., Singapore
Editora Prentice-Hall do Brasil, Ltd., Rio de Janeiro

ACKNOWLEDGMENTS

The authors both gratefully acknowledge the following people for granting permission to include their software with this book: Kris Coppieters (TextToHTML), John Cope (HTML ColorMeister), Norman Franke (SoundApp), Niklas Frykholm (HTML Pro), Rick Giles (HTML Editor), Maynard Handley (Sparkle), Peter Hardman (wwwstat4mac), Michael Herrick (HTML Grinder), Rik Jones (Site Writer Pro), Pete Keleher (Alpha), Scott Kleper (HTML Markup and HTML Markdown), Thorsten Lemke (GraphicConverter), Bill Melotti (httpd4mac), Kevin Mitchell (Gif Converter), Eric Lease Morgan (Email.acgi), Terje Norderhaug (Interaction), Jochen Schales (Webtor), and Lutz Weimann (Mac-Imagemap). We also thank Yves Piguet for answering questions about GifBuilder.

We would also like to thank our readers: Dr. Stephen J. Marshall, Eric Lease Morgan, Thomas Stiehm. Their insights helped to make this book more useful and understandable. We would

like to thank our more adventurous friends for contributing lively source materials: Jim Herson, Neil Larsen, and Nancy Marx. Ray Curiel helped with the JavaScript chapter, and reviewed many pieces of the book. Tomás and Alejandro Neou-Curiel contributed the artwork for the KidArt Gallery. Our editor, Mary Franz, and our production supervisor, Lisa Iarkowski, guided this book through the production process.

Mimi would like to thank Jim Pitkow for sharing his enthusiasm for and in-depth knowledge of the Web, and Marina Volkov for commenting on early writing. Her thanks go to the warm folks at the UTDC, Victoria University of Wellington (Cedric Hall, Joanna Kidman, Lorna Murray, and Iivi Turner) for maintaining her sanity by dragging her away from her keyboard for those all-important tea breaks. She would also like to thank her parents, Dede and Bruce, for continual support and encouragement.

Vivian would not have been able to write her portion of the book were it not for her husband, Ray Curiel, and his willingness to take care of the important things in life while she worked on this book. And of course thanks to "the important things in life," her kids, Tomás and Alejandro, for occasionally allowing her to write.

INTRODUCTION

When Thomas Jefferson first conceived of public libraries, he could not have imagined a world where people would have instant access to vast, globally distributed repositories of information. Today, the Internet is making this possibility a desktop reality. However, until recently much of the information on the Internet was difficult to locate and use. Fortunately, the World Wide Web and its browsers, such as Mosaic and Netscape, are leading the way in providing easy-to-use, seamless methods for navigating, and finding information on, the Internet.

The World Wide Web, commonly known as the Web, has made many gigabytes of digital data available to Internet users with a few mouse clicks. Data on the Web consists of documents. These documents, sometimes called Web pages, may contain text, images, video, audio, even executable programs. The Web is thus called a multimedia system. In addition, Web documents often have embedded cross-references or *links* to

other Web documents. This automatic cross-linking of documents to other relevant documents is called hypertext. Because the Web links data presented in many media, it is called a hypermedia system.

For example, a document on the Web about tandem bicycles may include pictures of the author's bicycle, a recording of *A Bicycle Built for Two,* and some information about spoke tension in wheels. The author of the document may know of another document located somewhere on the Internet that has extensive information about bicycle wheels. Rather than quoting the other document or merely listing its location, the author of the tandem document makes a link to the document about wheels. Now, when reading the tandem document, the reader can click (or issue the appropriate command) on the link to view the wheel document.

Documents on the Web such as the one we just described are written in HyperText Markup Language (HTML). If you want to make your own documents available through the Web, you need to learn how to use this language. HTML conforms to the Standard Generalized Markup Language (SGML) standard, which is an international standard (ISO 8879) for defining structured document types and the markup languages used to represent those document types.

In addition to HTML Version 2, this book covers what is commonly known as HTML Version 3. This version of HTML is still under discussion by the standards committee, but many of the planned features for this version are so useful that many browsers already support them. Thus, although HTML 3 is still evolving, we have included information about those elements that are already in use. We also cover the Netscape extensions to HTML and provide an introduction to JavaScript.

Who Needs HTML?

The most obvious use for HTML documents is to make information available on the Internet. The World Wide Web is the fastest growing Internet resource, and HTML is its "language." This book will provide guidance for your HTML project—whether you are writing an extensive document to advertise your company's products or want to link some personal documents into the Web.

Even if you do not plan to publish documents on the Internet, HTML can still be useful. Documents written in HTML can be viewed on almost all computer platforms thanks to the vast number of WWW browsers available (both free and commercial versions) for almost every type of computer system. Thus, HTML is an excellent choice for authoring on-line manuals or company documents for in-house use.

What This Book Can Do for You

By the time you are done reading this book, you should be able to write sophisticated, snazzy-looking documents in HTML. You'll learn about all the basic formatting commands, as well as how to use links and forms. We'll also teach you how to add pictures and sound to your documents. We go beyond the plain mechanics of HTML document creation—we also show you how to organize and lay out your documents so that they look as good as possible.

But that's not all! We also show you how to convert existing documents into HTML. You will learn how to set up a Web server so that you can publish your HTML documents on the Web. Best of all, you will find the tools to do all of these things on the included CD—you don't need to get anything else to produce and publish HTML documents.

Conventions Used in This Book

When we refer to actions within browsers, we will say to "click" on the item. If you are not using a mouse with your browser (for example, if you are using a line-mode browser), you should use the command that is equivalent to "clicking" on an item with a mouse.

We use a couple of icons throughout the book to point out important information:

We use this *tips* icon to point out useful tips and tricks. You should pay close attention when you see this icon.

We use this *warning* icon to draw your attention to areas where you can get into trouble. Follow our advice to keep from drowning in the rapids!

In chapters where HTML elements are discussed, we close with a section called *The Good, the Bad and the Ugly*. In these sections you will find a summary of the design tips and warnings introduced in the chapter.

Freeware and Shareware

This book comes with a cornucopia of freeware and shareware HTML tools. Before using the software on the CD, you should understand the difference between these two types of software. Freeware is just that—free. It is software that generous programmers have made publicly available. Since the software is free, there is usually no support for it, although some authors welcome comments. Shareware lies between commercial software and freeware. Shareware authors make their work available for evaluation purposes. If you try out a shareware package and decide to use it, you will need to register the package. Registration usually includes product support, and may include additional manuals. Registration details for each package are available with each package.

Contents of the CD

This book comes with a cornucopia of HTML tools. You will find everything you need to turn a Macintosh into a complete HTML authoring and publishing system—even servers and connectivity tools that will enable you to publish your HTML documents on the Internet. Here's a summary of the CD's contents.

HTML Editors

- ***Alpha***
- ***HTML Editor***
- ***HTML Pro***
- ***Site Writer Pro***
- ***Webtor***

HTTP Servers and Associated Software

- ***Interaction***, a collaborative add-on for MacHTTP
- ***Mac-Imagemap***, an image map processor for MacHTTP

- ***Email.acgi***, a forms-processing script
- ***httpd4Mac***, a freeware HTTP server
- ***wwwstat4Mac***, a log file processing program for use with httpd4Mac

HTML Converters and Maintenance Tools

- ***HTML Markdown***, a shareware tool for removing HTML tags from a document
- ***HTML Markup***, a shareware tool to add HTML tags to a plain text document
- ***TextToHTML***, a freeware tool to add HTML tags to a plain text or RTF document
- ***HTML Grinder***, a multipurpose HTML document set maintenance tool

Utilities

- ***HTML ColorMeister***, a color picker for setting background, text and link colors
- ***WebMap***, an image-map maker
- ***Sparkle***, an MPEG and Quicktime player and converter
- ***SoundApp***, a sound file player
- ***GraphicConverter***, an image manipulation tool
- ***GifConverter***, a tool to convert images between formats
- ***MacPerl***, a popular interpreted language for CGI applications

HTML Document Treasure Chest

One of the best ways to learn about HTML is to look at HTML documents. We've provided a "treasure chest" of HTML pages, including:

- Templates for personal home pages
- Sample business home page templates

- JavaScript examples
- HTML element demonstration pages so you can see how different HTML elements look in different browsers
- Form templates (order forms and response forms)
- HTML document to download over 10 Windows Web browsers—including Mosaic, Netscape, Interlink and more
- Free icons and images

and much more!

We have incorporated real links to documents on the Internet in some of the documents. These links all worked at the time the documents were written. However, the Internet is constantly changing, and since documents often move or are deleted, we cannot guarantee that all of the links will work when you try them.

What You Should Know

This book will teach you everything you need to know about HTML. Before starting this book you should already have a basic understanding of the Internet and World Wide Web. Although we will go over some basic Internet and Web applications in this book, you should get and read one of the general reference books on the Internet if you plan to do HTML publishing on the Internet.

However, you may just want to use HTML to develop in-house documentation or information manuals; for that, you should find everything you need in this book.

IN THIS CHAPTER YOU WILL LEARN

- HOW HTML ALLOWS YOU TO PUBLISH MULTIMEDIA DOCUMENTS ON THE WORLD WIDE WEB
- HOW HTML AND DOCUMENT DISPLAY VARIES AMONG WEB BROWSERS
- HOW TO DOWNLOAD A VARIETY OF WEB BROWSERS

THE WORLD WIDE WEB AND BROWSERS

What's In This Chapter

In this chapter we will explain more about the World Wide Web and its relation to HTML. We'll explain how HTML is dependent on Web browsers. We will also explain how to download a variety of Web browsers on the Internet using the browser document included on the CD. If you are already familiar with the Web and Web browsers, skip to the section on the HTML templates on the CD at the end of this chapter.

HTML and the Internet

As we mentioned in the introduction, HTML is a hypermedia document description language used to publish documents on

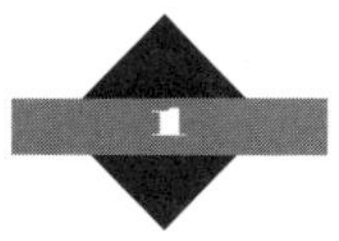

the World Wide Web. Since the Web spans the Internet, and the Internet is a global network, HTML documents can be, and frequently are, connected internationally. You might think of HTML documents as looking something like Figure 1–1.

From a practical standpoint this means that if you live in California and a colleague lives in New Zealand, the two of you could publish your work together—even though your portion of the work remains on a computer in California and your colleague's on a computer in New Zealand. How? It's simple—by using *links* to join your pieces of the work together. Thanks to the seamless integration of documents on the Web, your readers would not be affected by the geographic separation of the physical pieces of actual work (although they may notice differences in transmission times between different pieces of the document).

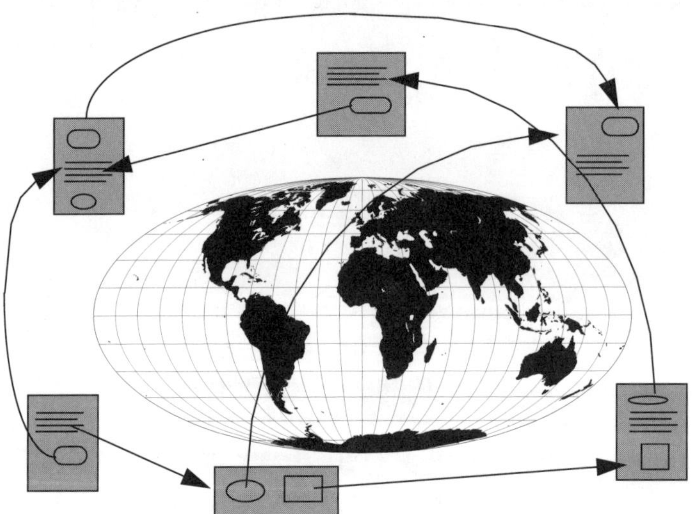

FIGURE 1–1 *HTML Documents on the Internet*

Let's look at a hypothetical set of documents in HTML to get a better understanding of how all of this fits together. It's time to introduce you to Kelly Kayaker. We will be developing a set of HTML pages for Kelly in this book to illustrate how HTML works. Kelly's pages can be found on the CD, so you can use them as templates for your own HTML projects.

First, let us give you a little background on Kelly. She writes travel books for a small publishing company named Ozone Books. Kelly lives in Canada, and Ozone is based in New Zealand. Kelly will be breaking new ground for Ozone by developing a document on kayaking that will be published on the Web. Ozone is also planning to begin selling books on the Internet.

One part of Kelly's book will consist of pictures and descriptions of hot kayaking spots. She has friends all over the world who are helping her with these descriptions. Some of these friends would like to provide seasonal updates of their descriptions, so they want to keep their portions of the document on their own computers. Kelly is also planning to let people who read her document add comments to a "guest book." As a result, Kelly's document will be in pieces that are linked in this fashion:

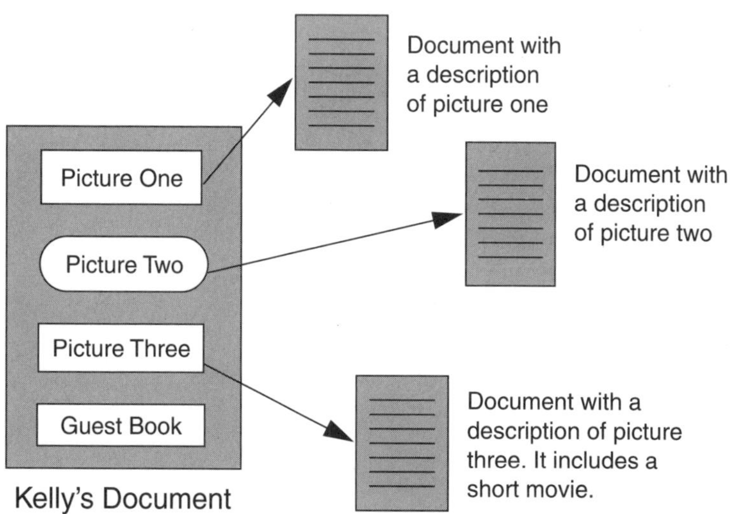

When readers look at Kelly's document with a browser (we'll tell you more about browsers in the next section), they will see a page of pictures. To read the descriptions that correspond to

the pictures, the reader clicks on the picture, and the browser then gets the document with the description and displays it. The documents with the descriptions do not have to be on the same computer as Kelly's picture document—they don't even have to be the same type of computer! Even though the actual pieces of the work may be scattered on different computers all around the world, from the reader's standpoint the document is a single, cohesive piece of work.

The guest book will appear as a form, and people reading the document will have the opportunity to sign in and leave comments about it.

Browsers

We've mentioned browsers a number of times. Where do they fit into the picture? Browsers are the applications used to display HTML and other kinds of formatted documents. They understand HTML commands and interpret the commands to format the document for display. Although there are many types of browsers now, the first widely used graphical browser was Mosaic from the National Center for Supercomputing Applications. Currently Netscape Navigator from Netscape Communications—a browser with roots from members of the NCSA team—is acknowledged as the most popular browser. As a result, many people now refer to Web browsers as "Netscape," although Netscape is actually just the name of one type of Web browser. Figure 1–2 shows how the Web browser fits into the Web.

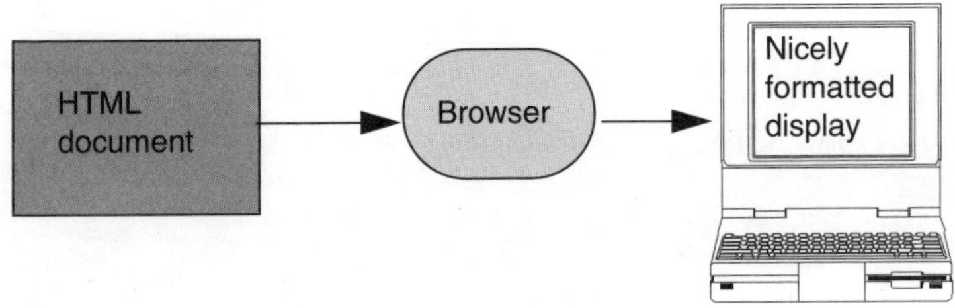

FIGURE 1–2 *Web Browser*

If you are already familiar with the Web, you may be thinking, "Hey, they left something out!" You are right. Figure 1–2 illustrates the flow of information for a local on-line help system and local review of HTML files (for example, you will probably use a browser to review your document before publishing it on the Internet). There is another piece in this picture, the Web server. If your eyes are starting to glaze over because you thought you were going to learn about HTML in this book, not computer networking, please stick with us. You actually need to know this to effectively use HTML. We'll keep the networking stuff short and simple.

Browsers are applications called *clients.* They get most of their information from *servers.* We say most rather than all because browsers can get their information directly from local files, as illustrated in Figure 1–2. Servers are the applications that allow HTML files to be linked across the network. A Web server is a program that waits for requests to get documents; when it receives a request, it gets the appropriate document and sends it to the browser that made the request. Requests can come from the computer the server is on, or from computers on the other side of the world. The server doesn't care—as long as the request is valid, it will return the requested document. Figure 1–3 shows the flow of information when HTML documents are shared across a network.

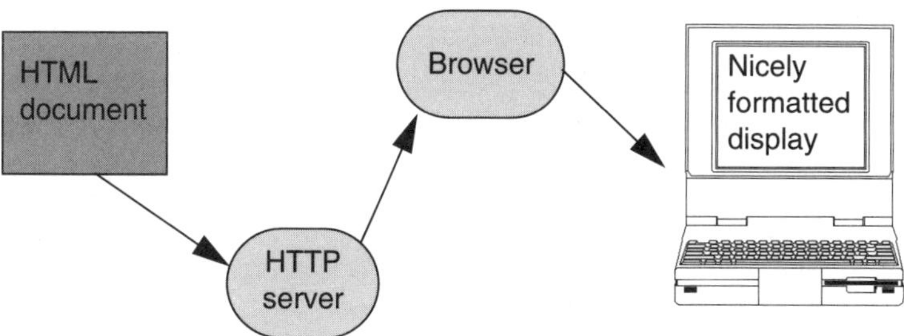

FIGURE 1–3 *Web Browser and Server*

Web servers talk to browsers by using a network protocol called the Hypertext Transport Protocol (HTTP). Protocols are the languages used by different applications on networks to talk to each other. Although HTTP is the primary protocol used to support the Web, Web browsers can actually get information from other types of servers that use different protocols, such as FTP, mail or gopher. As a result, you can put links in your HTML documents that will allow your readers to download documents and applications or to make a telnet connection to another computer. We'll explain how to do this in the section on Uniform Resource Locators (URLs) in "URLs and Links" on page 57.

Whew. That was a lot of jargon and acronyms. But now we're done with the network for a little while. Let's take a closer look at browsers.

HTML and Browsers

HTML is used to define the *structure* of a document. However, the browser used to display the document dictates how each structural element should be rendered. *Although general element display guidelines are provided in the HTML specification, in practice there is wide variation in display between browsers.*

Browsers also vary widely in their recognition of HTML elements. Most browsers try to support Version 2 of HTML; some browsers do not recognize anything above Version 1, while others (most notably Netscape Navigator) use vendor-specific extensions to HTML. To muddy things even further, most browsers are also willing to accept documents that violate all of the specifications for HTML. When a browser encounters a noncompliant document, it will typically ignore noncompliant portions of the document and do its best to interpret the rest.

In other words, there is nothing to force you to write HTML documents that fully adhere to any of the HTML specifications. In fact, if you are writing for an audience that will be using a specific browser (for example, you may be writing in-house documentation for which your company has chosen a specific browser), you may want to become familiar with the way that browser handles HTML so you can tailor your documents in an appropriate fashion. However, if you are writing documents that will be published on the Internet, you will need to make sure that your documents look okay on a broad range of browsers.

To complicate things even more, the same browser may have different features or slightly different ways of doing things from platform to platform. There are also differences between the way that the same browser may do things from one version of the browser to the next. While there is still much debate about which browser is used by which percentage of the Internet population, at the time this book was written the most popular browser was widely recognized as being Netscape Navigator, and the most popular platform was Windows.

To help you understand how much variation there is between browsers, we will show you pages in different browsers in cases where there are significant differences between browsers. We have also provided a document on the CD that will help you locate and download a wide variety of browsers across the Internet. We urge you to install at least two or three browsers to review your documents.

As an incentive, let's take a quick look at the way different browsers display a simple HTML document. The HTML source we will display is this:

```
<P>The logical tags in HTML are:
<DL>
<DT><STRONG>Citation:&lt;CITE&gt;</STRONG>
<DD><CITE>This paragraph is in a citation tag, and is
typically rendered in an italic font.</CITE>
<DT><STRONG>Code: &lt;CODE&gt;</STRONG>
<DD><CODE>CODE is intended for code examples, and is
typically displayed in a fixed-width font.</CODE>
<DT><STRONG>Emphasis: &lt;EM&gt;</STRONG>
<DD><EM>This paragraph is in an emphasis tag. It is usually
displayed in italics.</EM>
<DT><STRONG>Keyboard: &lt;KBD&gt; </STRONG>
<DD><KBD>This paragraph is in a keyboard tag. It is typically
displayed in a fixed-width font.</KBD>
<DT><STRONG>Sample: &lt;SAMP&gt;</STRONG>
<DD><SAMPLE>This paragraph is in a sample tag. The sample tag
is intended for sequences of literal characters and is
typically displayed in a fixed-width font.</SAMPLE>
<DT><STRONG>Emphasis: &lt;STRONG&gt;</STRONG>
<DD><STRONG>Strong Emphasis. It is usually displayed in a
boldface font.</STRONG>
<DT><STRONG>Variable Name: &lt;VAR&gt;</STRONG>
<DD><VAR>Variable Name. This is intended for variable names,
and is typically displayed in an italic font.</VAR>
</DL>
```

Now let's see how it looks in different browsers.

Netscape

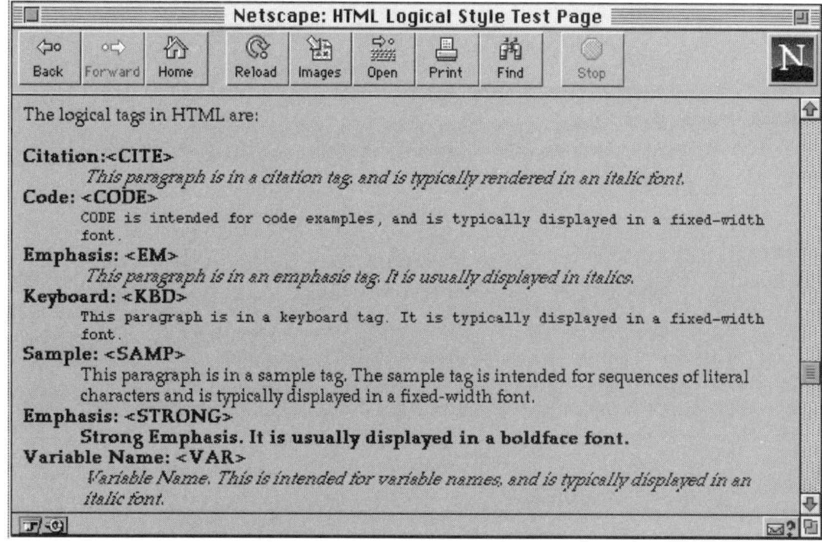

Microsoft Internet Explorer

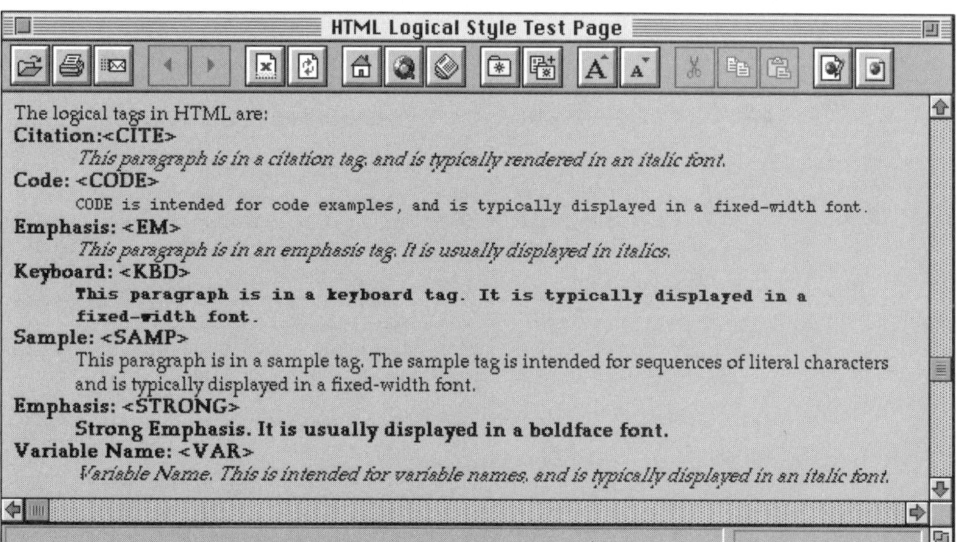

Lynx (A line-mode browser)

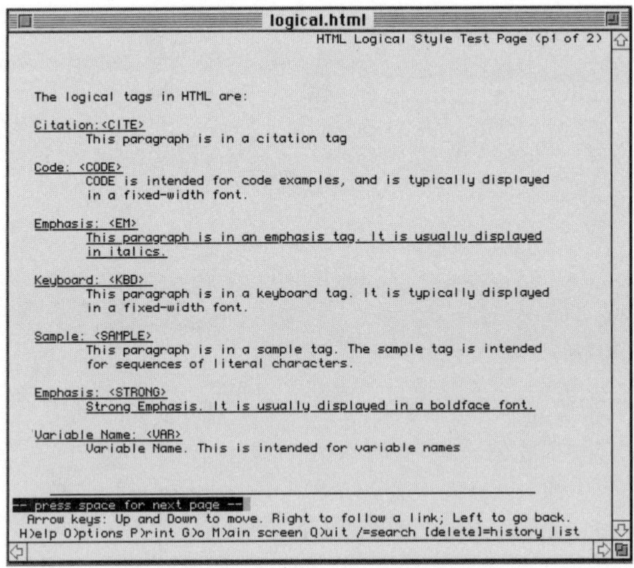

MacWeb (EiNET)

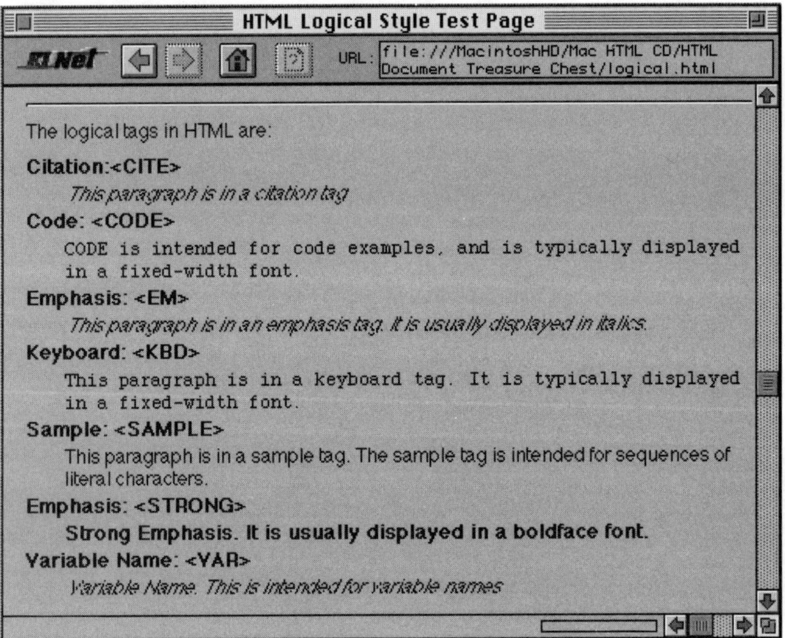

NCSA Mosaic

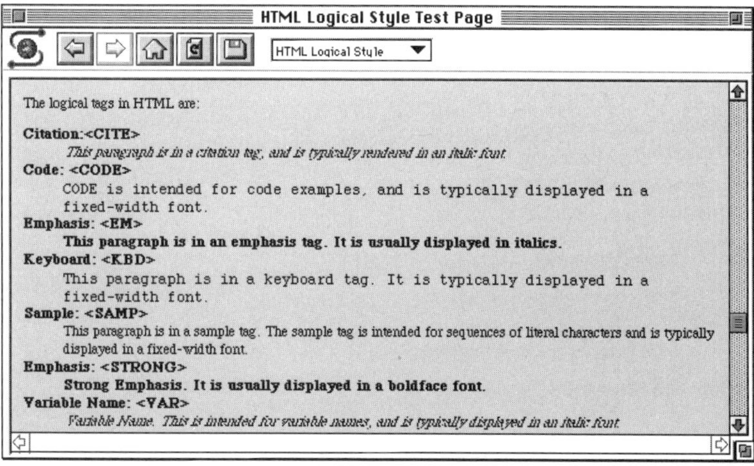

As you can see, these browsers display the same simple document in a variety of ways. From the background to line spacing to the fonts, you cannot count on anything to be consistent between browsers.

Compare the Lynx display with the graphical browsers. If you've only used a graphical browser, the way that a document looks in a line-mode browser may seem like going back to the dark ages. However, as a designer of Web pages, it is important for you to keep line-mode browsers in mind. There are still many people using these types of browsers—for example, in the libraries in San Francisco, California, there is public Web access—but only through line-mode browsers.

Many browsers also allow users to customize the way that various HTML elements are displayed, causing even greater discrepancies between the way a document may be displayed from one browser to another. For example, compare the following display of our document in Netscape with the way that Netscape displayed it on page 9.

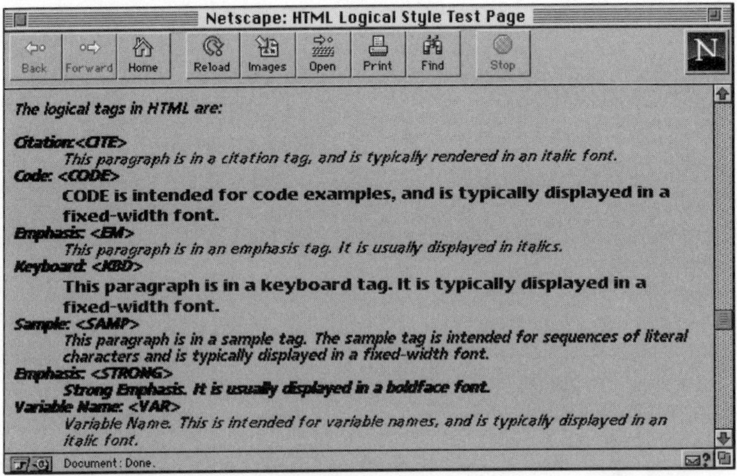

In more complex documents, especially ones that incorporate multimedia elements, the differences between browsers become even more pronounced. Unfortunately, there is no simple solution to this problem. As we introduce new HTML elements, we make design recommendations that will help you to author documents that will look good regardless of the browser used to display them.

You can preview your document in most browsers by specifying the Open Local *or* Open File *command, which can usually be found in the* File *menu.* This allows you to see your document as it is being developed and to correct potential errors. If you find a problem, correct it within the editing environment. Then use the *Reload* command to see if your changes have fixed the problem.

Getting Browsers

If you do not have any browsers, or only one, you are probably anxious to get some more now. We've included a browser document on the CD that will help you to locate a number of Mac browsers including:

- NCSA Mosaic
- Netscape Navigator
- Microsoft Internet Explorer
- MacWeb

Since Windows is the most popular Internet platform, you should try to check your documents on a Windows system as well. Our browser document includes information on downloading these Windows browsers:

- NCSA Mosaic
- Netscape Navigator
- SPRYNET Mosaic
- Cello from Cornell Law School
- Microsoft Internet Explorer
- Winweb from Trade Wave (formerly EINet)
- Oracle's PowerBrowser
- Quarterdeck Mosaic
- SlipKnot

A line-mode browser for DOS, Unix or VMS:

- Lynx

To download most of these packages, all you need to do is load browser.html into your favorite browser. You will see the list of browsers along with some information about each one. When you choose the link in a browser's description, either the browser will be downloaded to your system, or you will be placed at a homepage for the browser that will provide you with information about the browser and an opportunity to download it.

Now let's see how to start an HTML document.

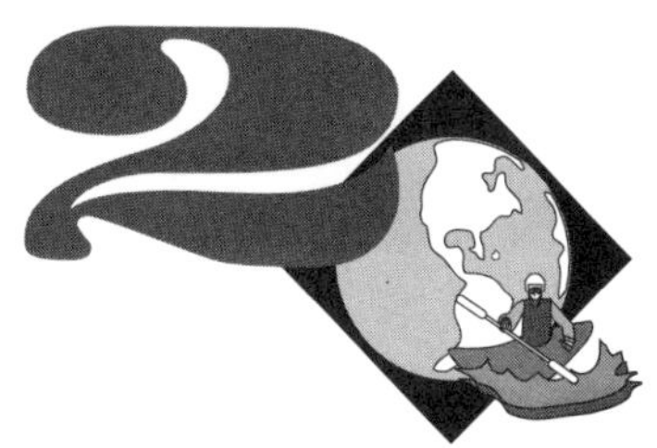

In this chapter you will learn

- How to author a basic HTML document
- How to use basic HTML commands
- How to use Netscape extensions to these commands
- How basic HTML elements look in a browser

The Basics

What's In This Chapter

This chapter shows you how to create a basic HTML document. It discusses setting up your document and introduces the basic formatting commands. We also describe Netscape extensions to these commands.

Creating an HTML Document

HTML documents are written in plain text (ASCII). There are a number of ways to create an HTML document:

1. You can use your favorite editor and add in the HTML commands yourself.
2. You can use an HTML editor that inserts the commands in the appropriate locations for you.
3. You can also use a conversion utility that takes a document from some other format and converts it to HTML.

We discuss all of these methods in this book. We start with the text editor method, since it is important to understand how HTML works, even if you do use a system that inserts HTML commands for you.

The first step is to create a file to hold your HTML document. On a Macintosh you need to create a file with the *.html* file extension. *Browsers and servers make some decisions on the way they deal with documents based on the file extension, so it is important to choose the correct extension for your document.*

In this chapter we will author a document on the sport of kayaking as an example. Hence, we call this file, kayak.html. We have included a copy of this document on the CD.

Document Tags: <HTML>, <HEAD>, and <BODY>

Several tags do not affect the presentation of documents but convey important information to browsers and users. As you will find, most browsers do not complain if you forget to put these tags in your document, but it is safer to include them.

First, HTML documents should contain an <HTML> tag. Note that the document should have a corresponding </HTML> at the end. HTML is *not* case sensitive. <HTML> is treated the same as <html> or <HtMl>.

The document should be organized into <HEAD> and <BODY> sections. Like an electronic mail message, the <HEAD> tags surround the introductory section, while the <BODY> tags surround the main part of the document.

Although these tags do not affect the presentation of a document, they are important. The HTTP protocol includes a "HEAD" command, which returns the information included in the head of a document. Although most browsers do not currently use this feature, many Web-searching robots use it to build their databases. If you want your documents to be catalogued in an understandable fashion, make sure that you include a HEAD section.

The TITLE element in a document must occur within the <HEAD> tags of the document, and it is the only element that goes in the head section. Within the <BODY>, the document can be structured in paragraphs, lists and so on, using HTML tags. The basic framework for our kayak document is shown in Figure 2–1.

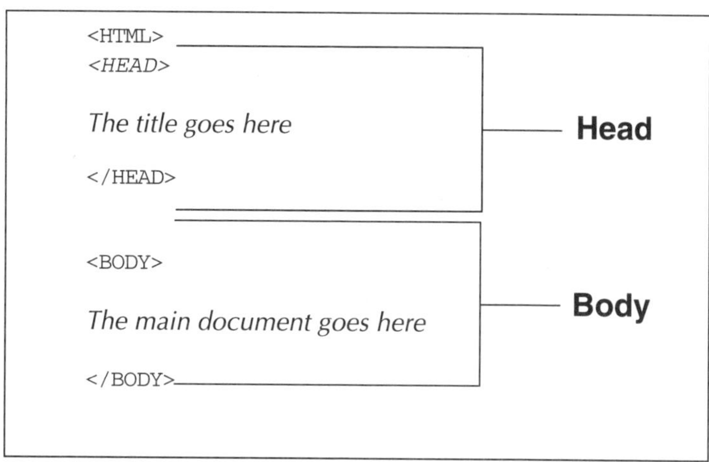

FIGURE 2–1 Basic Document Framework

Document Type: <!DOCTYPE>

In theory, every HTML document should begin with a document type identifier. This statement should be placed before the <HTML> tag and contain information about the version of HTML used in the document. For example, the official document type declaration for HTML 2 is:

```
<!DOCTYPE HTML PUBLIC "-//IETF//DTD HTML 2.0//EN">
```

This tag is intended to help browsers make useful inferences about the type of tags it will find in the document. Unfortunately, in practice using DOCTYPE can be difficult. As a result of the intensive development work going on with the HTML language, there are many variations of HTML—including vendor-specific extensions—and evolving official standards. Some of these extensions do not have official DOCTYPEs. Additionally, some documents include a mix of extensions from different sources. In these cases, it is almost impossible to decide which DOCTYPE to use.

However, it is likely that you have seen or will eventually see it in an HTML document, especially since some HTML editors automatically add it to the documents that they create. We mention DOCTYPE here primarily so that you will know what it is when you encounter it.

Markup Tags

If you've used a WYSIWYG (What You See Is What You Get) word processing program such as Microsoft Word, you have probably formatted your documents so that some words are displayed in italics or boldface. You have also probably designated portions of your text as titles, headings or lists.

HTML provides some of this functionality for documents that are published on the Internet. However, there is a significant difference between HTML and a WYSIWYG word processing system. Like many word processing systems, HTML allows you to define the *structure* of a document—you can specify such things as lists, titles, headings and so forth. However, the way these things will be displayed to the reader is determined by the browser used to display the document.

If you like to have complete control over the look of your document (for example, adjusting font sizes, or placing text on the page in a specific location), you will probably find working with HTML a bit frustrating. HTML was designed so that authors could mark up the text in documents to indicate *types* of text. However, since HTML was designed to allow the same document to be meaningfully displayed on a wide variety of platforms with vastly different capabilities, it is left up to the browser (which understands the limitations and abilities of the platform on which it is running) to decide how each type of text will be displayed.

Thus, you cannot specify that text should be displayed in a 9-point Courier font, or that an item designated as a heading will be centered and displayed in a bold 20-point font. These decisions are left up to the browser—and, as you will see, even on the same platform there is wide variation in how different browsers display the same document. In Chapter 3 we will provide some guidelines to make your documents look as good as possible in the wide variety of browsers that may be used to display them. But first, let's look at how different types of text are defined in HTML.

HTML commands use *markup tags* to specify structural elements in a document. These tags tell the browser about the type of text being displayed, such as headers, titles, lists or plain text.

HTML markup tags consist of a left angle bracket (<), followed by the name of the tag, and then a right angle bracket (>). Tags usually come in pairs in order to act as *containers* of the affected text. The second tag in a pair looks just like the first, except that a slash precedes the name. This second tag tells the browser that the command is done. Thus, an HTML statement looks something like this:

```
<TagName>Some Text</TagName>
```

Title: <TITLE>

The first essential item you should include in an HTML document is a title. We start our document with this title line:

```
<TITLE>The Sport of Kayaking</TITLE>
```

As you can see in this example, the markup tags for the title are <TITLE> and </TITLE>. Of course, since HTML is not case sensitive, we could have written our tags in lower-case:

```
<title>The Sport of Kayaking</title>
```

We will use upper-case letters in the rest of our examples, but it is fine to use lower-case tags if you prefer. In the above example, the title of the document is "The Sport of Kayaking." In Netscape Navigator it would look like this:

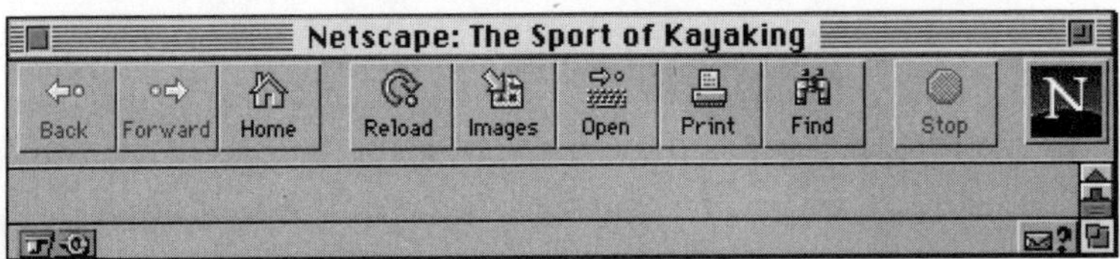

As you can see, Netscape, like most browsers, displays the title of a document in a special area of the window.

A DOCUMENT MAY HAVE ONLY ONE TITLE.

You should include only one title in your document. Including multiple TITLE tags in the same document not only violates the official HTML standard but also forces browsers to choose one tag to display since most do not have a place to display multiple titles.

You may have seen documents that violate this rule. Most such documents that we have encountered were due to an attempt by their authors to take advantage of an unfortunate feature in Version 1 of Netscape. This version allowed multiple title tags in a document to be displayed in succession in the title bar. Some writers took advantage of this feature by including titles such as:

```
<title>K</title>
<title>Ka</title>
<title>Kay</title>
<title>Kaya</title>
<title>Kayak</title>
<title>Kayaki</title>
<title>Kayakin</title>
<title>Kayaking</title>
```

in their documents. This would result in the title appearing to scroll into the title bar. Fortunately Netscape has corrected this problem in Version 2 of Navigator, which displays only the first title tag in the document. Authors trying to use the scrolling features will find that their documents appear with a single-letter title in newer versions of Netscape.

USE DESCRIPTIVE YET SUCCINCT TITLES.

Any HTML document should have a title that succinctly describes its contents. This title, like the title of a book, can be used by readers to decide if they wish to view the entire document. If the title is too generic, the reader will be unable to determine whether the document is of any interest. For example, a bad title would be:

```
<TITLE>Introduction</TITLE>
```

This title does not tell the reader anything about the contents of the document. Since links (we'll explain more about links in the next chapter) may be made to any document from any other document, this title makes it difficult for readers to decide whether the document contains information they want. A better title would be:

```
<TITLE>Introduction to Kayaking</TITLE>
```

The following two titles are also poor choices. Although they tell something about the content of the document, they are too general to be useful:

```
<TITLE>Security</TITLE>
<TITLE>Games</TITLE>
```

Better alternatives would be:

```
<TITLE>Computer Security Hints</TITLE>
<TITLE>Games on the Internet: MUDs</TITLE>
```

KEEP TITLES SHORT!
TITLES WITH NO MORE THAN FIVE OR SIX WORDS HAVE THE GREATEST IMPACT.

Although the HTML standard does not set a limit on the number of characters that may be included in a title, most browsers display only as much as will fit into the section of the window reserved for the title. This area is typically no longer than one line. If you keep your title under 64 characters, you can be reasonably well assured that it will fit into the allocated space.

DO NOT PLACE ANY MARKUP TAGS IN A TITLE!

A title may not contain anchors, highlighting or paragraph tags (these types of tags are described later). If you try to include these tags, the behavior from browser to browser is unpredictable (and, in most cases, undesirable). Some browsers may show the tags as part of the title, while others may actually pull the text out of the title area and display it as part of the document.

We've provided a document on the CD that deliberately violates the guidelines for good title composition. You can find the file in longtitle.html. Here's the beginning of the document:

```
<HTML>
<HEAD>
<TITLE>Here's a Title That Won't Show Up</TITLE>

<TITLE>This Is A Very Very <H1>Long Title</H1> That Tells You
Nothing About The Document And May Not Fit In The Area That
Browsers Set Up For Titles.</TITLE>

</HEAD>
<BODY>
<H1>Hints about Titles</H1>
<P>An HTML document can only have one title.</P>
```

And here's what happens when we load this document into Mosaic:

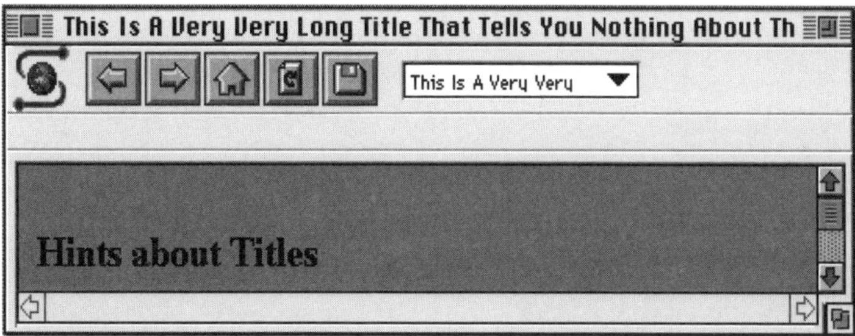

As you can see, our first title vanished without a trace, and the title that does show up is too long to fit into the title box. Of course, every browser will get confused in different ways when you violate the rules. Try loading this document into several different browsers and see for yourself.

Headings: <H1> through <H6>

Now we'll tell you about header tags. The next tag we use is H1:

```
<H1>White Water Kayaking</H1>
```

This is an example of a header tag, denoted by <H1>. The first header in our document is "White Water Kayaking." HTML allows you to specify up to six levels of headers, <H1> through <H6>. The first header, H1, is the largest, most prominent header. It is typically displayed in a large and bold font, while each subsequent header is displayed in an increasingly smaller size.

Here are how the six levels of headers look in Mosaic:

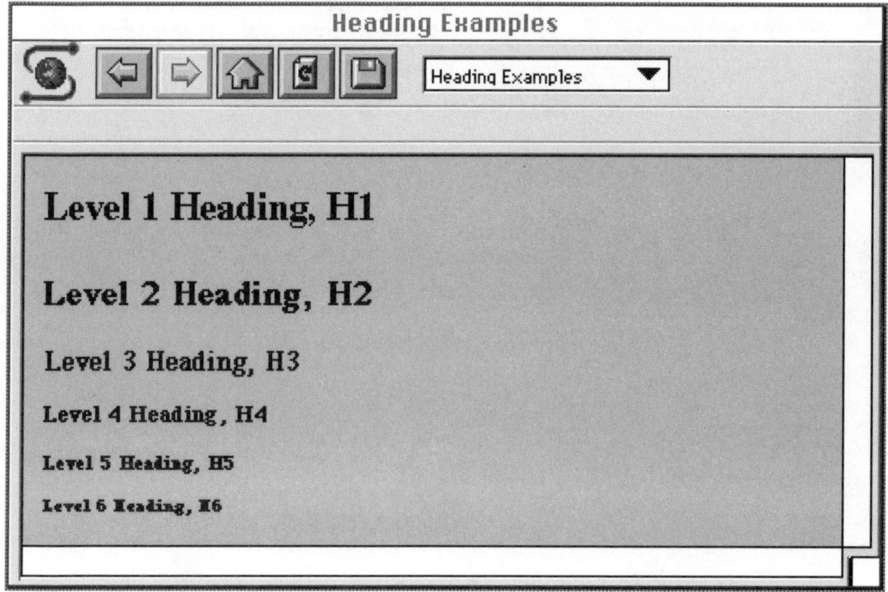

You can find this test document in heading.html on the CD. Try loading it in several browsers to see the difference in the ways various browsers choose to display headings.

Paragraphs: <P>

Now we want to include some general text:

```
<P>Kayaking is an outdoor sport, practiced by adrenaline
junkies, in which enthusiasts paddle wild rivers and creeks
in small, enclosed boats. Most people are a bit nervous the
first time they kayak.</P>
```

The <P> specifies a paragraph break. Unlike most tags, it is an example of an *empty container* since it does not require an end tag. HTML performs automatic word wrap in documents and ignores carriage returns. Therefore, you must explicitly signal paragraph breaks in text with the <P> tag. *If you do not include any paragraph breaks in your HTML text, it will appear as one long paragraph.* Some exceptions do exist, as we will explain later. Let's digress from our kayaking document for a moment to illustrate this point.

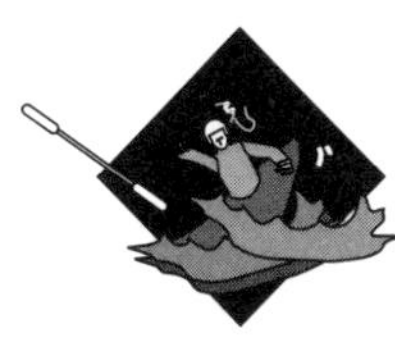

Let's look at a short and simple HTML document. The document source looks as if there should be three paragraphs. However, notice that there are no P tags in this document.

```
<HTML>
<HEAD>
<TITLE>Paragraph Break Test Document</TITLE>
<HEAD>
<BODY>
<H1>Paragraph Break Test Document</H1>
This document illustrates the need to include paragraph tags in
your HTML sources. If you do not include &lt;P&gt; tags in your
documents, your document will appear as one long paragraph
(perhaps with some breaks if you use other elements such as
lists or headers). This document does not include any P tags.

Although there is a blank line before this sentence in the HTML
source, there is no P tag, so the browser will not recognize
the start of a new paragraph. It should appear as one long
paragraph in your browser.

In HTML 2, there is no requirement to close a P tag. However,
it is good practice to do so since HTML 3 introduces extra
attributes for the P tag (such as center) that will work more
cleanly if P tags are closed.
</BODY>
</HTML>
```

Now let's see how it looks in NCSA Mosaic:

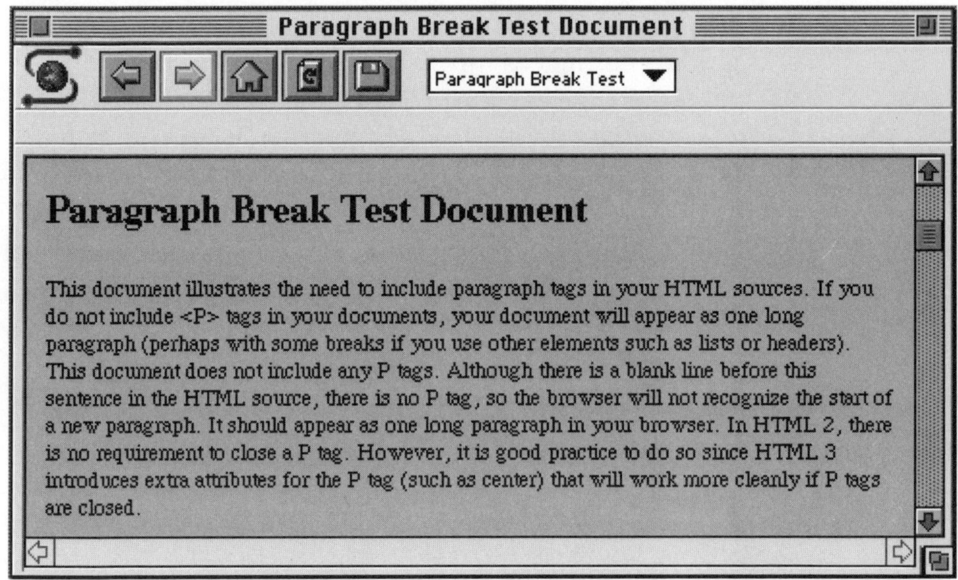

As you can see, the browser did not pay any attention to the blank lines in our HTML source and placed the whole document in one long paragraph.

In future versions of HTML, the paragraph markup tag will be extended to include alignment attributes. As a result, it will become a container, like most other tags (although, for compatibility with old documents, the requirement for a closing tag will not be enforced). Thus, a paragraph of text should be contained within <P> and </P> markers.

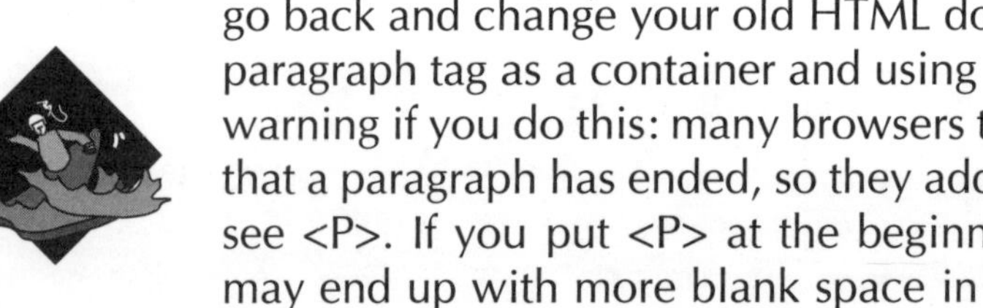

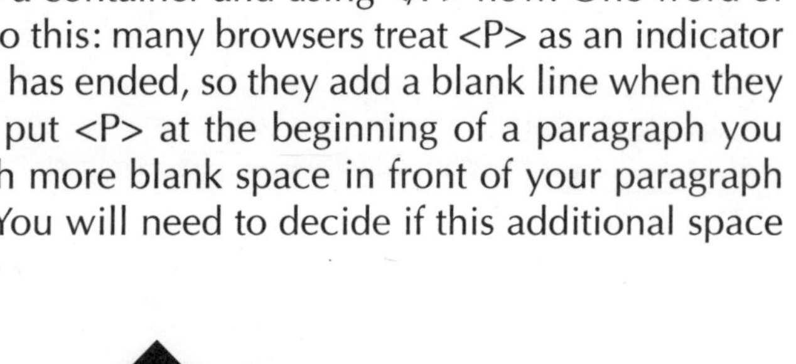

Since most browsers accept </P>, you can avoid having to go back and change your old HTML documents by treating the paragraph tag as a container and using </P> now. One word of warning if you do this: many browsers treat <P> as an indicator that a paragraph has ended, so they add a blank line when they see <P>. If you put <P> at the beginning of a paragraph you may end up with more blank space in front of your paragraph than you want. You will need to decide if this additional space is acceptable.

Text Alignment (HTML 3): ALIGN Attribute

In HTML 3 an ALIGN attribute has been defined for the paragraph tag that allows you to specify how the text is to be aligned. ALIGN may take one of four values: CENTER, LEFT, RIGHT, or JUSTIFY. We did not find any browsers that supported the JUSTIFY value, but the rest were supported in the latest version of the Netscape browser:

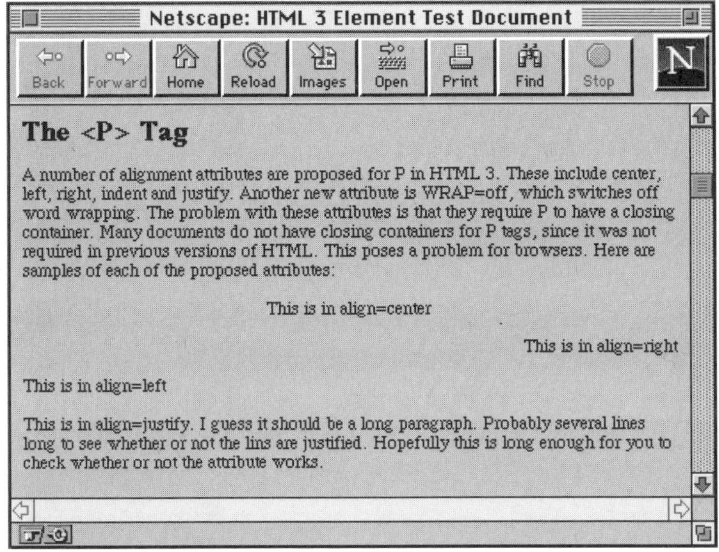

Horizontal Lines: <HR>

Sections between documents are often separated by a horizontal line that runs the length of the browser window. The <HR> tag produces a horizontal line in HTML. In our kayak document, we placed a line between the introductory paragraph and the rest of the document.

Netscape HR attributes

Netscape has added four custom attributes to the HR tag:

SIZE A number giving an indication of how thick the rule should be.

WIDTH	A number or percentage. The number is the number of pixels, the percentage is the width relative to the page size.
ALIGN	This may take one of three values: left, right or center (the default).
NOSHADE	Use a plain line—no shading.

It is easier to see an illustration than to go into detail on what each of these attributes does. Here are some samples:

```
A plain &lt;HR&gt;<HR>
&lt;HR SIZE=5&gt;<HR SIZE=5>
&lt;HR SIZE=50&gt;<HR SIZE=50>
&lt;HR WIDTH=200&gt;<HR WIDTH=200>
&lt;HR WIDTH=70%&gt;<HR WIDTH=70%>
&lt;HR WIDTH=70% ALIGN=LEFT&gt;<HR WIDTH=70% ALIGN=LEFT>
&lt;HR WIDTH=70% ALIGN=RIGHT&gt;<HR WIDTH=70% ALIGN=RIGHT>
&lt;HR NOSHADE&gt;<HR NOSHADE>
```

Notice that we have used symbol names for "<" and ">" so that each line in our example will be labeled with the tag used to make it. Let's see how this looks:

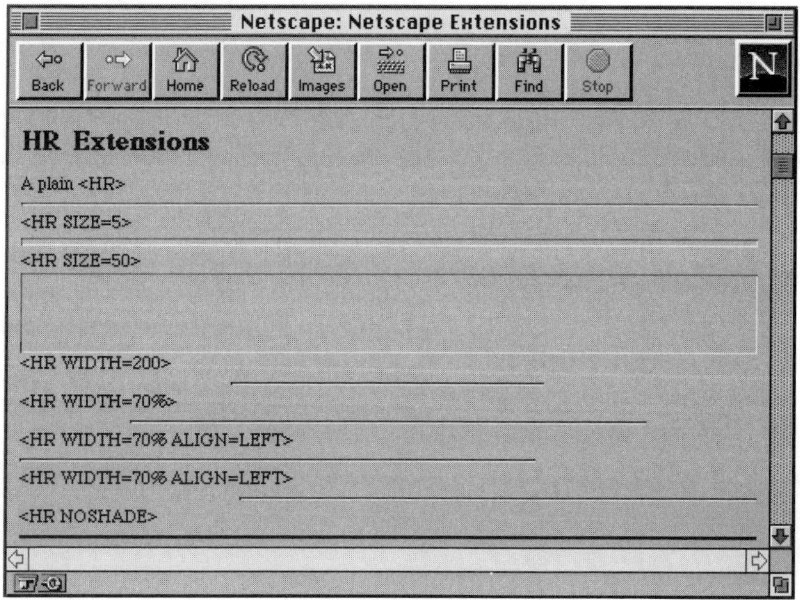

Lists

HTML provides several ways to display information in lists. These include:

- Unnumbered lists
- Numbered lists
- Menu lists
- Directory lists
- Definition lists

Specifying Items in Lists: <LI>

Lists share a common format. Like most HTML objects, they should start and end with the appropriate markup tags. However, the tags used to mark items within a list are empty container tags (like paragraph tags, they only need a start tag). For example:

```
<OL>
<LI>Paddles
<LI>Kayaks
</OL>
```

As you can see in this example, another markup tag is used to label each item in the list. With the exception of definition lists (which need two types of item tags since they have two types of items), items in lists are specified with the <LI> tag. You indicate that something is an item by starting it with the <LI> tag. Since this is an empty container tag, there is no need to close the item (although you can add a closing </LI> if you prefer).

With the exception of items in a directory list (which should be kept under 20 characters), items in a list can be longer than a single sentence. If you wish to have multiple paragraphs within a list item, don't forget to separate them with the <P> paragraph separator.

Creating a List

The process of creating a list is simple. Here are the basic steps:

1. *Begin with the opening list tag for the type of list you wish to create.*
2. *Enter the <LI> tag, followed by a list item.*
3. *Continue entering list items, with an <LI> tag preceding each item. No closing tag is needed for items.*
4. *End the list by typing the appropriate closing container tag for your list.*

Unnumbered Lists: <UL>

Unnumbered lists, which are also known as unordered lists, are typically displayed by browsers with a bullet in front of each item. The markup tags for unnumbered lists are <UL> and </UL>. For example, in our kayak.htm document, we would specify an unordered list as follows:

```
<P>There are many types of kayak paddles:</P>
<UL>
<LI>Feathered
<LI>Dihedral
<LI>Break-down
</UL>
```

When viewed with a browser, the above snippet would look like this:

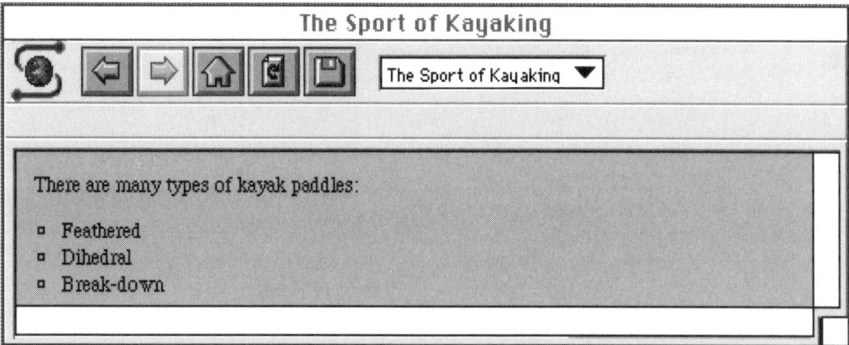

Netscape has added a TYPE attribute to unordered lists. This attribute allows you to specify the type of bullet you would like to use with your list. Possible values are DISC (the default), CIRCLE and SQUARE.

Here is an example:

```
<UL TYPE=DISC>
<LI>type=disc
<LI>Life
</UL>
<UL TYPE=CIRCLE>
<LI>type=circle
<LI>The Universe
</UL>
<UL TYPE=SQUARE>
<LI>type=square
<LI>Everything
</UL>
```

And here is how it looks.

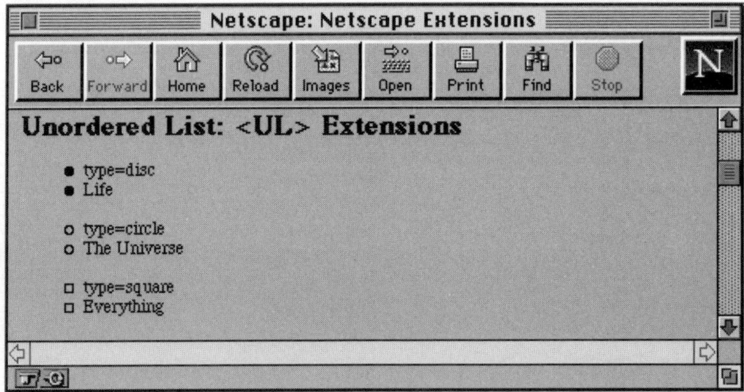

As with most Netscape extensions to HTML, keep in mind that this attribute will be ignored by other browsers, so when viewed in a non-Netscape browser your lists will be displayed with whatever bullet that browser uses by default. Even earlier versions of Netscape did not distinguish between DISC and CIRCLE.

Numbered Lists: <OL>

Numbered, or ordered, lists have numbered items. The markup tags for ordered lists are <OL> and </OL>.

For example, in our kayak.html document, we would specify an ordered list as follows:

```
<P>Kayaking and other river sports are very popular
recreational activities in New Zealand. Popular rivers for
these sports are</P>
<OL>
<LI>The Shotover River, South Island
<LI>The Buller River, South Island
<LI>The Karamea River, South Island
<LI>The Rangitikei River, North Island
<LI>The Mohaka River, North Island
</OL>
```

When viewed in NCSA Mosaic, our ordered list looks like this:

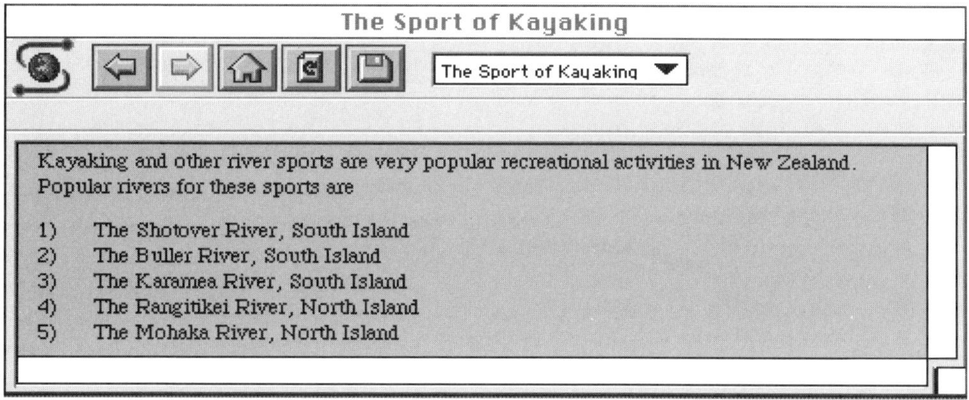
The Sport of Kayaking
The Sport of Kayaking
Kayaking and other river sports are very popular recreational activities in New Zealand.
Popular rivers for these sports are
1) The Shotover River, South Island
2) The Buller River, South Island
3) The Karamea River, South Island
4) The Rangitikei River, North Island
5) The Mohaka River, North Island

Netscape Extensions to OL

Netscape has added a couple of attributes to ordered lists. A TYPE attribute has been added, with possible values being:

A Upper-case letters

a Lower-case letters

I Large Roman numerals

i Small Roman numerals

1 Numbers—the default

A START attribute has also been added so that you can designate a starting place other than one. The start should always be specified as a number—the browser will automatically translate it into whatever type is specified for the list.

Here is our sample list:

```
<OL TYPE=A>
<LI>one,<STRONG>TYPE=A</STRONG>
<LI>two</OL>
<OL TYPE=a START=3>
<LI>three, <STRONG>TYPE=a START=3</STRONG>
<LI>four</OL>
<OL TYPE=I START=5>
<LI>five, <STRONG>TYPE=I START=5</STRONG>
<LI>six</OL>
<OL TYPE=i START=7>
<LI>seven, <STRONG>TYPE=i START=7</STRONG>
<LI>eight</OL>
<OL TYPE=1 START=9>
<LI>nine, <STRONG>TYPE=1 START=9</STRONG>
<LI>ten</OL>
```

And here is how it looks:

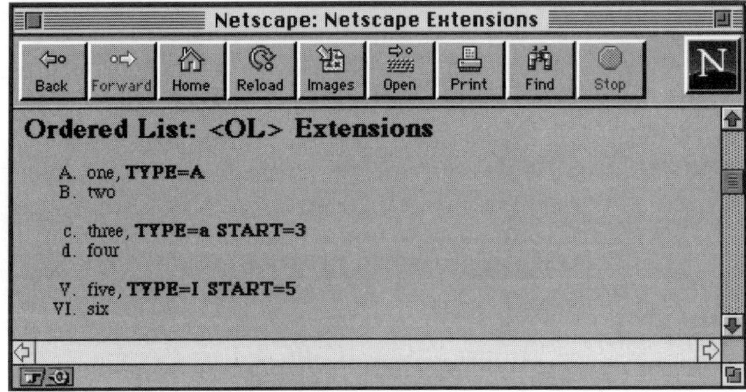

Remember that these extensions will only be used if your documents are viewed with Netscape. If other browsers are used, your lists will be displayed in the normal fashion. This is especially important if you use the START attribute, since numbering will start at 1 in other browsers even if you use START to specify something else.

Netscape Extensions to LI

A TYPE attribute has been added to the LI element. It takes the same values as TYPE for UL or OL (depending on the type of list you are in), and it changes the list type for that item and all subsequent items in that list. A VALUE element has also been added for ordered lists so that you can change the count on the fly. Here's our test document:

```
<H2>LI Extensions</H2>
<H3>An Unordered List</H3>
<UL>
<LI TYPE=CIRCLE>CIRCLE
<LI TYPE=SQUARE>SQUARE
<LI TYPE=DISC>DISC
</UL>
<H3>An Ordered List</H3>
<OL>
<LI TYPE=A>TYPE=A
<LI TYPE=A>TYPE=a
<LI TYPE=I VALUE=100>TYPE=I VALUE=100
<LI TYPE=i>TYPE=i
<LI TYPE=1>TYPE=1
</OL>
```

And here is how it looks:

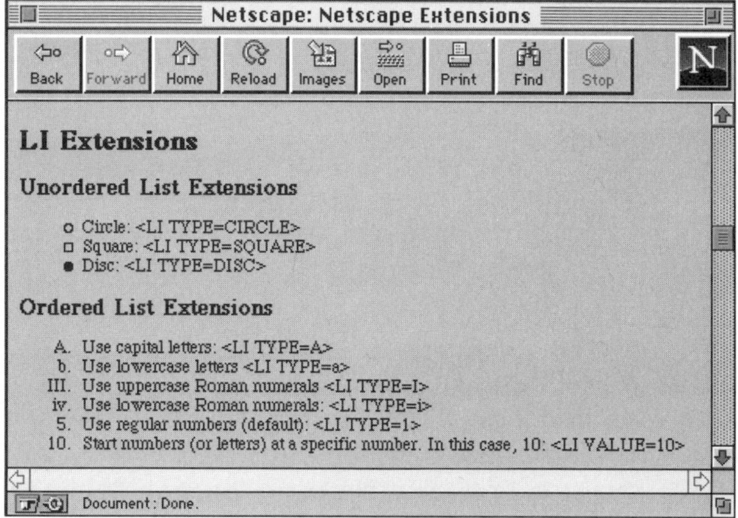

Directory List: <DIR>

Directory lists are intended for short lists. They should be enclosed in <DIR> and </DIR> tags. Each item should be no more than 20 characters. If space is available, the HTML specifications recommend that browsers try to display directory lists in multiple columns. However, in our tests with various browsers we have yet to find one that does this.

```
<P>Following is a list of kayaking resources you will find in
this document:</P>
<DIR>
<LI>Books
<LI>Magazines
<LI>Outfitters
<LI>River descriptions
<LI>Travel agencies
</DIR>
```

Now let's see how this looks in Mosaic:

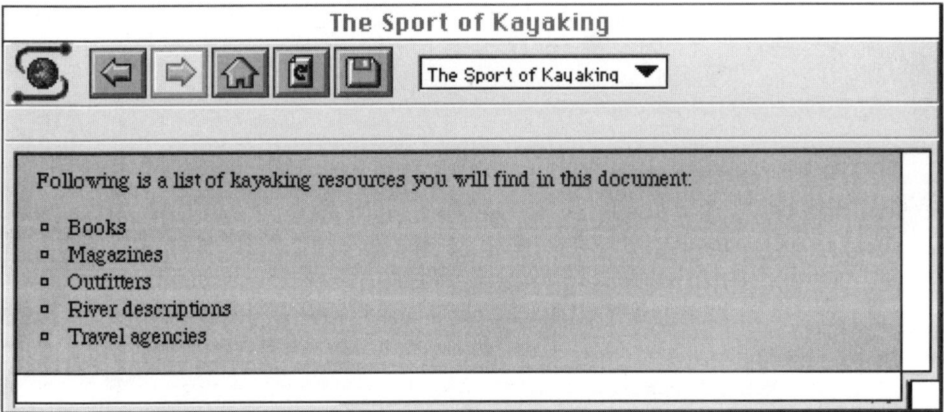

Menu List: <MENU>

A menu list functions much like an unordered list, except it is supposed to be displayed in a more compact style by browsers. We've found that menu lists look exactly like unordered lists in many browsers. However, as development on browsers continues, this may change.

A menu list is enclosed in <MENU> and </MENU> tags, and each item in the list is preceded by the <LI> tag.

```
<P>Kayaking is especially rewarding on those rivers in the
United States that have been designated by Congress as part
of the Wild and Scenic River system. These rivers include:</P>
<MENU>
<LI>The Tuolumne River, California
<LI>The Chattooga River, Georgia
<LI>The Rogue River, Oregon
<LI>The Illinois River, Oregon
<LI>The Middle Fork of the Salmon, Idaho
<LI>The Selway River, Idaho
</MENU>
```

Now let's see how this section looks in NCSA Mosaic:

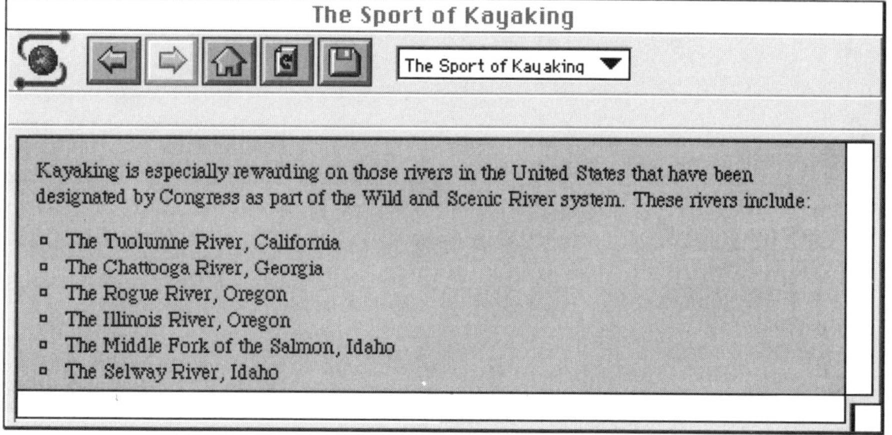

As you can see, the latest version of Mosaic at the time this book was written displays menu items in the same way that it displays directory lists. However, keep in mind that readers may tailor their browsers to use different formats for different types of lists.

Definition Lists: <DL>

Definition lists should be used when specifying a set of terms followed by their definitions. Most browsers format the definition text on a new line. Definition lists are specified as follows:

1. *Begin with an opening definition list <DL> tag.*
2. *Enter the <DT> tag, followed by the text for the defined term.*
3. *Enter the <DD> tag, followed by the text for the definition.*
4. *Continue entering definition terms with the <DT> tag, followed by their definitions, with the <DD> tag. No closing tags are needed.*
5. *Type the closing container tag, </DL>.*

For example, in our kayak.htm document, we would specify a definition list as follows:

```
<P>Essential items to have while kayaking:</P>
<DL>
<DT><EM>Life jacket</EM>
<DD>A life jacket is essential while kayaking as it provides
flotation.
<DT><EM>Helmet</EM>
<DD>A helmet protects the head against blows against rocks.
<DT><EM>Spray skirt</EM>
<DD>The spray skirt fits between the torso of the kayaker and
the boat, and prevents water from swamping the kayak.
<DT><EM>Paddle</EM>
<DD>A paddle allows the kayaker to navigate in the water.
</DL>
```

When viewed in Mosaic, the previous snippet would look something like this:

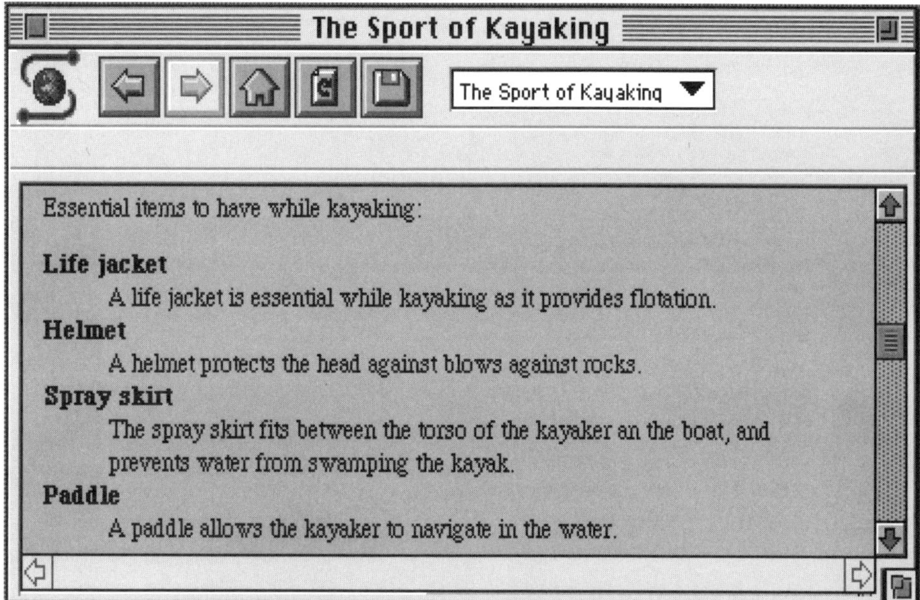
The Sport of Kayaking
The Sport of Kayaking
Essential items to have while kayaking:
Life jacket
A life jacket is essential while kayaking as it provides flotation.
Helmet
A helmet protects the head against blows against rocks.
Spray skirt
The spray skirt fits between the torso of the kayaker an the boat, and prevents water from swamping the kayak.
Paddle
A paddle allows the kayaker to navigate in the water.

tips

As with all list items, the <DT> and <DD> items can be multiple paragraphs. To make a multiple-paragraph item, use paragraph tags—do not do it by using multiple <DD> tags within a single definition.

Definition lists may also include the *compact* attribute, which tells browsers that compact rendering should be used. If you want to use the compact attribute, the start of your list should be:

```
<DL COMPACT>
```

This attribute should be used when the list is large or you would like the items in the list to be small. When the attribute is on, browsers are supposed to reduce the amount of white space between successive DT/DD pairs and may also reduce the width of the DT column. Although it doesn't hurt to include the compact attribute if you want your list to be displayed in this fashion, we have found that most browsers display description lists with the compact attribute no differently than a description list without it. Table 2–1 describes the various tags used to create lists.

TABLE 2–1 List Tags

Command	Description
<OL></OL>	Numbered or ordered list.
<UL></UL>	Unnumbered or unordered list.
<DIR></DIR>	Directory list. Looks like an unordered list in most browsers. List entries should be no longer than 20 characters.
<MENU> </MENU>	Menu list. This list also looks similar to an unordered list in most browsers. The display is supposed to be more compact.
<LI>	Item in a list.
<DL></DL>	Definition list.
<DT>	Defined item in a definition list.
<DD>	Definition of an item in a definition list.

Nested Lists

The lists you use can be nested to an arbitrary level. When you nest lists, keep your poor readers in mind. Nest too deeply, and not only will you have an ugly document, you'll be guaranteed a confused audience!

We might use a nested list in our kayak document as follows:

```
Kayaking uses a dizzying array of specialized gear:
<OL>
<LI>Kayaks
<UL>
<LI>White water kayaks
<LI>Sea kayaks
<LI>Squirt kayaks
</UL>
<LI>There are many types of kayak paddles:
<UL>
<LI>Feathered
<LI>Dihedral
<LI>Break-down
</UL>
</OL>
```

Our HTML source looks like this in NCSA Mosaic:

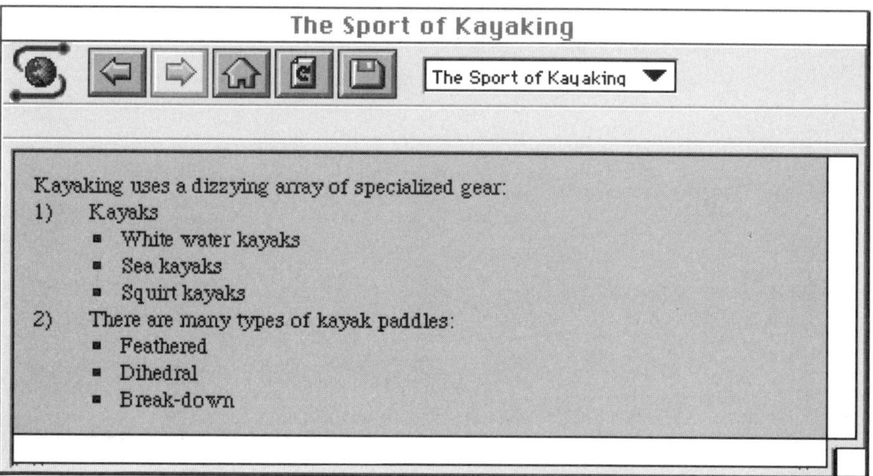

WHEN NESTING LISTS, DON'T FORGET TO CLOSE EACH LIST AND SUBLIST WITH THE APPROPRIATE TAG.

We found an interesting difference in the way that browsers display nested, unordered lists. Some browsers choose a different type of bullet for each level of nesting. We made a little test list to illustrate this:

```
<P>You can also nest unordered lists within each other.
Notice how some browsers change the bullets each level:</P>
<UL><LI>Level One
<UL><LI>Level Two
<UL><LI>Level Three
<UL><LI>Level Four
<UL><LI>Level Five
</UL></UL></UL></UL></UL>
```

Our favorite bullet changer is WinTapestry, a Windows browser from Frontier Technology. Here's how WinTapestry displays our test list:

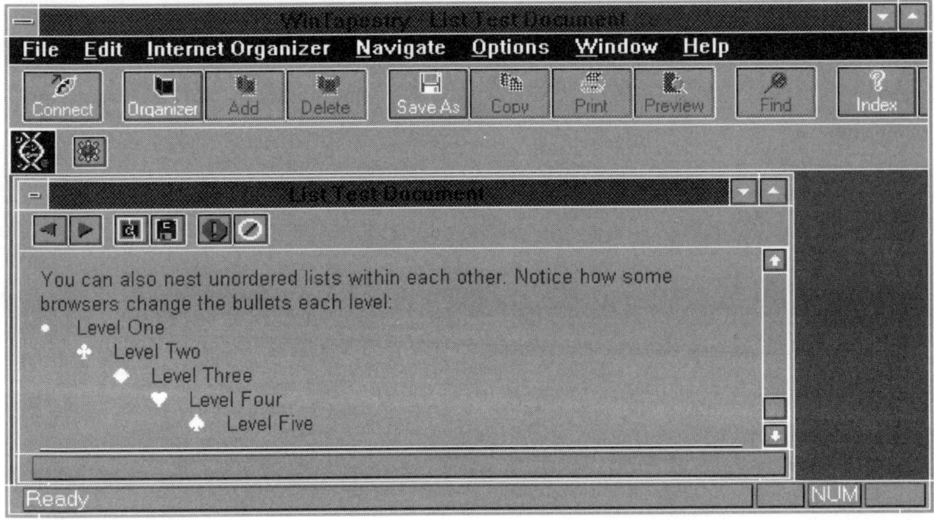

Although you can't count on it, this feature can add visual interest to your documents in some browsers.

Preformatted Text: <PRE>

Sometimes you don't want the Web browser to change the formatting of plain text. You may wish line breaks and spaces to be significant in a piece of text, not ignored by the browser. For example, you may need to display columns of data or show some computer program code. Another example would be a map drawn with ASCII characters. In all of these cases, you want the layout, spacing, and line breaks to be exactly reproduced by the browser.

The <PRE> tag tells the browser to display the text in a fixed-width font and to faithfully reproduce spaces, line breaks, and tabs. The closing tag is, not surprisingly, </PRE>.

You should not nest other kinds of tags within preformatted text because browsers may interpret such tags strangely. The only exception is the anchor tag, <A>, which is explained in the next chapter.

ANCHOR TAGS ARE THE ONLY TAGS THAT ARE ALLOWED IN PREFORMATTED TEXT.

For example, in our kayaking document, we might want to have a silly ASCII drawing of a kayak paddle. In this example, spaces and line breaks are crucial:

```
<P>Kayaks are navigated using a long paddle, which looks
something like this:</P>
<PRE>
```

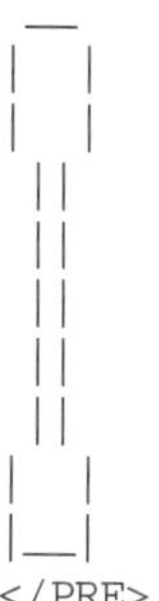

```
  __
 |  |
 |  |
  ||
  ||
  ||
  ||
  ||
 |  |
 |__|
</PRE>
```

This would be displayed in the browser as:

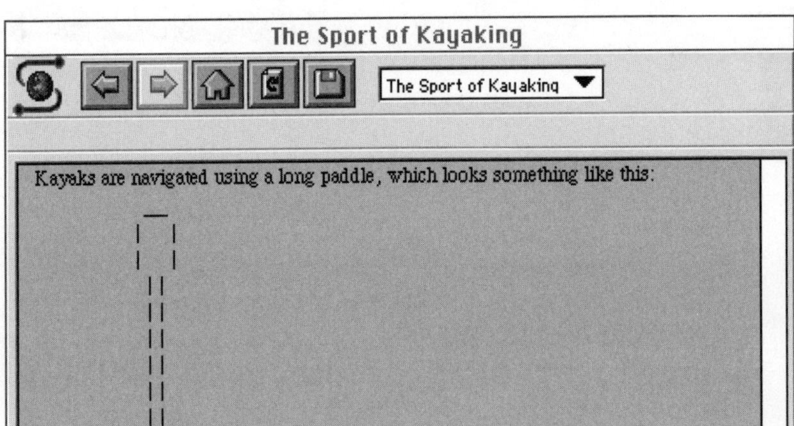

Long Quotations: <BLOCKQUOTE>

The <BLOCKQUOTE> tag is used to mark long quotations in documents. Browsers typically display quotations as indented text. For example, to include a quotation in our kayak document:

```
A first-time kayaker describes his experiences:
<BLOCKQUOTE>
<P>Sir William Francis Butler (1872) explains the thrill of
kayaking:</P>
<BLOCKQUOTE>
It is difficult to find in life any event which so
effectually condenses intense nervous sensation into the
shortest possible space of time as does the work of shooting,
or running an immense rapid.
</BLOCKQUOTE>
```

The resulting text is displayed as:

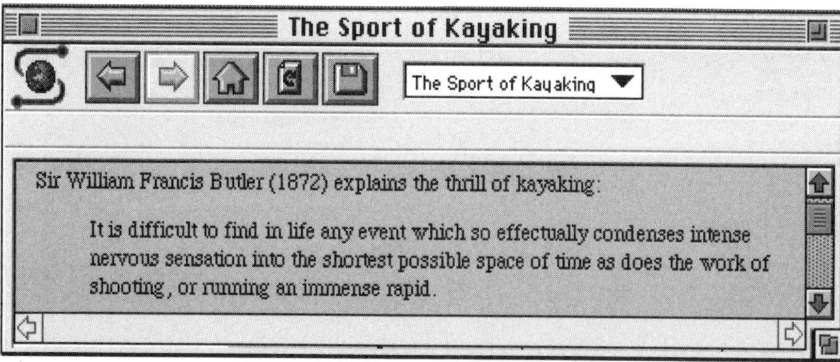
The Sport of Kayaking
The Sport of Kayaking
Sir William Francis Butler (1872) explains the thrill of kayaking:
It is difficult to find in life any event which so effectually condenses intense nervous sensation into the shortest possible space of time as does the work of shooting, or running an immense rapid.

Line Breaks:

A line break is indicated by the <BR> tag. Unlike the <P> tag, the <BR> tag does not insert an extra blank line. The <BR> tag simply forces a line break in the text.

Netscape Extensions to BR

Added functionality was added to the BR tag to accommodate the addition of floating images. A CLEAR attribute was added, which breaks the line and moves down vertically until there is a clear margin. Values that CLEAR may take include ALL, LEFT or RIGHT. You should use the option that matches the side on which you placed your image. So if you have an image with ALIGN=RIGHT, use a BR tag with CLEAR=RIGHT to break the line and move down vertically until there is a clear right margin. If you have images on both sides of your paragraph, use CLEAR=ALL. Let's look at an example now.

```
<P> Here is an example using the CLEAR attribute with the BR
tag. <IMG SRC=gif/tallsail.gif ALIGN=left BORDER=2>
We'll use a slightly taller boat so that you can see the
break. Since our image is on the left, let's use the LEFT
option to break this line.<BR CLEAR=LEFT>
<IMG SRC=gif/tallsail.gif ALIGN=right BORDER=2>
Now let's try a right linebreak. If it works correctly, there
should be clear space from the end of the paragraph and down
to the image's baseline. <BR CLEAR=RIGHT>
```

Here is how this snippet looks in Netscape Navigator:

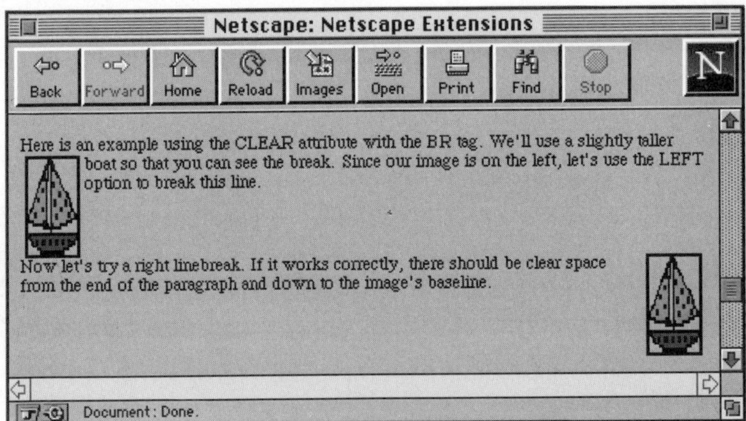

For comparison, let us look at a similar paragraph when we omit the CLEAR attribute:

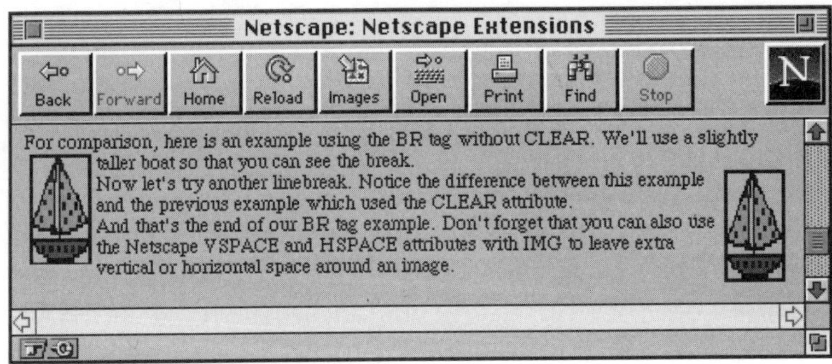

As you can see, the CLEAR attribute can be useful for putting comments about an image next to the image.

Addresses: <ADDRESS>

The <ADDRESS> tag is used to mark—surprise—addresses. Typically, it occurs at the end of documents and is used to enclose the author's name and electronic mail address. Browsers usually display addresses in italic style. For example, the author of the kayak document might include the address as follows:

```
<P>For more information, contact:</P>
<ADDRESS>
Kelly Kayaker<BR>
kayaker@kayak.com
</ADDRESS>
```

This would be displayed in NCSA Mosaic as:

Comments: <! -->

Comments may be included in HTML documents by using the comment tags, <!-- and -->. Text appearing within comment tags will be ignored by browsers. *Comments cannot be nested within one another.* Comments are useful for embedding information for authors, such as document creation date. For example:

```
<!-- The file was created on Jan 1, 1995, by Kelly Kayaker-->
```

Many browsers do not treat embedded HTML tags in a comment correctly. Let's write some lines of HTML that have a nested comment line and a comment line containing several HTML tags.

```
<P>The following line is &lt;!-- Comment --&gt; It should not
be displayed</P>
<!-- Comment -->
<P>Now we try a comment that contains a tag: &lt;!-- Testing
&lt;H1&gt;test&lt;/H2&gt; --&gt; If your browser handles tags in
comments, nothing should appear between the end of this
sentence and the word "Now" in the next paragraph.</P>
<!-- Testing <h1>test</h1> -->
<P>Now we try nesting some comments: &lt;!--&lt;!-- Testing
&lt;H1&gt;test&lt;/H2&gt; --&gt; Note that we only nest the
starting tag for the comment. Since "--&gt;" is defined to be
the end of a comment, the comment should end as soon as the
browser sees one -- there is no provision for nesting end tags
in the HTML standard. Nothing should appear between this
sentence and the horizontal rule if your browser can handle
nested comments.</P>
<!-- <!-- Testing <h1>test</h1> -->
```

NCSA Mosaic handles our test comments without any problems:

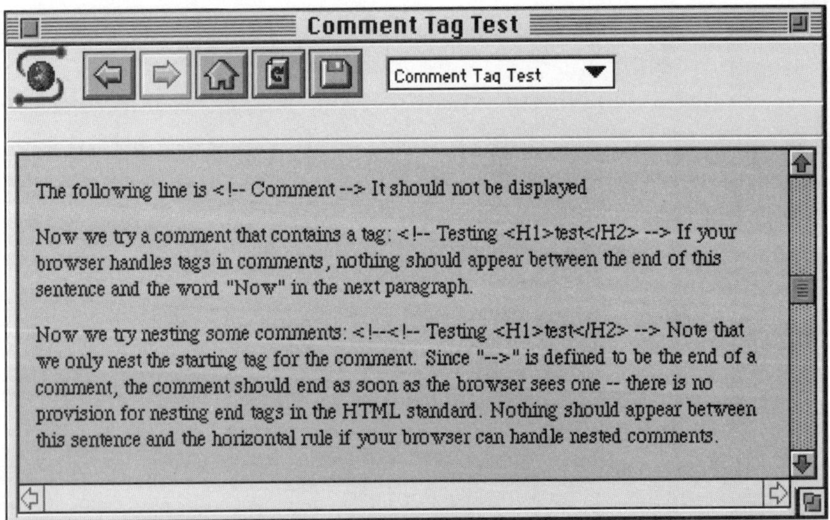

One of the Windows browsers that we tested, WebSurfer, is confused by our nested comments:

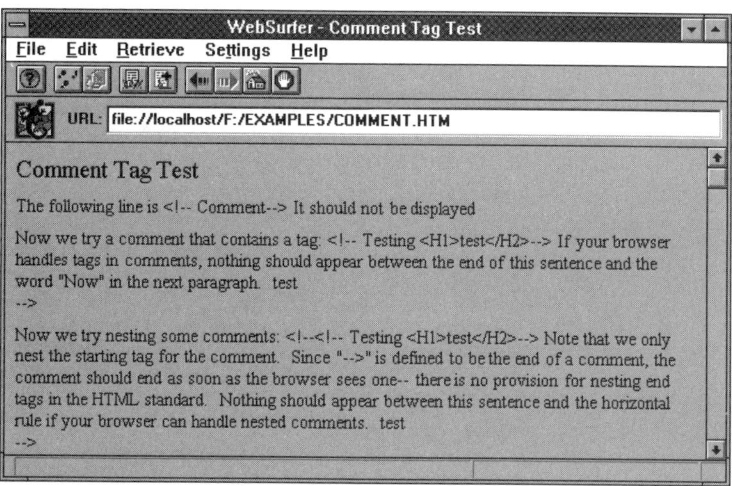

Although the HTML specification does not restrict you from including HTML tags in a comment, it is better to be safe and avoid placing any tags in a comment. This means that you should not try to use a comment to prevent sections of a document from being displayed!

Logical and Physical Styles

The <CITE> tag is an example of a logical tag. It is intended to demark a bibliographic citation, and it is left to the browser to determine how to display such a field. Most browsers choose to display addresses in italics, but this is not enforced; hence, it is called a logical style. Moreover, users may modify their browsers to display a logical style to their preferences. You can find a list of logical style tags in Table 2–2. In our tests of various browsers, we have found that browser support for the logical tags listed in this table is very uneven. The only tags consistently supported were STRONG and EM. Use the other tags with caution. You can check browser support for these tags by loading the logical.html document (which we used to illustrate differences in browsers in Chapter 1).

TABLE 2–2 Logical Style Tags

Style Marker	Description
<CITE>	Used for bibliographic citations. Browsers usually display citations in italics.
<CODE>	Used to display snippets of computer code. Browsers usually display in a fixed-width font.
<EM>	Used to denote emphasis of the affected text. Browsers usually display emphasis in italics.
<KBD>	Used to denote user keyboard entry. Browsers often display in a bold fixed-width font.
<SAMP>	Used to denote a sequence of literal characters.
<STRONG>	Used to denote strong or important text. Browsers usually display in bold font.
<VAR>	Used to indicate a variable name.

Physical styles, on the other hand, specify the desired physical appearance of the affected text. Physical styles in HTML are listed in Table 2–3.

TABLE 2–3 Physical Style Tags

Command	Description
<B>	Bold style.
<I>	Italic style.
<TT>	Use typewriter text or fixed-width font.
<U>	Underline the text.

For both logical and physical styles, don't forget to include the closing tag to denote the end of the style.

Let's see how we can use these tags to dress up our documents. We'll go back to our description list, and add some physical and logical style commands:

```
<P>Essential items to have while kayaking:</P>
<DL>
<DT><STRONG>Life jacket</STRONG>
<DD>A life jacket is essential while kayaking as it provides
flotation.
<DT><B>Helmet</B>
<DD>A helmet protects the head against blows against rocks.
</DL>
<P>Other things you need include:</P>
<DL>
<DT><EM>Spray skirt</EM>
<DD>The spray skirt fits between the torso of the kayaker and
the boat, and prevents water from swamping the kayak.
<DT><I>Paddle</I>
<DD>A paddle allows the kayaker to navigate in the water.
</DL>
```

Now let's see how this looks in Mosaic:

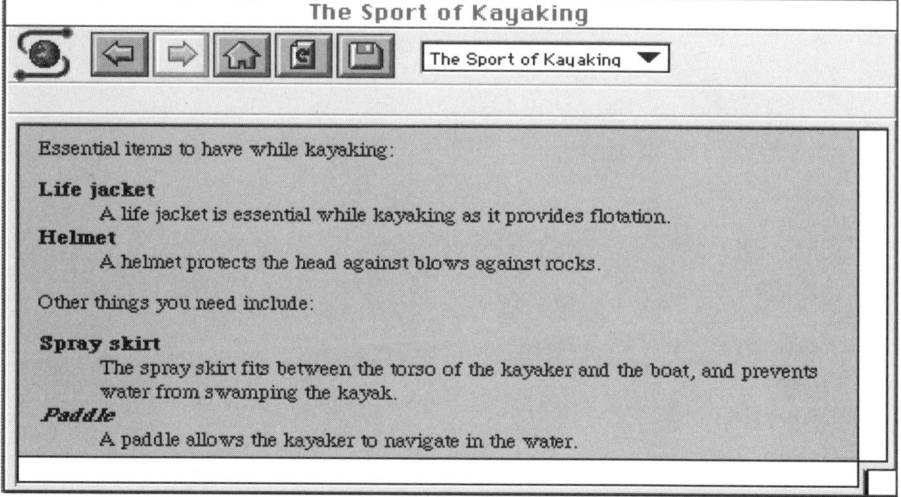

Notice that we used a different style command for each term in our list. As you can see, in this version of Mosaic, the logical tags STRONG and EM and the physical tag B are all displayed in a boldface font. The physical tag I is displayed in an italic font. Now let's see how these tags are treated in other browsers. First let's check Netscape Navigator:

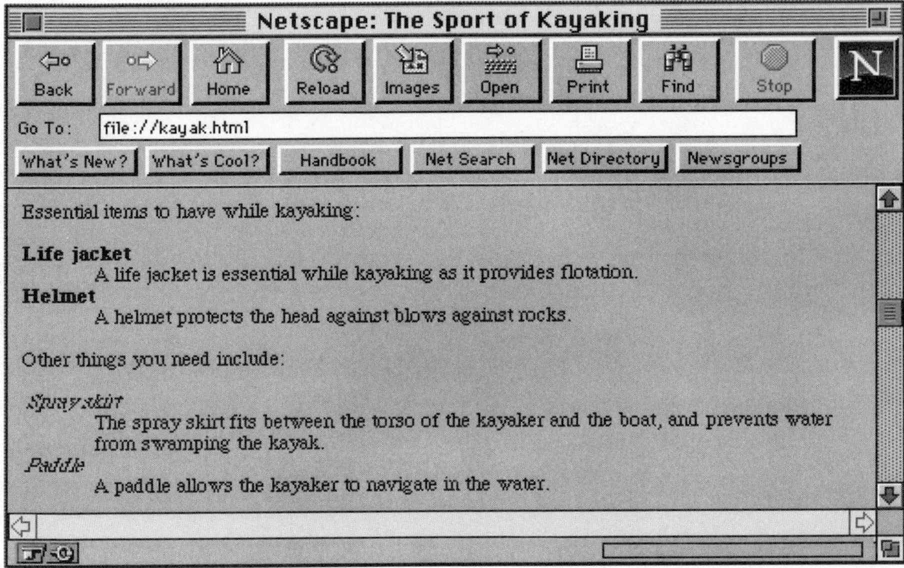
Netscape: The Sport of Kayaking
Back
Forward
Home
Reload
Images
Open
Print
Find
Stop
Go To: file://kayak.html
What's New?
What's Cool?
Handbook
Net Search
Net Directory
Newsgroups
Essential items to have while kayaking:
Life jacket
A life jacket is essential while kayaking as it provides flotation.
Helmet
A helmet protects the head against blows against rocks.
Other things you need include:
Spray skirt
The spray skirt fits between the torso of the kayaker and the boat, and prevents water from swamping the kayak.
Paddle
A paddle allows the kayaker to navigate in the water.

In this version of Netscape Navigator, STRONG and B are treated in the same fashion. However unlike Mosaic, EM and I are displayed in the same font. Now let's see how it looks in Lynx:

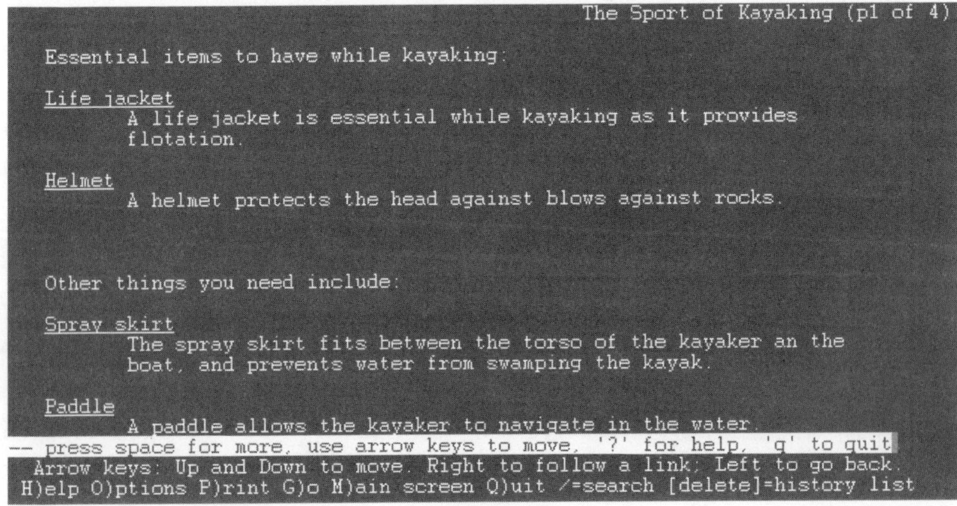
The Sport of Kayaking (p1 of 4)
Essential items to have while kayaking:
Life jacket
A life jacket is essential while kayaking as it provides flotation.
Helmet
A helmet protects the head against blows against rocks.
Other things you need include:
Spray skirt
The spray skirt fits between the torso of the kayaker an the boat, and prevents water from swamping the kayak.
Paddle
A paddle allows the kayaker to navigate in the water.
-- press space for more, use arrow keys to move, '?' for help, 'q' to quit
Arrow keys: Up and Down to move. Right to follow a link; Left to go back.
H)elp O)ptions P)rint G)o M)ain screen Q)uit /=search [delete]=history list

Not surprisingly, all four tags are displayed in the same way in Lynx.

Since logical and physical styles can produce the same end result, there is some debate in the HTML community regarding the desirability of one form over the other. The consensus is that logical style markers should be used whenever possible since they give browsers greater flexibility in choosing the appropriate display for different elements. However, there are times when it might be necessary to use physical tags. For example, if you are providing instructions, you may want to put optional portions of commands in italics and include a statement in your document explaining this convention. In this case you would need to be sure that certain portions of text really are in italics. Since browsers have more leeway on the rendering of <EM>, it would be safer to use <I> in a case like this—although, as you can see in our Lynx illustration, you cannot even count on I to be displayed in italics.

We have included two documents—physical.html and logical.html—on the CD that you can use to check how different elements look in different browsers.

Special Characters

HTML reserves four special ASCII characters for its own use. These are the left angle bracket (<), right angle bracket (>), ampersand (&) and quote ("). The alert reader will have noticed that the angle brackets are used to mark tags. The ampersand is used to signal the start of an escape sequence, while the quote is used around file names and URLs. These characters are frequently used in HTML documents, and browsers rely on these characters to interpret the documents.

If you wish to display these characters in your documents, you must use the escape sequences listed in Table 2–4.

TABLE 2–4 *Special Characters*

Escape sequence	Description
<	The escape sequence for <
>	The escape sequence for >
&	The escape sequence for &
"	The escape sequence for "

For example, you might want to display a section of HTML code in a document:

```
<P>Here are the escape sequences for some HTML characters:</P>
<PRE>
The escape sequence for &lt; is &amp;lt.
The escape sequence for &gt; is &amp;gt.
The escape sequence for &amp; is &amp;amp.
The escape sequence for &quot; is &amp;quot.
</PRE>
```

Here is how this looks in Mosaic:

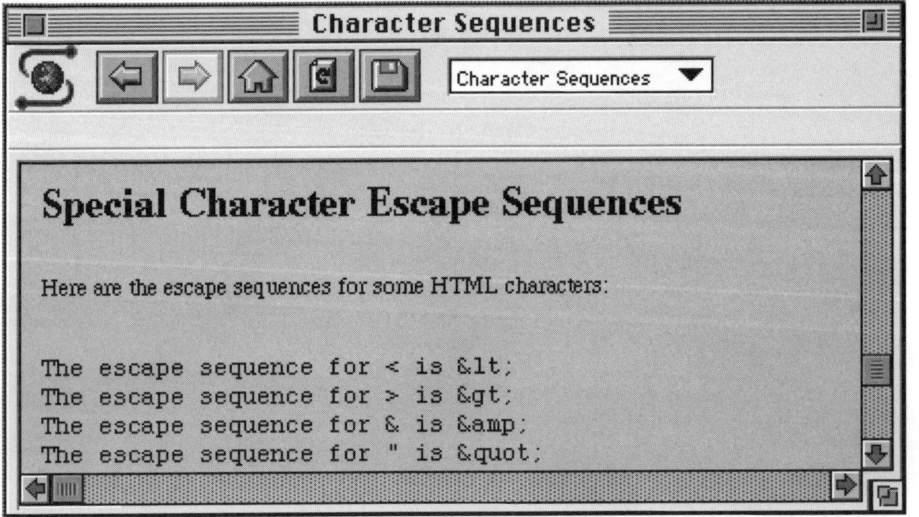

Unlike other HTML markers, escape sequences *are* case sensitive. Escape sequences are also used in HTML for accented characters that occur in other languages. You can find a table of these in Appendix A.

The Good, the Bad and the Ugly

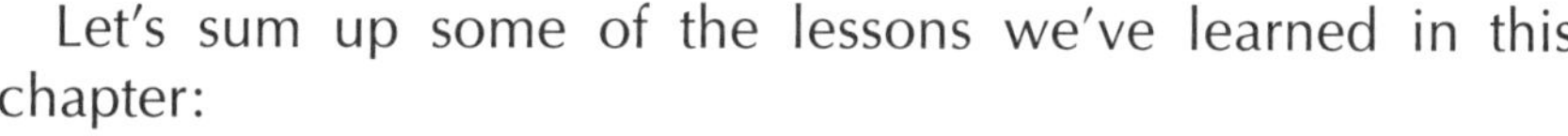

Let's sum up some of the lessons we've learned in this chapter:

- Divide your documents into head and body parts.

- Don't forget closing tags.
- Never use more than one title in a document.
- Never use other tags in a title.

- Keep your titles fairly short—no more than 64 characters.
- Make your titles meaningful. For example, "Games" is a poor choice for a title; "Games on the Internet: MUDs" is better.
- When nesting lists, don't forget to close each list with the appropriate tag.
- Avoid HTML tags in comment fields—it is not a good idea to place portions of your document in a comment field to try to prevent it from being displayed. Browsers do not always handle tags within comment fields correctly.
- Look at your documents in more than one browser. Different browsers may display the same elements in dissimilar ways.

In this chapter you will learn

- What a URL is
- How to link documents with URLs—the "hyper" part of HTML
- How to link to other popular network protocols in your documents

In this chapter we will be using the Netscape browser to display our documents. At the time this book was written, some network surveys indicate that Netscape was the most widely used Web browser—with around 70% of the market.

URLs and Links

What's In This Chapter

This chapter introduces links—the "hyper" part of HTML. We also explain URLs and how to use them in links. As a hypertext system, HTML allows you to link portions of a document to other locations that can be in either the same document or other documents. The links may be made from regions of text, icons, or graphics. They may point to a specific location within another document, or even to another section in the original document.

When a Web browser sees a link, it signals its availability to the user by underlining or coloring the link region. The link destination is communicated to the browser via a uniform resource locator (URL).

Uniform Resource Locators

In the previous chapters we have mentioned URLs a number of times. You can think of URLs as addresses for documents on the Internet. In order to make links you will need to understand what the different parts of a URL are. There are usually three parts in a URL: *protocol, hostname* and *filename*. These three parts are put together to make a URL as follows:

```
protocol://hostname/filename
```

A typical URL looks something like this:

```
http://www.ozone.com/kayak/top.html
```

In this example, "http:" indicates the name of the protocol that should be used for transfer, "www.ozone.com" is the name of the host, and "/kayak/top.html" is the name of the document.

Markup Tag: <A>

The link markup tag in HTML is <A> (denoting "anchor"). This is followed by the URL of the destination document. Then the content or name of the hypertext link (that is, the pointing link) is entered. The closing anchor tag is, of course, </A>.

Specifically, you specify a hypertext anchor in a document with the following somewhat cumbersome set of commands:

- Begin your anchor with "<A ". Don't forget the space after the A.
- Enter the URL of the destination document by typing HREF="*URL*".
- Enter ">".
- Enter the text that serves as the name or pointer to the destination document.
- Enter the closing container tag, </A>.

For example, we might wish to add to our kayak document a pointer to an FAQ on sea kayaking. The FAQ document is stored on another Web server, named www.intelenet.com, and the document is called /clubs/ckf/seakayaker. This link would be entered as follows:

```
Sea kayaking is also exciting. You can find out more about sea
kayaking in the
<A HREF="http://www.intelenet.com/clubs/ckf/seakayaker.html">
sea kayaking FAQ</A>.
```

Let's see how this looks in Netscape:

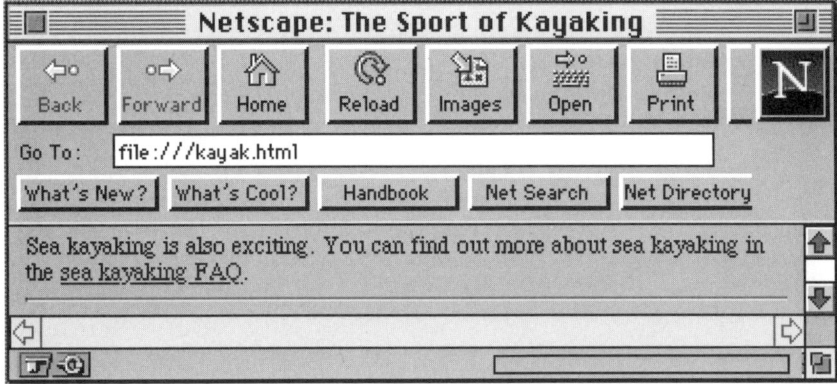

As you can see, the link shows up with an underline. It is also displayed in a different color.

The anchor tag is not supposed to be case sensitive, but many systems (mostly UNIX) will not be able to find the file unless the pathname portion of the URL is treated in a case-sensitive fashion. This is not supposed to be the case according to the HTML specification, but in practice it is. Thus, http://ozone.com/myfile.html is not necessarily the same as http://ozone.com/MyFile.html. Make sure that you check your capitalization as well as spelling for URLs!

Partial Links

You can also make a link that points to a file that is stored on the same machine and is in the same directory or subdirectory as the original document. In this case, you use a partial, or relative, URL as follows:

```
A number of <A HREF="magazine.html">kayaking magazines</A>
are also available to help you learn more about the sport.
```

In this case, the browser assumes that the pointed-to document, magazine.html, is located in the same directory as the original document, kayak.html. It also assumes that the http protocol is used to retrieve the document.

In general, you should use partial links when pointing to related sets of documents. This way, it is easy to move entire sets of documents to a new location on the server if it becomes necessary. Be careful about trying to use relative URLs when your files are not on the same partition as your original file. These URLs may work correctly while checking your files with a browser locally, but will almost always fail when you try to access them through a server. For example, using an anchor that looks like this:

```
<A HREF="/HardDisk1/html/magazine.htm">kayaking
magazines</A>
```

may work correctly when you test your document with a browser locally; but when you move it to a server, you will probably find that the link no longer works. You should also use caution when trying to traverse a directory tree in an upward direction with "..". For example, you might be tempted to try something like the following:

```
<A HREF="../html/magazine.htm">kayaking magazines</A>
```

Like our previous example, this anchor works when the file is checked locally, but may not work correctly when moved to a server (depending on the server used). If you know that you will be using a server that can handle ".." as a means for traversing the directory tree, then it is an easy convention for accessing files in different subdirectories. Be sure to check whether you can do this with your server before including it in many documents—otherwise you may have to make extensive changes later.

Rather than trying to use relative URLs when pointing to documents that are in neither the same directory nor one of its subdirectories, you could use complete URLs. Note that some servers (primarily on UNIX systems) allow links to be made

between unrelated directories. If you wish to make links between documents in unrelated directories, check with your site's webmaster to see whether this capability is supported by the local server.

YOU SHOULD USE COMPLETE URLs WHEN POINTING TO UNRELATED DOCUMENTS, OR DOCUMENTS ON OTHER MACHINES.

Specific Locations in Other Documents

In addition to pointing to other documents, links can be used to jump to specific locations within other documents, or even to another location within the same document.

For example, let's add a link within our kayak.htm document that specifically points to information about our favorite kayaking magazine in magazine.htm. To do this, we need to insert a named anchor to mark the location within magazine.htm. We name the destination location as follows:

```
<A NAME="wave">Wave~Length</A>
```

Then, when we create our link in the original document, kayak.htm, we include the URL pointing to the destination document, magazine.htm, as well as the name of the pointer to the desired destination anchor within the document. This is done using the hash mark (#), as follows:

```
<A HREF="magazine.htm#wave">Wave~Length</A>
```

Now when the reader clicks on the link "Wave~Length," not only will the reader be taken to the new file, magazine.htm, but directly to the specific location within that document. This is an especially useful feature when the destination document is long, and we don't want our reader to have to wade through a long document in order to find the section of interest.

Specific Locations within the Current Document

This notion of marking specific locations within documents using named anchors also applies within one document. Thus, we may choose to name several locations in one document, then have pointers to these locations within the same document. This is a quite useful feature if we wish to have a table of contents at the top of a long document. Readers may select an item in the table of contents and be taken directly to that section of the document.

Naming anchors within one document works exactly the same way, except that the name of the destination document is omitted. Only the name of the anchor is included. For example, we may wish to put a pointer to the kayaking resource section at the top of the kayak document. First, we add a label to the beginning of the resource section, as follows:

```
<H2>Kayaking <A NAME="resources">Resources</A></H2>
```

Then, at the beginning of the document we add a link to this label:

```
<A HREF="#resources">kayaking resources</A></P>
```

Be careful when you reference links in the same document. Unlike links to other sites or files, which will usually cause browsers to leave your reader in the same location if something is wrong at the other end (for example, the other host is down or the browser is unable to find the file), browsers will not treat your readers kindly if something is wrong with the other end of a same-document link. Some browsers will dump your reader at the end of the document, while others may not do anything. Unlike links that go to other sites or files where you may have no control over the other end, you *do* have control over both ends of links within the same document. Make sure that you get it right!

Special Characters

URLs may include any alphanumeric character and the symbols: hyphen (-), dollar sign ($), period (.), plus (+), exclamation point (!), star (*), left parenthesis "(", right parenthesis ")", single quote (') and underscore (_), typed in directly.

However, you may occasionally want to make a link to a file on some other operating system that allows authors to be more creative with filenames. It is common for Macintosh filenames to include spaces, and it is not uncommon to find files with even more unusual characters in their names. When you run into this problem, you will need to encode the character. You encode characters by preceding the ASCII code for the character with a percent sign (%). For example, the ASCII code for the space character is 20. Thus, the URL for a file named "My Kayak" would be:

```
http://ozone.com/My%20Kayak
```

You can find an ASCII table in Appendix B, and on the CD in characters.html.

Other Ways to Use Links

Although at the beginning of this chapter we said that you can think of URLs as addresses for documents on the Web, they are actually much more than that. The key is the protocol portion of the URL. So far, all of our examples have used the Hypertext Transfer Protocol (http). However, you can specify protocols other than http, such as ftp, gopher, telnet, news or mail. By specifying the appropriate protocol in the URL, you can use links to ask the browser to send mail, transfer files or even make a telnet connection. Keep in mind that some browsers do not support all of these actions, so readers using them will not be able to use these links.

One significant difference between the specification of the protocol and markup tags is that some browsers treat the protocol specification in a case-sensitive fashion. Therefore, it is not safe to assume that FTP is the same as ftp.

ALWAYS SPECIFY PROTOCOLS IN LOWER CASE.

A note of caution about the use of protocols other than http: as with markup tags, it is up to the browser to take the appropriate action for each protocol. Some browsers may not support all of the protocols. In these cases the browser will probably just ignore the reference.

We'll explain now how to use some of the most popular protocols in URLs.

FTP

When you specify FTP as the protocol in a URL, the browser will automatically make an anonymous FTP connection to the specified location, and transfer the requested file or provide a directory listing (depending on what you specify). Here is the format for an anonymous FTP URL:

```
ftp://hostname/directoryname/filename
```

Let's look at a few examples to see how this works. The following link will transfer a file called "kayak.hqx" from the host ozone.com:

```
<A HREF="ftp://ozone.com/kayak.hqx">Kayak Trip Planning
Program</A>
```

If a reader chooses this link, the browser will try to open an FTP connection to the host ozone.com and download the file kayak.hqx. If you do not specify a filename, a directory listing will be provided:

```
Here are the files in our <A HREF="ftp://ozone.com/"> kayak
repository </A>.
```

Although ftp uses anonymous FTP as a default, you can also have the URL specify a particular user. We'll explain how to do this, but first a word of caution. After opening an FTP connection, browsers do not offer you the option of entering a password for the account if one is not provided. This means that you must include the password and account name as part of the URL if you want to use a specific account. This is a huge security hole since the password is not encrypted—anyone reading your document will be able to see it. Unless you have some special application that requires the use of a specific account, we strongly recommend that you avoid using this feature. The format for a URL that includes an account and password is:

```
ftp://username:password@hostname/path
```

For example, if we want to see a directory listing of Kelly Kayaker's account we could include the following in our kayaking document:

```
<p>Here is a <A HREF="ftp://kayaker:badidea@ozone.com/">
directory listing</A> of Kelly's account.
```

We have made extensive use of the ftp protocol in our browser.html document (this is the document that you can use to get a variety of browsers) on the CD. You should look at this document for more examples of this protocol.

File

The file protocol is for accessing files on a local disk. It is related to ftp because it will try to use FTP if you have specified a host other than the one on which the browser is being used. Here is the format for a file URL:

```
file://localhost/pathname
```

Mail

Using a link to send e-mail is an easy way to allow your readers to provide feedback about your document. The name for this protocol is *mailto*. Thus, the format for e-mail URLs is:

```
mailto:username@hostname
```

Two of the best places to put this option are in a short request for feedback at the beginning of the document, or as part of the address at the end of the document. Let's modify our kayak document to allow readers to send Kelly a message:

```
For more information contact:
<ADDRESS>Kelly Kayaker<BR>
<A HREF="mailto:kayaker@ozone.com"> kayaker@ozone.com </A>
</ADDRESS>
```

If the reader is using a browser that can send e-mail, kayaker@ozone.com will be highlighted in some fashion. If the reader clicks on it, it will provide a mail window that looks something like this:

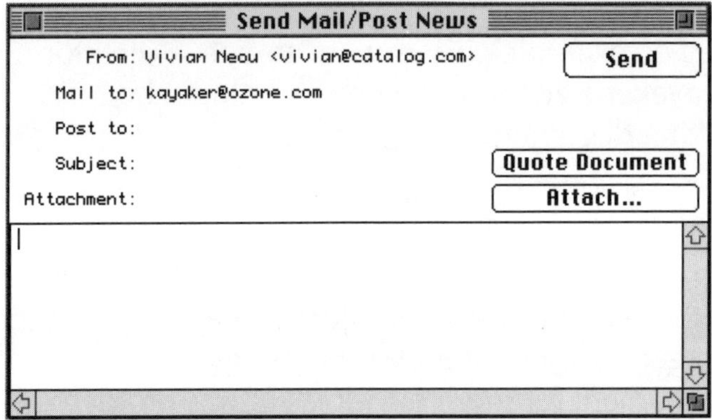

As you can see, the browser inserts the address specified in the URL in the "To" field.

Telnet

You can also use URLs to provide a telnet connection to the site of your choice. Telnet URLs appear in this format:

```
telnet://hostname:portnumber
```

You do not need to specify a port number if you want a connection made to the default telnet port. However, if you are making a link to a special service at a certain port, you will need to make the connection directly to that port. For example, the University of Michigan offers weather information on port

3000 on the host downwind.sprl.umich.edu. Let's incorporate this information in our kayak document:

```
It is important to know what the weather will be like
before going on a kayak trip. You can get National
Weather Service forecasts for any location from the <A
HREF="telnet://downwind.sprl.umich.edu:3000"> University of
Michigan WEATHER UNDERGROUND</A>. <P>
```

When the reader chooses this link, the browser will call a helper application to make a telnet connection to port 3000 on the host downwind.sprl.umich.edu. You can try this yourself by loading the kayak document into a browser and choosing this link.

Gopher

Gopher is an information service developed at the University of Minnesota. It provides easy transfer of files because it encodes information about many types of files. However, since the Web includes similar file transfer facilities, it is usually easier to access files through http if a site offers both types of services. However, some sites still only offer gopher service. In this case, you will need to make a link through gopher. A gopher URL looks like this:

```
gopher://hostname:port/gophertype[item]
```

A Gophertype is a single character indicating the type of thing to expect (see Table 3–1).

TABLE 3–1 Gophertypes

Type	Description
0	A text file.
1	A directory.
2	A CSO phone-book server.
3	Error.
4	A BinHexed Macintosh file.
5	A DOS binary archive of some sort.

TABLE 3–1 Gophertypes (Continued)

Type	Description
6	A UNIX uuencoded file.
7	An Index-Search server.
8	The item points to a text-based telnet session.
9	The item is a binary file.
g	The item is a GIF format graphics file.
T	The item points to a text-based tn3270 session.
I	The item is some kind of image file.

The two most commonly used types are 0 (text) and 1 (directory). Let's add a link to a gopher site with kayaking information to our kayak document:

```
You can get more kayaking information from this <A
HREF="gopher://ftp.std.com/11/nonprofits/canoe.kayak">goph
erserver</A>.
```

News

Newsgroups are an extensive set of electronic bulletin boards. There are newsgroups covering almost every conceivable topic. The news protocol allows you to make a link to a specific newsgroup. The format for URLs using this protocol is:

```
news:newsgroup
```

For example, we might want to make a link to the newsgroup rec.boats.paddle in our kayak document:

```
You can find more information about kayaks in the newsgroup
<A HREF="news:rec.boats.paddle"> rec.boats.paddle</A>.
```

You can also specify specific articles by replacing the name of the newsgroup with an article ID in the URL. However, since news turns over so rapidly, this link would remain valid only a short time.

In order to use a newsgroup link, the reader's browser must support some news-reading mechanism and must be configured to use a news (NNTP) server. This is a fairly new feature, and many browsers do not support it. While it is not your responsibility to make sure that your reader's browsers are set up correctly, if you make heavy use of news URLs, it might be helpful to your readers to include a warning about configuring their browsers to use an NNTP server before trying those links.

Link Trivia

There are a few things about links that we have not yet mentioned. We've left them for last, not because they are the best, but because right now they are not terribly important. Feel free to skip this section. We've told you about the attributes HREF and NAME in the anchor tag. We expect these tags to be the only ones you'll ever need to use. However, there are actually a number of other attributes that can be used with anchor tags, and so for completeness they are listed in Table 3–2. Browser support for these attributes is fairly spotty, and there is still

TABLE 3–2 Additional Anchor Tag Attributes

Attribute	Description
REL	This is currently only proposed. It is supposed to give the relationship described by the link.
REV	Another proposed attribute. It is supposed to give the relationship described by the link in the opposite direction to REL.
URN	This stands for Uniform Resource Number, and is supposed to help the browser avoid reloading a document it has already acquired.
TITLE	This is only for information. It should provide the title of the document whose address is in the HREF attribute.
METHODS	This is supposed to provide information regarding the functions that the reader may perform on the object.

debate about these attributes in the Web development community. For now, use them at your own risk.

The Good, the Bad and the Ugly

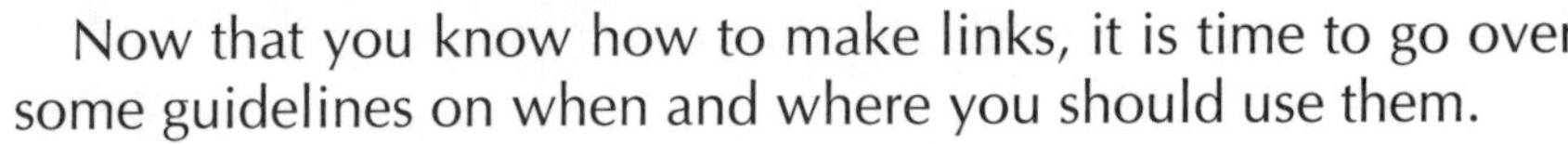

Now that you know how to make links, it is time to go over some guidelines on when and where you should use them.

Don't fall into the *click here* trap. Many people have chosen to make links that look like this:

```
If you want to see my document on kayaking click <A
HREF="kayak.htm">here</A>.
```

While one "click here" in a document isn't necessarily a bad thing, it does not make good use of the browser's display features. Since most browsers highlight links, the links in a document are more conspicuous than the rest of the text. If most of your links are made to the same word, there is no way for the reader to quickly distinguish between the links. For example:

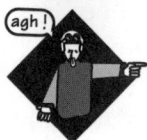

```
<UL>
<LI>Click <A HREF="bird.htm">here</A> for a document on birds.
<LI>Click <A HREF="cat.htm">here</A> for a document on cats.
<LI>Click <A HREF="dog.htm">here</A> for a document on dogs.
<LI>Click <A HREF="fish.htm">here</A> for a document on fish.
</UL>
```

When we see this in a browser, the word "here" leaps out. It is difficult to see what the links are actually for.

However, simply shifting the link over to the subject of each document and slightly rewriting each line clears up the problem.

```
<UL>
<LI>A document about <A HREF="bird.htm">birds</A>.
<LI>A document about <A HREF="cat.htm">cats</A>.
<LI>A document about <A HREF="dog.htm">dogs</A>.
<LI>A document about <A HREF="fish.htm">fish</A>.
</UL>
```

Now we have:

In our new and improved version, the topic of the document behind each link is easy to see.

It is easy to make links in inappropriate places. There are so many resources on the Internet, you may be tempted to make a link every time you mention something for which you have an Internet resource. Only place links where they really contribute something to the content of your document.

Finally, don't make your anchor text too long. While there is nothing to stop you from making a whole sentence into a link, doing this is unsightly and does not make it any easier for your reader to follow the link. Rather than using a long phrase as a link, choose the words in the phrase that most clearly describe the link and place your anchor tags around them.

IN THIS CHAPTER YOU WILL LEARN

- HOW TO INCLUDE IMAGES IN YOUR HTML DOCUMENTS
- HOW TO PICK THE CORRECT GRAPHICS FORMAT FOR THE IMAGES IN YOUR WEB PAGES
- HOW TO MAKE IMAGES WITH "CLICKABLE" HOT SPOTS
- HOW TO MAKE ANIMATED GIF IMAGES
- HOW TO INTEGRATE VIDEO AND SOUND INTO YOUR HTML IMAGES

MULTIMEDIA: IMAGES, VIDEO AND SOUND

What's In This Chapter

This chapter explains how to turn your HTML documents into multimedia presentations. We begin the chapter with a discussion of image formats, and explain why some are better than others for use within HTML documents. We will show you how to manipulate images to improve their appearance in Web documents, and show you how to use GraphicConverter. We explain how to include images in your HTML documents. And for Netscape-oriented documents, we explain how to include images as backgrounds. We also show you how to make images with clickable "hot spots." We'll also discuss video and sound, and explain how to best incorporate them into your documents.

Images in HTML Documents

We spent much time discussing how to format text in your documents—but HTML also supports multimedia authoring on the Web. To make the best use of HTML's power, you also want to have pointers to or include multimedia elements such as images in your documents.

Graphics Formats

Images may be stored in many formats. Table 4–1 displays many of the common file formats used on the Web and their recognized filename extensions. Browsers use the filename extension to determine which viewer is needed for a particular image, so images *must* be given a filename extension that matches the image type.

Choosing an Image Format

As shown in Table 4–1, there are many formats that may be used to store images. However, most browsers only have built-in or "inline" support for one or two formats. While most browsers may be configured to support additional formats, it is up to the user to do so. Additionally, when a browser must use an external program to display an image, the image does not appear in the browser window; instead, the browser runs the viewer program, and the image is displayed in the viewer program's window rather than in the browser window with the rest of your document.

Since you cannot count on your readers to configure their browsers to support additional image formats, it is advisable to choose one of the widely supported formats for your images. Many tools exist to convert images from one format to another (including our favorite Mac image tool, GraphicConverter), so even if you have images in a less common format it is a fairly straightfoward task to convert them to one of the popular formats.

TABLE 4–1 Common Multimedia File Extensions

Description	Extension
GIF image	.gif
JPEG image	.jpg or .jpeg
TIFF image	.tiff
XBM bitmap image	.xbm
Computer Graphics Metafile	.cgm
Windows Bitmap image	.bmp
Encapsulated PostScript	.eps
PostScript file	.ps
PICT image	.pict
Progressive JPEG image	.pjpg
Adobe Acrobat file	.pdf
AIFF sound	.aiff
AU sound	.au
QuickTime movie	.mov
MPEG movie	.mpeg or .mpg

At this time this book was written the two most widely supported image formats were GIF and JPEG.

Graphics Interchange Format (GIF)

The most common format for images on the Web is Graphics Interchange Format (GIF), which was developed by CompuServe. You can be fairly sure that if you provide images in GIF format, as long as the browser supports any image display, it will be able to display your image. If you already have a collection of images in some other format, consider converting them to GIF. You will find an application called GraphicConverter on the CD that can be used to convert many formats to GIF.

Interlaced GIFs

Interlaced GIF images are images in which the scan lines have been rearranged so that a low-resolution version of the image can quickly be displayed. The rest of the image is then filled in over several passes. Although storing images in this format does not speed up their transmission time (in fact, it typically takes slightly more space to store the interlaced version of an image than the noninterlaced version), it does provide readers with a quick preview of the final image and helps to provide the impression that your document has loaded quickly. GraphicConverter can be used to convert noninterlaced images into interlaced images.

Keep in mind that some browsers do not take advantage of this feature, waiting until the entire image has been downloaded before displaying it. However, for browsers such as Netscape Navigator that do support this feature, it substantially improves the time in which readers can begin to see your images.

JPEG

JPEG stands for Joint Photographic Experts Group, which is the group that originally developed this standard. There is a related standard called MPEG that is used for video. We will discuss MPEG later, in the section on video.

JPEG stores information about the image by keeping track of the color changes in the image, rather than storing information about each pixel in the image. It is what is known as a *lossy* format because the final image is not exactly the same as the original. However, the human eye does not usually perceive the tiny differences introduced by JPEG. The big advantage offered by the JPEG storage format is that for certain types of images JPEG images typically take less storage space (and hence require less transmission time) than do equivalent GIF images. For example, the picture of Kelly Kayaker on the CD in JPEG format requires 26 kb of storage space, while the same picture in GIF format requires 122 kb of space. This dramatic difference in the storage requirement illustrates JPEG's strength in storing photographs and other images with a wide variety of shadings. This advantage does not hold for line drawings. For those types of images, GIF images may require less storage space.

Although JPEG is popular, GIF formatted images are still the most common and have the widest support. To reach the widest possible audience it is safest to provide your images in GIF format whenever possible (there are a few exceptions that we'll explain later).

Progressive JPEG

There is a good chance that progressive JPEGs may become the most popular way to store plain images for the Web. Why? Because this format offers the advantages of interlaced GIF images accompanied by the low storage requirements of the JPEG format. Additionally, progressive JPEG files are frequently smaller than a regular (baseline) JPEG file containing the same image.

The downside? Progressive JPEG files are not readable by regular JPEG decoders. This means that special support has to be added before a browser can display a progressive JPEG image. At the time this book was written browser support for this format was fairly limited—Version 2 of Netscape Navigator was the first popular browser to support it. However, other browsers such as Microsoft's Internet Explorer were also planning to add support, and we expect even more browsers to support it as the format gains in popularity.

You will find references in the utilities.html document to a number of tools that you can download over the Internet to convert your images into this format.

Image Tips and Tricks

Choosing the basic format for your image is only the first step in making the images in your documents look as good as possible. There are also many other things you can do to make your images more appealing in HTML documents.

We've included a number of GIF and JPEG images in the Images folder on the CD that you can use to experiment with images in documents. You are welcome to use these images as you wish.

Transparent Backgrounds

Some images look better if their own backgrounds do not appear, giving them the appearance of floating on the browser's background. For example, if you have made a red button for your links, it would detract from the look of the button to have a white square background appear in back of it. If your image is in GIF89a format (or is in a format that can be converted to GIF89a), you can modify it so that the background is "transparent." What this means is that one color in the image is designated as the transparency color. When the image is displayed, this color is replaced with whatever background color is used by the display window.

Let's see what a difference this can make. In the following figure, the image does not have a transparent background:

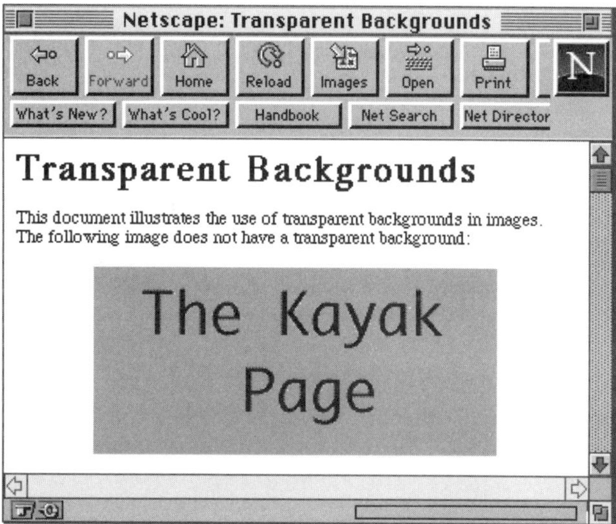

As you can see, there is an unsightly background square behind the text in the image. It would be preferable to display the image without having to see the background, as you can see here:

The key to transparency is in the version of GIF. Many GIF images are in GIF87 format, an old version of GIF that does not support transparency. Fortunately it is a fairly simple process to convert your GIF87 images to GIF89a using GraphicConverter. We'll explain how to do this in the section about GraphicConverter that's coming up.

Since there is no way to indicate that only the background is to be made transparent, your image's background should be a solid color, and the color should not be in use elsewhere in the image. For this reason transparent backgrounds are not suited for many types of images. In particular, photographs do not work well with transparent backgrounds, since their backgrounds are rarely solid colors and it is difficult to make sure that the background color is not used elsewhere in the image. However, as mentioned, this technique is an excellent one to use with buttons and other icons.

A note of warning about design decisions for transparent backgrounds: not all browsers currently provide support for them. If a browser does not support transparency, it will display the image's own background. One way to partially get around this problem is by choosing the background to be the gray color many browsers use for their own backgrounds. This way, the image's background will still blend in with the browser's background even if the browser does not support transparent images. However, not all browsers use gray as a background color, so this is not an infallible technique.

Reducing Image Size

Keeping image storage size as small as possible is an important element of creating graphics for the Web. One way to reduce image size is to reduce the number of bits allowed for the storage of color information. When you reduce the number of bits you also reduce the number of colors that can be used in the image. Table 4–2 shows a list of the number of colors that may be stored for a given bit depth. If you are working

with a simple image that only uses a few colors, you can reduce to a bit depth of 3. Even with more complex images it is often possible to reduce the depth with only a small reduction in picture quality. It is worth spending some time comparing your images at different bit depths to see if the trade-off between picture quality and storage space (which of course translates into transmission time) is worthwhile for a particular image.

TABLE 4–2 *Bit Depth vs. Number of Colors*

Bit Depth	Number of Colors
3	8
4	16
5	32
6	64
7	128
8	256

You can create 1, 2, 3, 8, and 16 bit files with GraphicConverter (choose Color from the Picture menu). Some other image manipulation programs such as Adobe Photoshop allow you to choose almost any bit depth you want.

Netscape Navigator's Window Color Palette

You may be wondering why we are discussing the way that Netscape supports colors on its Windows browser in a book on Macintosh HTML support. Even though you may be doing all of your design on a Macintosh, it is likely that a large portion of your readers will be viewing your document on a Windows system. Unfortunately there is a little quirk in the way that Netscape supports graphics on Windows systems (3.1, 95 and NT) running in 8-bit mode that can make your images look awful.

The quirk? Netscape uses a 216-color palette on these systems. This means that colors that are in the palette will appear as expected, while other colors are "dithered" to approximate the actual color. Dithering means nonpalette colors are represented by intermingling pixels with colors from the palette. Sometimes dithered colors look fairly close to the color they are supposed to represent, but often they can produce some fairly ugly results. Before we explain how to get around this problem, we need to explain a little about the way that computers store color information.

Colors are stored in a set of three numbers, representing the amounts of the primary colors—red, green and blue—used to compose that color. This is known as the RGB representation for a color. The size of the color palette is determined by the range of values that each number in the RGB set may take. For reference, Table 4–3 shows some RGB color codes.

TABLE 4–3 RGB Color Codes

Code	Color
#000000	Black
#FFFFFF	White
#0000FF	Blue
#FF0000	Red
#00FF00	Green
#FFFF00	Yellow
#FF00FF	Purple

The Netscape Windows color palette is composed of RGB values where the values are always 0, 51, 102, 153, 204, 255 (decimal) or 00, 33, 66, 99, CC, FF (hexadecimal). RGB values are typically represented in hexadecimal. For example, an RGB value of 003399 would be in the Netscape color palette. Whenever possible, you should try to restrict the color tables for your images to values in this palette.

Thumbnails

It has been said that a picture is worth a thousand words. In the case of HTML and pictures, a picture can be worth much more than a thousand words—at least in the amount of time it takes to transfer the picture to your reader's system. Pictures can make a document look great, but if it takes your reader a couple of hours to transfer the document, odds are pretty high that he or she won't be willing to wait, no matter how great your pictures are. Image files are usually fairly large, and many people are still reading documents over slow phone lines. The answer? Thumbnail copies of your images. A thumbnail copy of an image is a small version (typically around one inch wide) that your readers can use to decide whether they want to get the full-size version.

As an example, we have a GIF picture of Kelly in her kayak. The full-size picture is approximately 122 kb, but our thumbnail version is only 5 kb. By putting the thumbnail picture in our document with a link to the full-size picture, we have saved our readers over 100 kb (unless they decide to get the full-size picture). If your reader is using a 14,400 bps modem, this translates to approximately one minute. While one minute is not a lot of time, you can see how this adds up if you have any number of images at all.

GraphicConverter

How do you make thumbnail copies of pictures, use transparent backgrounds, and make sure that your images are in GIF format? A nifty shareware program called GraphicConverter can solve all of these problems for you. GraphicConverter is an image file editor that can load and save image files in many common Macintosh, IBM, Amiga, and Atari formats. It also allows you to edit pictures, so you can use it to create images as well.

Installing GraphicConverter

You will find the GraphicConverter folder in the Utilities folder on the CD. To install it on your hard disk, simply drag the folder to your hard disk.

Starting GraphicConverter

After Setup is done, you can access GraphicConverter by clicking on the GraphicConverter icon in the GraphicConverter Folder:

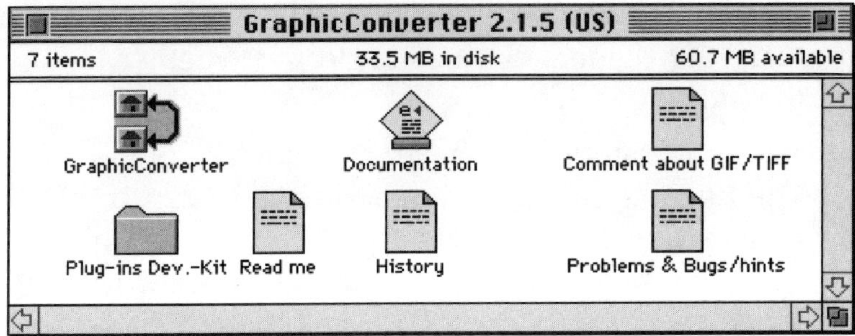

After GraphicConverter starts, it will display a registration status window:

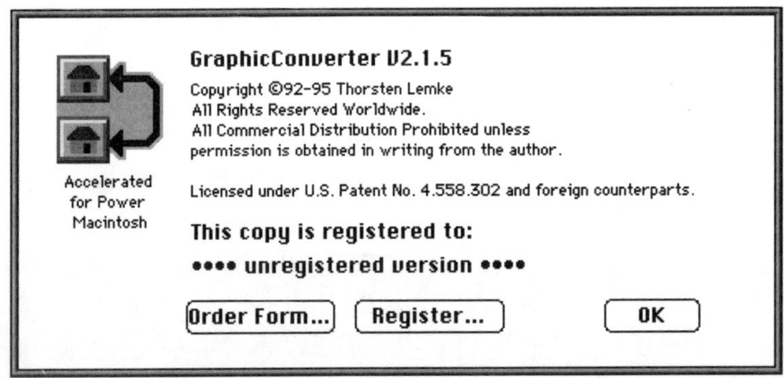

GraphicConverter V2.1.5
Copyright ©92-95 Thorsten Lemke
All Rights Reserved Worldwide.
All Commercial Distribution Prohibited unless
permission is obtained in writing from the author.
Licensed under U.S. Patent No. 4.558.302 and foreign counterparts.
Accelerated for Power Macintosh
This copy is registered to:
•••• unregistered version ••••
Order Form...
Register...
OK

There will be a 5-second countdown before you are permitted to choose an option (the delay is removed after you register the package). To start the program, click on the "OK" button.

Converting Between Formats

As we've mentioned, graphics in Web pages will work the best if they are stored in GIF or JPEG format. GraphicConverter makes it easy to convert images you may have in other formats to either GIF or JPEG. To convert an image, first open it by choosing Open from the File menu and entering the name of the file:

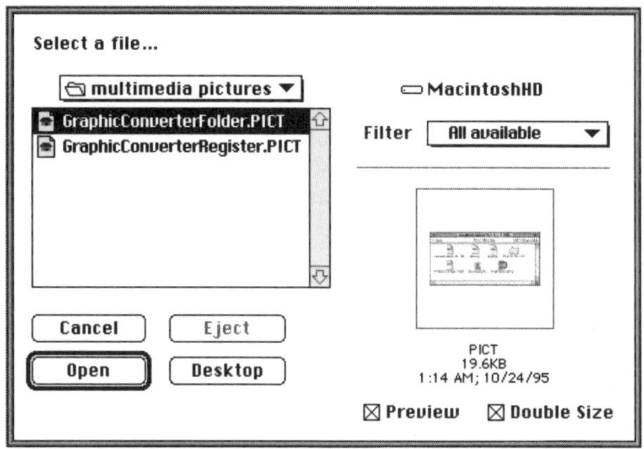

Notice that you can preview the files before you open them—a convenient feature if you have large number of images.

After you open the file, you can use GraphicConverter to modify it, or if you only want to convert format, choose Save As from the File menu:

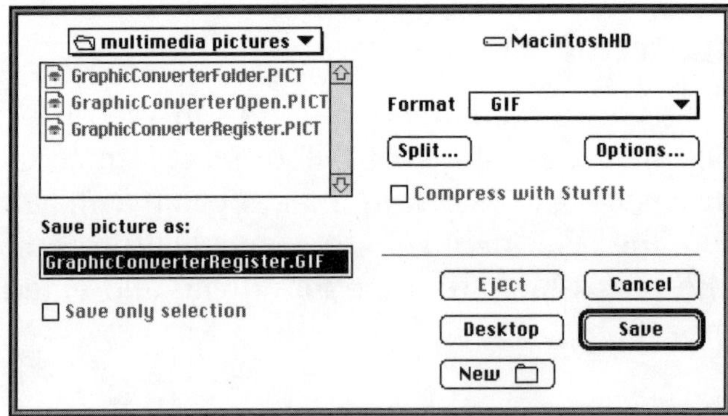

Pick the new format for your image from the Format menu. Notice that GraphicConverter will add a new extension to your file name to correspond to the new format.

Creating Interlaced Images

GIF files in either GIF87a or GIF89a format may also be saved with interlaced rows. To do this, click on the Option button:

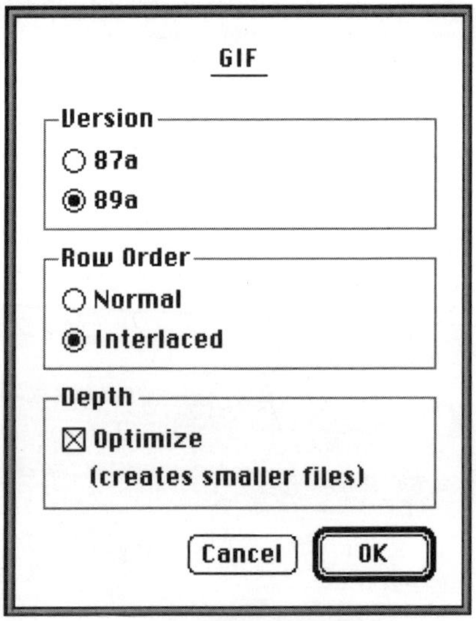

Choose Interlaced under Row Order (note that if you plan to use a transparent background you should also choose 89a under Version). Then click on OK to return to the Save box. Save your image in the new format, and you're done.

Making Thumbnails

If you plan to incorporate many images in your documents, one of the things you will undoubtedly need to do is to create a thumbnail version of some of your images. Let's see how to make a thumbnail copy of Kelly's image. First, we load the image by choosing Open from the File menu. We enter the name of the file and then get the following screen:

To make a thumbnail version of our image, we choose "Size" from the Picture menu and "Scale" from the Size menu:

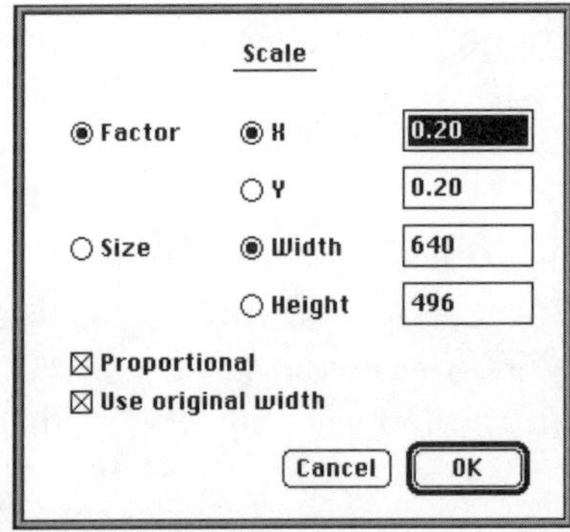

In this example we choose to reduce the picture by using Factor, which does a percentage reduction. However, if you have a specific target size (perhaps if you wish to make a row of same-size thumbnails), you can choose Size and then specify the target width or height. Note that you need only choose one dimension—as long as the Proportional box is checked, the other dimension will be set for you automatically. Unless you want to distort your picture, it is best to use the Proportional setting. Click on "OK" after you are done, and the thumbnail version of your image will be displayed:

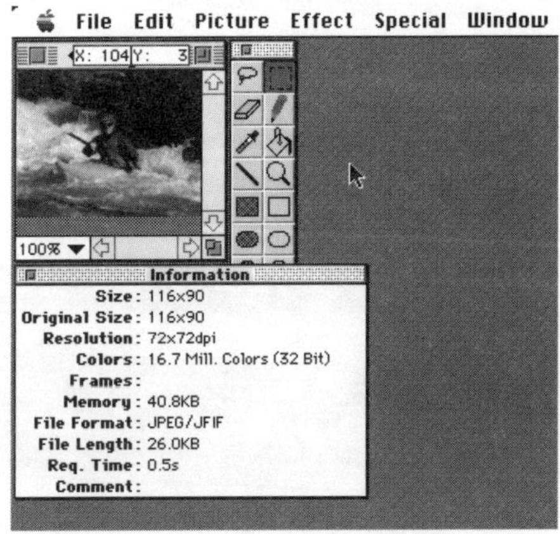

Now choose "Save as" from the File menu and choose a new filename for the thumbnail image.

Creating Transparent Backgrounds

As we mentioned in the section on transparent backgrounds, GraphicConverter can save an image with transparent color information. The procedure is fairly simple. First, use the Open command in the File menu to load your image into Graphic-Converter. Next, choose Colors from the Picture menu, and then choose Transparent GIF Color from the Colors menu:

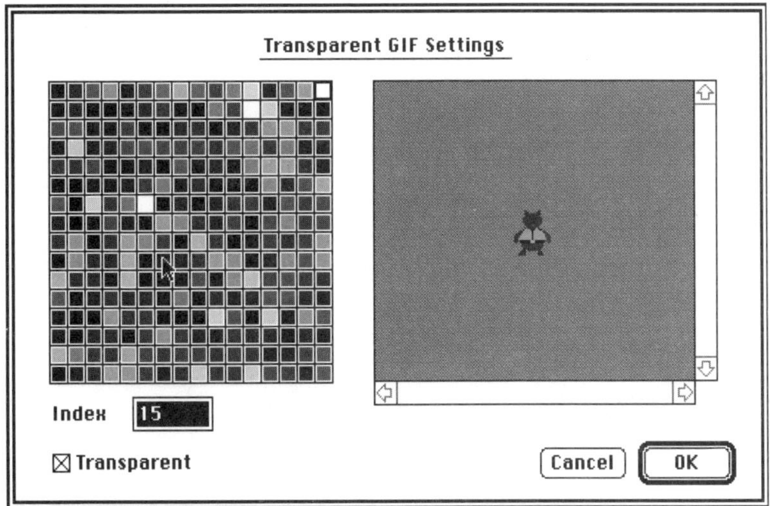

Select the palette entry for the color that you wish to make transparent. You do this by either clicking on the box with the color you want or entering the number for the color index. The display will show you how the image looks with the current setting. You should load the image in a browser that supports transparent backgrounds (such as NCSA Mosaic or Netscape Navigator) to verify that the image is in the correct format.

GraphicConverter can be used to manipulate your images in many other ways as well. For more information about this useful tool, read the Documentation file in the GraphicConverter folder. Finally—don't forget to register it if you choose to use it. At $35 for a US registration, it is a bargain!

Image Tag: <IMG>

HTML supports the ability to display embedded images within textual documents. The syntax for an embedded image is similar to the one used for links. The image itself is pointed to with a URL, as follows:

```
<IMG SRC=URL_of_image>
```

Let's use this element to add some pictures to our kayak document. It would be nice to have some pictures next to the choices in the table of contents at the beginning of the document. As you may recall, we had a table of contents that looked like this:

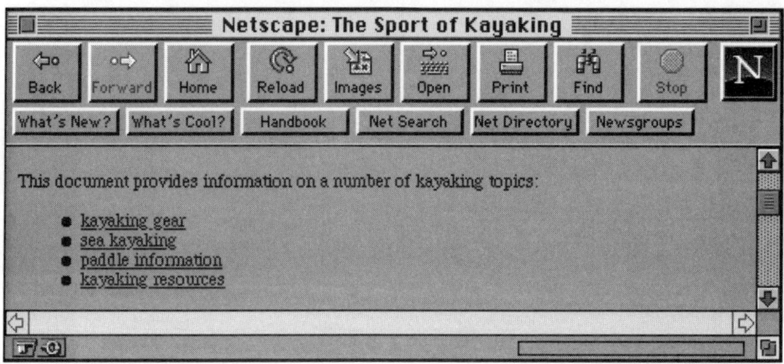

Those bullets are pretty boring, and we just happen to have some small GIF pictures that would work well in their place. We will put the image in the file kayak.gif next to "kayaking gear," and the image in sea.gif in next to "sea kayaking." Here are the commands we use to add these images:

```
<PRE>
<A HREF="kayak.htm#gear"><IMG SRC="gif/kayak.gif">
kayaking gear</A>
<A HREF="kayak.htm#seakayak"><IMG SRC="gif/sea.gif"> sea
kayaking</A>
```

If you look carefully at this example, you will see that we have placed both the images and the descriptive text inside an anchor tag. Although the images did not have to be inside the anchor, placing them includes them in the link. Now the reader can click on either the picture or the text to make the jump. As you will see, Netscape also frames images that are links to let the reader know that the link is there. Most other browsers use a frame to indicate the presence of a link, although some browsers may use other methods to display the link.

Now let's see how our changes affected the document:

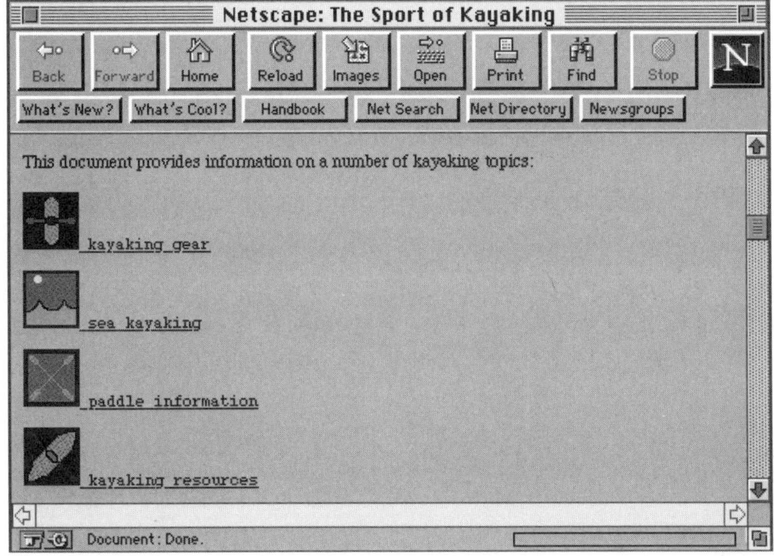

It's much fancier than our original list! Unfortunately there is a lot of wasted space, since HTML 2 doesn't provide a way to line things up in columns. This will change in the next version of HTML, but for now let's see how to do it using only HTML 2. We do this by enclosing our table of contents in <PRE> tags and adjusting our spacing to line up the images. Remember that line breaks are significant in areas that are tagged with <PRE>, so be careful not to accidentally insert extra lines. The lines in our document are too long to show here in their entirety, but you can look at them on the CD in the document kayak.html. Here we show you as much as will fit on the page:

```
<PRE>
<A HREF="#gear"><IMG SRC="gif/kayak.gif"> kayaking gear</A>...

<A HREF="#paddle"><IMG SRC="gif/paddle.gif"> paddle ...
</PRE>
```

We are going to make one more adjustment to the image and show you how it looks.

Aligning Images: ALIGN Attribute

Browsers generally display an embedded image with the bottom of the image aligned with the text in the document. For those of you who wish to align your images in some other manner, the IMG tag offers the ALIGN option. For aligning text with the top of an image, use ALIGN=TOP. For aligning text with the center of an image, use the ALIGN=MIDDLE tag. For example, if we want our kayak images to be aligned with the middle of the text baseline, we would change the image tags to include ALIGN=MIDDLE:

```
<IMG SRC="kayak.gif" ALIGN=MIDDLE>
```

Now let's take a look and see how PRE and ALIGN changed our document:

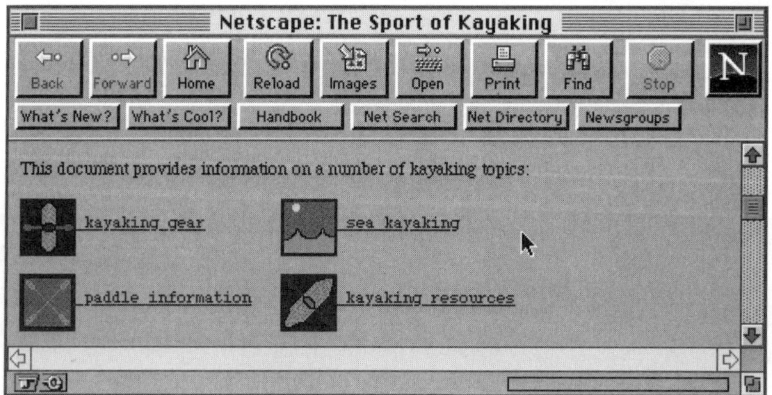

Images and Text-Only Browsers: ALT Attribute

Some browsers, such as Lynx, are not able to display images. Rather than simply ignoring those users, the ALT option allows you to display text to those users who use a browser that cannot display images.

With our kayak image, we may wish to substitute text indicating the content of the image for browsers that cannot display it, as follows:

```
<P><A HREF="#gear"><IMG SRC="gif/kayak.gif" ALT="[Kayak
Icon]"> kayaking gear</A>
<P><A HREF="#seakayak"><IMG SRC="gif/sea.gif" ALT="[Sea
Icon]"> sea kayaking</A>
<P><A HREF="#paddle"><IMG SRC="gif/paddle.gif" ALT="[Paddle
Icon]"> paddle information</A>
```

Users reading this document with a text-only browser will, instead of the embedded image, see the alternate text, such as "[Kayak Icon]." The following image shows how this section looks in Lynx.

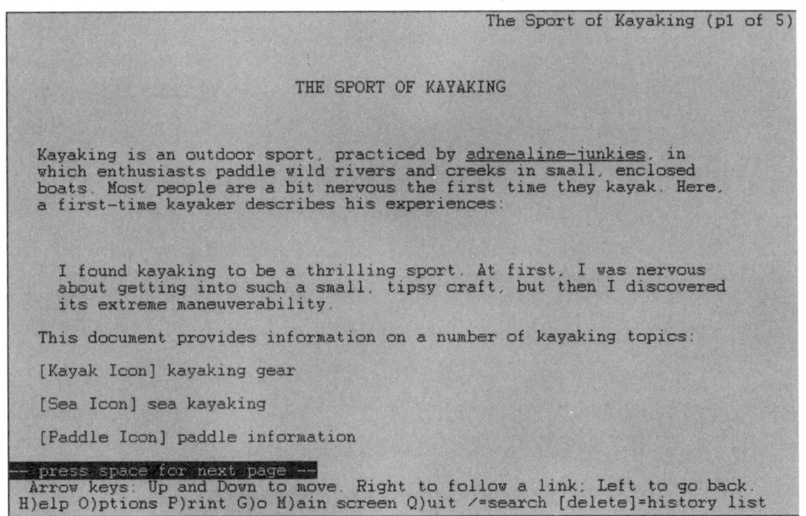

The Sport of Kayaking (p1 of 5)
THE SPORT OF KAYAKING
Kayaking is an outdoor sport, practiced by adrenaline-junkies, in which enthusiasts paddle wild rivers and creeks in small, enclosed boats. Most people are a bit nervous the first time they kayak. Here, a first-time kayaker describes his experiences:
I found kayaking to be a thrilling sport. At first, I was nervous about getting into such a small, tipsy craft, but then I discovered its extreme maneuverability.
This document provides information on a number of kayaking topics:
[Kayak Icon] kayaking gear
[Sea Icon] sea kayaking
[Paddle Icon] paddle information
-- press space for next page --
Arrow keys: Up and Down to move. Right to follow a link; Left to go back.
H)elp O)ptions P)rint G)o M)ain screen Q)uit /=search [delete]=history list

Netscape Extensions to IMG

For those of you who wish to tailor your documents for readers using the Netscape Navigator browser, there are many additional attributes available for the IMG element. These extensions include greater control over alignment, borders, and size declarations (to help the browser display documents more quickly).

Netscape extended the alignment attribute for IMG. In addition to the original top, middle, and bottom options, Netscape has added left, right, texttop, absmiddle, baseline and absbottom. Four of these new options are:

TEXTTOP
: Align the image with the top of the tallest text in the line (this is usually, but not always, the same as ALIGN=top).

ABSMIDDLE
: Align the middle of the current line with the middle of the image. The difference between this option and the standard HTML middle option is that middle aligns the baseline of the current line with the middle of the image.

BASELINE
: Align the bottom of the image with the baseline of the current line (identical to ALIGN=bottom). Since ALIGN=bottom is standard HTML, it is better to use it than this Netscape-only option.

ABSBOTTOM
: Align the bottom of the image with the bottom of the current line.

Here is an example to illustrate the way these options place images:

```
<P>In the following examples notice how the alignment commands
affect the location of the baseline. If you plan on including
more than one image in a line, you should be careful of your
use of these alignment commands</P>
<PP>These images are aligned
<IMG SRC=gif/sailb2.gif ALIGN=texttop>
<IMG SRC=gif/sailb2.gif ALIGN=baseline>
<IMG SRC=gif/sailb2.gif ALIGN=absbottom>
<IMG SRC=gif/sailb2.gif ALIGN=absmiddle>
in this order: texttop, baseline, absbottom, absmiddle.</P>
<P>These images are aligned
<IMG SRC=gif/sailb2.gif ALIGN=baseline>
<IMG SRC=gif/sailb2.gif ALIGN=absmiddle>
<IMG SRC=gif/sailb2.gif ALIGN=absbottom>
<IMG SRC=gif/sailb2.gif ALIGN=texttop>
in this order: baseline, absmiddle, absbottom, texttop.</P>
<P>These images are aligned
<IMG SRC=gif/sailb2.gif ALIGN=texttop>
<IMG SRC=gif/sailb2.gif ALIGN=absmiddle>
<IMG SRC=gif/sailb2.gif ALIGN=absbottom>
<IMG SRC=gif/sailb2.gif ALIGN=baseline>
in this order: textop, absmiddle, absbottom, baseline.
```

Here is this section of the document:

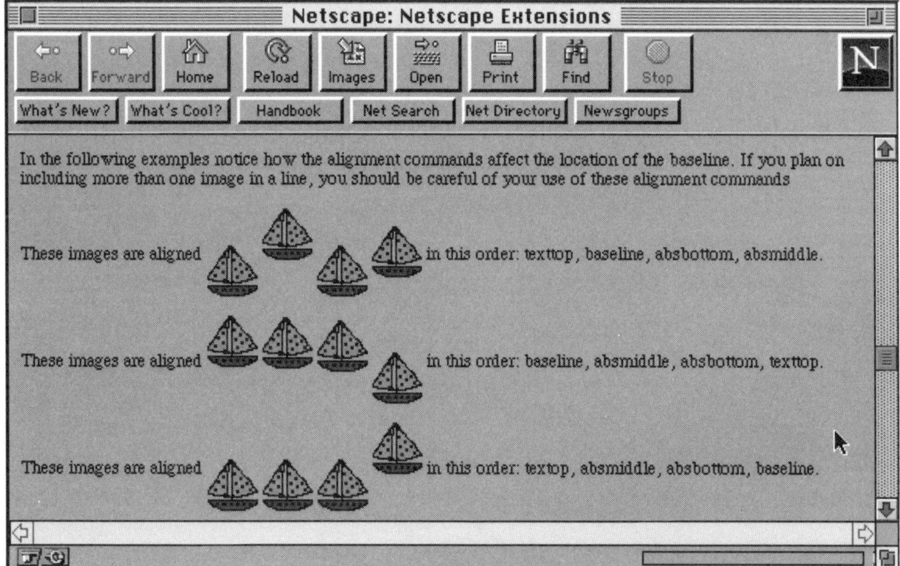

There are two more Netscape alignment options: left and right. These options "float" the image to the left or right margin rather than displaying it at the point in the text where the tag is placed.

LEFT

Floats the image down and over to the left margin (into the next available space there). Subsequent text will wrap around the right-hand side of that image.

RIGHT

Aligns the image with the right margin and wraps the text around the left.

Here is a paragraph using these options:

```
<P><IMG SRC=gif/sailb2.gif ALIGN=left> Now let's sail our
little boat on the left and right of this paragraph. This is an
example of floating images, where text will just go next to the
image rather than leaving space around it.
<IMG SRC=gif/sailb2.gif ALIGN=right> New attributes have been
added to the BR tag to allow you to cause the lines to be
displayed under the image. You can also use the Netscape VSPACE
and HSPACE attributes with IMG to leave extra vertical or
horizontal space around an image. </P>
```

Here is the way this paragraph looks in Netscape:

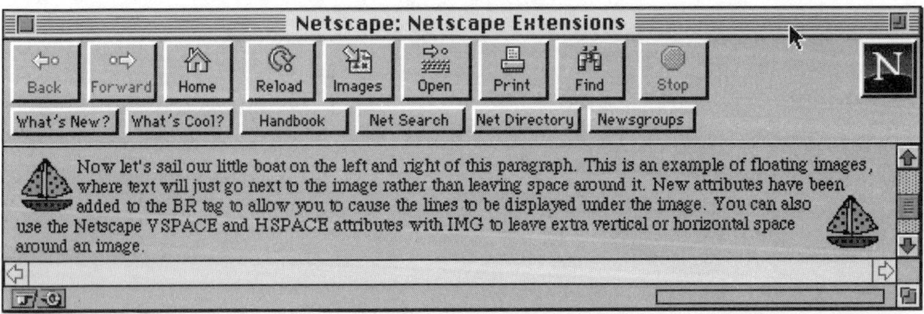

Other Netscape attributes include:

WIDTH and HEIGHT

These attributes allow you to specify the size of the image. They are used to allow the browser to display documents with images more quickly by reserving space for the image without having to wait for the image to be downloaded to calculate the size.

BORDER

This attribute lets you control the thickness of the border around an image. You can confuse readers by setting BORDER=0 on images that are also part of anchors, since this will eliminate the colored border normally placed around an image to indicate the presence of a link.

Since the WIDTH and HEIGHT attributes affect only the way images are loaded by the browser, we can't show you an example here. However, we can show you an example of BORDER:

```
<P>Now we will place our <IMG SRC=gif/sailb2.gif ALIGN=left
BORDER=6> little sailboat on the left, and give it a thick
border (BORDER=6)</P>
```

Here is this paragraph in Netscape:

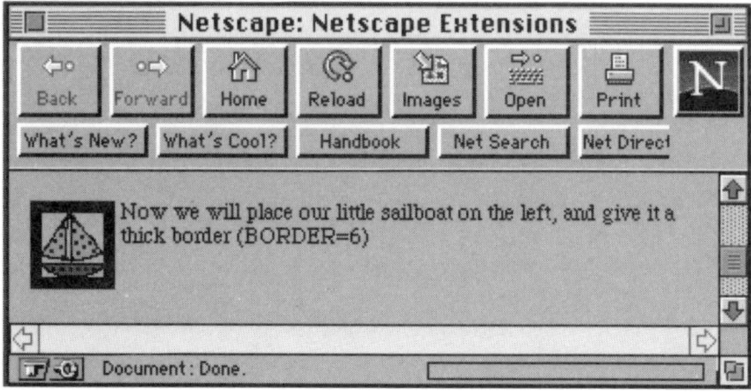

For the sake of completeness, we mention two other attributes here: VSPACE and HSPACE. These attributes are supposed to allow you to create empty space around floating images. However, although these attributes are described in Netscape's documents, and although we found support for these attributes in some earlier versions of Netscape, the latest version of the browser at the time this book was written no longer supported them. We recommend that you avoid these attributes.

Image Maps, Images with Clickable Spots

We've explained how to make images that are links. Now we'll show you how to do even fancier linking with images. Rather than making the entire image a single link, it is possible to make images with "hot spots" that have links. Readers can click on these spots to follow the link. For example, you could include the image of a map with hot spots that link points on the map to documents which describe those locations; or a picture of a car with each part of the car linked to a document describing how that part works.

Clickable images work by being associated with a coordinate map of the image that has links associated with specific coordinates. The association between the map and image is made by the server, so clickable images only work through a server. Here are the basic steps of making a clickable image:

1. *Get an image. The best images for this purpose should have well-defined sections and be in GIF format.*

2. *Decide what links you want to make to which sections of your image.*

3. *Make a coordinate map for your image. Different servers use different formats, so you will need to know the appropriate format for your server before you do this. You can make a map manually or with an application such as WebMap. We strongly recommend using an application to make the map.*

4. *Add information about your coordinate map to your Web server. If you are running your own server, you can do this yourself. If not, you'll need to ask the person in charge of your Web server to do it for you.*

5. *Make a document that includes your clickable image. You specify the image as being clickable by including the ISMAP attribute with the IMG tag.*

6. *Load your document in a browser and check it.*

Choosing Images for Image Maps

Not all images are suitable for use with image maps. In general, the more clearly the areas within the image are delineated from each other, the better the image is for use as an image map. Most photographs make poor image maps, since areas in photos are usually not well defined, making it difficult for users to know where to click to make the jump. Graphics with numerous buttons make good image maps.

If you wish to use a photograph for an image map, you should consider using an image processing program such as Adobe's Photoshop to make clear-cut areas in the image. However, remember that clickable areas in image maps are constrained to certain shapes, so that irregularly shaped areas will have to fit within one of these shapes.

Another way that photographs may be incorporated into an image map is to put several photographs together and have each photograph be a separate hot spot.

Image Map Formats

There are two formats for image map files—one for CERN-based servers and another for NCSA-based servers. Different servers use different formats for these maps, so you need to know which format your server uses. To further complicate matters the allowable shapes for hot spots differ between these two formats: rectangles, circles and polygons for CERN, and rectangles, circles, points, and polygons with NCSA-based servers.

NCSA image maps are in the format:

```
#Comment lines may be included
default URL
rect URL x,y,x2,y2
circle URL x,y,r
poly URL x1,y1,x2,y2,x3,y3,x4,y4...
point URL x,y
```

CERN image maps are in the format:

```
#Comment lines may be included
default URL
rectangle (x,y) (x2,y2) URL
circle (x,y) r URL
poly (x,y) (x1,y1)....(xn,yn) URL
```

For example, here is a map file in NCSA format:

```
default http://localhost/kayak.html
rect /kelly/kayak.html#resources 285,1 379,127
rect /kelly/kayak.html#paddle 192,0 283,125
rect /kelly/kayak.html#seakayak 102,1 191,127
rect /kelly/kayak.html#gear 1,0 101,127
```

And the same map in CERN format:

```
default http://localhost/kayak.html
rectangle (1,0) (101,127) /kelly/kayak.html#gear
rectangle (102,1) (191,127) /kelly/kayak.html#seakayak
rectangle (192,0) (283,125) /kelly/kayak.html#paddle
rectangle (285,1) (379,127) /kelly/kayak.html#resources
```

The process of figuring out the coordinates for each area in your image map by hand can be very tedious. Fortunately, we have included a program on the CD that automates this process for you.

WebMap

WebMap automates the process of image map creation. It allows you to outline polygons, circles and rectangles on top of your GIF and PICT images, and link a URL to each item. WebMap also allows you to go back and delete these "hot spots," set a default URL for clicks outside of the "hot" areas and associate comments of arbitrary length with each object. It even knows about the formats for the NCSA and CERN servers.

You will find WebMap in the Utilities Folder on the CD. To install it simply drag its folder to your hard disk. You can find updates for WebMap on the Internet at:

```
http://www.city.net/cnx/software
```

Running WebMap

To start WebMap, open the WebMap folder and click the WebMap icon:

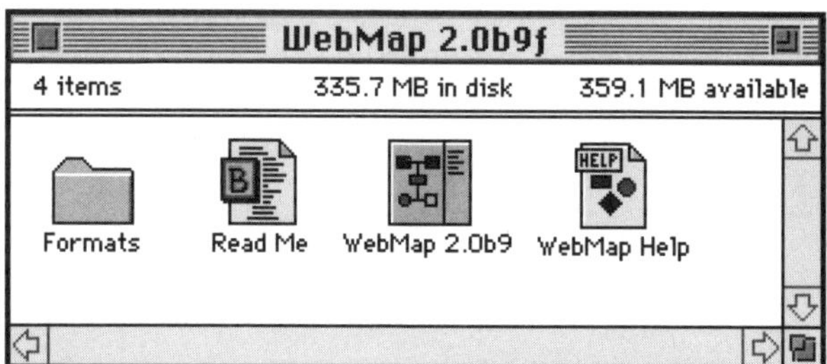

Using WebMap

Let's see how to use WebMap by going through an example. Rather than using separate images in our table of contents, let's combine our images into one and turn it into an image map. Before proceeding however, a word of caution should you decide to use an image map as a table of contents: remember to provide a corresponding text-based table of contents in

addition to your image map. If you don't you will lose readers who are browsing with image loading turned off, and readers who are unable to view images.

Our image is in kayakmenubar.gif:

The first step is to load our image into WebMap. From the File pulldown menu, we choose Open, enter the name of our image file, and get this screen:

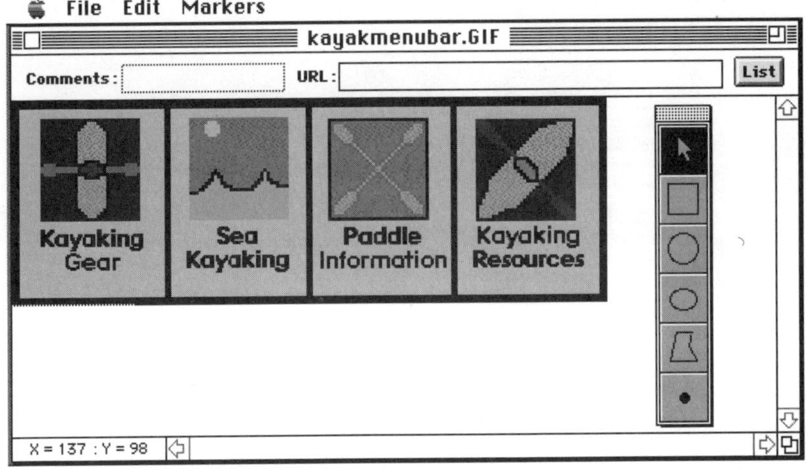

Next we make a link to the appropriate section of the image for each topic in our table of contents. To do this we need to outline the section of the image that we wish to link, and then associate the appropriate URL with it. We choose the rectangle from the shape menu bar, since our image has a rectangular section for each topic. Now we are ready to start making "hot spots." We outline each section of the image that we wish to link. As we outline the area, we enter the URL for the link in the URL box, and a description of the link in the Comments box. After we are done creating the regions and associating URLs with them, we click on the LIST button to review our list:

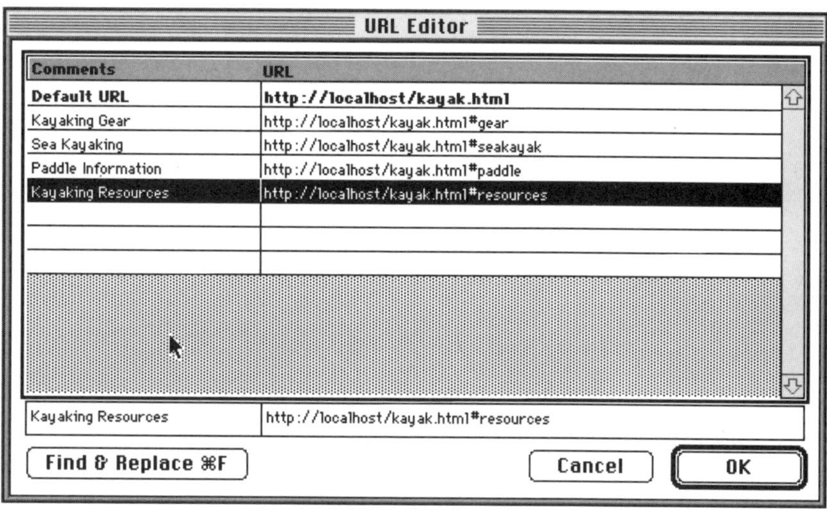

After we are done, we choose "Export As Text" under the File menu to save the map into a text file.

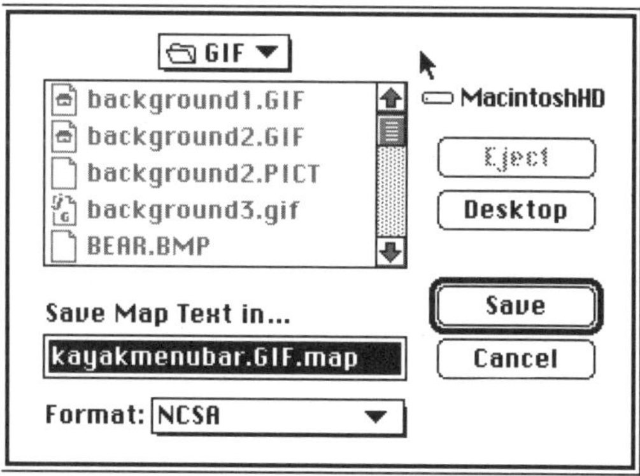

Here is how our finished map looks:

```
# Created by WebMap 2.0b9
# Monday, November 13, 1995 at 11:13 AM
# Format: NCSA
#
rect http://localhost/kayak.html#resources 285,1 379,127
rect http://localhost/kayak.html#paddle 192,0 283,125
rect file://localhost/kayak.html#seakayak 102,1 191,127
rect file://localhost/kayak.html#gear 1,0 101,127
default http://localhost/kayak.html
```

WebMap stores the markers for the links in the resource fork of the image file. If you wish to remove all of the markers, you can remove the file, which should be found in "filename*m*". For example, the file for our image kayakmenubar.GIF is kayakmenubar.GIFm.

Clickable Images: ISMAP

Now we are ready to add the image to our document. We use the IMG element ISMAP attribute to indicate that this is a "clickable image." ISMAP is an attribute that identifies an image as an image map. We place the image in an anchor tag that links it to the imagemap application in the server area. You will need to get the appropriate command for the imagemap program on your Web server from the person in charge of it. In our case, the line for the imagemap would be:

```
<A HREF="http://ozone.com/imagemap/kayakmenubar"><IMG
SRC="kayakmenubar.GIF" ISMAP></A>
```

Since we are using the MacHTTP server, and have control over it, we can add information about our image ourselves (you may need to coordinate this with the person in charge of your Web server). We go to the file "imagemap.config" in the imagemap folder in the MacHTTP folder, and add the line:

```
kayakmenubar : :kayak:kayakmenubar.gif.map
```

You will not be able to test a clickable image if you open a file locally with a browser. The server handles the mapping, so you can only access the hot spot functionality through a server.

A new Netscape attribute, USEMAP, is similar to ISMAP, but provides a way to create clickable images without a server. You can find more about this attribute in Chapter 6.

Background Images and Color

HTML 3 and Netscape offer new attributes to the BODY tag that allow you to include a background image or to change the background and text color used to display your document.

Image Backgrounds: BACKGROUND

In HTML 3 an attribute has been added to the BODY tag to allow you to specify an image to be used as a background for your document. The format for this attribute is:

```
<BODY BACKGROUND="background.gif">
```

Background images are displayed by tiling the image to fill up the background.

Not every image is suitable for a background. If you are using a textured image, make sure that it has been created so that the edges meet smoothly. Otherwise you will end up with seams where the "tiles" meet. Image size is also important. Since your document won't be displayed until the image is loaded, you should try to keep the image fairly small. If you are using GIF images, don't interlace them. Interlacing slightly increases the size of the image file, and unlike single images in a document, interlacing doesn't add anything to the appearance during the loading of the image. If you plan to use a photograph or some other highly textured image as a background, compare the file size between JPEG and GIF. All the browsers that we've found which support BACKGROUND also support JPEG, so you may be able to reduce your file size by using JPEG rather than GIF format.

Finally, check to make sure that your text is visible. If you use a dark image, the default text color may make your text difficult or impossible to read. You can use the TEXT attribute described later in this chapter to get around this problem. However, keep in mind that the attributes for setting colors for the text in your documents are Netscape extensions and may not be supported in other browsers (we did find support for image backgrounds in Internet Explorer).

Netscape offers a number of GIF-format images suitable for backgrounds on its server. You can find these images at the URL:

```
http://home.netscape.com/assist/net_sites/bg/backgrounds.html
```

Background Color (Netscape): BGCOLOR

In addition to support for the HTML 3 BACKGROUND attribute, Netscape added a number of additional attributes that allow you to specify background, foreground, and link colors for your document. This is important, since it is easy to obscure the default text color with many background images. The background attribute is BGCOLOR and is specified as follows:

```
<BODY BGCOLOR="#rrggbb">
```

#rrggbb is the hexadecimal red-blue-green triplet that represents the color to be used. Each pair of letters is a hexadecimal number between 00 and FF that represents one of the shades of a color.

Text Colors (Netscape): TEXT, ALINK, LINK and VLINK

The foreground (text) color is specified with the TEXT attribute:

```
<BODY TEXT="#rrggbb">
```

Link colors are specified with the ALINK, LINK, and VLINK attributes:

```
<BODY ALINK="#rrggbb" LINK="#rrggbb" VLINK="#rrggbb">
```

ALINK stands for the active link, VLINK controls the color for visited links, and LINK specifies the color for all other links.

HTML ColorMeister

If you wish to set a background or text color, finding the correct code for the colors you wish to use can be a painful process. Fortunately for you the CD includes HTML ColorMeister, a handy freeware utility by John Cope. This application not only translates colors into their corresponding numerical codes but can create your document framework with the appropriate information. If you prefer to use an image rather than a background color, it offers that option as well. To start ColorMeister, click on its icon:

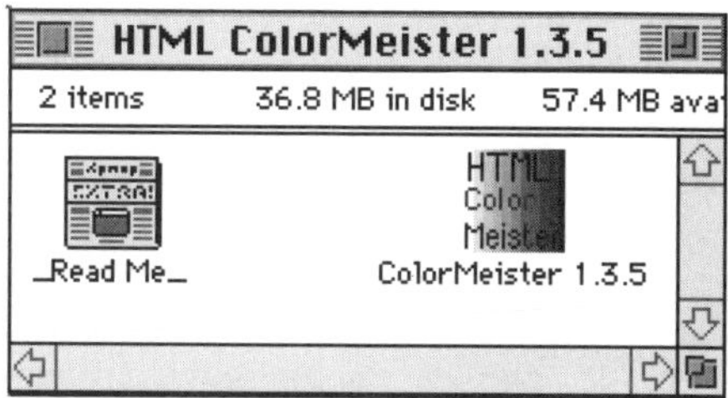

It will present you with a form:

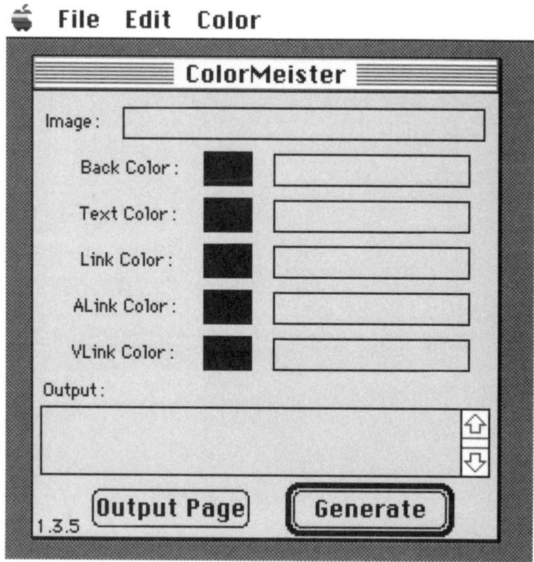

If you wish to use a background image, enter the URL for the image in the Image box. Keep in mind that a background image will prevent a background color from being seen. However the background color may show briefly while the document is being loaded into a browser. It is generally a good idea to choose a background color that matches the main color in your background image so that the document has a consistent look while loading.

For each item's color you wish to set, click on the color box next to the item. You will be given the following form:

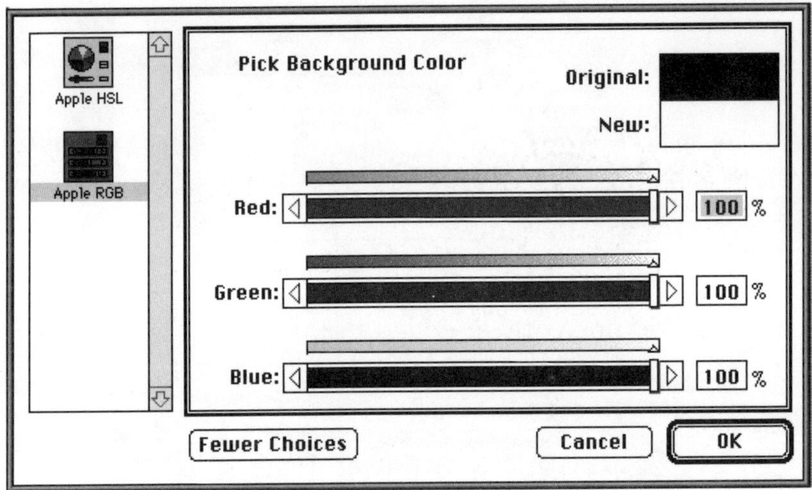

Select the color you want by moving the slide on the color. The color you have chosen will be displayed in the "New" box. Click "OK" to return to the main form. Repeat the procedure for each attribute you wish to set. You can pull up a preview window by choosing Show Preview from the File menu:

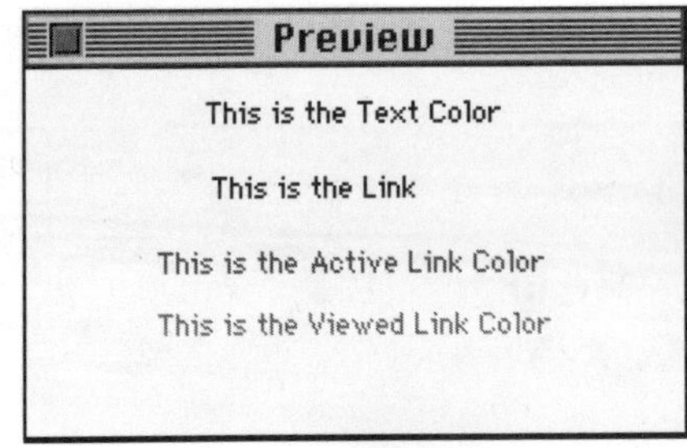

When you have set the colors and images to your satisfaction, click the "Generate" button to see the BODY line that corresponds to your choices:

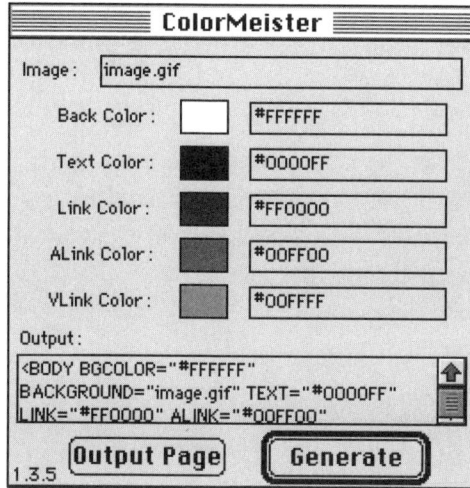

You can copy the line in the Output box directly into your document, or if you wish, you can have ColorMeister create a document template for you by clicking "Output Page."

GIF89a Animations

Beginning with Version 2, Netscape browsers support GIF89a animations. If your readers are using this version (or higher) of the Netscape browser, GIF98a animation provides a simple way to add animation to your pages.

There are many advantages to using GIF89a animations over animation through server-push or client-pull. Some of them include:

- Everything is in one file. Once the image file is loaded, no further network connections are needed (vs. multiple connections for client pull, or a lengthy connection for server push).
- Small file size. The spinning globe we will use as an example takes only 17kb.

- Unlike animation that is done with client pull, there is no need for multiple HTML files. It's all contained in a single image file.
- No need for access to the CGI directory. These are just images and can be used like any other image. If the viewing browser doesn't support animation, only the first "frame" will be displayed.
- No additional overhead if you reuse the image in a document. Once the image is loaded, you can use it over and over in the same document, and it doesn't need to be reloaded over the network.

GifBuilder

Yves Piguet has created a terrific freeware application that allows you to quickly create a GIF animation. At the time this book was written he had just released it and was still making frequent updates. We have not included it on the CD, but you can find a pointer to download it across the Internet in our utilities.html document. We don't expect the basic interface to change, so we'll explain briefly how to create an animation with this utility.

The animation that we'll create is a spinning globe. We have ten small GIF images showing a globe in different steps of the rotation. Our goal is combine these images into a single GIF89a file along with the appropriate control information for Netscape. Our example uses GifBuilder 0.2:

Probably the easiest way to start your build is to choose all the files that you wish to use and then drop them onto the GifBuilder icon. In our case, we are using files named globe1.gif through globe10.gif. After we choose them and drop them on the icon, GifBuilder starts, and opens a frame window that looks like this:

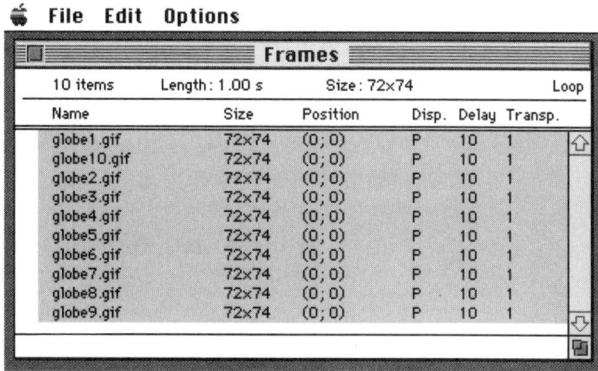

File Edit Options

Frames

10 items   Length: 1.00 s   Size: 72x74   Loop

Name	Size	Position	Disp.	Delay	Transp.
globe1.gif	72x74	(0; 0)	P	10	1
globe10.gif	72x74	(0; 0)	P	10	1
globe2.gif	72x74	(0; 0)	P	10	1
globe3.gif	72x74	(0; 0)	P	10	1
globe4.gif	72x74	(0; 0)	P	10	1
globe5.gif	72x74	(0; 0)	P	10	1
globe6.gif	72x74	(0; 0)	P	10	1
globe7.gif	72x74	(0; 0)	P	10	1
globe8.gif	72x74	(0; 0)	P	10	1
globe9.gif	72x74	(0; 0)	P	10	1

As you can see, the files show up in alphabetical order. Since we want globe10.gif to be displayed after globe9.gif, we move it by control-clicking to choose it, and then dragging it to the correct position. A black bar should show up under the line of the image being moved.

Now that we have the images in the desired order, we need to add a loop block so that Netscape Navigator will know what to do with it. This is done by going to the Options menu and making sure that "Looping" is checked.

We make two more adjustments. First we set up a transparent background. Even if the original GIF images are saved with transparent backgrounds, transparency will not work unless it is also set in the final GIF file's control blocks. For our images, the first pixel in each image is part of the background, so we choose "Based on first pixel" from the "Transparent Background" option. Our final change is to turn off interlacing in the options menu.

Now we are ready to build our animated GIF image. To do this we simply choose "Build" from the File menu. It brings up a dialog box to provide a filename for the output file. We chose spinning-globe.gif for our output file. That's it! You can see our final globe by looking at the animated-gif.html document.

GifBuilder provides other options such bit depth control, color palette. It can also take PICT and TIFF files as input. If you'd like to try building a globe yourself, you will find the individual globe images in the spinning-globe folder, which is in the gif folder.

Video

Video and animations are two of the most dramatic and eye-catching elements that you can include in your Web documents. The two most common formats used on the Web are Quicktime and MPEG (Moving Picture Expert Group).

Quicktime is a format originally developed by Apple, which allows users to view and edit digital video, animation, sound, text, music, and other dynamic information. From a technical point of view, Quicktime supports two kinds of files: image files and time-based movie files. Apple maintains a Quicktime Web site at:

```
http://quicktime.apple.com
```

MPEG is a standard for digital video and audio compression. MPEG is expected to become the industry standard for delivery of interactive television. Note that older versions of MPEG do not support digitized audio. These MPEG file using the older standard sometimes come with accompanying sound files in WAV format. Quicktime also supports MPEG compressed video.

On the CD we have provided examples of movies in both Quicktime and MPEG formats, so that you can compare the two.

In this next section we describe three aspects of video usage: preparing video for Web use, incorporating video in Web documents, and viewing video within Web documents.

Preparing Video

There are many ways to compose digital video in a Macintosh environment. For example, the small QuickCam camera, made by Connectix, will plug directly into most Macintoshes. Or, if you have an AV Mac, you can plug a VCR directly into your computer.

While the actual process of making high-quality video is beyond the scope of this book, we mention one critical aspect for Web publishing. Many tools for creating and editing Quicktime movies may create documents that reference other movie documents and resources. In the Macintosh world, this is called a multifork file. Since this is a Mac-specific implementation, it is not supported by the Web protocol. Therefore, to create Quicktime movies that contain all the necessary data for Web use, you must make sure that your movie is "self-contained" and "flattened."

Creating a "self-contained" movie usually involves selecting this option when saving the movie file.

Flattening combines all resources used by the movie into one data fork. Some applications will include flattening as an option when saving the movie. Otherwise, you must use a separate tool. The most reliable application we have found is a shareware tool called "FlattenMooV." You simply open your movie document within the FlattenMooV application, then save it again as a flattened movie.

Once you have flattened and made your movie self-contained, it is ready to be incorporated into Web documents.

Incorporating Video

Incorporating video in your Web documents is no different than including other multimedia elements. As usual with Web documents, the use of video and its format is specified via the filename extension. For Quicktime, use .qt or .mov as the extension. For MPEG, use .mpg, .mpeg, or .mpe as the file name extension.

A video link is also specified in the usual way, with the <A> tag. For example, suppose Kelly wanted to include a link to a Quicktime movie on kayaking, called kayaking.mov. She would write her link as follows:

```
<A HREF="kayaking.mov">My kayaking movie</A>.
```

Viewing Video

If you are using one of the popular Web browsers, all you need in order to view video is the appropriate "helper" application. If your browser is properly configured, it will automatically download the video with the correct viewer.

To view Quicktime movies, use Apple's MoviePlayer application or Sparkle. Sparkle is a shareware application which can play both MPEG and Quicktime movies. You can also use this application for converting between formats. This software requires the Threads Manager (which comes with System 7.5) and works better with Quicktime 2.0 (which also comes with System 7.5). You can find a copy of Sparkle on the CD in the Utilities folder.

A document named video.html is provided on the CD that includes a number of videos. The Quicktime video that is part of this document was made with a black-and-white digital video camera called QuickCam, made by Connectix. Although it is a short clip—only about eight seconds long—it takes up 880K of disk space. If it were color, the clip would take up even more space. This should drive home the point that video storage requires large amounts of disk space.

We translated the clip into MPEG format, and now it only takes up about 180K. If you view the clip, you will see that we've lost both quality and sound!

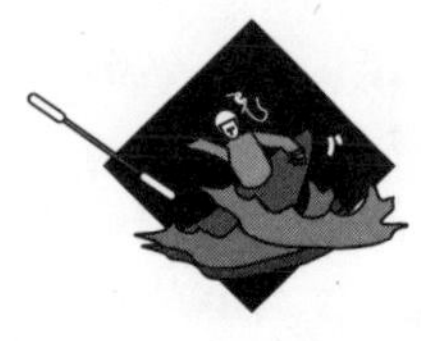

In sum, if you plan to incorporate video into your Web documents, you must ensure that you have adequate disk space. In addition, you'll probably also want to have a fast server machine and a fairly high-bandwidth network connection. Otherwise, Web clients trying to retrieve video documents risk

having to wait a long time while the video is transferred. Worse, if it takes too long, their network connection might abort partway through the process!

Links to Images, Sounds, Movies

Instead of embedding images, you may wish to include pointers in your document to external images, sound, movies and so on. This way, users can decide if they wish to load and view large nontext documents. To include a pointer to such files, the usual link syntax is used, and the external document is referred to via a URL. As with embedded images, the filename extension must be used to specify the file type. Browsers need to know the file type of a nontext document in order to use the appropriate viewer to display them. It is also desirable to include the size of the file that is being linked so that readers can decide ahead of time if they have the time and space to download the document.

The Good, the Bad and the Ugly

Turning a Web document into a multimedia presentation can be fun, but it is easy to get carried away. Here are some guidelines to keep your documents under control:

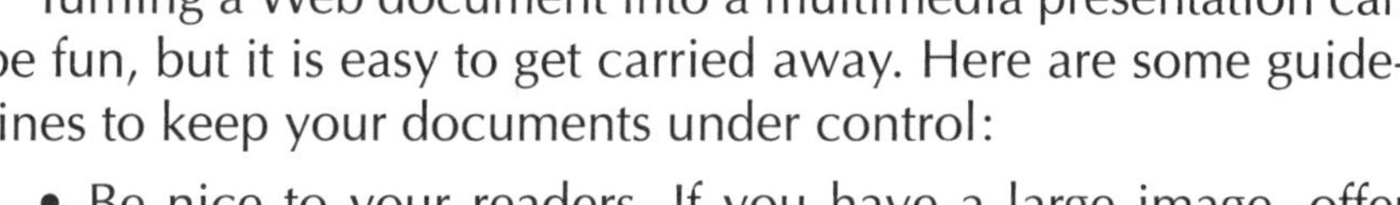

- Be nice to your readers. If you have a large image, offer either a thumbnail or a plain-text link to it. On a related note, for video and sound as well as images, it is a good idea to include the size of the multimedia element next to the link that will be used to retrieve it.

- Remember to use the ALT attribute so that readers without a graphical browser are not left out.
- If is often possible to reduce an image's storage requirements by reducing the number of colors in its palette. You can do this with GraphicConverter. Reducing the number of colors also reduces the likelihood that all of the available colors on your reader's system will get used up.

- Generally speaking, you should try to offer your images in GIF format.
- Interlaced images will allow readers with a browser that supports this format to see what the image looks like more quickly.

In toc.html on the CD you can see the versions of the kayak table of contents we've gone over in this chapter.

Desktop digital video has only recently become widely available. This means that the technology is rapidly evolving. It also means that there are many factors that can affect the quality and effectiveness of video within Web documents.

First, digitized video takes up a significant amount of disk space. If you plan to make extensive use of video, you need to make sure you have enough disk space available. You can reduce disk-space usage by using higher compression rates, though the resulting quality of the video will suffer.

In the network's Web environment, other factors will also affect the quality of video playback. Some of these factors are:

- The power of the server machine. A more powerful server will serve large files faster.
- The speed of the network connection. With large video files and slow network connections, downloading will take a long time, and may even time-out!
- The power of the client machine. A more powerful client will play movie files faster.
- The "helper" viewer application used. These vary in how well they implement and support the video standards.
- The options set by the user in the viewer application. Different settings will affect playback quality and speed.

In this chapter you will learn

- How to create documents supporting user input
- About the Common Gateway Interface (CGI)
- About server push and client pull for making animated pages

Creating Interactive and Dynamic Documents

What's In This Chapter

In this chapter we describe how to create interactive and dynamic documents. We first describe how to create documents that contain tags supporting user input (via Forms). We describe how to write scripts (or programs) that process user input and send new output to users back through the Web server, via the Common Gateway Interface (CGI). We then discuss dynamic documents. Such documents can be created on the fly to contain tailored information, such as the current date and time. Similarly, with the use of Java and VRML, documents can contain nonstatic information, such as animations and executable programs. We also provide and explain how to use a JavaScript script that creates a scrolling message in the status bar.

Introduction

By definition, Web documents are interactive. If a document contains a hyperlink, users can individually select links and choose their own pathway through the information.

The Web also supports other ways for users to interact with documents. HTML Version 2.0 and higher provide support for several kinds of user interactions. For example, Web documents can contain graphics with clickable regions and support keyword searches of databases. Documents can also cause a program to be executed with the input to the program supplied by the user. The output from the program is then displayed to the user, typically in a new Web document. We call these kinds of documents highly interactive documents.

In a typical scenario, user input and output is processed in the following manner. A Web document uses special set of HTML tags, called forms, to collect user input. This document also specifies the name of the program on the Web server that should process the user input. After the user has entered the desired input, it is then packaged by the browser and sent to the server. The Web server recognizes that this particular browser request contains a user query and specifies a program. Accordingly, the server ships the user input to the responsible program and continues being a Web server. In turn, the program is run using the input from the user. If the program has output—for example, a new Web document—the program sends the output to the server, which then ships it back to the requesting browser. In this way, the Web documents returned to users are specifically tailored to users' input. Figure 5–1 illustrates this process.

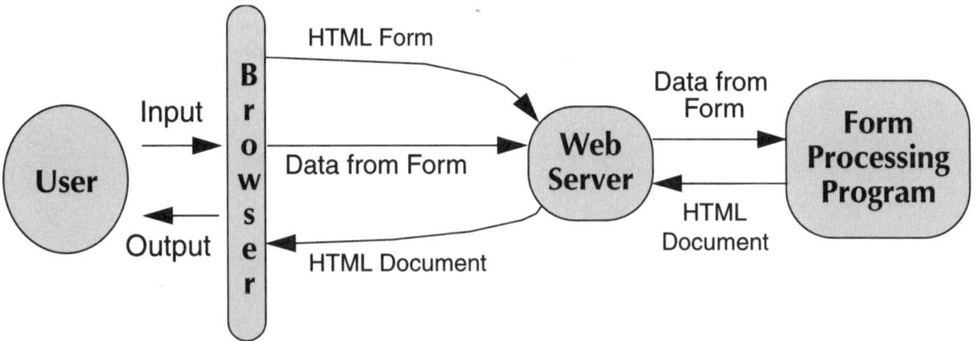

FIGURE 5–1 *Flow of Information for Forms.*

In this chapter we first describe markup tags that support higher levels of interaction with the user. We then describe the latest in Web technologies for supporting the creation of dynamic pages.

Forms

Our description begins with the FORM tag. As with all HTML elements, forms depend on browsers, and their support varies wildly from browser to browser. This is one area where testing your documents in several browsers is especially important. We will display each of our examples in at least two browsers to give you some idea of the variety you can expect.

Although most browsers we tested support forms in some fashion, there are still many browsers that don't. When you use form elements in a document, you should warn your readers that they may not be able to access all the features by including a line stating that forms support is required.

Forms: <FORM>

The form element is an HTML tag that is used to demark a data input form (or fill-in-the-form). A region using forms is enclosed within the <FORM> </FORM> pair of markup tags. A

Web document can contain several forms, but the form element itself cannot be nested within other form elements. However, forms can be embedded within other HTML tags. Similarly, within a forms region, the usual HTML formatting tags can be inserted.

The form element allows three possible attributes. They are ACTION, METHOD, and ENCTYPE. We explain ACTION and METHOD in the following example.

Suppose we wish to author a user-survey questionnaire within a Web document. We begin our form as follows:

```
<HTML>
<HEAD>
<TITLE>Testing Forms</TITLE>
</HEAD>
<BODY>
<H1>User Survey</H1>
<FORM METHOD="POST" ACTION="http://ozone.com/cgi/survey.cgi">
</FORM>
```

The ACTION attribute specifies the destination URL to which the form should be submitted once it has been completed by the user. If no URL is specified, the URL of the current document containing the form is used. Here, our destination URL is:

```
http://ozone.com/cgi/survey.cgi
```

In this example the file "survey.cgi" is a CGI script that parses and collates users' responses. We have located the program in the folder called "cgi". The actual location of CGI scripts or programs is dependent on how the server is set up and must be discussed with your server administrator.

The method used to transmit the user's response is defined by both the access method contained in the URL and the value of the METHOD attribute. Thus, the value contained in the METHOD attribute must be compatible with the access method defined in the URL. The method attribute specifies the way in which the data from the user is encoded; the program that receives the user input naturally expects the user data to be encoded in this manner.

The default METHOD is GET. However, for most applications, we prefer the POST method. The reason for this preference will become clear in the section on CGI scripts. Note that the value of the METHOD attribute is case sensitive on some servers!

As we will describe, a form is generally submitted by the user once the "Submit" button or "Return" key is pressed. When a form is submitted, the destination URL receives a string containing the selections and text entry made by the responding user. The method you choose (GET or POST) determines how the data is sent to the server. The selection of a method is a server-side issue and must be discussed with your Web server administrator. In the section on CGI scripts we explain how to use CGI scripts to decode data sent via forms.

Each field within a form is defined by the following nested elements: INPUT, TEXTAREA, SELECT, and OPTION. These are described next. These fields must use the NAME attribute to identify the value selected by the user when the form is completed and submitted by the user. Thus, the submitted contents usually contain a stream of name/value pairs. The name is equal to the NAME attributes of the various elements within the form. The value is equal to the entries made by the responding user.

Input: <INPUT>

The Input tag is a nested element within a form, denoted by <INPUT>. It specifies the kind of input field presented to the user. The contents of the input field are then modifiable by the user.

The Input tag uses the following, optional attributes: NAME, TYPE, CHECKED, ALIGN, MAXLENGTH, SIZE, SRC, and VALUE. A summary of these attributes may be found in Table 5–1.

TABLE 5–1 Input Attributes

Attribute	Description
NAME	The name of the particular form item. This attribute is required for most input types. When parsing a user's input, the NAME value is used to provide a meaningful identifier for a field.
CHECKED	Indicates that a checkbox or radio button is selected.
ALIGN	When an image is used, this specifies the vertical alignment of the image. The syntax is the same as that of the <IMG> tag.
MAXLENGTH	Indicates the maximum number of characters that can be entered by users in a text field. If this attribute is not set, there is no limit on the number of characters.
SIZE	Specifies the size of the field and depends on its type.
SRC	Denotes URL for an image. This is used only with IMAGE type.
VALUE	Contains the initial value displayed to users. This attribute is required for radio buttons.
TYPE	Defines the type of data used in the field. The default is free-text input. The following types are definable: CHECKBOX, RADIO, HIDDEN, IMAGE, TEXT, PASSWORD, SUBMIT and RESET.

Input TYPE attribute

The TYPE attribute is used to specify the type of data used in an Input field. The other attributes that are applicable to a particular field depend on the field's TYPE attribute. For example, the MAXLENGTH attribute specifies the number of characters that may be entered in a field. It should only be used with fields that allow text entry (such as TEXT), since it has no meaning with other types such as RADIO or CHECKBOX. If no type is specified, TEXT is used.

CHECKBOX Type

A checkbox is an item where several values can be selected at the same time. This type is submitted as separate name/value pairs, with a name/value pair submitted for each selected value. The default value for checkboxes is *on*.

You should always set both a NAME and a VALUE for each checkbox. Since each checkbox will cause the form to return two pieces of information to you, there are two ways you could set up checkboxes that are grouped together:

- set a unique *name* for each checkbox
- set a unique *value* for each checkbox.

The more common choice is to use the same name while setting a unique value for each checkbox in a group. It is vital that you do at least one of these things; otherwise, you will not be able to distinguish what was selected in the different boxes. For example:

```
<B>Why do you browse the Web?</B><BR>
<input NAME ="browse" TYPE=checkbox>Fun
<input NAME ="browse" TYPE=checkbox >Work
<input NAME ="browse" TYPE=checkbox>Research
<input NAME ="browse" TYPE=checkbox>Education
```

In this example no value is set, so all of the checkboxes would be returned with the name that we assigned along with the default value. Thus the name/value pair that is returned for any checkbox in this group would be "browse/on". There is no way to tell the difference between the boxes. One way to set up this set of checkboxes would be:

```
<B>Why do you browse the Web?</B><BR>
<input NAME="browse" VALUE="fun" TYPE=checkbox>Fun
<input NAME="browse" VALUE="work" TYPE=checkbox>Work
<input NAME="browse" VALUE="research" TYPE=checkbox>Research
<input NAME="browse" VALUE="education" TYPE=checkbox>Education
```

Now each checkbox will be submitted with a unique value. Be careful to use different names for different groups of checkboxes. Otherwise, if the same value is used in two groups, it will be impossible to tell which set of checkboxes returned the data. In the following example we have a couple of true/false questions. Since we use values of true and false for the questions, we make sure that there is a different name for each set of checkboxes:

```
<p>I like cats.
<input NAME="cats" VALUE="true" TYPE=checkbox>True
<input NAME="cats" VALUE="false" TYPE=checkbox>False
<P>I like dogs.
<input NAME="dogs" VALUE="true" TYPE=checkbox>True
<input NAME="dogs" VALUE="false" TYPE=checkbox>False
```

You can also define the initial setting for a checkbox by including the CHECKED attribute. When this attribute is set, the checkbox will appear to be selected when the form is first displayed or after the reset button is chosen. The reader can deselect the box by clicking on it.

RADIO Type

The RADIO type defines an item where only one value can be selected from a set of possibilities. A set is defined as the group of radio boxes with the same NAME attribute. Only the name and the selected value is returned. Note that you must set a value for each radio box. You can also set a default box by using the CHECKED attribute. However, you should be careful never to set more than one CHECKED radio box in the same name set. Here is a sample set of radio boxes:

```
<B>What is your gender?</B> <BR>
<INPUT NAME="gender" VALUE="male" TYPE=radio>Male
<INPUT NAME="gender" VALUE="female" TYPE=radio>Female
<P><B>Why do you browse the Web?</B><BR>
<input NAME="browse" VALUE="fun" TYPE=checkbox>Fun
<input NAME="browse" VALUE="work" TYPE=checkbox>Work
<input NAME="browse" VALUE="research" TYPE=checkbox>Research
<input NAME="browse" VALUE="education" TYPE=checkbox>Education
```

Let's see how these elements look in browsers. Here our source is displayed in Netscape:

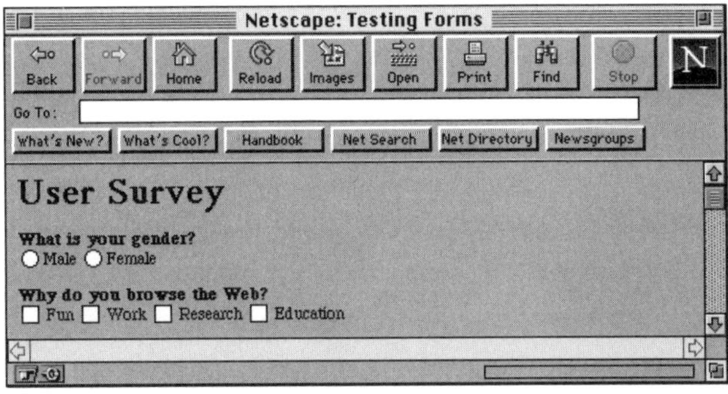

This is how the same source is displayed in NCSA Mosaic:

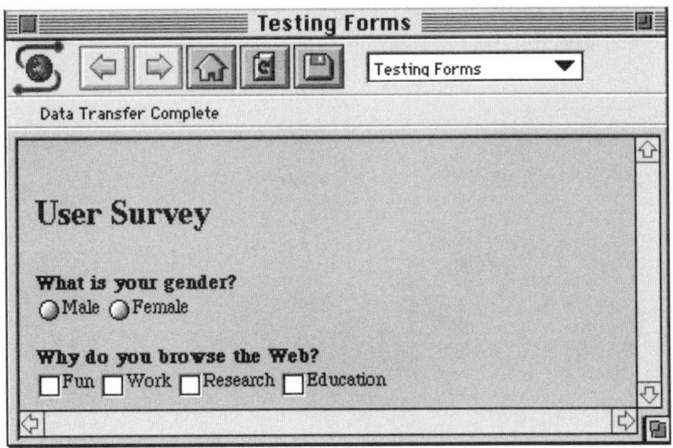

HIDDEN Type

No field is presented to the user (although a user looking at the source will be able to see that the field is there), but the contents of the field are returned in the submitted data. You might wonder what use there could be for an invisible field that does not allow user input. The primary use for this field is record keeping for programs that may parse user input from forms.

TEXT Type

This enables single-line text entry fields; it is used in conjunction with the MAXLENGTH and SIZE attributes. As you may recall, MAXLENGTH allows you to specify the number of characters that may be entered in the field, and SIZE allows you to specify the size of the field on the form.

Be careful to set MAXLENGTH to a value equal to or greater than SIZE. Otherwise, readers will be presented with an entry box that cannot be filled out completely.

Let's take a look at an example. Here is our document:

```
<P><B>First Name:</B> <INPUT NAME="fname" TYPE=text
MAXLENGTH=30 SIZE=30></P>
<P><B>Last Name:</B> <INPUT NAME="lname" TYPE=text
MAXLENGTH=30 SIZE=30></P>
<P><B>E-mail Address:</B> <INPUT NAME="eaddr" TYPE=text
MAXLENGTH=50 SIZE=50></P>
```

In Netscape Navigator, this source looks like this:

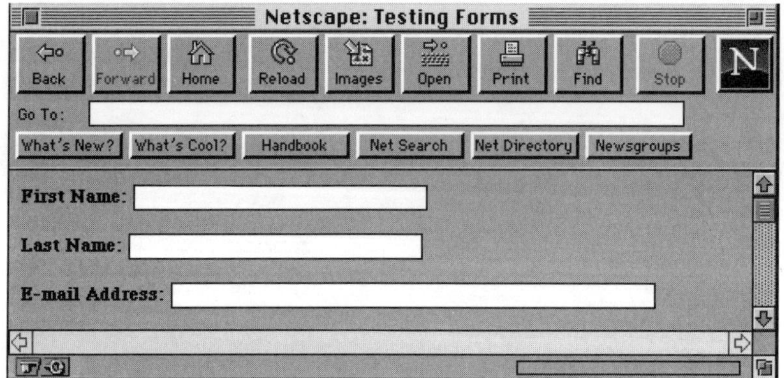

This is how it looks in MacWeb:

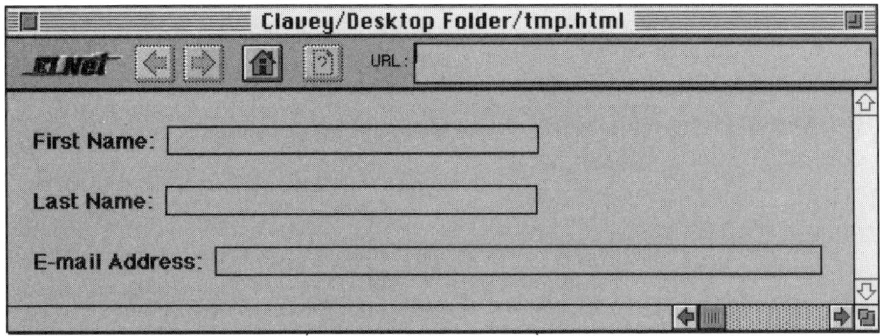

If you want a multiline text entry, use TEXTAREA (see below).

PASSWORD Type

Password is the same as text, except the text is not displayed to the user. Like text, you can use the SIZE and MAXLENGTH attributes with this field.

```
<P><B>Enter a password to be used to retrieve survey
results:</B><BR>
<INPUT NAME="password" TYPE=password MAXLENGTH=50 SIZE=50></P>
```

This section in Netscape Navigator looks like this:

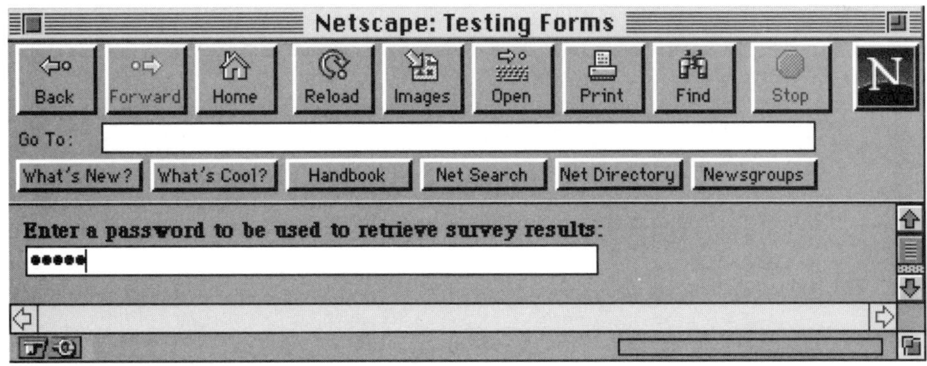

Do not allow the nonechoing characteristic of this field to lull you into a false sense of security. Although the reader (and anyone peeking over the reader's shoulder) will not be able to

see whatever is typed in the field, the information is still exchanged with the server in a nonsecure fashion. You cannot rely on this field to provide real security.

SUBMIT and RESET Types

The SUBMIT button is used to submit the form's contents, as specified by the ACTION attribute. RESET resets the fields to their initial values. Both buttons may be used with the VALUE attribute to set the text that is displayed in the button. If you do not use the VALUE attribute, the buttons will be displayed with either SUBMIT or RESET. For example, we might end our survey with the following:

```
<P>Thank you for responding to this questionnaire.
<INPUT TYPE=SUBMIT>
<INPUT TYPE=RESET>
</FORM>
```

This looks like the following in Mosaic:

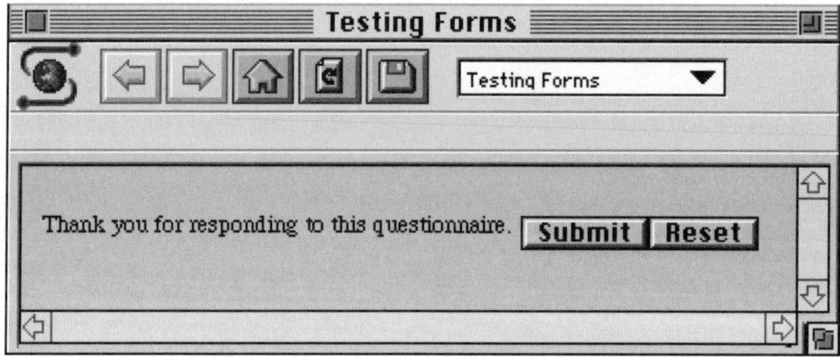

Now let's see how the addition of the VALUE attribute changes the buttons:

```
<P>Thank you for responding to this questionnaire.</P>
<P><INPUT TYPE=SUBMIT VALUE="Finished - Submit">
<INPUT TYPE=RESET VALUE="Restart - Clear All Fields"></P>
```

Here's how it looks now:

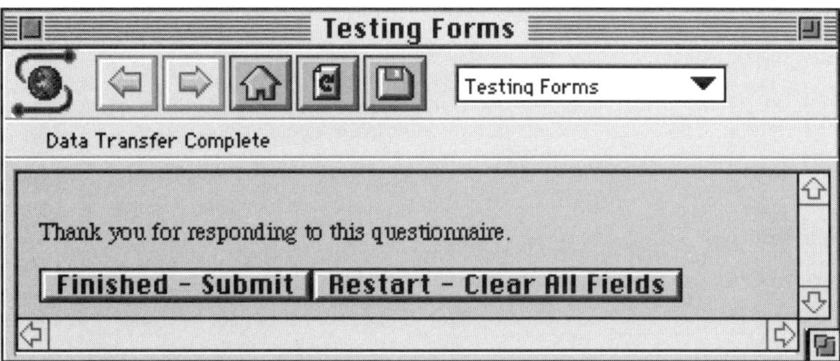

IMAGE Type

If you do not like the look of the plain button used with SUBMIT, you may use the IMAGE type along with an image as an alternative to SUBMIT. The image type defines an image field that can be clicked on by the user with a pointing device, causing the form to be immediately submitted. The coordinates of the selected point are measured in pixel units from the upper left corner of the image. These are returned (once the form is submitted) in two name/value pairs. The *x*-coordinate is submitted under the name of the field with an *x* value appended, while the *y*-coordinate is submitted under the value of the field with a *y* value appended. This is discussed in greater detail in Chapter 4.

Let's look at an example now. We have the image of a submit button that we prefer over the standard submit button. Our image is in the file SUBMIT.GIF, located in the GIF folder.

```
<P>Thank you for responding to this questionnaire.</P>
<P><input NAME="submit" TYPE=IMAGE SRC="GIF/SUBMIT.GIF"
ALIGN=TOP></P>
```

Here is how this looks in Mosaic:

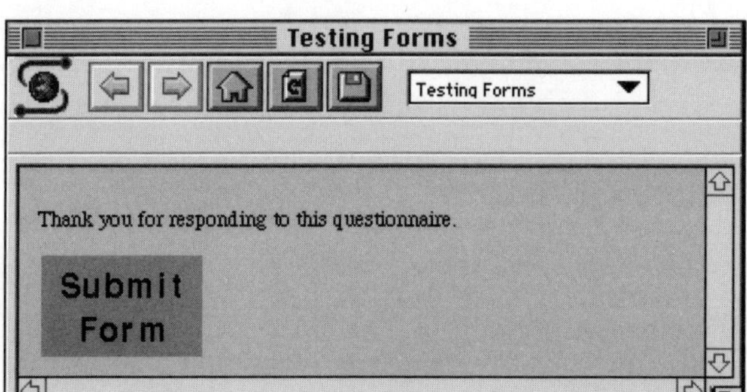

Note that the standard way for submitting forms is with the SUBMIT button, described earlier. In future versions of HTML, the IMAGE type is supposed to be folded into the SUBMIT type. Also, there is no way to use this to reset your form. Resetting may only be done with the RESET type.

Textarea: <TEXTAREA>

The TEXTAREA tag is a nested element within a form. It is used when we wish to let users define more than one line of text. The tag creates a multiline text input region, which can contain prespecified text. The end tag, </TEXTAREA>, is required, even if the form is initially blank. The TEXTAREA tag uses two arguments, ROWS and COLS, to specify the height and width of the text box.

The following example displays a scrollable box into which the user can type text. The box begins with the following text:

```
<P>Please enter any additional comments here:
<TEXTAREA NAME="comments" ROWS=10 COLS=60>
</TEXTAREA></P>
```

This source looks like this in Netscape Navigator:

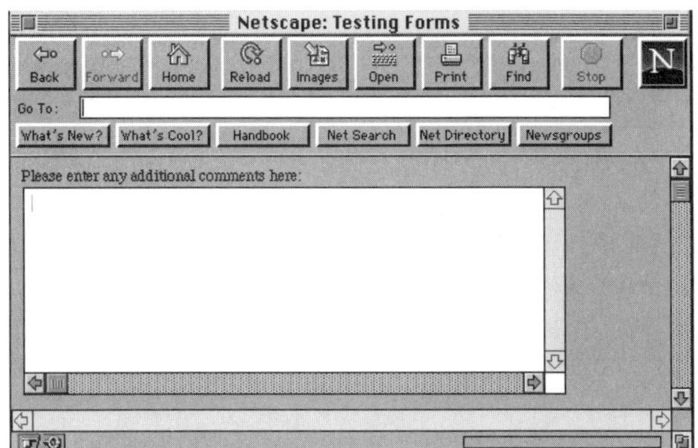

If you want to include default information, it should be placed within the <TEXTAREA> and </TEXTAREA> tags. Note that default information can be erased by the user. If default information is not erased, it will be returned as data by the form.

Netscape Extension: WRAP

With Versions 2 and above of Netscape, an additional attribute, WRAP, is available with TEXTAREA. This attribute allows you to control how word-wrapping for text input should be handled. The default condition for TEXTAREA is for text to scroll until the person entering the data enters a carriage return. With WRAP, you can change this behavior. The following values may be used:

OFF
The default setting. No wrapping. Lines are sent exactly as typed.

VIRTUAL
The display word-wraps, but long lines are sent as one line without new-lines.

PHYSICAL
The display word-wraps, and the text is transmitted at all wrap points.

Select: <SELECT> and Option: <OPTION>

The SELECT and OPTION tags are used to create enumerated lists of values. In other words, the SELECT element allows the user to choose one (or possibly more) items from a list. The items, which are specified with the OPTION element, are generally displayed in a compact manner as a pulldown list. The OPTION element can only occur within a SELECT element. It represents one choice in a list of alternatives. Once the user has selected an option from the list, it becomes the visible element in the pulldown list.

SELECT may be used with three attributes:

MULTIPLE

This attribute allows the user to choose more than one option.

NAME

This is the name of the field. This attribute should always be included.

SIZE

This attribute is used to specify the number of items that should be displayed. If no size is specified, typically only one option is displayed.

For example, in our survey we might have the following:

```
<P><B>Please select your occupation from the following
list</B>
<BR><SELECT NAME="occupation">
<OPTION>Unemployed
<OPTION>Student
<OPTION>Administrative
<OPTION>Professional
</SELECT><P>
```

In Netscape, the reader would see something like this:

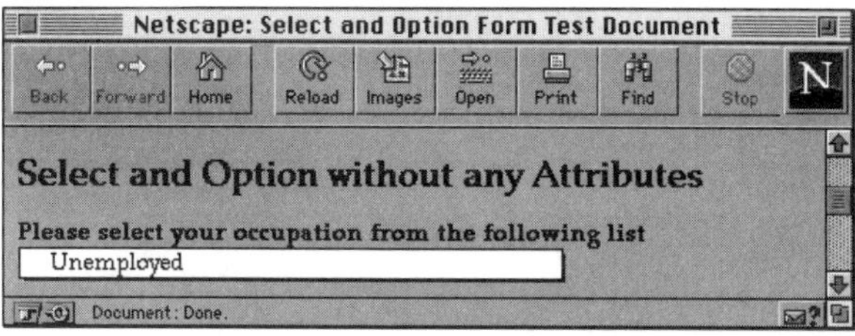

When the reader clicks on the select box, the list of options will be displayed. Note that some browsers will display the first choice in the box, while others leave the box empty until the reader makes a choice.

The SIZE attribute allows you to tell the browser the number of options you wish to be displayed. For example, if we add the attribute SIZE=3 to our SELECT tag:

```
<SELECT NAME="occupation" SIZE=3>
```

it will be displayed like this:

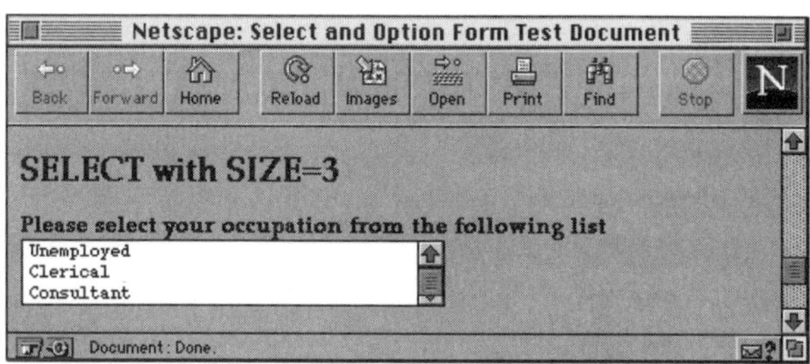

Notice that SIZE=3 does not provide enough space for the scroll bar to be displayed properly. Should you decide to use the SIZE attribute, make sure that you choose a size that is large enough to accommodate the scroll bar.

You can use the MULTIPLE attribute with SELECT to allow readers to choose more than one option. We could modify our example to use the MULTIPLE attribute:

```
<BR><SELECT NAME="occupation" MULTIPLE>
```

Now let's see how this changes the display for this field:

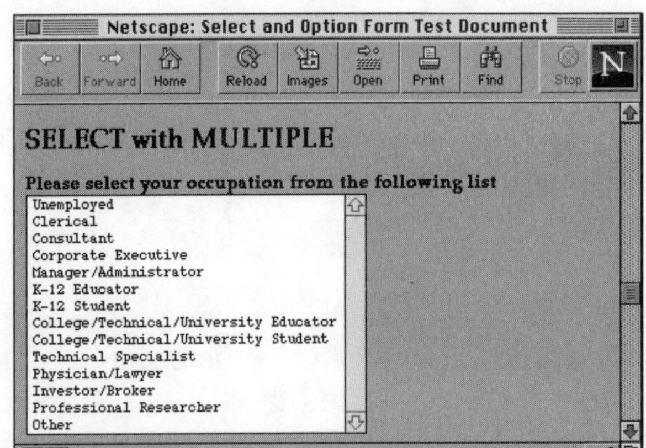

As you can see, all of the options are displayed. You can use the SIZE attribute to limit the number of options displayed at one time if your list is very long.

Two attributes may be used with OPTION:

SELECTED

This attribute causes the option to be selected until the user chooses another option.

VALUE

Specifies a value to be returned if the option is chosen. If no value is specified, the content of the OPTION element is returned.

We strongly advise using the SELECTED attribute no more than once with each group of options. In our tests with different browsers we found that even if the MULTIPLE attribute is used with the SELECT tag, specifying SELECTED with more than one option did not have the desired effect. For example, with Netscape, we found that all the options with SELECTED attributes would appear as being selected when the form was displayed, but the information returned by the browser when the form was submitted only included the last option with the SELECTED attribute.

The VALUE attribute allows you to set the value that is returned if a particular option is chosen. For example, we may want to place the results of our form directly into a database in which occupations are given a single letter code. We can have the form return the appropriate code letter by using the VALUE attribute:

```
<P><B>Please select your occupation from the following
list</B>
<BR><SELECT NAME="occupation">
<OPTION VALUE="U">Unemployed
<OPTION VALUE="S">Student
<OPTION VALUE="A">Administrative
<OPTION VALUE="P">Professional
<OPTION VALUE="O">Other
</SELECT><P>
```

HTTP File Upload

Netscape browsers Version 2 and above support a new attribute, ENCTYPE, that allows you to write forms that take files as input. An example of such a form would be:

```
<FORM ENCTYPE="multipart/form-data"
ACTION="http://ozone.com/cgi/form" METHOD=POST>
<P>Send this file: <INPUT NAME="inputfile" TYPE="file">
</FORM>
```

HTTP File Upload is not a Netscape innovation and is under consideration by the HTML standards committee.

The Complete Form

Our complete survey example, with three questions and a text-entry box, looks like the following:

```
<HTML>
<TITLE>Form Test Document</TITLE>
<H1>User Survey</H1>
<FORM METHOD=POST ACTION=""http://ozone.com/cgi/survey.cgi">
<P><B>First Name:</B> <INPUT NAME="fname" TYPE=text
MAXLENGTH=30 SIZE=30></P>
<P><B>Last Name:</B> <INPUT NAME="lname" TYPE=text
MAXLENGTH=30 SIZE=30></P>
```

```
<P><B>E-mail Address:</B> <INPUT NAME="eaddr" TYPE=text
MAXLENGTH=50 SIZE=50></P>
<P><B>Enter a password to be used to retrieve survey
results:</B><BR>
<INPUT NAME="password" TYPE=text MAXLENGTH=50 SIZE=50></P>
<P><B>What is your gender?</B></P><BR>
<INPUT NAME="gender" VALUE="male" TYPE=radio>Male
<INPUT NAME="gender" VALUE="female" TYPE=radio>Female

<P> <B>Why do you browse the Web?</B><BR>
<input NAME="browse" VALUE="fun" TYPE=checkbox>Fun
<input NAME="browse" VALUE="work" TYPE=checkbox>Work
<input NAME="browse" VALUE="research" TYPE=checkbox>Research
<input NAME="browse" VALUE="education"
TYPE=checkbox>Education</P>

<P><B>Please select your occupation from the following
list</B>
<BR><SELECT NAME="occupation">
<OPTION>Unemployed
<OPTION>Clerical
<OPTION>Consultant
<OPTION>Corporate Executive
<OPTION>Manager/Administrator
<OPTION>K-12 Educator
<OPTION>K-12 Student
<OPTION>College/Technical/University Educator
<OPTION>College/Technical/University Student
<OPTION>Technical Specialist
<OPTION>Physician/Lawyer
<OPTION>Investor/Broker
<OPTION>Professional Researcher
<OPTION>Other
</SELECT><P>

<P>Please enter any additional comments here:<BR>
<TEXTAREA NAME="comments" ROWS=2 COLS=60>
</TEXTAREA>
</P>
<P>Thank you for responding to this questionnaire.</P>
<P><INPUT TYPE=SUBMIT VALUE="Finished - Submit">
<INPUT TYPE=RESET Value="Restart - Clear All Fields"></P>
</FORM>
</HTML>
```

You can also find a copy of this form on the CD in form2.html.

HTML Tags: ISINDEX, ISMAP

Two additional HTML tags supporting user input are ISMAP and ISINDEX. ISMAP is an attribute that can be used with the IMG tag to make images with "hot spots." It is described in the multimedia chapter.

ISINDEX: <ISINDEX>

The ISINDEX element in a document signals to the browser that the requested document also serves as an index document. This tag should be placed in the HEAD portion of a document. The presence of the ISINDEX tag indicates that the user can perform a keyword search. From a user's point of view, the browser displays a text-entry box in which the user may type search keywords. The ISINDEX tag will be described only briefly here since its use requires close interaction with the Web server and its administrator.

We have added the ISINDEX tag to a short HTML document to illustrate the way some browsers provide a search box. Here is our document:

```
<HTML>
<HEAD>
<TITLE>ISINDEX Test Document</TITLE>
<ISINDEX>
</HEAD>
<BODY>
There is an ISINDEX tag in the head of this document. If your
browser has the capability to submit a search request, a
search box should appear when this document is displayed even
though there is no server with a search engine to do anything
with the text entered in the box.
</BODY>
</HTML>
```

Let's see how this looks in Netscape Navigator:

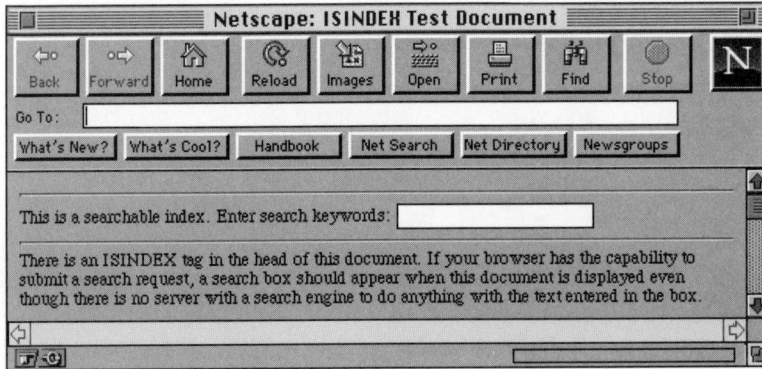

and in MacWeb:

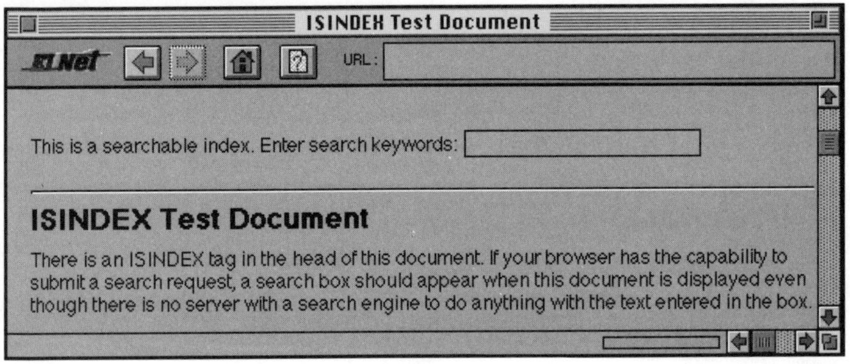

Different browsers may present the search box in different ways. Notice that the lack of a server and a search engine does not stop the browser from displaying the search box.

If everything has been set up correctly, the browser will capture the user input and send the query to the server. The browser does this by adding a question mark at the end of the document URL, followed by the list of desired keywords. These keywords are separated by the plus (+) sign.

Documents containing the ISINDEX tag are often generated dynamically by a CGI script on the server, so there is no confusion about searchability. Since the document is generated on the fly by the script, the user may only access it through the CGI script's URL. The data provided by the user is then returned to the script for processing. We realize that this can be confusing, so let's look at an example.

Suppose we encounter a searchable Web document on the server OZONE.COM that lists the addresses of kayak stores throughout the world. The document is generated by a CGI script named "findkayak". This particular CGI script has been written so that it returns a query form when it gets an empty request. Thus, when we access the document through the path:

```
http://ozone.com/cgi-bin/findkayak
```

it does not see a query, so it returns a form asking for search keywords. As a user, we can look for store locations within California by entering "California" in the keyword box. The query is sent by the browser to the server, as follows:

```
http://ozone.com/cgi-bin/findkayak?California
```

This passes the user input "California" back to the CGI program, which then processes the query and returns the matches from the database.

If you choose to add the ISINDEX tag to a document manually, you should be careful to add it only if the document is really set up for searches. Since it is unlikely that a static HTML document would be able to process a database query, you will probably need to use it in conjunction with the BASE tag. By setting a location with the BASE tag, the query can be directed to the correct search location. For example, rather than having our query document for the kayak stores be generated by the CGI script, we could create a static document named kayak-stores.html and include:

```
<ISINDEX>
<BASE HREF=http://ozone.com/cgi-bin/findkayak>
```

This will cause the user data to be sent to the findkayak CGI script rather than to the static kayak-stores.html document.

Please note that in order for any ISINDEX query to work, the document or script receiving the query must already be configured to perform keyword searches, and its Web server must already possess search-engine software. On the Macintosh, AppleWebSearch (a free search engine by Chuck Shotton for use with licensed versions of MacHTTP) is a powerful way to make Web documents searchable via the Web.

ISINDEX vs. FORM

Much of the functionality offered by ISINDEX is also available through FORM. ISINDEX is good for short keyword searches, but since it only uses a single input field, it does not provide a way to add modifiers to the search as you can do with a form. Since forms offer more flexibility with user input, you should review your requirements to make sure that ISINDEX rather than a FORM is the most appropriate way to submit your data.

Netscape Extension: PROMPT

Netscape has added a PROMPT attribute to ISINDEX. If you do not like the default message (i.e., "This is a searchable index. Enter search keywords:"), you can use this attribute to enter an alternate message.

```
<H2>ISINDEX</H2>
<P>Here is the default prompt:
<ISINDEX>
<P>Here it is with the Netscape PROMPT attribute:
<ISINDEX PROMPT="Enter the name of the celebrity you would
like to find here: ">
<HR>
```

In this example, we have set the prompt to "Enter the name of the celebrity you would like to find here:"

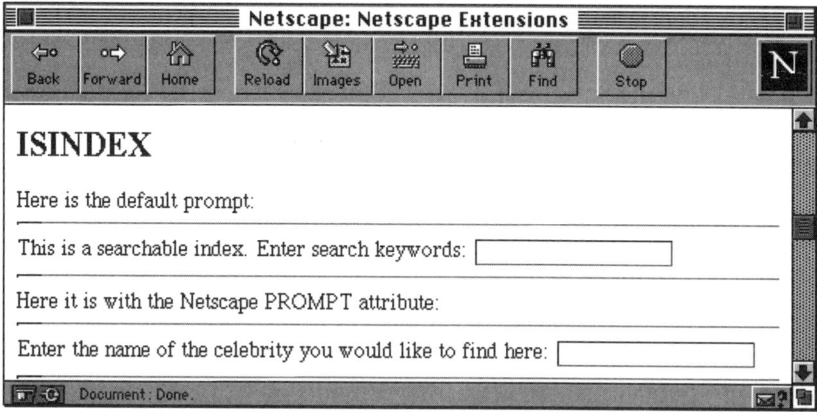

CGI Scripts

The Common Gateway Interface, or CGI, is a standard developed to allow external computer programs to interface with information servers, such as Web servers (Figure 5–2). The MacHTTP server included on the CD is a CGI-compliant server. The implementation of CGI scripts requires close interaction with the Web server and its administrator.

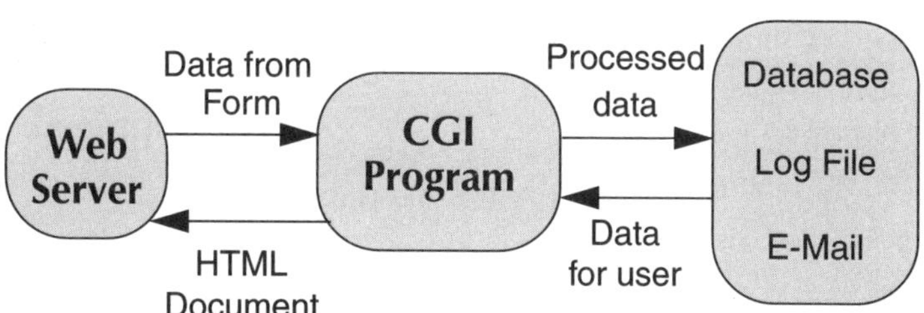

FIGURE 5–2 CGI Data Flow

Essentially, the standard allows a Web browser to execute a program on a Web server. This program then sends back information to the server, which returns it in a format readable by the browser. Some things you might use a CGI program to do include:

- Process the information from an order form and return a confirmation along with the total cost of the order
- Provide an interface to a searchable database and return the result of a search to the client in HTML
- Process input from a guestbook, including logging information to a database or file, and return a message to the client
- Provide the current hit count as part of a page each time someone accesses that page

CGI programs can be written in any programming or scripting language. On the Macintosh, the most popular options are AppleScript, Frontier, MacPerl, C, and Hypercard. If you are using MacHTTP as your server, the language you choose must handle Apple events (Mac's way of communicating between Mac applications).

CGI programs are executed on a server through the use of URLs. The URL in the ACTION attribute points to the desired Web server and the executable program. For example, the URL

```
http://ozone.com/cgi/guestbook.cgi
```

requests that the CGI program named "guestbook.cgi" in the folder named "cgi" be run. The METHOD attribute specifies the method for sending the user's input to the program that will be run. Thus, a form tag using this URL along with the POST method would be:

```
<FORM METHOD=post ACTION="http://ozone.com/cgi/guestbook.cgi">
```

Upon receiving the form's output, the server hands off control to the executable program. This program is run with the user's input. The server then returns the output from the program to the browser, usually as another Web document.

POST and GET

As previously mentioned, two methods can be used to send data from your form. These methods are POST and GET. The way in which the server receives the encoded results of the form depends on which method is specified in the form. With GET, the data are appended to the URL, much like the ISINDEX tag. With POST, the program receives the user's data from standard input.

Note that the maximum length of a URL is limited by the browser and the server. With the POST method there is no length limitation, since user data come from standard input. We therefore recommend using the POST method if the number of user input parameters is large, or if there is a <TEXTAREA> in your form. With the POST method you do not run the risk of the URL length exceeding what the browser or server can handle. Of course, you can always write your script such that it handles both methods.

POST Method: (METHOD="POST")

If you use the POST method, your CGI script or program receives the encoded form input in its standard input stream. The server will not send an end-of-file (EOF) at the end of the data input. Therefore, you can use the CONTENT_LENGTH environment variable, which specifies how much data should be read from standard input. If you haven't already gotten our message, this is the method we recommend.

GET Method (METHOD="GET")

If you use the GET method, your CGI program receives the encoded form input in the QUERY_STRING variable, which follows the '?' in the URL that calls the script.

Recall that in the above ISINDEX example the query from the browser was sent to the server as:

```
http://ozone.com/cgi-bin/findkayak?California
```

If we use the GET method in this example "California" will be placed in QUERY_STRING.

Form Data

We have now told you where to find the output data from a form. Next, you need to decode this data. Recall that each form item should have a NAME tag. When the user enters information in that particular form item, this information is encoded in the form data. The name of the information is simply the NAME of the item tag, while the value is the information entered by the user.

Form data is then returned to the user as name/value pairs. Each pair is separated by the ampersand (&) character, while each pair of name and value is separated by the equal (=) character. These data are also URL encoded (see Chapter 3 for more information on URLs). For example, the space character becomes the plus character.

Let's look at a specific example now. We'll use an abbreviated version of the form that we developed in the previous section. Here is the completed form with answers checked off.

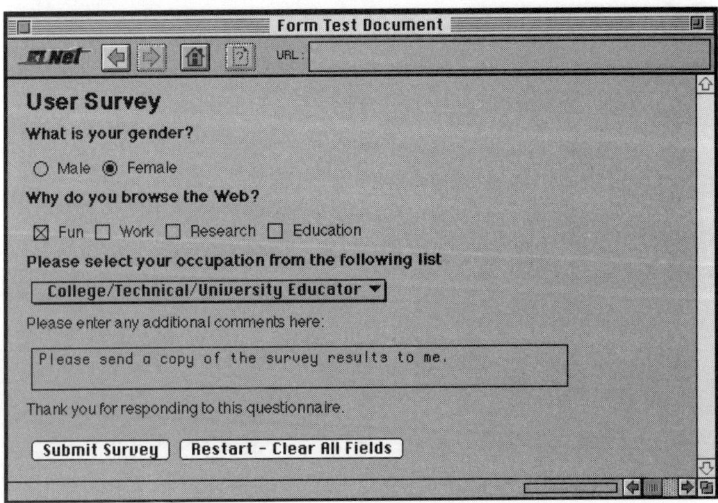
Form Test Document
URL:
User Survey
What is your gender?
Male
Female
Why do you browse the Web?
Fun
Work
Research
Education
Please select your occupation from the following list
College/Technical/University Educator
Please enter any additional comments here:
Please send a copy of the survey results to me.
Thank you for responding to this questionnaire.
Submit Survey
Restart - Clear All Fields

The output from these answers would look like this:

```
?gender=female&browse=fun&browse=research&occupation=College%2
FTechnical%2FUniversity+Educator&comments=Please+send+a+copy+o
f+the+survey+results+to+me.
```

Notice how each pair is separated by the & character. Each pair consists of the NAME, as specified in the form, and the VALUE selected by the user. The name/value pairs are separated by equal (=) signs, and spaces in the input fields are replaced with plus (+) signs.

The basic process in a CGI script is to split up the elements separated by ampersands. Each of these elements represents a name and value pair. Then each element is parsed to determine the value for each NAME item. Your program can then use these values to decide how to respond to the user.

On the CD you will find several FORM examples. We have also included a general-purpose CGI-compliant script that will send the contents of any HTML form to a prespecified electronic-mail address. This application, email.acgi, is described in the next section.

Email.acgi

Email.acgi, kindly provided by Eric Morgan, is an AppleScript that uses the CGI standard to deliver the contents from any HTML form to a prespecified e-mail address. The contents are sent in human-readable form, with each name-value pair separated by a colon (:). The data is thus easily imported into a database. You will find Version 3.0.6 of email.acgi in the email-cgi folder on the CD. The latest version is always available at:

```
ftp://ftp.lib.ncsu.edu/pub/software/mac/email-cgi.hqx.
```

To use email.acgi, simply point to it within the ACTION attribute of your form and include required details (such as the destination e-mail address) in prespecified tags. We explain in detail below.

Installation

Installing email.acgi is easy. Simply drag the script from the CD and place it into your MacHTTP server application folder or any subfolder.

System Requirements

Email.acgi requires the following:

- MacHTTP (or WebStar, its commercial cousin)
- AppleScript

Two shareware OSAXes (Open Scripting Architecture Extensions, written in AppleScript) are also required:

- Parse CGI, a useful shareware OSAX for decoding arguments sent as part of a POST in a form available at:

  `http://marquis.tiac.net/software/home.html`

- TCP Scripting Additions Version 1.1.2 or higher, an OSAX providing access to TCP/IP communications. It is available at:

  `http://www.mangotree.com/tcpscripadd.html`

Email.acgi and Required Tags

To correctly use email.acgi, you must embed six required tags into your form. These tags, which may appear in any order, must use specified name values and attributes in order to collect the necessary information. As an example, we've entered Kelly Kayaker's information into the tags. The required name values are:

to_address

Specifies the e-mail address of the person who is to receive the contents of the FORM. Use the INPUT tag and HIDDEN type as follows:

```
<INPUT TYPE="hidden" NAME="to_address"
VALUE="kayaker@ozone.com">
```

to_name

Specifies the name of the corresponding the email address. Use the INPUT tag and HIDDEN type as follows:

```
<INPUT TYPE="hidden" NAME="to_name" VALUE="Kelly Kayaker ">
```

mailer

Specifies the host name or IP address of the machine acting as your mail (SMTP) server. Unless you have an SMTP server running on your Macintosh, don't put your Macintosh's name in this box! Use the INPUT tag and HIDDEN type as follows:

```
<INPUT TYPE="hidden" NAME="mailer" VALUE="mailer.ozone.com">
```

from_address

Creates a text-entry box into which the person filling out the form enters his/her e-mail address. Use the INPUT tag and TEXT type as follows:

```
<INPUT TYPE="text" NAME="from_address" SIZE="40"
MAXLENGTH="40">
```

from_name

Creates a text-entry box into which the person filling out the form enters his/her name. Use the INPUT tag and TEXT type as follows:

```
<INPUT TYPE="text" NAME="from_name" SIZE="40"
MAXLENGTH="40">
```

subject

Specifies the subject line of the e-mail message that is sent. Use the INPUT tag and HIDDEN type as follows:

```
<INPUT TYPE="hidden" NAME="subject" VALUE="Simple Form
Results">
```

Using Email.acgi in a Form

If you already have a form and want to link it to email.acgi, modify your FORM tag to use the POST method and to have the ACTION attribute point to email.acgi. Remember, email.acgi must be placed in the server's application folder or subfolders, and the URL should point to it relative to the server's location. The tag should be in the format:

```
<FORM METHOD="POST"
ACTION="http://your.site/email-cgi/email.acgi>
```

Once your forms are set up, you do not need to run email.acgi to process incoming data from your forms—the server will run it automatically when it is needed. At this point, if your server is running and you have a valid Internet email address, you should be able to test your form by firing up a browser, loading the form, filling it out and submitting it.

Email.acgi Example

Let's look at an example now. This example form is available on the CD in the file called form-to-email.html, in the email-cgi folder. The complete form is as follows:

```
<HTML>
<HEAD>
<TITLE>Form to Email Test</TITLE>
</HEAD>
<BODY>
<H1>My Simple Form Example </H1>
<P>This form takes in information and uses the email.acgi
script to return it as email.
<HR>
<H2>My test Form</H2>
<P>Click the "Submit" button to send form data.

<FORM METHOD="POST"
ACTION="http://ozone.com/email-cgi/email.acgi">
<INPUT TYPE="hidden" NAME="to_name" VALUE="Kelly Kayaker">
<INPUT TYPE="hidden" NAME="to_address"
VALUE="kayaker@ozone.com">
<INPUT TYPE="hidden" NAME="mailer"
VALUE="mailer.ozone.com">
```

```
<P>What is your name?<BR>
<INPUT TYPE="text" NAME="from_name" SIZE="40"
MAXLENGTH="40"><P>

<P>What is your email address?<BR>
<INPUT TYPE="text" NAME="from_address" SIZE="40"
MAXLENGTH="40"><P>

<INPUT TYPE="hidden" NAME="subject" VALUE="simple form
results"><P>
<INPUT TYPE="Submit" VALUE="Send"> <p>
</FORM>
</BODY>
</HTML>
```

Suppose Bob Biker fills out this form and enters his e-mail address as bob@ozone.com. Kelly Kayaker will then get an e-mail message that looks like the following:

```
To: Kelly Kayaker <kayaker@ozone.com>
From: Bob Biker <bob@ozone.com>
Subject: simple form results
```

Upon submitting the form, Bob will see a new Web page, containing something like the following:

```
Bob Biker, your message has been successfully queued for
delivery.
Below is a report listing of what was sent.
Envelope
Addressee's name: Kelly Kayaker
Addressee's address: kayaker@ozone.com
Your name: Bob Biker
Your address: biker@ozone.com
Subject: simple form results
Contents
```

Debug Mode

You can run email.acgi in a debug mode, where the contents of the form are simply sent back to the browser as a new Web page, and no e-mail is sent. To do this, simply add the following tag to your form:

```
<INPUT TYPE="hidden" NAME="debugMode" VALUE="on">
```

Errors

Upon encountering errors, email.acgi generates the following diagnostic messages:

PARSE ERROR

An error was found while parsing the form data. Make sure you are using the required name values.

DEBUGGING ERROR

An error was found while returning the debugging information.

COMMUNICATIONS ERROR

An error was found while trying to send e-mail. Make sure the mailer and e-mail address are complete and accurate.

FEEDBACK ERROR

Contact the author.

Security

CGI scripts are one of the most vulnerable aspects of the Web. These scripts are susceptible to tampering by malicious users, and transmitted data can be snooped on. We urge you to consult with Web administrators during implementation, because Web security is an area of active development.

Creating Dynamic and Animated Documents

The Web was originally conceived as a document distribution system. As you might imagine, this was soon not enough. People want to be able to send documents that contain customized information, or change dynamically. They want to be able to send animations. Lately, they even want to send programs that are executed on the browser's computer! In the fast-changing world of the World Wide Web, it is impossible to predict what tomorrow will bring. But we can give you a taste of some of the exciting dynamic capabilities, including Netscape's Push and Pull, Server-Side Include, Sun's Java, Netscape's JavaScript, and VRML.

CGI Scripting

The most obvious way to create a customized document is through the use of a CGI script. On the CD, we have provided a simple AppleScript that demonstrates how you can embed the current date and time in a document. The script is called, time.script, and is located in the CGI Scripts folder.

```
-- Demonstration of embedding current date and time.

property crlf : (ASCII character 13) & (ASCII character 10)
set datestamp to current date

--this builds the normal HTTP header for regular access
set http_10_header to "HTTP/1.0 200 OK" & crlf & ¬
"Server: MacHTTP" & crlf & "MIME-Version: 1.0" & crlf &¬
"Content-type: text/html" & crlf & crlf

return http_10_header & ¬
"<Head>" & ¬
"<title>Demo of Dynamic Document</title></HEAD>¬
<BODY><h2>Demonstrating a Dynamic Document</h2>" & ¬
"<HR>Hello, World. <p> The current date and time: " & ¬
(current date) ¬
& "</BODY>"
```

Move the script onto a Macintosh computer running a Web server (if you are running MacHTTP, you must put the script within the MacHTTP folder structure). Load the document by using the following URL:

```
http://your.site/time.script
```

and you will see a document with the current date and time. If you keep hitting the "Reload" button, you will see the contents correspondingly updated.

This kind of approach can be used to create documents on-the-fly.

Frontier: An Alternative CGI Scripting Language

Much like AppleScript, Frontier is an environment for scripting the Macintosh. The environment has a scripting language, called UserTalk, a debugger, and a suite of development tools. This environment allows you to customize and automate your Macintosh, including its file system, networking, and applications.

Recently, Frontier added support for writing CGI scripts in UserTalk. Frontier also will run any AppleScript CGIs that you may have.

While our experience with Frontier is limited, we found that it provides better performance and a more complete development environment than AppleScript.

Detailed information and software can be found at the following URL:

```
http://www.hotwired.com/staff/userland/aretha/
```

Information and software on using Frontier's CGI framework can be found at the following URL:

```
http://www.webedge.com/frontier/
```

Netscape's Push and Pull

Netscape has been experimenting with ways of repeatedly sending new data from a Web server to a browser. These methods are only guaranteed to work with Netscape's server and client, although we have found support for them in other browsers such as Microsoft's Internet Explorer.

The first method, server push, keeps open the connection between a server and a browser so that the server can keep sending new data to the browser. Server push is not supported by httpd4mac or MacHTTP, so if you want to implement server push, you will need to purchase a full-featured Web server, like Webstar, or buy space from a service provider that supports server push. Server push provides a more seamless way to do animation than client pull, since it allows only a small portion of a window to be redrawn.

In the second method, client pull, the client requests new data from the server after a prespecified interval. In particular, the server sends a document to the browser, which includes a directive telling the browser to wait a specified number of seconds, then to reload the document or fetch a new one.

You do this by using the <META> tag, as in the following example:

```
<META HTTP-EQUIV=Refresh CONTENT=1>
```

This HTTP header tells the browser to "Refresh" after 1 second. If we wanted a refresh after 5 seconds, we would use "Content=5", as follows:

```
<META HTTP-EQUIV=Refresh CONTENT=5>
```

If we wanted the browser to refresh after 1 second with a new document called newdoc.html, we would use the following tag:

```
<META HTTP-EQUIV=Refresh
CONTENT="1;URL=http://your.site/newdoc.html">
```

Important Notes

- The URL in the CONTENT field must be fully qualified, containing the name of the server site and the name of the document.
- The <META> tag must be contained within the <HEAD> portion of your document.
- The Refresh directive is one time only. If you want the document to be repeatedly refreshed, you must embed the appropriate <META> tag within each newly loaded document.

On the CD we have provided a simple AppleScript that demonstrates client pull, again by embedding the current date and time in a document. The script is called pull-example.script and is located in the CGI Scripts folder. Here it is:

```
-- Variables available for use:
-- http_search_args - stuff in the URL after a ?
-- post_args - stuff in the URL after a $
-- method - GET, POST, etc. Used to tell if post_args are valid
-- client_address - IP address or domain name of remote
--     client's host
-- from_user - non-standard. e-mail address of remote user
-- username - authenticated user name
-- password - authenticated password
-- server_name - name or IP address of this server
-- server_port - TCP/IP port number being used by this server
-- script_name - URL name of this script
-- referer - the URL of the page referencing this document
-- user_agent - the name and version of the WWW client software
--     being used
-- content_type - MIME content type of post_args

set crlf to (ASCII character 13) & (ASCII character 10)
set datestamp to current date

--this builds the normal HTTP header for regular access
set http_10_header to "HTTP/1.0 200 OK" & crlf & "Server:¬
 MacHTTP" & crlf & ¬
"MIME-Version: 1.0" & crlf & "Content-type: text/html" & ¬
crlf & crlf

return http_10_header & ¬
"<HEAD><META HTTP-EQUIV=Refresh CONTENT=1>" & ¬
"<title>Test Client Pull</title><HEAD><BODY>¬
<h2>Testing Client Pull</h2>" & ¬
"<HR><I>Results generated  at: " & (current date) ¬
& "</I></BODY>"
```

Move the script onto a Macintosh computer running a Web server (if you are running MacHTTP, you must put the script within the MacHTTP folder structure). Load the document in Netscape Navigator (Version 1.1 and later) by using the following URL:

```
http://your.site/pull-example.script
```

and you will see a document with the current date and time. Since the document has a refresh rate of 1 second, you will see Netscape reload the document, with the updated date and time. Netscape will keep reloading the document, until you expressly hit the "Stop" button or close the window.

Client pull is a useful feature for displaying documents with changing content. For example, a stock trader may wish to view a document containing updated stock prices every five minutes. Client pull can even be used to implement a "low-tech" animation. Each frame of the animation contains a refresh directive and a URL pointing to the next frame in the animation. Of course, given network delays, this won't be a movie-quality production!

Commercial Software: Netcloak

Netcloak, by Maxum, is a software product that adds functionality to your Macintosh Web server (MacHTTP and Webstar). Essentially, by installing the software, you get approximately 30 new HTML commands that you can embed in your Web documents. These commands are interpreted by the server before serving up the document to a requesting client, allowing you to dynamically tailor the document's content to the situation.

For example, in your documents you can:

- include counters containing the number of visits
- insert the current time and date
- determine the type of browser used by the requesting client (thus allowing you to customize document layout to the type of browser)

More information and software (commercial and shareware) is available at:

```
http://www.maxum.com/NetCloak/
```

Sun's Java and HotJava

In addition to documents, Java and HotJava allow programs to be sent via the Web. These programs, called applets, are then run locally on the browser's computer. The applets can be embedded within HTML documents. Or they can be standalone applications.

Developed by Sun Microsystems, HotJava is a Web browser that knows how to run these applets. These are written in the Java object-oriented programming language.

At the present time, Java and HotJava are in beta mode. But the ability to send running programs within Web documents, adding untold spice and life, clearly adds enormous potential to the kinds of documents that will become available. Time will only tell to what extent this approach will catch on.

At the time this book was written the HotJava browser was freely available for various kinds of Unix platforms and Windows 95 and NT. A port to Macintosh system 7.5 was due soon. In addition, Netscape has added support for Java applets in new versions of Netscape Navigator (Version 2.0 and later), including the Macintosh version. Two Macintosh development environments for Java applets were available:

- Natural Intelligence. You can find more about this product, which is called the Roaster Integrated Development Environment, at http://www.natural.com/ or by sending e-mail to info@natural.com.
- Sun Microsystems. A free Java Developer's Kit as well as more information about Java and demonstration applets are available at http://java.sun.com.

JavaScript

JavaScript is an interpreted language developed by Netscape. An early version of this language was called LiveScript, and you may still occasionally see references to it under the old name. We provide a JavaScript tutorial and some basic uses for it in Chapter 7.

VRML: Virtual Reality Markup Language

The Virtual Reality Modeling Language is a developing standard for delivering interactive three-dimensional scenes with Web hyperlink. Like the Web, these can be delivered across the Internet, making it a kind of HTML for Virtual Reality. It is widely expected that the next generation of Web browsers will understand and interpret VRML.

With VRML, 3-D interactive scenes can be displayed. As with Virtual Reality, users can explore and interact with these scenes in order to gain a sense of a new environment. More information and demonstrations are available at:

```
http://www.sdsc.edu/vrml
```

Macromedia's Shockwave

Macromind has created a plug-in for browsers that allows Director movies to be played on the Web. This plug-in is part of the Shockwave extensions for Director. If your readers will be using browsers that have been configured with the Shockwave plug-in, adding multimedia elements with Shockwave is a great way to add snap to your pages. Since Director movies can include both animation and sound, it is a much cleaner method for incorporating these elements into a document than some of the more traditional methods that require browsers to launch an external application.

However, the drawback is that before a reader can see your creation, the reader must have downloaded the Shockwave plug-in and installed it in their browser. Since it does take an extra step (and a machine with a fair amount of memory), it may be awhile before the average Internet user has a browser with the Shockwave plug-in. Of course if you decide to go this route and are worried about losing readers, you can encourage people to install Shockwave by adding a link to the Macromedia plug-in page.

You can find more information about Shockwave at:

```
http://www.macromedia.com
```

The Good, the Bad and the Ugly

Test your forms with as many browsers as possible. Some form tags are not supported as universally as others, and if you use default values (such as CHECKED or SELECTED) you may find that different browsers will return different data if users leave the defaults alone. For example, when using SELECT in a form, be sure that you do not specify more than one option with the SELECTED attribute. If you try to specify more than one, you will probably find that some browsers will only return one anyway.

Do not place an ISINDEX tag in a document unless you are certain that it has been correctly set up for searches.

Never set the CHECKED attribute for more than one item in a set of radio boxes.

Make sure that you set a value for every radio box.

Don't forget to include name and value attributes for your input tags. If you don't, how will you decode the user's data?

Remember to include a submit button in your forms even if you only have one input field in your form. Some browsers such as Netscape automatically submit the form if there is only one field, so you may be tempted to leave the submit button out. If you do this readers using browsers like Lynx will not be able to use your form.

When using client pull, keep in mind the additional network overhead that will result.

IN THIS CHAPTER YOU WILL LEARN

- HOW TO USE TABLE ELEMENTS
- THE KEY FEATURES OF THE NETSCAPE EXTENSIONS TO HTML INCLUDING FRAMES, CLIENT-SIDE IMAGE MAPS, AND MORE!

BEYOND HTML 2

What's In This Chapter

This chapter discusses new elements introduced since HTML 2 became a standard. It also includes descriptions of all the nonstandard HTML elements available in the Netscape browser that we were able to find. We urge you to use these nonstandard HTML elements with caution, since it is difficult to make documents that use nonstandard elements look good when viewed by different types of browsers. Additionally, unlike official HTML elements, these elements have bypassed the rigorous screening process that official HTML elements must pass. Instead they rely on a single company for advocacy and support.

HTML Evolution

HTML itself is evolving to meet the needs of the Internet. At the time this book was written Version 2 of HTML had only recently completed the process for official recognition as the definition for HTML. Even so, a substantial amount of work had already been done on a standard that was to be called Version 3 of HTML. Some of the features introduced in this new version of HTML included support for tables, client-side image maps, and mathematical equations. It also was to have provided better support for layout of images and text.

However, the committee in charge of the development of this version of HTML realized that the lack of functionality in HTML 2 was causing many browser vendors to develop incompatible custom extensions to HTML. Clearly the rapid release of formal standards for these new functions (such as tables and client-side image maps) was needed. To reduce the time needed to develop and release a complete standard, the committee decided to pursue the development of new additions to HTML in separate tracks. Thus, what many call "HTML 3" no longer exists—instead there are merely extensions to HTML 2. To give you an idea of just how unsettled things are, even the decision on what to call these extensions (HTML 2.1 vs. "HTML 2 with the table extension" and so on) has still not been resolved.

One of the most important new HTML features is the addition of support for tables. Although the final details are still under discussion, some browsers such as NCSA Mosaic and Netscape have already included support for some of the changes. If you choose to use any of these elements in your documents, keep in mind that they are not supported by all browsers, and the definitions themselves may still change before being accepted officially.

New Elements and Attributes

We will describe a number of new features here: text alignment, tables and frames. As with any HTML element, the usefulness of an element is dependent on support for that element by browsers. After extensive testing, we have found support in some commercial browsers for the elements described here. There is an experimental browser called Arena specifically for HTML 3 that provides better support, but it is currently only available on UNIX systems and is not in wide use.

We have included a document on the CD named "html3.html" that includes samples of each of the features described in this chapter. You can easily determine whether a browser supports these features by loading this document into the browser you want to test. We expect that support for these features will be added to many browsers in the near future.

Tables: <TABLE>

The addition of tables is one of the most important extensions to HTML 2. The table tag allows you to format tables in your document. A table should be enclosed in the <TABLE></TABLE> tags. Within the table, the <TR> tag is used to designate rows. Individual cells are designated by <TH> for a header cell or <TD> for a data cell. A caption may also be included by using the <CAPTION></CAPTION> tags. You can find the tables presented in this section on the CD in the documents table.html and toc.html.

Attributes that are available with TABLE include:

ALIGN

This specifies horizontal alignment for the table itself. It can take one of five values: CENTER (center table between text margins, the default value), RIGHT (flush with right margin), LEFT (flush with left text margin), JUSTIFY (size the table to fill the space between left and right margins), and CHAR (used to specify an alignment character such as ".").

BORDER=*n*

Render borders around the table. *n* is the width of the border and is optional. This attribute is supposed to be superseded by the FRAME attribute.

CELLSPACING=*n*

Cell spacing. *n* should be a value in pixels.

CELLPADDING=*n*

Cell padding. *n* should be a value in pixels.

CHAR

This is used to specify the character to be used with the ALIGN=CHAR attribute. It is case sensitive.

COLS

Specifies the number of columns in the table. It is intended to allow a browser to display the table as data is received rather than waiting to get the entire table to determine the total number of columns.

FRAME

This attribute is used to specify which sides of the cell to display. It is supposed to take the place of BORDER, which was the original attribute used to control this function. FRAME may take the following values: VOID (no borders), ABOVE (top border), BELOW (lower border), HSIDES (top and bottom borders), LHS (left-hand border), RHS (right-hand border), VSIDES (left and right borders), BOX (all four borders) and BORDER (all four borders, same as BOX).

RULES

This is used to specify where rules should be drawn in the interior of the table. It may take the following values: NONE (no rules), GROUPS (place rules between groups), ROWS (horizontal rules between all rows), COLS (vertical rules between all columns), or ALL (lines between everything). Note that setting the BORDER attribute is equivalent to setting RULES=ALL.

VALIGN

Sets the default vertical alignment for the table cells. It may take one of four values: TOP, MIDDLE, BOTTOM and BASELINE. This alignment may be overridden for individual cells by specifying an alignment attribute with the cell tag.

WIDTH=*n* or *n*%

Allows you to specify the width for the table. The width may be entered as a total number of pixels or as a percentage of the page width. A WIDTH attribute is also available for TD and TH. The width may be expressed in pixels or as a percentage of the table width.

Because the table-element specification was still evolving at the time this book was written, browser support for it was uneven. Our example illustrates only the use of borders and a caption, since we found these to be the most consistent support elements. However, as the attributes become finalized we expect that browsers will begin to provide support for them. As a result, we've included other attributes in our example on the CD so that you can check the browsers that you expect your readers to use:

```
<TABLE BORDER UNITS=en COLSPEC="C20, D50" WIDTH 70>
<CAPTION><H3>Internet Growth<H3></CAPTION>
<TR><TH>Date <TH>Number of Hosts
<TR><TD>8/81 <TD> 213.0
<TR><TD>5/82 <TD> 235.0
<TR><TD>8/83 <TD> 562.0
<TR><TD>10/84<TD> 1,024.0
</TABLE>
```

In Netscape, this table is displayed as follows:

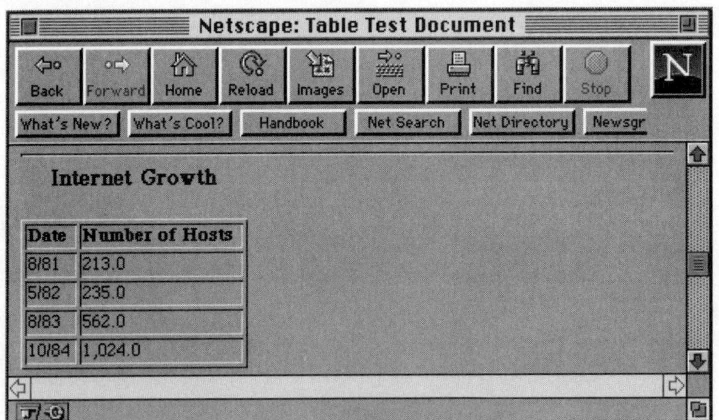

Within the table, elements are marked by the TD and TH tags, and rows are marked by TR. Here are two of the attributes that may be used with these tags:

ALIGN

The ALIGN attribute allows you to specify the horizontal alignment of paragraphs within a table row. In the absence of this attribute, the default may be overridden by the presence of an ALIGN attribute on the parent TR element, or by the COLSPEC attribute on the TABLE element. The COLSPEC attribute takes precedence over the TR element. It may take one of five values:

left	Flush left, the default for data cells (TD)
center	Center the paragraphs, the default for header cells (TH)
justify	Justify if practical, otherwise leave like left
right	Flush right
char	Align on the first occurrence of the specified character in the line. Use the CHAR attribute to set the alignment character.

VALIGN

This attribute is used to explicitly specify the vertical alignment of material within a table row. Using it with an individual cell will override the setting for a row. It can take one of the following four values: top (align contents with the top of the cell—the default), middle (center contents vertically), bottom (place contents at the bottom of the cell), and baseline (ensure that all cells in a row share a baseline—applies only to the first text line for each cell).

Two more attributes that can be used with TH and TD to control cell size are:

COLSPAN

The number of columns spanned by the cell. It allows you to merge cells across columns. It defaults to one.

ROWSPAN

The number of rows spanned by the cell. This allows you to merge cells across rows. It defaults to one.

Let's look at a table example that uses some of these attributes. Here is a rather silly table:

```
<P>Here is a table with funny alignment and spanning columns
and rows:</P>
<TABLE BORDER>
<CAPTION><H3>A Very Silly Table</H3></CAPTION>
<TR><TH>Column One<TH>Column Two<TH>Column Three<TH>Column
Four
<TR ALIGN=CENTER><TD>La<TD>De<TD>Da<TD>Ta Dum!
<TR><TD COLSPAN=2>Next cell is right justified<TD
ALIGN=RIGHT>Da<TD>Ta Dum!
<TR><TD ROWSPAN=2>La De<TD>Da<TD>Ta Dum!<TD>Ta Dum!
<TR ALIGN=RIGHT><TD>Da<TD>Ta Dum!<TD>Ta Dum!
</TABLE>
```

And here is how our silly table looks:

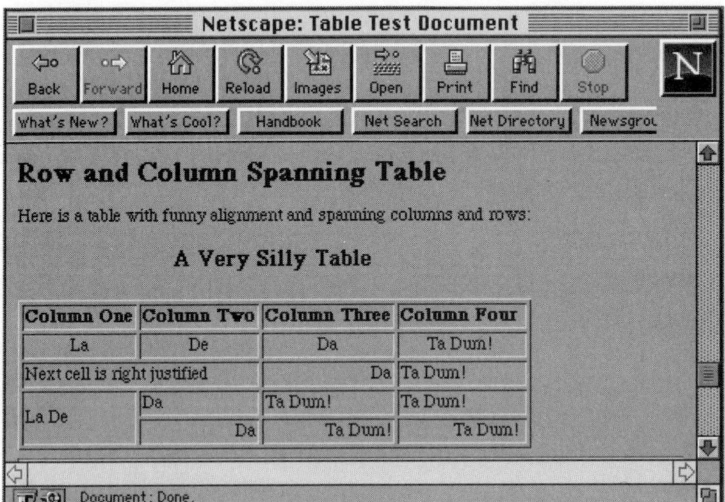

As you may recall from our chapter on images, we were having problems lining up our icons in the table of contents for our kayaking document. We ended up using the PRE tag to put things in neat columns, but the HTML source looked pretty messy. With the TABLE attribute, it is easy to make a table of contents in columns. We use the following snippet instead of our original:

```
<TABLE>
<TR><TD><A HREF="#gear"><IMG SRC="gif/kayak.gif" ALIGN=MIDDLE>
kayaking gear</A>
<TD><A HREF="#seakayak"><IMG SRC="gif/sea.gif" ALIGN=MIDDLE>
sea kayaking</A>
<TR><TD><A HREF="#paddle"><IMG SRC="gif/paddle.gif"
ALIGN=MIDDLE> paddle information</A>
<TD><A HREF="#resources"><IMG SRC="gif/kayak2.gif" ALIGN=MIDDLE>
kayaking resources</A>
</TABLE>
```

This then appears as follows:

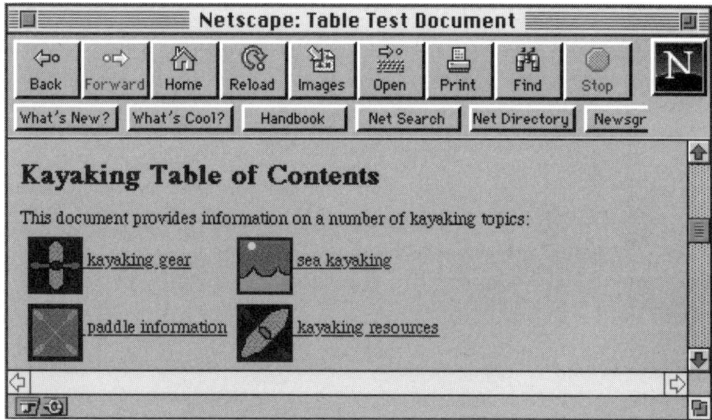

If you compare the source and the result with our HTML 2 version on page 92, you will see that both the source and output are better when using tables.

Now let's see how we can use the BORDER attribute to make a menu bar for our table of contents. By using a wide border, we can get the effect of buttons with beveled edges. Here is the HTML:

```
<TABLE border=10>
<TR>
<TD ALIGN=CENTER VALIGN=MIDDLE CELLPADDING=0 WIDTH=25%><A
HREF="kayak2.htm#gear"><IMG SRC="gif/kayak.gif"
ALIGN=MIDDLE><br>kayaking gear</A></TD>
<TD ALIGN=CENTER VALIGN=MIDDLE CELLPADDING=0 WIDTH=25%><A
HREF="kayak2.htm#seakayak"><IMG SRC="gif/sea.gif"
ALIGN=MIDDLE><br>sea kayaking</A></TD>
<TD ALIGN=CENTER VALIGN=MIDDLE CELLPADDING=0 WIDTH=25%><A
HREF="kayak2.htm#resources"><IMG SRC="gif/kayak2.gif"
ALIGN=MIDDLE><br>kayaking resources</A></TD>
<TD ALIGN=CENTER VALIGN=MIDDLE CELLPADDING=0 WIDTH=25%><A
HREF="kayak2.htm#paddle"><IMG SRC="gif/paddle.gif"
ALIGN=MIDDLE><br>paddle information</A></TD>
</TABLE>
```

And here is how it looks:

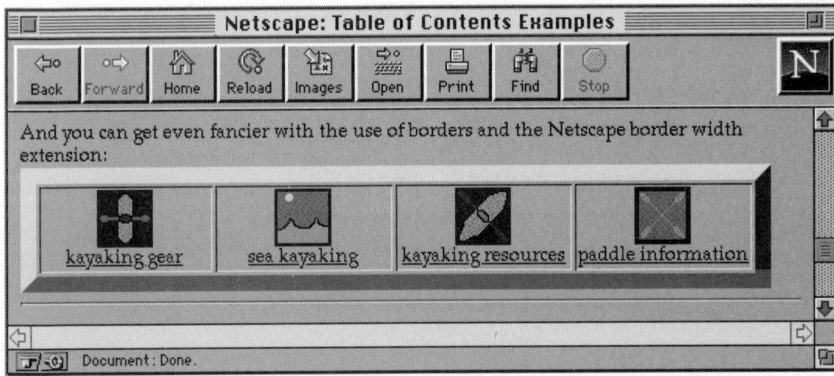

DIV

DIV is a separator that allows you to specify how a section of text should be aligned. It has one attribute: ALIGN, which may take the values LEFT, RIGHT or CENTER. Netscape Navigator 2 and above supports this tag. Here is an example:

```
<DIV ALIGN=RIGHT>
Right aligned section of text.
<UL>
<LI>One
<LI>Two
</UL>
</DIV>
<DIV ALIGN=CENTER>
Center aligned section of text.
<UL>
<LI>One
<LI>Two
</UL>
</DIV>
<DIV ALIGN=LEFT>
Left aligned section of text.
<UL>
<LI>One
<LI>Two
</UL>
</DIV>
```

And here is how it looks in Netscape Navigator:

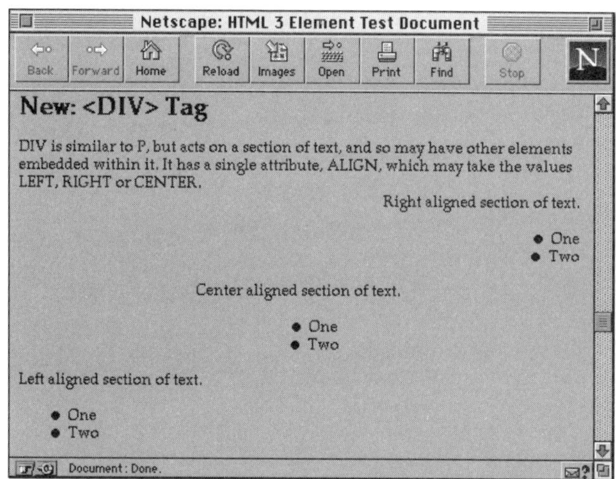

Netscape and HTML

This section describes the nonstandard HTML elements that are available (at least at the time of this writing) in the Netscape browser. As we mentioned before, Netscape appears to be the most widely used browser, and these extensions allow you to have much greater control over the "look" of your document than does standard HTML—but only if your readers are using Netscape Navigator.

However, at present these extensions are almost all guaranteed *not* to work with other browsers. Netscape has said that they will work with the standard bodies and other browser writers to try to make these extensions available in other browsers, so it is possible that at least some of these extensions may someday make it into the standard. Nevertheless, if your goal is to produce documents that look good in a wide variety of browsers, use these extensions to HTML at your own risk. You can check to see if any changes have been made to these extensions since this book was written by looking at:

```
http://home.netscape.com/home/services_docs/html-extensions.html
```

Blink: <BLINK>

The BLINK tag does exactly that—makes your text blink on and off. In earlier versions of Netscape this tag would cause the text to disappear momentarily and then reappear. The newer versions of Netscape just seem to flash a box around the text. Here's a sample from our netscape document:

```
<P><BLINK>Blink on...<BLINK></P>
<P>Blink off</P>
```

And here is how it looks:

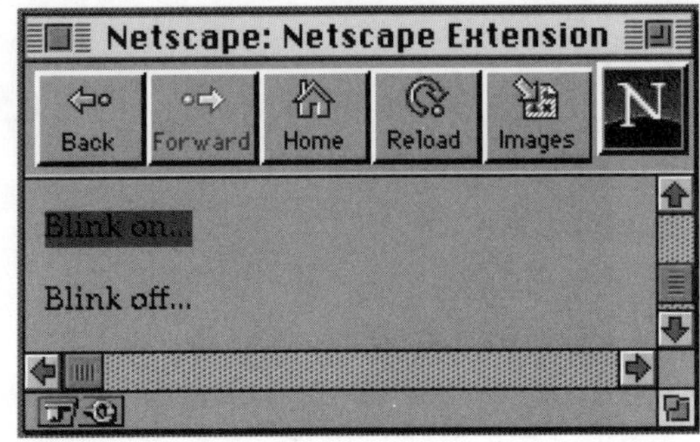

No Break: <NOBR>

The NOBR element stands for no break. This means all the text between the start and end of the NOBR elements cannot have line breaks inserted. As with PRE, long text strings inside of NOBR elements probably will force readers to scroll the window horizontally to see the entire line.

Word Break: <WBR>

The WBR element stands for word break. This is for the very rare case when you have an NOBR section and you know exactly where you want it to break. It is also useful any time you want to give the Netscape Navigator help by telling it where a word is allowed to be broken. The WBR element does not force a line break (BR does that); it simply lets the Netscape Navigator know where a line break is allowed to be inserted if needed.

Font Size: <FONT SIZE=value>

The FONT SIZE tag allows you to change font size. Valid values range from one to seven, with the default being three. The value given to size can optionally have a '+' or '-' character in front of it to specify that it is relative to the current base font size. Here's our test document:

```
<H2>FONTSIZE</H2>
<FONT SIZE=1>1
<FONT SIZE=2>2
<FONT SIZE=3>3
<FONT SIZE=4>4
<FONT SIZE=5>5
<FONT SIZE=6>6
<FONT SIZE=7>7
<FONT SIZE=+3>6
<FONT SIZE=+2>5
<FONT SIZE=+1>4
<FONT SIZE=+0>3
<FONT SIZE=-1>2
<FONT SIZE=-2>1
```

In the first half of the document we use absolute values for the font size, and in the second half we use relative values to produce the same result. The relative values are based on the default base font size of 3. Now let's see how this looks:

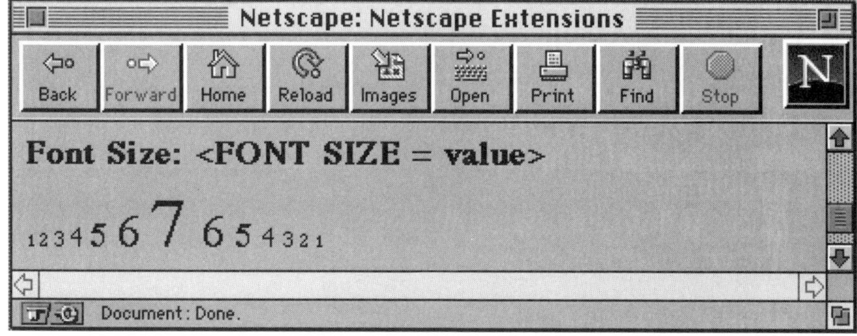

Base Font Size: <BASEFONT SIZE=value>

BASEFONT SIZE changes the base size of the font. Relative font size changes are based on this value, which defaults to 3 and has a valid range of 1-7. Here is an example that shows how the same font size can be set using either the FONT SIZE tag, the BASEFONT SIZE tag, or a combination of the two:

```
<BASEFONT SIZE=1>1
<FONT SIZE=+2>3
<BASEFONT SIZE=3>3
<FONT SIZE=+2>5
<BASEFONT SIZE=5>5
<FONT SIZE=+2>7
<BASEFONT SIZE=7>7
<FONT SIZE=-2>5
<BASEFONT SIZE=5>5
<FONT SIZE=-2>3
<BASEFONT SIZE=3>3
<FONT SIZE=-2>1
<BASEFONT SIZE=1>1
```

And here it is:

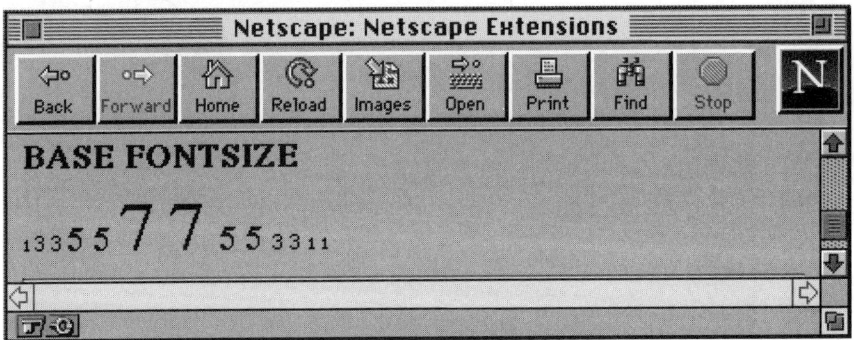

If the base font size is already set to the maximum, trying to set a greater relative font size has no effect.

Font Color: <FONT COLOR=###>

The COLOR attribute for the FONT tag allows you to specify a color for a specific range of text. The tag should be used as follows:

```
<FONT COLOR=#rrggbb>
```

The *#rrggbb* in this example represents a color code. For a detailed explanation of the codes please refer to the multimedia chapter. To find the code for a specific color, you can use the HTML Color Meister application which is included on the CD. You can find more information on HTML Color Meister in the multimedia chapter. You should also be familiar with the discussion of the use of color in HTML documents in the multimedia chapter.

Center: <CENTER>

This tag allows you to center text. The text to be centered should be placed in <CENTER></CENTER> tags. At the time that Netscape created this tag, there was no other way in HTML to center text. However, since that time an "ALIGN=CENTER" attribute for the <P> and <H*n*> tags has been added to the HTML standard under development. Since Netscape also supports the ALIGN=CENTER attribute, we recommend using it over <CENTER> for compatibility with other browsers.

```
<CENTER>Here is some centered text!</CENTER>
<CENTER>We've finally reached the end!</CENTER>
<CENTER>Adi&oacute;s!!!</CENTER>
<CENTER>Auf Wiedersehen!</CENTER>
```

And here it is:

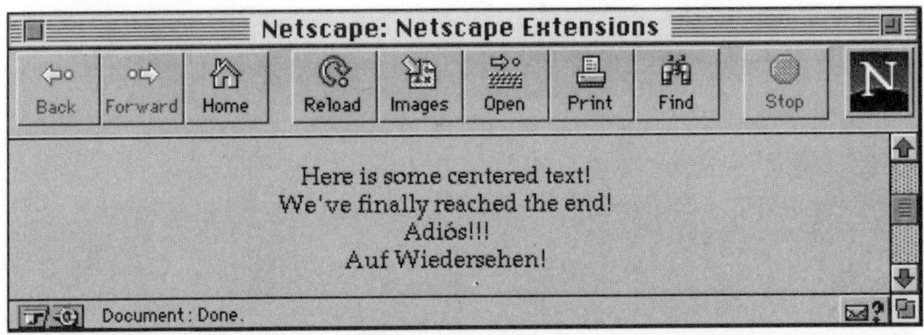

Let's see how the ALIGN=CENTER attribute compares with the CENTER tag for support. We review the following bit of HTML in Netscape, Microsoft Internet Explorer and NCSA Mosaic:

```
<CENTER><H1 ALIGN=CENTER>Centered Heading - with
&lt;CENTER&gt;</H1></CENTER>
<H1>Centered Heading - with ALIGN=CENTER</H1>
```

As you can see, in Netscape CENTER and ALIGN=CENTER both do the trick:

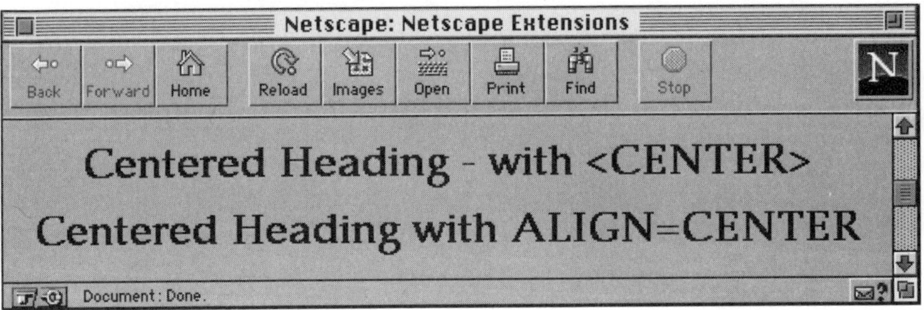

The same is true in Microsoft Internet Explorer:

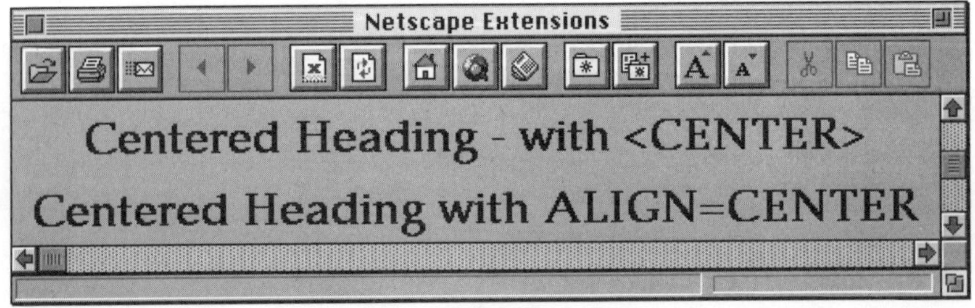

But NCSA Mosaic is a different story:

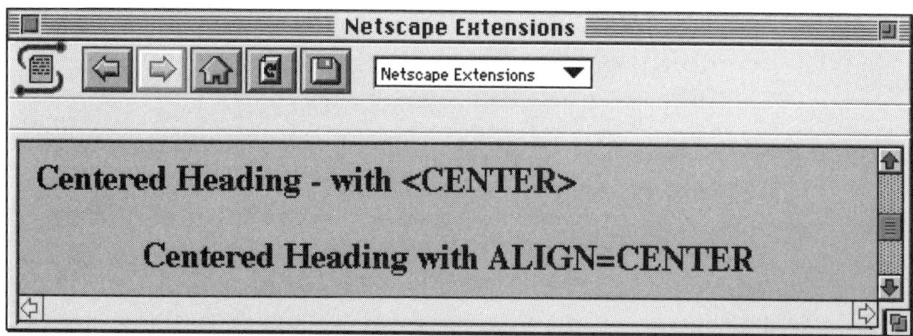

As you can see, ALIGN=CENTER worked in all three browsers, while the Netscape CENTER tag didn't. The bottom line? Use CENTER=ALIGN attribute with H1. The CENTER tag provided functionality that was unavailable elsewhere at the time it was introduced, but now that there is a way to do centering in standard-track HTML, there is no need to use it.

Standard-track Netscape Extensions

Unlike most of the Netscape extensions just described, there is a good chance that the following elements will eventually make it into an official HTML specification. This distinction may not matter to you if you are already making extensive use of the features in the previous section. However, if your goal is to create HTML documents that will look good in many browsers, using tags that are likely to make it into the official HTML standard increases the likelihood that your document will look good in any browser. Note that the following elements are only supported in Version 2 and above of Netscape Navigator, so you will not see any change in the display of your document if you add them and then view your document with earlier versions of the browser.

Big and Small Print: <BIG>, <SMALL>

The <BIG> and <SMALL> elements specify that the enclosed text should be displayed, if practical, using big or small fonts relative to the current font size. Here is a little example to illustrate this:

```
<p>The BIG and SMALL tags specify that the enclosed text
should be displayed in big or small fonts relative to the
current font size. Here is some <BIG>big text</BIG> and
here is some <SMALL>small text</SMALL>.
```

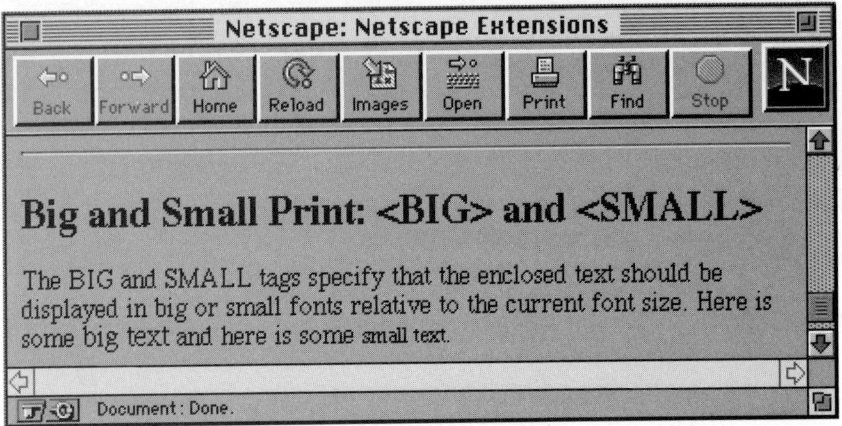

Subscript and Superscript: <SUB>, <SUP>

The <SUB> element specifies that the enclosed text should be displayed as a subscript, while the <SUP> element specifies that the enclosed text should be displayed as a superscript. Both will be displayed in a smaller font relative to the regular font size.

```
<p>The SUP and SUB tags specify that the enclosed text
should be displayed in a superscript or subscript. The
font size will also be reduced relative to the current
font size. Here is some <SUP>superscript </SUP> and here
is some <SUB>subscript</SUB>.
```

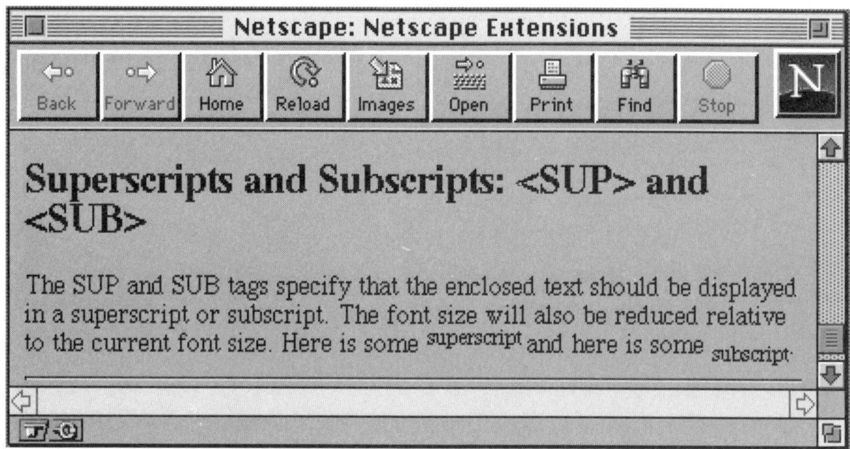

Client-Side Image Maps

Beginning with Netscape Navigator Version 2, Netscape browsers have support for client-side image maps. As you may recall from our discussion on image maps in the multimedia chapter, you need to have a server in order to use or test standard image maps. With client-side image maps, the processing is done by the browser, so you can use them without a server.

The HTML extensions to support this functionality are composed of two parts: a new attribute, USEMAP, for the IMG tag, and new MAP and AREA tags. The USEMAP attribute is used to specify the location of the map and is specified in the same format as the source for an HREF.

The Map

MAP tags are used to contain a map and have one attribute: NAME, which is used to specify the name of the map so that the image can refer to it. The map itself is composed of a number of AREA tags. The AREA tag is in the form:

```
<AREA SHAPE=rect COORDS="x,y,x1,y1" HREF="destination">
```

or

```
<AREA SHAPE=rect COORDS="x,y,x1,y1" NOHREF>
```

The NOHREF tag indicates that clicks in this region should perform no action. An HREF tag specifies where a click in that area should lead. Note that a relative anchor specification will be expanded using the URL of the map description as a base, rather than using the URL of the document from which the map description is referenced. If you keep your maps in a separate document, you can use the BASE tag to change this if you wish.

At the time this book was written, the only values supported for SHAPE were RECT (rectangle) and DEFAULT. DEFAULT specifies the destination for spots on the image that are not covered by the map. When you specify RECT, you will also need to include a COORDS attribute to specify the rectangle's coordinates. The coordinates are in the form "x,y,x1,y1" where:

- x=left
- y=top
- x1=right
- y1=bottom

This is the same coordinate structure used in server-side map files. It is fairly easy to convert server-side map files into a client-side map document (so you can use an application like WebMap to find the coordinates for you). If two areas defined in a map intersect, the one which appears first will take precedence in the overlapping region. Any region of the image that is not defined by an AREA tag is assumed to be NOHREF.

You may recall that we had a server-side image map menu bar for our kayaking document from the multimedia chapter. Here is one of the lines from the NCSA map file for this document:

```
rect file://localhost/kayak.html#gear 0,0 101,127
```

For our client-side map, we need to convert the information in this line into an AREA tag. We do this by taking the coordinates at the end of the line

```
<AREA SHAPE=rect COORDS="0,0, 101,127" HREF=kayak.html#gear>
```

If we were to convert it into a client-side map it would look like this:

```
<MAP NAME=kayakmenubar>
<AREA SHAPE=rect COORDS="0,0, 101,127" HREF=kayak.html#gear>
<AREA SHAPE=rect COORDS="102,1, 191,127"
HREF=kayak.html#seakayak>
<AREA SHAPE=rect COORDS="192,0, 283,127"
HREF=kayak.html#paddle>
<AREA SHAPE=rect COORDS="285,1, 379,127"
HREF=kayak.html#resources>
<AREA SHAPE=default HREF=kayak.html>
</MAP>
<P><IMG SRC="GIF/kayakmenubar.GIF" USEMAP="#kayakmenubar">
```

As you can see in this example, the "map" portion of the document is composed entirely of tags. Browsers that are not able to handle client-side image maps will simply ignore that portion of the document. The map may be placed either in the document using the map or in a separate document (useful if you wish to use the map with a number of documents, such as in the case of a menu bar).

IMG and USEMAP

Adding a USEMAP attribute to an IMG element indicates that it is a client-side image map. Note that even if you use the USEMAP attribute in an IMG tag, you can still include the ISMAP attribute to allow the image to be processed as either a client-side or server-side image map. When both attributes are specified the USEMAP attribute takes precedence, so the ISMAP will be ignored if USEMAP is supported. This allows you to provide a fallback for people with browsers that support server-side image maps but not client-side maps.

USEMAP takes a single argument—the name of the map. The name of the map should be specified in the same format as an HREF anchor. For example, let's say we have a map named "kayakmenumap" in a file "kayak.html":

Same file:

```
<IMG SRC=menubar.gif USEMAP="#kayakmenumap">
```

A different file:

```
<IMG SRC=menubar.gif USEMAP="kayak.html#kayakmenumap">
```

If you don't have access to server-side map support, and want to provide an alternative in case your document is viewed in a browser that does not handle client-side maps, you can place a regular link around the image. This way, when the user clicks on your map, if there is no support, the link document will be displayed. For example:

```
<A HREF="kayak-nomap.html><IMG SRC=menubar.gif
USEMAP="kayak.html#kayakmenumap" ISMAP></A>
```

Frames: <FRAMESET>, <FRAME>, <NOFRAME>

Frames provide a way for you to divide a window into separate sections or "frames" and load a different document into each window. Documents in one frame may update other frames, allowing you to create an index in one frame that will display the requested topic in another frame. If this seems like it can't work without departing from standard HTML, you're right. Documents that use frames have a structure that looks like this:

```
<HTML>
<HEAD>
</HEAD>
<FRAMESET>
</FRAMESET>
</HTML>
```

As you can see, BODY has been replaced by FRAMESET. Framesets allow you to set up the layout for a window. It takes two attributes: COLS and ROWS. Both attributes take a list of values. The values may be in:

- number of pixels
- percentage

- *number** where * indicates that the frame corresponding to this value gets whatever space is not used by the other frames. *Number* is optional and indicates the percentage of remaining space to be allocated to that frame (if there is more than one such frame).

For example, to make a simple window divided into equally sized quarters, you could use:

```
<FRAMESET ROWS="50%,50%" COLS="50%,50%">
```

The result would be:

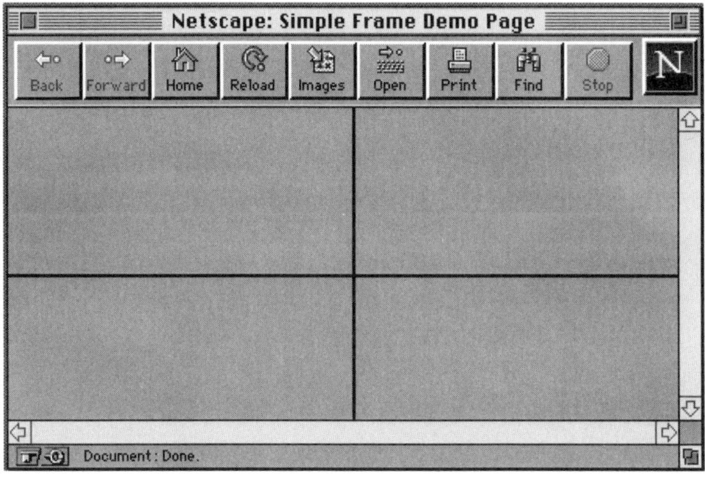

You can nest FRAMESET tags to create just about any layout you want. For example, if you wanted to have a narrow frame across the top of your window for a banner or introductory material, and another narrow banner at the right of your window, to hold an index, you could use the following:

```
<FRAMESET ROWS="20%,80%">
<FRAMESET COLS="80%,20%">
</FRAMESET>
</FRAMESET>
```

Here is how this looks:

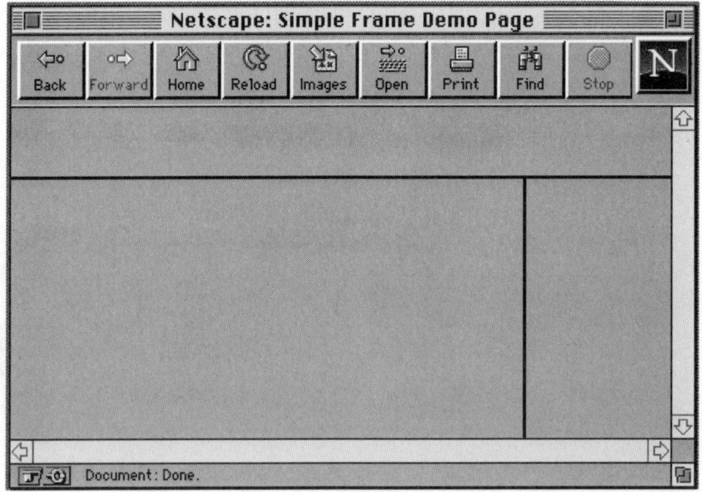

Actually we cheated a bit. This snippet would not display anything because there are no frames in it. Before anything is displayed, you need to specify what will go in the frames you laid out. You do this with the FRAME tag.

Frames: <FRAME>

Once you have finished the layout for your window, you will need to place content in each frame. You do this with the FRAME tag. FRAME takes a number of attributes:

SRC=*URL*

This attribute allows you to specify the URL of the document that is to be displayed in the frame. If you do not specify an SRC, the frame will be left empty (as in our examples above).

NAME=*window-name*

NAME is used to give the frame a name so that it may be updated by links in other documents. Names must begin with a number or letter.

MARGINWIDTH=*value*

Used to control the width of the left and right margins, *value* should be expressed in pixels, and may not be less than one (so the frame's contents do not touch the edge of the frame).

MARGINHEIGHT=*value*

Same as marginwidth, except that it controls the width of the top and bottom margins.

SCROLLING=*yes / no / auto*

This attribute controls whether a scroll bar will be available for that frame. AUTO is the default; it will cause a scrollbar to be placed only if it is needed. YES causes scrollbars to be displayed even if the frame is not full, and NO prevents scrollbars from being displayed even if some of the information cannot be displayed. NO is a dangerous choice since it can create situations in which readers may be unable to see the entire document.

NORESIZE

This prevents readers from resizing a frame. (Readers are normally permitted to resize frames by dragging frame edges using their mouse.)

Content for Browsers without Frame Support: <NOFRAMES>

Since the content of frames is completely contained within FRAME tags, browsers that do not have frame support will not display anything. Since many browsers do not have frame support (including early Netscape browsers), you can lose a substantial number of readers unless you provide some content that does not require frame support. You do this with the <NOFRAMES> tag.

You place your content in a <NOFRAMES> tag:

```
<NOFRAMES>
<P>This should be visible if your browser does not support
frames, while an alternative set of documents will be
displayed if your browser does support them.
</NOFRAMES>
```

When this is viewed by a frame-aware browser, it will not be displayed. Other browsers will not recognize the <NOFRAMES> tag and simply display the content as any other HTML document.

Frame Navigation: TARGET and <BASE>

Navigating around a document that uses frames can be confusing for readers. This is because documents that do not include appropriate navigational control may leave readers stuck with a window divided into multiple frames even though they are no longer viewing a frame document. This happens when links in a frame document do not include directives for the placement of the new document. Without a target directive, new documents are loaded in the current frame, leaving the other frames in the window intact. Making matters even worse, if the reader wants to return from the link, the familiar "Back" button in the browser will not be of any help, since the browser considers the top-level frame document the one that is loaded in the window. As a result, a click on "Back" would return the reader to the document that was loaded before the top-level frame document rather than returning the frame to the previous document loaded in it.

There are a number of methods for specifying where a link should be displayed. These methods allow you to create links in any frame that can update another frame (or window), which is known as the target. When a reader clicks on a link for which a target has been specified, the requested document will appear in the target frame or window.

The default target frame is the current frame, so if you do not specify a target, the document will be displayed in the current frame. If you specify a target frame that does not currently exist, a new frame (in a new window) will be opened and given that name.

Target names must begin with a number or a letter. They are also case sensitive, so be careful when you enter the name. For example, the target names Frame, fRame, frAme, and fraMe are not the same.

You can set a default target for all of the links in a document by using the BASE tag with the TARGET attribute. This tag sets a named target window for every link in a document that does not have an explicit TARGET attribute. The format for this tag is:

```
<BASE TARGET="default_target">
```

You can set a target for a specific link by using the TARGET attribute with the A tag. The syntax for this attribute is:

```
<A HREF="url.html" TARGET="window_name">Click here and open a
New Window</A>
```

Predefined Targets

As we said in the previous section, the names that you choose for targets must start with a number or letter. This is in part because other characters are reserved for predefined target names. At the time this book was written, the predefined targets shown in Table 6–1 were available:

TABLE 6–1 *Predefined Targets*

Target	Description
_blank	Load this link into a new unnamed window
_self	Load link into current window (default)
_parent	Load link over parent (self if no parent exists)
_top	Load link at the top level (self if you are currently at the top)

Notice that all of these target names begin with an underscore. They are also composed of lower-case letters. As we stated before, target names are case sensitive, so be sure that you enter the names exactly as they appear in Table 6–1.

Frame Document Example

Let's look at an example. We've created a set of documents for a Kid's Art Gallery. You can find the document in netscape-frames.html. We divide our window into three frames. The top frame contains the logo for the Gallery, and clicking on the logo will refresh the welcome message in the main frame. The rest of the window is divided into two parts—one for the welcome message and display of full-size images, and the other for an index to the art. Clicking on thumbnail images in the index will cause a full-size version of the image to be displayed in the main window.

Our top-level frame document looks like this:

```
<HTML>
<HEAD>
<TITLE>Netscape Frames Test Document</TITLE>
</HEAD>
<FRAMESET rows="15%,85%">
<FRAME SRC=kidbanner.html SCROLLING=NO MARGINHEIGHT=0
MARGINWIDTH=0 NORESIZE>
<FRAMESET cols="75%,25%">
<FRAME SRC=kidwelcome.html NAME=artwindow>
<FRAME SRC=kidindex.html>
</FRAMESET>
</FRAMESET>
<NOFRAMES>

NOFRAMES portion of the document removed for brevity
</HTML>
```

The NOFRAMES portion of the document duplicates the information in the documents referenced by the FRAMES. Although we do not show this part of the document here, you can see it on the CD. It is very important to include a NOFRAMES section in your frame documents, since readers viewing the document in a browser that does not support frames will not see anything (other than the title) if you do not have a NOFRAMES section.

Notice that we have set a name for only one of our three frames, since this is the only frame that we plan to refresh. The other two frames contain documents with links that target this frame.

Now let's look at two of the documents loaded by our top-level frame document. Our top frame contains only a logo for our gallery. We use the NORESIZE attribute with this frame, since there is no reason for readers to resize it. First, our banner document, kidbanner.html:

```
<TITLE>Kid Gallery Banner</TITLE>
<BODY BGCOLOR=#0000FF VLINK=#0000FF>
<CENTER>
<A HREF=kidwelcome.html TARGET=artwindow><IMG
SRC=kidbanner.GIF ALT="Kid Gallery Logo"></A>
</CENTER>
```

Since we only have one link in this document, we do not bother including a BASE tag. Instead, we include a TARGET attribute in our link tag to specify that the linked document should be displayed in the frame named artwindow.

The second document is our gallery index, kidindex.html:

```
<HTML>
<HEAD>
<TITLE>KidGallery Index</TITLE>
</HEAD>
<BODY BGCOLOR=#000000 TEXT=#FFFF00>
<H1>Kids Art Gallery</H1>
<BASE TARGET=artwindow>
<P><A HREF="kidpictures/kidpict10.gif"><IMG
SRC="kidpictures/kidpict10-thumb.gif" ALT="[Picture
1]"></A><br>187Kb image
<P><A HREF="kidpictures/kidpict2.gif"><IMG
SRC="kidpictures/kidpict2-thumb.gif" ALT="[Picture
2]"></A><br>44Kb image
<P><A HREF="kidpictures/kidpict3.gif"><IMG
SRC="kidpictures/kidpict3-thumb.gif" ALT="[Picture
3]"></A><br>33Kb image
```

Additional image links removed for brevity

```
<HR>
<P><A HREF="index.html" Target="_top"><IMG
SRC=pictures/CDTHUMB.GIF ALT="[HTML CD Home Page]"></A></P>
<ADDRESS>Vivian Neou, <A
HREF="mailto:vivian@catalog.com">vivian@catalog.com</A><BR>
Copyright &#169; 1995 Vivian Neou</ADDRESS>
</HTML>
```

Notice that each thumbnail image is linked to a large image, and that the link is targeted to be displayed in the artwindow frame. Our final link goes to the index for the HTML CD. Since this document has nothing to do with the Kids Gallery, we target this link to the predefined target "_top", which will cause the document to be loaded in the whole window rather than in one of the Kid Gallery frames. Now let's see how our document looks:

Clicking on any of the images in the index will cause a full-size version of the image to appear in place of the "Welcome to Kids Art Gallery" message. For example, if we were to click on the second image, the resulting window would look like this:

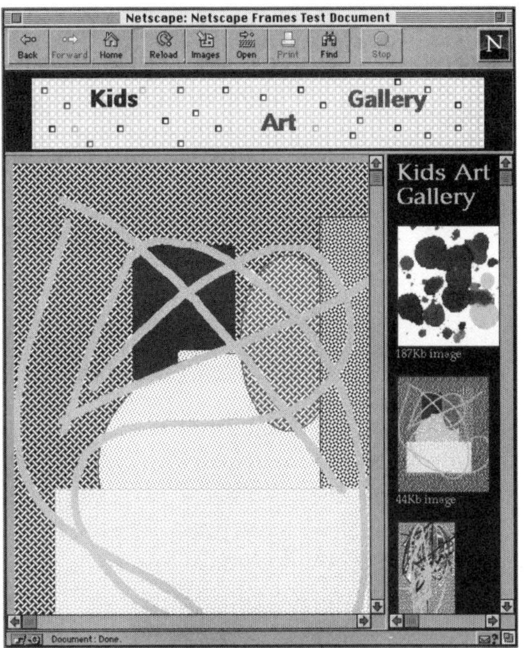

Readers may click on the banner at the top of the window at any time to have the welcome message reloaded in the large frame. Finally, readers can return to the HTML CD index by scrolling to the end of the gallery index and clicking on the link to the CD index. Since the link to the CD index is targeted for loading to "top," it will then be loaded using the entire window rather than in an individual frame.

Embedded Objects: <EMBED>

The EMBED tag allows the insertion of arbitrary objects directly into an HTML page. Embedded objects are supported by application-specific plug-ins. EMBED can take arbitrary attributes. Table 6–2 lists the attributes available for EMBED.

TABLE 6–2 EMBED Attributes

Attribute	Description
SRC	Specifies source URL. Required.
HEIGHT	The object's image will be scaled to fit the specified height and width.
WIDTH	The object's image will be scaled to fit the specified height and width.

The Good, The Bad and The Ugly

This chapter covers new and "unfinished" areas in HTML. While many people using the Internet upgrade their browsers frequently so that they can access the latest and greatest enhancements, there are still a significant number of people out there who are not using browsers that support the features described in this chapter. If you create documents that make heavy use of the features described here, you should try to offer alternative documents for people that do not have browsers that support these elements. This is especially true for FRAME documents, since even pre-Version 2 Netscape browsers do not support this element.

IN THIS CHAPTER YOU WILL LEARN

- ABOUT THE DIFFERENCE BETWEEN JAVA AND JAVASCRIPT
- HOW TO CREATE A FORM-CHECKING APPLICATION IN JAVASCRIPT
- HOW TO USE JAVASCRIPT TO CREATE A SCROLLING MESSAGE ON THE STATUS BAR

JAVASCRIPT

What's In This Chapter

In this chapter we introduce Netscape's JavaScript language. We explain the differences between JavaScript and Java, and show you how to create applications in JavaScript.

Using This Chapter

It is not our intention to provide a complete tutorial on JavaScript here, since that would take an entire book. Since this is a book on both HTML and JavaScript, our goal here is to provide information that will be of use to programmers and people without any programming experience.

The first part of this chapter presents basic concepts and language structure. The second half of the chapter contains four complete JavaScript examples:

- Simple database look-up
- Scrolling status bar message
- A forms checker
- Basic animation

If you are a programmer, we recommend going through the entire chapter and then reviewing the JavaScript Appendix. If you are not a programmer, but would like to incorporate the features offered by one of these scripts, you should first read the section introducing JavaScript and then go directly to the section describing the script you wish to use.

We will explain how we created these scripts and how they may be customized for your use. Programmers may use this information to create new scripts, while those of you without a programming background should be able to copy the scripts from the CD and make the appropriate changes for your own use.

Introduction

As mentioned in the previous chapter, the age of static HTML documents has passed. Now, we want our documents to contain running animations. We want them to contain live, interactive content. In short, we want our documents to contain real applications.

Traditionally, applications are written in programming languages such as C or C++, then compiled to run on specific platforms, such as the Macintosh or Windows. This means that you need to compile an application for every target platform. And as applications become more full-featured, they take up increasing amounts of disk space. In an environment requiring high-performance, networked computing on multiple platforms—like the Internet—the traditional approach simply won't work. There is too much overhead in creating applications for multiple platforms, and users don't have the patience to wait for large applications to download.

Enter Java and JavaScript. While the Java programming language, designed by researchers at Sun, was not intended for the Internet, it proved to be a natural fit. JavaScript, a scripting language developed by Netscape, came along later to make the power of Java accessible to nonprogrammers.

To better understand JavaScript, we must first describe Java. Unlike other programming languages, Java is both *compiled* and *interpreted*. This means that the programmer's Java source code is first compiled into what is known as Java Bytecode. This Bytecode isn't native machine code, but is closer to machine code and is platform independent. Then, when the client downloads the Bytecode, it is efficiently translated by the Java Interpreter into native code for the particular machine. This means that each client, no matter what its platform is, only needs the Java Interpreter to run the Java application. Similarly, a programmer can write a Java application for the Internet, called an applet, which can be embedded in HTML documents. When downloaded by the client browser, the applet is interpreted by a Java-aware browser, such as Netscape 2.0 and HotJava, and run on the client.

JavaScript is a scripting language based on Java. While Java is like C++, JavaScript is more like AppleScript or HyperTalk (the scripting language behind Hypercard).

JavaScript scripts are directly embedded as text in HTML documents, using the <SCRIPT> tag. When a JavaScript-aware browser, like Netscape 2.0, encounters the tag, it interprets the script that follows. *Interprets* means that the computer translates the script as it is run. Thus, programs written in JavaScript are distributed without first being translated into native code.

In addition, Netscape Web servers now support server-side JavaScript. These scripts are also embedded in HTML documents but are first interpreted by the server when the document is requested. The results of interpreting and running the script are then sent to the client. This chapter does not describe server-side JavaScript, since currently only Netscape Web servers support server-side JavaScript.

Programming for the Web

What does programming for the Web mean? For most of the examples in this book, any necessary processing is done by the server. For example, if you wished to check the input sent from a form, you would use a CGI application that would perform the check *on the server* and return the results to the browser. This results in a slow and cumbersome interaction. With Java and JavaScript, you can create programs that will take care of some of these actions on the browser's machine, without going out on the network.

Java vs. JavaScript

Since Java and JavaScript are both intended for the creation of dynamic and interactive documents for the Web, how does one decide which of these languages to use? Let's look at some strengths and weaknesses of each language.

It is much easier to start working in JavaScript than in Java. From a programming standpoint, JavaScript is a much simpler language than Java. It is a scripting language that you insert directly into HTML documents. To write JavaScript, all you need is a browser that supports JavaScript (Netscape Version 2.0 was the only browser that fit into this category at the time this book was written), and a text editor. Essentially, the tools that you use to author plain HTML documents will probably also work for authoring documents that contain JavaScript.

Also, future versions of JavaScript will enable you to control the appearance and behavior of Java applets and Netscape plug-ins. In essence, your scripts can acts as the glue for applets and plug-ins.

Unfortunately there are also problems with JavaScript. Among them:

- Limited browser support reduces the number of readers that can use the features you offer with JavaScript.
- It is not always easy to integrate a non-JavaScript alternative in your documents for readers who view the document with browsers that are not JavaScript aware.
- Some browsers that are not JavaScript aware do not always recognize the JavaScript portion of the document as being a script that should not be displayed. As a result they may display the script as part of the document (we will show examples of this problem later in this chapter).

With Java, on the other hand, you can create multiplatform stand-alone applications, or applets, for the Web. These applets can be more cleanly integrated with regular HTML documents. Since only the Java Bytecode is distributed, Java applets may be incorporated in HTML documents through the use of a few specific tags. Although browsers that are not Java-aware will not understand these tags, they will not display the tag or its contents. As a full-fledged, object-oriented language, Java also provides much more functionality and much faster performance than JavaScript.

On the down side, if you lack experience with languages such as C++, learning Java requires commitment. In addition, you will need a development environment so that you can compile your Java applications or applets before distributing them. Although a Java Developer's Kit (JDK) is freely available from Sun Microsystems, you may prefer to purchase a third-party development environment that provides more features than Sun's JDK.

In the final analysis, JavaScript has an important niche in Web documents. For example, JavaScript can:

- Perform data validation. It can, on the client, quickly check the validity and integrity of form data entered by the user.

- Create special features such as scrolling messages on the status bar.
- Perform the functionality of a simple database by sending data to the client and searching the data in response to user queries.

For advanced development issues, it will probably be necessary to use Java rather than JavaScript.

Some Concepts

Before presenting our examples, we define some important concepts in JavaScript:

- **Objects** are tangible elements in the browser environment. Examples of objects include windows, frames, documents, and forms. Objects in JavaScript follow a hierarchy that is based on the structure of the HTML page. The topmost object is the window. Subobjects in the window are the location (the current URL), the history list, and the current document. The document object has many subobjects, including the document's forms and links. Finally, the form has its many subobjects, including text fields, text areas, and checkbox, radio, password, submit, and reset buttons.
- **Properties** describe the attributes of objects, such as the background color of a document.
- **Methods** are functions (or procedures) associated with objects, such as writing some text to a document or frame, or opening and closing a window.
- **Event handlers** signal user events that occur on the client. Important events include loading a document, clicking the mouse button, or submitting a form.

The JavaScript Appendix provides a list of the more commonly used objects, properties, methods, and handlers.

Starting Your Script: <SCRIPT>

JavaScript scripts are delineated from the rest of your document through the <SCRIPT></SCRIPT> tags. You should also use the optional LANGUAGE="JavaScript" attribute to specify the language used in the script. At present the JavaScript-aware browsers will correctly choose JavaScript as the language to interpret, since it is the only scripting language supported. However, it is likely that other scripting languages will be supported in the future, making it important to let the interpreter know which language is being used.

Scripts consist of a series of statements that optionally are terminated with a semi-colon. If you wish to put more than one statement on a line, you must separate them with a semicolon. Your script should be placed in the HEAD portion of your document to insure that it is completely loaded into memory before anything tries to use it. Let's look at a simple script that simply prints out a few lines. Here it is:

```
<HTML>
<HEAD>
<TITLE>JavaScript Demo Document</TITLE>
<SCRIPT LANGUAGE="JavaScript">
// My simple JavaScript script
{
document.write("<TITLE>A New Title</TITLE>")
document.write("<H1>Simple JavaScript Document</H1>")
document.write("<P>This is a simple JavaScript")
document.write("demonstration.</P>")
}
</SCRIPT>
</HEAD>
<BODY>
</BODY>
</HTML>
```

Notice that our entire script is in the head portion of the document. Now look in the body portion of the document. As you can see, it is empty. Yet, when we load the document into Netscape Navigator, here is what is displayed:

What happened? Our script is interpreted when the document is loaded, and the document.write commands in the script cause their arguments (which are lines of HTML) to be displayed in our document. As used here, the *document* object refers to the currently loaded document, and the *write* method specifies that the argument should be displayed in the document.

There are a few important points to consider here. Although we included a TITLE tag in our document, the title that is displayed is the one that our script produced. If you try loading this script yourself (you can find it in simple-script.html on the CD), you will find that the original title flashes on the title bar but is quickly replaced by title printed by the script. Had we included some lines of text in the body of the document, they too would have been replaced. In practice, our script has created a new HTML document and loaded it over the one that was there. However, although it appears to be a plain HTML document, there is a significant difference. This brings us to our second point.

If you were to try to print this document from the browser, you would get a blank piece of paper. This is because output that is generated by JavaScript cannot be printed by the current version of Netscape (Version 2.01). This may change in future versions of the browser. Nevertheless, you should not count on readers being able to print out a copy of a document generated by HTML. For example, don't generate a confirmation message from a form, and tell your readers to print it out and mail it in.

Basics

This section covers basic JavaScript constructs. JavaScript is a loosely typed language. This means that variables are not associated with a specific data type when they are created. The type is set when the variable is used, and for the most part, conversion between types is done automatically.

Although JavaScript does not explicitly type variables, it does distinguish between certain value types. These types include:

- Numbers (5, 3.14, and so on)
- Boolean values (true or false)
- Strings ("Kayaking is fun" and so on)
- null. This is a special keyword that denotes a null value. Since JavaScript is case sensitive, it must be in lower-case letters.

As we stated before, you do not need to specify the type. When a value is used, JavaScript automatically analyzes it to determine the type.

Literals are fixed values and may be integers, floating-point (real) numbers, logicals (true or false), or strings. Some examples include:

- 245
- 5.13242
- true
- "Ozone Books"

Converting Strings to Numbers

Although JavaScript is loosely typed, there are times when it is necessary to do explicit type conversion. For example, input from forms is considered to be in strings. If you are trying to get numerical input from a form, you will need to convert the strings into numbers.

JavaScript provides several special functions for converting strings to numbers. If the string cannot be converted, the functions will return an error value.

eval

Usage: eval(*variable_name)*

Evaluates a string representing any JavaScript literal or variable, converting it to a number. For example:

```
x = eval(test);
```

would assign the variable "x" the numerical value associated with the string contained in the variable "test".

parseInt

Usage: parseInt(*variable_name*)

Converts a string to an integer.

parseFloat

Usage: parseFloat(*variable_name*)

Converts a string to a floating-point number.

Variable Names

Variables in JavaScript are created with the "var" statement. To create a variable named "Kayak" that contains the string "Best rivers", you would use the var statement as follows:

```
var Kayak = "Best rivers";
```

As you can see from this example, you do not need to explicitly tell JavaScript that the variable will hold a string. Although you do not specify a type when you create a variable, the variable name itself must conform to certain rules. Specifically, variables:

- Must start with a letter ("A" through "Z" and "a" through "z") or underscore ("_").
- May have digits (0–9) in any position but the first one.

Remember that JavaScript is case sensitive. For example, the variable "Kayak" is considered to be a different variable than "KAYAK".

Special Characters

Special characters are included in strings through the use of special escape sequences. You can use the escape codes in Table 7–1 to represent special characters in JavaScript.

TABLE 7–1 *Special-Character Escape Codes*

Escape Code	Description
\b	backspace
\f	form feed
\n	new line character
\r	carriage return
\t	tab character

If you wish to include a quotation mark in a string, you will need to escape it with a backslash. For example, to create a variable named kellstring containing the string:

"Kelly said 'Kayaking is the best sport.' "

you would use:

```
var kellstring = "Kelly said \"Kayaking is the best sport.\""
```

Assignment Operators: =, +=, -=, *=, /=

Assignment of a value to a variable is done with the "=" sign. JavaScript also offers additional assignment operators, as listed in Table 7–2.

TABLE 7–2 Assignment Operators

Operator	Equivalent Statement using "="
x = y	x = y
x += y	x = x + y
x -= y	x = x - y
x *= y	x = x * y
x /= y	x = x / y
x %= y	x = x % y

Arithmetic Operators

JavaScript arithmetic operators take numeric values (which may be literals or variables) as their operands and return a single numerical value. JavaScript supports the standard arithmetic operators:

- addition: +
- subtraction: -
- multiplication: *
- division: /

In addition to the standard operators, the following operators are also available:

Modulus: %

Usage: x % y

It returns the remainder of dividing x by y. For example, 17 % 3 would return 2.

Increment: ++

Usage: x++ or ++x

It adds one to its operand. If it is used as x++, it returns the value before incrementing. Thus if x is 5, "y=x++" would result in y being set to 5 and x being set to 6. If it is used as ++x, it returns the value after incrementing. For example if x is set to 5, "y=++x" would cause both x and y to be set to 6.

Decrement: --

Usage: var-- or --var

It subtracts one from its operand. If it is used as x--, it returns the value before decrementing. For example, if x is 5, the statement "y = x--" would result in y being set to 5 and x being set to 4. If it is used as --x, it returns the value after decrementing. Thus if x is 5, "y=--x" would result in both x and y being set to 4.

Unary negation: -

Usage: -x

This operand returns the negation of its operand. For example, y = -x.

Logical Operators

JavaScript has support for a number of logical operators. These operators take boolean values as expressions and return a boolean value. Logical operators supported by JavaScript include those in Table 7–3.

TABLE 7–3 Logical Operators

<table>
<tr><th>Name</th><th>Operator</th><th>Usage</th><th>Description</th></tr>
<tr><td>And</td><td>&&</td><td>expr1 && expr2</td><td>Returns true if expr1 and expr2 are both true, and returns false otherwise.</td></tr>
<tr><td>Or</td><td>||</td><td>expr1 || expr2</td><td>Returns true if either expr1 or expr2 is true. Returns false if both expr1 and expr2 are false.</td></tr>
<tr><td>Not</td><td>!</td><td>!expr</td><td>Returns the negated value of expr. If expr is false, it returns true; if expr is true, it returns false.</td></tr>
</table>

TABLE 7–4 Comparison Operators

Name	Operator	Usage	Description
Equal	==	*expr1 == expr2*	True if the operands are equal.
Not equal	!=	*expr1 != expr2*	True if the operands are not equal.
Greater than	>	*expr1 > expr2*	True if left operand is greater than right operand.
Greater than or equal to	>=	*expr1 >= expr2*	True if left operand is greater than or equal to right operand.
Less than	<	*expr1 < expr2*	True if left operand is less than right operand.
Less than or equal to	<=	*expr1 <= expr2*	True if left operand is less than or equal to right operand.

Comparison Operators: ==, >, >=, <, <=, !=

A comparison operator compares its operands and returns a logical value based on whether the comparison is true or not. The operands may be numerical or string values. When used on string values, the comparisons are based on the standard lexicographical ordering. Comparison operators are listed in Table 7–4.

Concatenation Operator: +

The concatenation operator (+) can be used to join string values together. It returns a string that is a union of the strings being concatenated. For example,

```
"Ozone " + "Books " + "and Raging Wahine Adventure"
```

returns the string:

```
"Ozone Books and Raging Wahine Adventure"
```

The concatenation assignment operator (+=) can also be used to concatenate strings. For example, if the variable ozone contains "Ozone ", and the variable books contains "Books", then the expression:

```
ozone += books
```

evaluates to "Ozone Books" and assigns this value to the ozone variable.

Operator Precedence

The precedence of operators determines the order of their application when evaluating an expression. The default precedence may be overridden through the use of parentheses.

The precedence of operators, from lowest to highest is:

- comma (,)
- assignment (=, +=, -=, *=, /=, %=, <<=, >>=, >>>=, &=, ^=, |=)
- conditional (?:)

- logical-or (||)
- logical-and (&&)
- bitwise-or (|)
- bitwise-xor (^)
- bitwise-and (&)
- equality (==, !=)
- relational (<, <=, >, >=)
- shift (<<, >>, >>>)
- addition (+), subtraction (-)
- multiply (*), divide (/), modulus (%)
- not (!), negation (-), increment (++), decrement (--)
- call "()", member ([])

Statements

JavaScript statements consist of keywords used with the appropriate syntax. The following statements are available in JavaScript:

- break
- comment
- continue
- for
- for...in
- function
- if...else
- return
- var
- while
- with

With the exception of comment, which is described in the following section, you can find descriptions of these statements in the JavaScript Appendix.

Comments

Comments allow you make notes in your script. Like the comments in most programming languages they are ignored by the interpreter. Comments on a single line should be preceded by a double slash (//). Comments that span multiple lines should be preceded by a "/*" and followed by a "*/".

For example:

```
//This is a single-line comment
x = y;
/*This is a multiline comment.
This line is part of the comment
This is the last line of the comment */
```

Note that the interpreter will also ignore HTML comment lines.

Now that we've reviewed the basic concepts and constructs, let's look at a few JavaScript examples.

Simple Database Look-Up

This example shows how you can use JavaScript to provide simple database look-up functionality—all on the browser.

Ozone Books has been growing rapidly and the company is finding it hard to keep the current list of employee telephone extensions on everyone's desk. Kelly decided this problem can be neatly solved by JavaScript. She authored an HTML document, named phones.html, that contains a simple form. When someone wants to find out the telephone extension of a new employee, she loads Kelly's document, then types in the name of the employee.

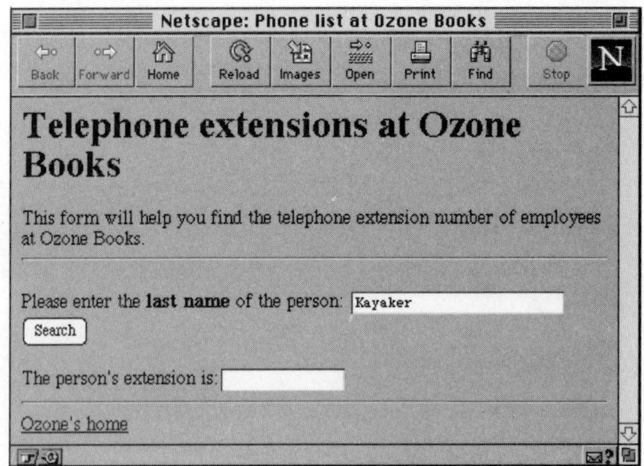

The JavaScript in phones.html contains a list of employee names and their extensions. When the user enters a query, the JavaScript searches its list and displays for the user the appropriate extension.

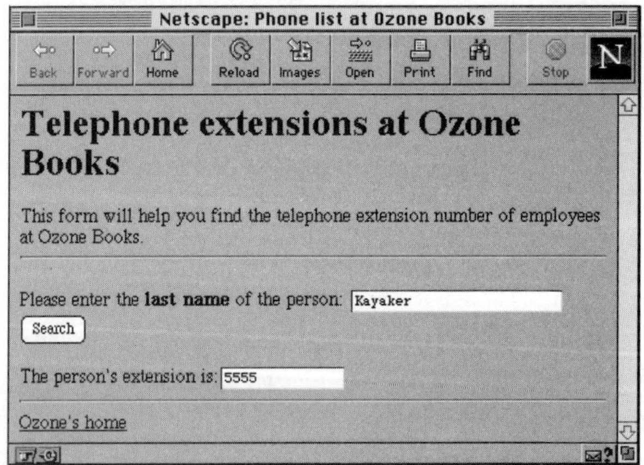

Conveniently, all of the processing takes place on the browser, so employees can store a copy of this document on a local disk for use even when they are not connected to the network. Moreover, when the master list needs to be updated, only one file needs to be changed, phones.html.

Let's look at the complete document, phones.html. Here are some things you should notice. First, we embed the JavaScript within the <SCRIPT></SCRIPT> tags and place it in the HEAD of the document. This way, the script is fully loaded before the user can enter information into the form. Second, comments in the script are preceded by "//". Here is the full document:

```
<HEAD>
<TITLE>Phone list at Ozone Books</TITLE>
<SCRIPT LANGUAGE="JavaScript">
// make an empty array of n items
function makeArray(n) {
    this.length = n
        for (var i=1; i <= n; i++)
            this[i] = null
        return this
}

//Total number of entries allowed in the database
var maxentries = 5

// create object listing last names
var lastname = new makeArray(maxentries)
lastname[1] = "Kayaker"
lastname[2] = "Biker"
lastname[3] = "Hiker"
lastname[4] = "Caver"
lastname[5] = "Swimmer"

// create object listing phone extensions
var extension = new makeArray(maxentries)
extension[1] = "5555"
extension[2] = "5556"
extension[3] = "5557"
extension[4] = "5558"
extension[5] = "5559"

// has input been entered by user?
function notempty(inputStr) {
```

```
    if (inputStr == "" || inputStr == null) {
        alert("Please enter a last name before clicking
Search.")
        return false
    }
    return true
}

// Main function for phones db lookup
function search(form) {
    var foundMatch = false
    var inputStr = form.entry.value
    if (notempty(inputStr)) {
        inputValue = inputStr
         for (var i = 1; i <= lastname.length; i++) {
            if (inputValue == lastname[i]) {
                foundMatch = true
                break
            }
        }
    form.result.value = (foundMatch) ? extension[i] : "No
match found"
    }
}
</SCRIPT>
</HEAD>
<BODY>
<H1>Telephone extensions at Ozone Books</H1>
This form will help you find the telephone extension number of
employees at Ozone Books.
<HR>
<FORM METHOD=post>
Please enter the <b>last name</b> of the person:
<INPUT TYPE="text" NAME="entry" SIZE=25>
<INPUT TYPE="button" VALUE="Search"
ONCLICK="search(this.form)">
<P>
The person's extension is:<INPUT TYPE="text" NAME="result"
SIZE=14>
<HR>
<A HREF="http://www.ozone.com">Ozone's home</A>
</BODY>
</HTML>
```

Let's briefly walk through the script. The script creates a new array called *lastname* via a call to the new operator. Five elements of this array are then assigned values with the last name of each of five employees. Similarly, a new *extension* array is created and assigned values for each of the employees' extensions. The order in which the names and their extensions are listed must correspond exactly.

Customizing the Database

If you wish to customize the script, you would replace each of the *lastname* and *extension* values with your own information, making sure to match the order. If you have more or less than 5 entries in your list, you will need to change the value for the maxentries variable to the number of entries you wish to have in your database. Thus, if your phone list has 10 entries, your script contains:

```
var maxentries = 10
```

The function *notempty* returns true if the string is nonempty. Otherwise it returns false and pops up an alert box to the user. This is a useful general function. The next function, *search*, contains the meat of the script.

Finally, the HTML part of the document contains some text and a form into which the user enters the name to search on. Notice how when the button "Search" is clicked, the function *search* is run. Results from the search are immediately displayed in the last form box.

Scrolling Status Bar

Now let's look at a script that scrolls a message across the browser's status line. Our scripts also include a stop button. Since we have found that scrolling messages can be quite annoying (especially when you want to see the messages that are normally displayed in the status bar), we like to offer our readers the ability to stop the message if they prefer.

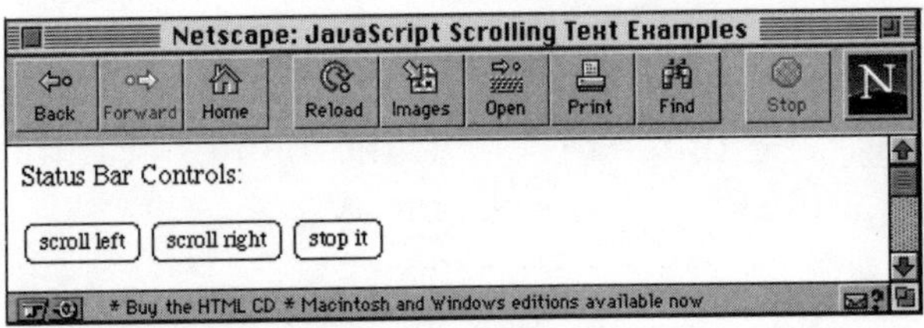

The document you will find on the CD, scrollcontrol.html, actually contains four scripts: left status bar scroll, right status bar scroll, left frame scroll, and right frame scroll. Since they are all very similar, we will go over the left status bar scroll here.

```
<HEAD>
<SCRIPT LANGUAGE="JavaScript">
// Print scrolling text on status bar
function scrollstatusleft(countdown, iteration) {
    var phrase1  = "Buy the HTML CD";
    var phrase2  = "Macintosh and Windows editions available
  now";
    var separator = " * ";
    var scrollmsg= phrase1 + separator + phrase2;
    var timewait = 60;
    if ((countdown < scrollmsg.length) &
  !(document.forms[0].stopit.value=="true")){
        var tmpcount = scrollmsg.length-countdown;
        window.status=
  scrollmsg.substring(tmpcount,scrollmsg.length) +  separator +
  scrollmsg.substring(0, tmpcount);
        countdown++;
        var cmd="scrollstatusleft(" + countdown + "," +
  iteration +  ")";
        cmdtimer=window.setTimeout(cmd,30);
    }
    else {
        if ((--iteration >= 1) &
  !(document.forms[0].stopit.value=="true")){
            var cmd="scrollstatusleft(0 ," + iteration + ")";
            cmdtimer=window.setTimeout(cmd,120);
        }
        else {
            window.status=scrollmsg;
```

```
        }
    }
}
// Done with the code -->
</SCRIPT>
<TITLE>JavaScript Scrolling Status Bar Example</TITLE>
</HEAD>
<BODY bgcolor="#FFFFFFF" >
```

-- Additional text removed for brevity --

```
<P>Status Bar Controls:
<form>
<input type=button
  onclick="document.forms[0].stopit.value=false;
  ScrollTime=window.setTimeout('scrollstatusleft(0,4)',0)"
  value="scroll left">
<input type=button
  onclick="document.forms[0].stopit.value=true;" value="stop
  it">
<input type=hidden name=stopit value="false">
</form>
```

Now let's see how we made the message appear. We placed our message on the status bar by setting the value of the status property for our window to the message that we wished to display. For example:

```
window.status=scrollmsg;
```

Since we want the message to scroll slowly enough for our readers to see and read it, we need to use a timer to adjust the speed of the scroll. The timer method is setTimeout. This method takes two arguments: the command to be evaluated, and the number of milliseconds to pause before the command should be executed. For example:

```
cmdtimer=window.setTimeout(cmd,120);
```

executes the command in the string "cmd" after 120 milliseconds.

Customizing the Status Bar Script

Now let's look at how the script may be customized for your use. As it currently stands, this script allows two phrases, although it is fairly simple to add additional ones should you desire. We split our phrases between different variables because JavaScript has problems with very long string assignments (although in this case, our strings are short enough to have been assigned in a single shot). The variables for the phrases are *phrase1*, and *phrase2*.

```
var phrase1  = "Buy the HTML CD";
var phrase2  = "Macintosh and Windows editions available now";
```

To add your own phrases, simply replace the text between the quotation marks with your own phrases. For example, if you wish to use "Late-breaking news..." as your first phrase, the line for phrase1 would become:

```
var phrase1  = "Late-breaking news...";
```

You should not place carriage returns or quotation marks in the phrases you create.

You can also customize the separation characters, which are kept in the variable *separator*.

```
var separator = " * "
```

As with the phrases, replace the text between the quotation marks with your preferred separation characters. Remember to leave spaces so that your phrases do not get pushed up against the separation character(s).

Next, copy the script (everything from <SCRIPT> to </SCRIPT>) into the HEAD portion of the document where you wish to use it.

We let our readers turn the message on and off through the use of forms. However, if you prefer to have a message begin as soon as the document is loaded, simply grab the command for the type of message that you want (the command is attached to the onclick attribute) and add an "onLoad" attribute to the BODY tag with that command. For example:

```
<BODY
onLoad="ScrollTimer=window.setTimeout('scrollstatusleft(0,3)',
0)">
```

This script takes two arguments. The first should always be set to 0, since it is used by the script as a countdown timer. The second argument is the number of times the banner should be displayed. Notice that we have set the banner to display 3 times. We chose to have the banner run a finite number of times because a problem with Version 2.0 of the Netscape browser caused it to run out of memory if the banner was allowed to loop indefinitely. It may also annoy readers if they lose control over the status bar and their view of the messages that normally appear there. If you prefer to have it run indefinitely, you can simply remove the check for loopnum.

That's it! To check your script, just load it into Netscape 2 or higher. If you made any errors, the browser will pop up a window with a message describing the error.

Animation

Doing animation with JavaScript is fairly easy, but also rather ugly. This is due to JavaScript's lack of a method for updating specific areas of a window. As a result, the whole document must be reloaded (this is similar to client pull animations). The resulting animation tends to be very jerky.

Given these limitations, if you are still interested in using JavaScript to add animation to your documents, we recommend using it in combination with frames. By placing your animation in a frame of its own (sized to the animation), only a single frame needs to be updated rather than the entire window. The other benefit this combination provides is a side-effect of the fact that the only browser that supports both of these features is Netscape (although this may change). By using a <NOFRAME> tag in your top-level frame document, you can provide users with a non-JavaScript, nonframe alternative—something that is difficult to do without frames.

Now let's look at an example. You may recall from our previous discussions about animation that we have a sequence of GIF images which can be used to create a spinning globe. Our images are in files named globe1.gif through globe10.gif. As with any animation method that requires a separate image file to be loaded for each frame of the animation, we strongly recommend that you give your files the same name followed by a number. This allows you to step through the images with a counter rather than having to build different file names (along with the appropriate order) into your script.

The first thing we do is to create an HTML document that lays out the frames in our window. We plan to display our globe in a square frame on the top left of the window. Our main document will be displayed in a frame to the right of our animation, and we leave the frame below the animation empty. Our initial document looks like this:

```
<HTML>
<HEAD>
<TITLE>Animation Examples</TITLE>
</HEAD>
<BODY>
<FRAMESET COLS="20%,80%">
<FRAMESET ROWS="20%,80%">
<FRAME SRC=empty.html NAME=JSAnimate>
<FRAME SRC=empty.html NAME=Empty>
</FRAMESET>
<FRAME SRC=jsanimate.html NAME=Source>
</FRAMESET>
</BODY>
</HTML>
```

As you can see, we have named the frame where we plan to display our animation "JSAnimate". The frame below it is named "Empty", and the main frame is named "Source". We preload the two lefthand frames with empty.html, an HTML file that does nothing more than set a background color. Our

"Source" window is loaded with "jsanimate.html", the document containing the JavaScript code for the animation. Let's take a look at jsanimate.html now. Here it is:

```
<HEAD>
<TITLE>Animation Control</TITLE>
<SCRIPT LANGUAGE="JavaScript">
function writeframe(countdown){
    var i = parseInt(countdown);
    if (i++ < 10) {
        parent.JSANIMATE.location.href="globe" + i + ".gif";
         var timerstring = "writeframe(" + i + ")";
        timer=setTimeout(timerstring,1000);
    }
}
{
writeframe("0");
}
</SCRIPT>
</HEAD>
<BODY BGCOLOR=#FFFFFF>
<H1>Animation Control</H1>
     -- Document text removed for brevity --
```

Our script makes use of the ability for a document in one frame to update information in a sibling frame. Thus, all we need to do to refresh the frame that is to contain our animation is to update the "location.href" property for that frame. The frame where we wish to place the animation is named JSANIMATE. We place our images in this frame by updating its URL through the *href* property:

```
parent.JSANIMATE.location.href="globe" + i + ".gif";
```

Here *parent* is a predefined name that refers to the "parent" of the current frame.

Customizing the Script

The first step in customizing the animation script is to set up a frame document. Reserve a frame for your animation and make sure that you name it JSANIMATE. If you are not sure how to do this, please refer to the section on frames in Chapter 6. Next you will need to have a set of images in either GIF or JPEG format that make up your animation. They should be placed in files with a name in the format: myimage1.gif, myimage2.gif, myimage3.gif and so on.

Place the script in a document that will be loaded into one of the other frames in the window. Replace "10" in this line:

```
if (i++ < 10) {
```

with the total number of images in your animation. In this line, replace "globe" with the name of your file:

```
parent.JSANIMATE.location.href="globe" + i + ".gif";
```

If you use JPEG images rather than GIF images, replace "gif" with "jpg" or "jpeg", depending on what you use in your image filenames. Load your frame document, and you should see your animation.

JavaScript Forms Checker

Our final JavaScript script does some preprocessing on Ozone Books' order form. The original form was processed by a CGI program. This meant that the form had to be transmitted to Ozone Books' server, the CGI program had to process it, and if any problems were found, a warning message was returned to the reader. As a result, a single transaction might require several network connections. Since network connections take time, this slowed things down for the customer. By shifting the burden of the processing to the local system, we reduce the time the customer must wait for the form to be processed. Our script adds the following functionality:

- **Order-total calculator**. We add a new button that allows readers to calculate and review their order total *before* submitting the form. Readers no longer need to calculate subtotals for themselves—all they have to do is enter the number of items and the cost of the items. The script takes care of the rest.

- **Required information check**. Rather than submitting a form that may be incomplete, we use the NotEmpty function developed for our database script to check whether readers have filled in certain fields (in this case we check for phone and e-mail). If the field is empty, the form is not submitted and a warning message is displayed.

Order-Total Calculator

We first look at the portion of the script that totals the order. Our goal is to create an extra button that will allow users to check their order total without having to submit the form. For example, a user may enter:

Product Number	Title	Qty	Price	Total
X12	Running the Rapids	1	10.50	
Y23	Climb High, Fall Far	3	12.73	
B31	Biking ABCs	5	15.43	
		Order Total:		

Total my order

and then click on the "Total my order" button to get:

Product Number	Title	Qty	Price	Total
X12	Running the Rapids	1	10.50	10.50
Y23	Climb High, Fall Far	3	12.73	38.19
B31	Biking ABCs	5	15.43	77.15
		Order Total:		125.84

Total my order

We achieve this with three new functions: PrintNumber, subtotal, and totalorder. We also use the notempty function from our database script.

Our first function, PrintNumber, addresses the problem of dealing with floating-point numbers. Floating-point numbers are not always treated precisely. For example, on some plat-

forms, 4.6 becomes 4.5999999.... Obviously we cannot display figures like this! To avoid this problem, we turn our floating-point number into integers and deal with the fractions in separate steps.

We accomplish this by using the Math object with the *round* method. This method takes a number or numeric expression and rounds it to the nearest integer. Here is PrintNumber:

```
// Round a floating-point number to the correct value and
// convert it to a string
function PrintNumber(InNum){
        var dollars = Math.round(InNum * 100);
        var pennies = (dollars % 10);
        dollars = Math.round((dollars - pennies)/10);
        var dimes = dollars % 10;
        dollars = Math.round((dollars - dimes)/10);
        return(dollars + "." + dimes + pennies);
}
```

Our next function, subtotal, takes two input strings. It first checks to see if there is anything in the strings using the notempty function we developed for our database application. If both strings contain input, it converts them to numerical values with the parseFloat method, multiplies the result, and uses the *return* statement to return the total. If either string did not contain input, it returns 0.

```
//Get a subtotal for an item. Input consists of two strings
// containing price and quantity. The function returns the
// sum of the two.
function subtotal(quantity,price){
    if (notempty(quantity) && notempty(price)) {
        var subtotal = parseFloat(quantity) *
           parseFloat(price);
    }
    else {
        var subtotal = 0;
    }
   return subtotal;
}
```

Before looking at the next function, let us first review the portion of the form that contains the list of books being ordered. We have abbreviated the form to allow space for only three items. Here it is:

```
<FORM METHOD=post NAME="OrderForm"
ACTION="mailto:orders@ozone.com">

-- Form address information removed for brevity --

<TABLE>
<TR><TH>Product
Number<TH>Title<TH>Qty<TH>Price<TH>Total
<TR><TD><INPUT NAME="PN1" TYPE=text MAXLENGTH=5 SIZE=5>
<TD><INPUT NAME="TITLE1"
TYPE=text MAXLENGTH=40 SIZE=40> <TD><INPUT NAME="QTY1"
TYPE=text MAXLENGTH=5
SIZE=5><TD><INPUT NAME="PRICE1" TYPE=text MAXLENGTH=6
SIZE=6><TD><INPUT NAME="TOTAL1"
TYPE=text MAXLENGTH=9 SIZE=9>

<TR><TD><INPUT NAME="PN2" TYPE=text MAXLENGTH=5 SIZE=5>
<TD><INPUT NAME="TITLE2"
TYPE=text MAXLENGTH=40 SIZE=40> <TD><INPUT NAME="QTY2"
TYPE=text MAXLENGTH=5
SIZE=5><TD><INPUT NAME="PRICE2" TYPE=text MAXLENGTH=6
SIZE=6><TD><INPUT NAME="TOTAL2"
TYPE=text MAXLENGTH=9 SIZE=9>

<TR><TD><INPUT NAME="PN3" TYPE=text MAXLENGTH=5 SIZE=5>
<TD><INPUT NAME="TITLE3"
TYPE=text MAXLENGTH=40 SIZE=40> <TD><INPUT NAME="QTY3"
TYPE=text MAXLENGTH=5
SIZE=5><TD><INPUT NAME="PRICE3" TYPE=text MAXLENGTH=6
SIZE=6><TD><INPUT NAME="TOTAL3"
TYPE=text MAXLENGTH=9 SIZE=9>

<TR><TD> <TD><TD COLSPAN=2><STRONG>Order
Total:</STRONG><TD><INPUT NAME="GRANDTOT" TYPE=text
MAXLENGTH=9 SIZE=9>
</TABLE>
```

Each order item has five input fields:

- PN*x*: the part number
- TITLE*x*: the book's title

- QTY*x*: the number of copies requested
- PRICE*x*: the book's price
- TOTAL*x*: the total cost for this item

Note that *x* represents the item number (e.g.: PRICE1, PN2, and so on). Our function, totalorder, looks at the QTY*x* and PRICE*x* input fields from our form to calculate a subtotal for each item. It accesses these fields by using the appropriate document subobject. When we created our form we used the NAME attribute to name it "OrderForm":

```
<FORM METHOD=post NAME="OrderForm" ...>
```

We use this name to access the form through the document object's *form* subobject. Since we want to access a specific field in the form, we also need to use the appropriate form subobject. Thus, to access the value in the PRICE1 field, we enter:

```
document.OrderForm.PRICE1.value
```

The totalorder function also sums the subtotals to provide the total cost for the order. It sends the output to the form by setting the *value* subobject for the fields that have been set up for this purpose: TOTAL1, TOTAL2, TOTAL3, and GRANDTOTAL. Since our concern is with the order's cost, we do not check the part number or title. Now here is the function itself:

```
//Calculates the total cost of the order, and writes it out
// to the appropriate place in the form.
function totalorder(){
    var total1 = subtotal(document.OrderForm.QTY1.value,
       document.OrderForm.PRICE1.value);
    document.OrderForm.TOTAL1.value = PrintNumber(total1);
    var total2 = subtotal(document.OrderForm.QTY2.value,
       document.OrderForm.PRICE2.value);
    document.OrderForm.TOTAL2.value=PrintNumber(total2);
    var total3 = subtotal(document.OrderForm.QTY3.value,
       document.OrderForm.PRICE3.value);
    document.OrderForm.TOTAL3.value=PrintNumber(total3);
   document.OrderForm.GRANDTOT.value=PrintNumber(total1+
       total2+total3);
}
```

Of course we do not want these functions to automatically calculate the order as soon as the reader enters information in the form's fields. Instead we set up a button field that will allow the reader to click on it to trigger this part of our script. Here is the HTML used to create the button:

```
<INPUT TYPE="button" VALUE="Total my order"
ONCLICK="totalorder()">
```

Note that the button type is not a part of standard HTML. It was added by Netscape so that custom buttons (rather than only the standard SUBMIT and RESET) could be tied to other actions.

Required Field Checker

Our form requests some contact information. Part of the information requested includes an e-mail address and phone number:

```
<B>ZIP:</B> <INPUT NAME="zip" TYPE=text MAXLENGTH=30 SIZE=10>
<TR><TD><B>E-mail:</B>        <TD><INPUT NAME="email"
TYPE=text MAXLENGTH=50 SIZE=50>
<TR><TD><B>Daytime Phone:</B> <TD><INPUT NAME="phonenum"
TYPE=text MAXLENGTH=30 SIZE=20>
```

We do not want readers to be allowed to submit the form unless the e-mail and phone number fields have been completed. Instead, we would like a warning message to be printed:

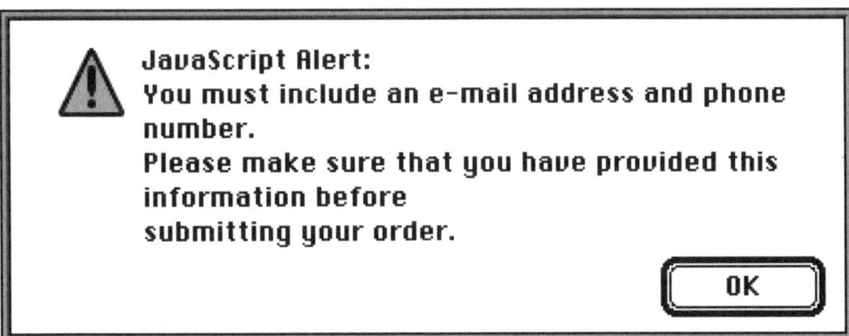
JavaScript Alert:
You must include an e-mail address and phone number.
Please make sure that you have provided this information before
submitting your order.
OK

We accomplish this by replacing the submit input field with a button field that calls our input checking function, requireinput:

```
<P><INPUT TYPE=button VALUE="Place My Order"
onClick="requireinput(document.OrderForm)">
```

When the user clicks this button, the function requireinput is called. requireinput uses our notempty function to check whether the e-mail and phonenum fields are empty. If they are, it uses the alert method to create an alert box with a warning message and does not submit the form. If the fields have been completed, requireinput uses the submit method to submit the form:

```
//Used when the form is submitted to see whether the e-mail
// and phone number fields have information. If they don't,
// it prints out a warning and does not submit the form.
function requireinput(CheckForm){
    if (!notempty(CheckForm.email.value) ||
        !notempty(CheckForm.phonenum.value)) {
        var alertmsg = "You must include an e-mail address
and phone number.\nPlease make sure that you have provided
this information before\nsubmitting your order.";
        alert(alertmsg);
    }
    else {
        CheckForm.submit()
    }
}
```

Adapting the Form

If you wish to use our script to check portions of your own order form in, you should start with the template from the CD. You will find it in order-verify.html. Copy the script (everything from <SCRIPT> to </SCRIPT>) at the beginning of the document to your order form.

Now modify the totalorder and requireinput functions to use the names of your form and input fields, rather than the names of our input fields. For example, if you have a form named "myform" with a quantity column named "quantity1" and a price column named "cost2", you would change the line:

```
var total1 = subtotal(document.OrderForm.QTY1.value,
   document.OrderForm.PRICE1.value);
```

to:

```
var total1 = subtotal(document.myform.quantity1.value,
   document.myform.cost2.value);
```

If you have more than three item lines in your form, you should copy the two lines of code used to process an item:

```
var total1 = subtotal(document.OrderForm.QTY1.value,
   document.OrderForm.PRICE1.value);
document.OrderForm.TOTAL1.value = PrintNumber(total1);
```

Place as many copies of these lines before the grand total line as you have items in your form. Then update the lines to reflect the correct field names for your items. Finally, update the grand total line to include all of your items. For example, if you added three items, you would change:

```
document.OrderForm.GRANDTOT.value=PrintNumber(total1 +
total2 + total3);
```

to:

```
document.OrderForm.GRANDTOT.value=PrintNumber(total1 +
total2 + total3 + total4 + total5);
```

To customize the requireinput function, replace *email* and *phonenum*:

```
if (!notempty(CheckForm.email.value) ||
    !notempty(CheckForm.phonenum.value)) {
```

with the names of the input fields you wish to check. You can add extra fields by adding the or operator (||) followed by the notempty function (remember to negate it!) acting on the field.

The Good, the Bad, and the Ugly

Here are some tips to keep in mind while creating documents that incorporate JavaScript scripts:

- Remember that JavaScript output will not be printed when the document is printed by a browser. Don't make the mistake of generating a confirmation notice and asking users to print it!
- Include HEIGHT and WIDTH attributes with any images that you include in a document that uses JavaScript. There have been reports that Netscape Navigator has problems with JavaScript and images if these attributes are omitted.
- If you don't want to take the time to maintain an alternate set of documents for JavaScript-challenged browsers, make sure that you review your documents with other browsers before releasing them! As you can see from our Internet Explorer examples, even when you take the time to try to hide your script with HTML comment lines, you may still run into other accessibility problems.

The biggest challenge when using JavaScript is to create documents that work cleanly with non-JavaScript-aware browsers. For example, here is our order form document in Internet Explorer:

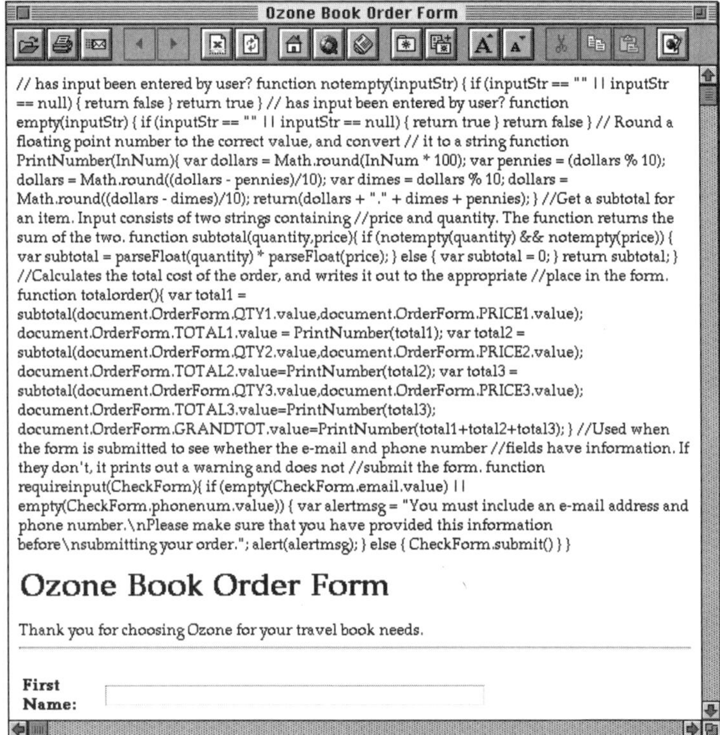

This is definitely not a very nice looking document. We can get rid of the JavaScript display by adding an open HTML comment line:

```
<!-- Start script hiding
```

at the beginning of our script (either immediately before or after the <SCRIPT> tag) and another closing comment line:

```
// Now we end our script -->
```

immediately before the closing script tag, </SCRIPT>. After making these changes, we find that Internet Explorer displays our document like this:

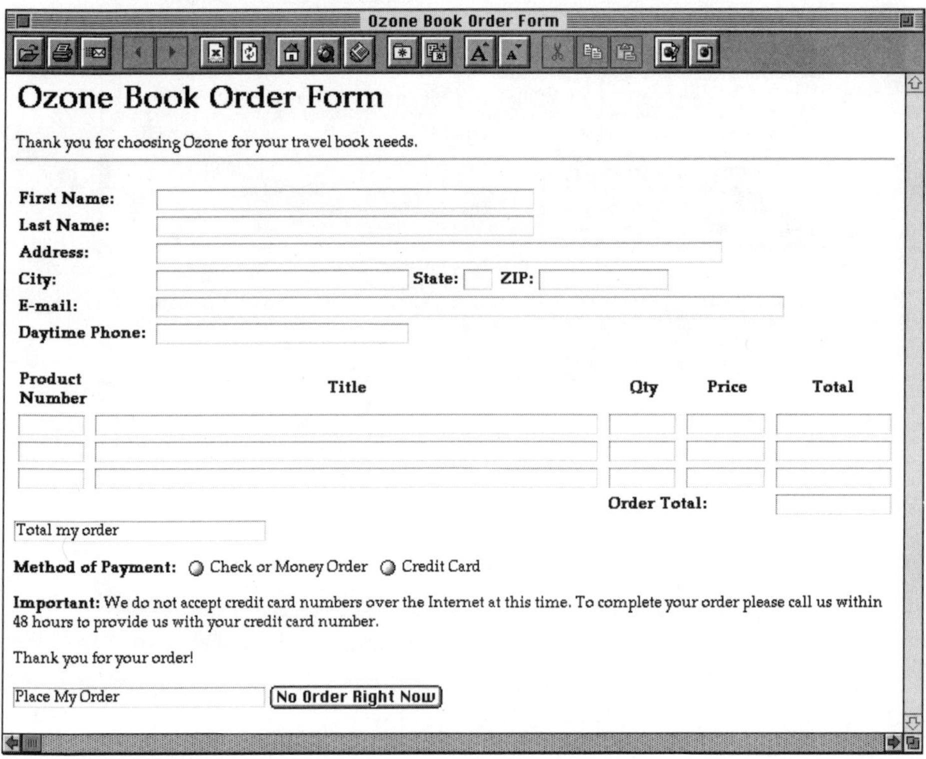

Now we have a new problem. Do you see a working submit button anywhere? Of course not—because we created our own submit button with the JavaScript input type "button," which Internet Explorer does not see as a submit field. Notice that our total button ends up as a text input field. This happened because Internet Explorer saw it as field with an unknown type and defaulted to a text input field.

To make matters worse, when we check our script in other browsers (such as Lynx), some of the script still shows up. Is there a solution to this mess? Is there something we can do other than place a big warning message at the beginning of our JavaScript documents, telling readers using something other than NetScape to go away?

Fortunately there is a partial solution—use JavaScript in combination with frames. This solution is based on the fact that the only browser that supports JavaScript also supports frames. With this in mind, to automatically direct your readers to the appropriate page for their browser, simply access the JavaScript document through a frame document. If your JavaScript document does not use multiple frames, just create a document that looks something like this:

```
<FRAMESET>
<FRAME SRC=javascript.html>
</FRAMESET>
<NOFRAME>
Alternate text for frame and JavaScript-challenged browsers
```

Your JavaScript document will be displayed only if the browser understands frames—and if it knows about frames, it will also have JavaScript support. (This was true at the time we wrote this book, though we can't guarantee that some browser creator won't decide to make a browser that understands frames, but not JavaScript.) If it doesn't understand frames, the document that you include in the <NOFRAMES> tag will be displayed instead.

The Future

There are still many areas in JavaScript that are unfinished—both in the development of the language specification and in the interpreter. For example, one of the rumored additions to the language will be the ability to separate JavaScript scripts into separate files, which would be included in documents through the use of an SRC attribute for the SCRIPT tag.

We have tried to present the most current information about JavaScript available at the time this book was written. However, since this is a rapidly changing field, we recommend referring to the on-line documentation at Netscape for the latest information. You will find it at:

```
http://home.netscape.com/comprod/products/navigator/version_2.
0/script/script_info/index.html
```

In this chapter you will learn essential guidelines for

- Designing and laying out Web pages
- Using graphics
- Supporting navigation in Web documents
- Efficiently using system resources

Design Guidelines, Styles and Tips

What's In This Chapter

This chapter pulls together the design guidelines mentioned as we described HTML tags in previous chapters, and introduces overall guidelines for laying out Web documents. In particular, we focus on the following aspects of Web document design:

- Designing and laying out Web pages
- Using graphics
- Supporting navigation in Web documents
- Efficiently using system resources

Introduction

Generally, books, magazine articles and papers are authored with particular audiences or readers in mind. Similarly, Web documents can be authored for a target audience. For example, Web documents containing company policy might be authored for members of that organization.

However, documents that are made part of the Internet World Wide Web are instantly available for browsing by its millions of global members. This means that the documents we author can be browsed by a hugely diverse population. In this case, it is almost impossible to know who our audience might be.

Moreover, users are not simply reading our Web documents—they are interacting with them. Our readers can select hyperlinks, navigate backward and forward between documents and Web sites, and generally choose their own pathway within information spaces in ways that we cannot fully anticipate.

These conditions present interesting and unique challenges for authors wishing to design interesting, appealing and effective Web documents. Although multimedia publishing is a recent desktop reality, little is known about the most effective ways to design digital documents that combine text, images, graphics, movies and sound in order to best present and convey the intended information.

Fortunately, fields such as human-computer interaction, graphic design, information design and instructional design combined with traditional typography contribute many useful techniques for improving the design and layout of effective Web documents.

Based on our experience in browsing and authoring documents for the Web, we have formulated a set of important authoring principles. Many of these principles have already been highlighted at appropriate spots in the book. In this chapter we review and discuss these design principles, which authors should bear in mind when authoring Web documents.

In particular, we focus on the design and layout of Web pages, the use of graphics and support of navigation in Web documents, and the efficient use of system resources.

Of course, many of these issues are related. For example, a set of documents that are well designed usually enable users to effectively navigate within pages. Similarly, designers wishing for a strong graphical impact will take system and network resources into account. In short, the guidelines we present in the following section should be considered together.

Page Design and Layout

When authoring a set of related documents, it is important to keep a consistent design style and organization across documents. When authors use a repeated organization of text and graphics across documents, readers will come to know what to expect and where to locate pertinent information. Such patterns will help make your documents more understandable and legible.

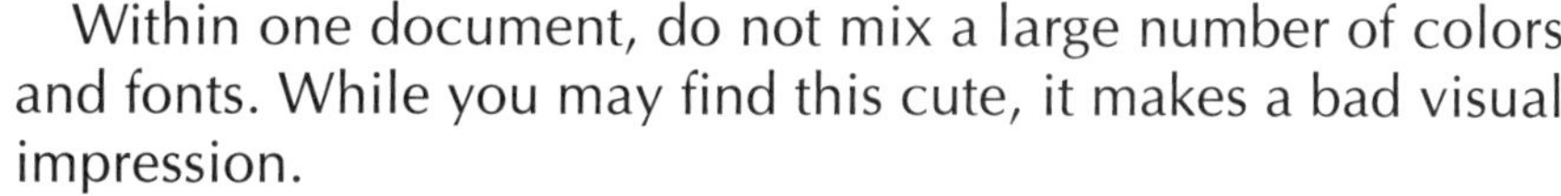

Within one document, do not mix a large number of colors and fonts. While you may find this cute, it makes a bad visual impression.

Header Elements

In particular, you should have the following header elements at the top of each document. These elements should be positioned with the same screen location in each document.

The Title of the Document

Do not confuse this with the title tag, which you should also include in the document. The title of the document should be included in a header tag at the beginning of the document.

Banner, logo, or seal identifying the organization or institution (if applicable)

This banner can also be a hyperlink that points back to the organization's top-level page, or it could be an image map that provides links to various locations within the organization's pages. If you choose to use an imagemap, make sure that you offer an alternative table of contents so that readers that cannot use graphics are still able to navigate through your pages.

For example, the following header is used on the top level of Kelly Kayaker's business pages:

```
<A HREF="/cgi/imagemap/obrwa>
<IMG SRC=wahine/obralogo.gif ISMAP ALT="[Ozone Books and
Raging Wahine Logos]"></IMG></A>
<H1 ALIGN=CENTER>Welcome to</H1>
<H1 ALIGN=CENTER>Ozone Books and Raging Wahine Adventures</H1>
```

Although it is not included here, a table of contents that provides equivalent navigational opportunities is included beneath the first paragraph in the document. Here is how this header looks in Netscape Navigator:

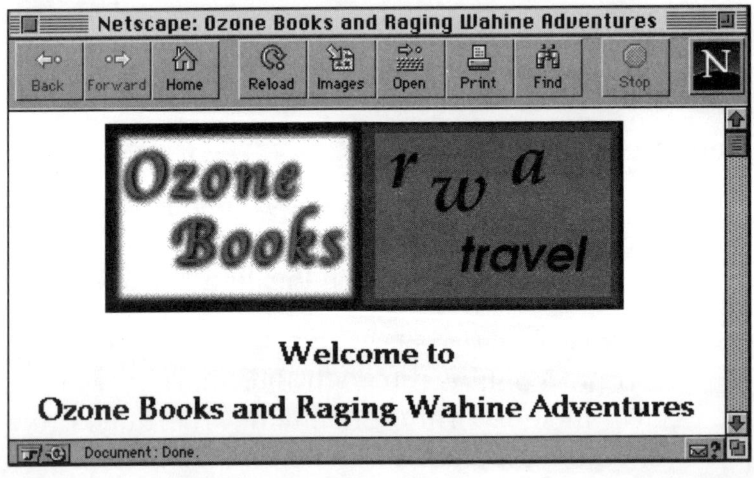

Footer Elements

You should have the following elements at the bottom of documents (sometimes called footers). To give your pages a consistent look, these elements should be similarly positioned in all documents.

The author's name and contact information

This information is typically placed within an <ADDRESS> tag. It is a good idea to include an e-mail address with a mailto link. You may also wish to include a hyperlink from the author's name to the author's personal home page.

Link to a top-level or home page

This is important! Remember that anyone can make a link to any page. If you don't include a link back to your top-level page, and someone gets to your page via a link outside your pages, it may not be easy for them to find your top-level page. If you want to encourage people to look at all of your pages, make it easy for them to get to your starting point!

Links to related documents (if applicable)

Like a link to your top-level page, links to related documents help your readers to navigate through your pages. These links don't have to go to other parts of your web, although typically links in footers do.

Last modification date of document

While this isn't absolutely necessary, it is often helpful for readers to know how recently information has been updated.

Copyright status of document (if applicable)

If you have disclaimers or other restrictions on your pages, you can avoid having to include your list on every page by making a page with this information and then linking a copyright notice to that page.

Let's look at the footer for Ozone Books' catalog. It includes an address, an e-mail contact, and links to relevant top-level pages. Since the catalog itself is dated, we do not include a last modification date, and since they want the catalog to be distributed as widely as possible, there is not copyright restriction notice on this page.

```
<ADDRESS>
Raging Wahine Adventures and Ozone Books<BR>
P.O. Box 600<BR>
Wellington, New Zealand<BR>
<A HREF="mailto:queries@ozwa.com">queries@ozwa.com.nz</A><BR>
</ADDRESS>
<HR>
<A HREF="../ozwatop.html"><IMG SRC="../images/ozwahome.gif"
ALT="[Ozone/Wahine Home Page]"></A>
<A HREF="../wahine/raging.html"><IMG
SRC="../images/wahihome.gif"
ALT="[Raging Wahine Home Page]"></A>
<A HREF="index.html"><IMG SRC="../images/ozhome.gif"
ALT="[Ozone Books Home Page]"></A>
```

Here is how our footer looks in Netscape Navigator:

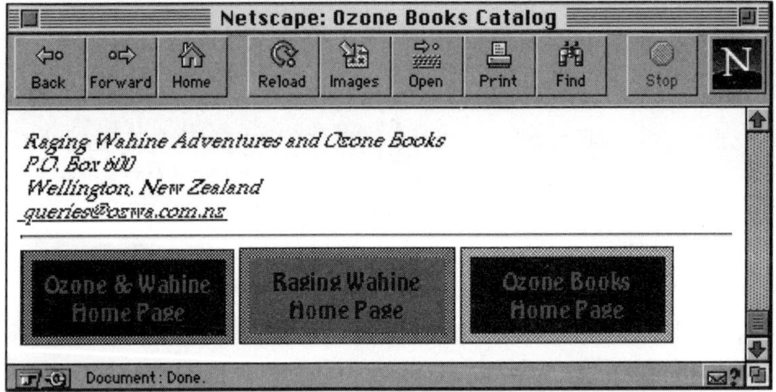

Using Graphics and Other Multimedia Items

The Web has made networked desktop publishing a reality for many people. Naturally, as authors, we are tempted to take maximum advantage of this new ability to integrate multimedia elements such as graphics, animations, audio and video into our documents.

However, there are many reasons to use such items with caution. Many users have limited network bandwidth and hence choose to browse the Web with images "turned off." Others access Web documents using text-only browsers, such as Lynx. These users are completely lost upon encountering a graphics-intensive page.

DON'T MAKE AN IMAGE MAP THE ONLY WAY FOR READERS TO NAVIGATE THROUGH YOUR DOCUMENTS.

Using image maps as a navigational tool for your web pages is a tempting way to make flashy-looking pages. However, don't make image maps the only way for readers to navigate through your documents. These graphics often take a long time to load for users connecting to the Web with a less-than-high-speed network connection. Many of these users will not have the patience for documents designed in this manner. Others will be incapable of viewing them.

This is especially important in your top-level document. While this kind of top-level navigation approach is visually appealing and supports graphical navigation, you will lose users browsing without images.

For example, our header example from page 234 includes a clickable image. We provide a text-based navigation option equivalent to this image later in the document. However, as you can see when we display the beginning of the document in Lynx, our readers would be unable to navigate to our other related documents if we did not do this.

```
                                 OZONE BOOKS and RAGING WAHINE TRAVEL (p1 of 3)

   [Ozone Books and Wahine Adventures Logos]

                       OZONE BOOKS & RAGING WAHINE TRAVEL


   Welcome to Ozone Books and Raging Wahine Adventures. Ozone Books and
   Raging Wahine have teamed together to provide for all your adventure
   travel needs. Ozone books is a publisher of travel books, specializing
   in adventure travel. For those of you that prefer firsthand
   experience, Raging Wahine Adventures provides travel expeditions.
     _________________________________________________________________

Ozone Books


   Ozone Books has been publishing and selling travel and adventure books
   since 1987. We are based in Alberta, Canada. We hope that you enjoy
-- press space for more, use arrow keys to move, '?' for help, 'q' to quit
  Arrow keys: Up and Down to move. Right to follow a link; Left to go back.
 H)elp O)ptions P)rint G)o M)ain screen Q)uit /=search [delete]=history list
```

One way to be sure that you do not lose readers who do not wish to view images is to offer two sets of pages—one with graphic-based navigational links, and another set with text-based links. Then, on your top-level page offer readers the choice of which set of pages to use.

If you do choose to keep only one set of pages that use images or image maps for navigation, be sure to offer an alternative text-based navigation route. You can use the ALT tag to show your readers what they are missing, and offer text-based links for users with text-only browsers.

Image Style Issues

From the point of view of style, you should use graphics only to improve and enhance the presentation and content of your document. You shouldn't cram your page full of graphics, icons and buttons simply for their sex appeal. Make sure these offer real added value to your document and your document Web space. For example, an inlined graphic of your organization's logo used as a banner at the top of every page is an effective use of graphics since it provides a visual identity for documents. This banner can also be used as a hyperlink back to the organization's home page.

When designing graphics for inclusion into Web documents, use a graphical format that most computer platforms can display. Presently, the two most common formats are GIF and JPEG. A new format, Portable Network Graphics (PNG), has been developed in response to the legal uncertainties surrounding GIF, and the limitations in the JPEG standard. Although support for the PNG format is very limited at this time, there is strong interest among developers to add PNG capabilities to their products. However, for now, GIF is the most widely supported format, with JPEG following closely behind.

KEEP THE SIZE OF INLINED IMAGES AS SMALL AS POSSIBLE.

Again, out of deference to network transfer time, try to keep the size of your inlined images as small as possible. If you have a large image, use a small icon representation to convey to users the content of a graphical image; then make the icon a hyperlink to the actual item. Using the icon representation, users can better decide if they wish to retrieve the entire image. You should also give users an estimate of the size of the full image. For example, next to the icon you might say "(Full image is 100K)." This will allow users to estimate network transfer time, and help them decide if they want the full image.

Here is a sample page for a children's art gallery that uses this technique:

```
<H1><IMG SRC=kidpictures/logo.gif ALIGN=BOTTOM ALT="KidArt
Logo"> Kids Art Gallery</H1>
<P>Welcome to our art gallery! These pictures were created by
children in local preschools. If your school would like to
participate in this gallery please <A
HREF="mailto:gallerymaster@kidstuff.org">contact us</A>.

<HR><P>Here are a couple of the most recent additions to our
gallery:</P>
<P><A HREF="kidpictures/kidpict1.gif"><IMG
SRC="kidpictures/kidpict1-thumb.gif" ALT="[Picture
1]"></A>33Kb image </P>
<P><A HREF="kidpictures/kidpict2.gif"><IMG
SRC="kidpictures/kidpict2-thumb.gif" ALT="[Picture 1]">
</A>44Kb image</P>
```

Here it is in Netscape:

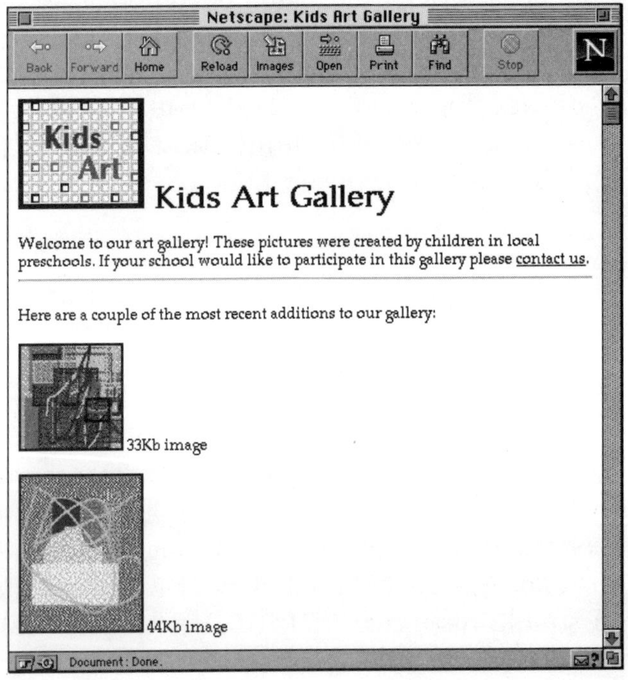

Notice that we included only two pictures besides the logo in our top-level page.

AVOID USING MANY SMALL IMAGES IN A SINGLE DOCUMENT.

Although small images can be transferred quickly, a new network connection must be initiated for each image. Since it takes additional time to open each connection, it ends up taking more transfer time than a single image that is equivalent in size to the total amount of space used by the small images. Additionally, some browsers have problems loading large number of images in a single document.

There are a couple of techniques that you should consider to minimize these problems. If you use multiple images for navigation, try to reuse the same images on all of your pages. Browsers usually keep copies of images in a local memory cache and will be able to reuse them without needing to download them repeatedly. Alternatively, you could combine your images into a single image map. This way, only a single image will need to be transferred.

If possible, provide your images in an interlaced format. Although interlacing does not speed up transfer time, it allows your readers to more quickly determine what the complete image will look like. This way they do not have to wait for the entire image to be transferred before deciding whether they want to see it.

Finally, many authors make the mistake of designing images that are too wide. The sides of these images then get chopped off when loaded in a browser set to the standard size. Avoid this problem by designing your graphics such that they fit within the standard browser size, which is usually on a 13-inch screen with 640 by 480 pixels.

Supporting Navigation

Navigation within and between sets of Web documents is an issue of paramount importance. Document design must support effective navigation among related documents, while avoiding the "lost in hyperspace" syndrome. In this syndrome, links are so convoluted and complex that users forget their location, cannot retrace their steps, and cannot locate items of interest. We now discuss supporting effective navigation for your users.

INCLUDE A TABLE OF CONTENTS.

Having to browse through a large document using a scroll bar is tiresome and disorienting and makes navigation slow and cumbersome. It is better to keep your documents short and put a table of contents at the top of each high-level, introductory document. Items in the table of contents should be hyperlinks to the actual items. The table of contents provides users with a overview of the document or set of documents and gives an estimate of the coverage. The hyperlinks allow users to quickly locate items of interest and form their individual information pathways.

There are a number of styles for tables of contents. For a fairly short table of contents it is popular to enclose the list in square brackets, with vertical bars separating the topics. For example:

```
<P>[<A HREF="kayak2.htm#gear">kayaking gear</A> |
<A HREF="kayak2.htm#seakayak">sea kayaking</A> |
<A HREF="kayak2.htm#paddle">paddle information</A> |
<A HREF="kayak2.htm#resources"> kayaking resources</A>]</P>
```

Another simple style uses an unordered list:

```
<UL>
<LI><A HREF="kayak2.htm#gear">kayaking gear</A>
<LI> <A HREF="kayak2.htm#seakayak">sea kayaking</A>
<LI> <A HREF="kayak2.htm#paddle">paddle information</A>
<LI> <A HREF="kayak2.htm#resources"> kayaking resources</A>
</UL>
```

Here is how these two styles for a table of contents look in Netscape:

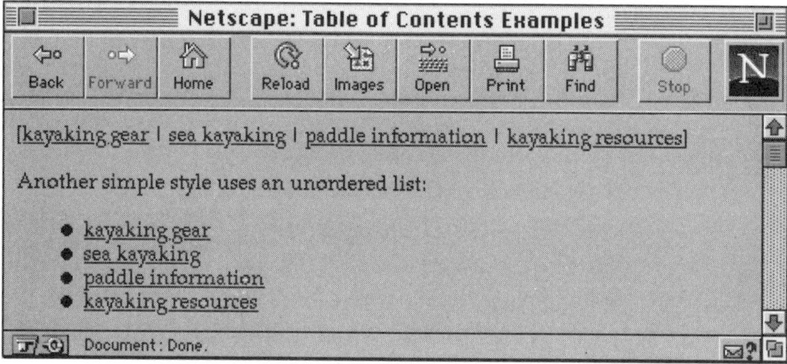

A fancier version of a table of contents uses clickable images. If you choose this style and your images do not explicitly tell readers what they are linked to, make sure that you include a text description along with the picture. You should also include an ALT attribute with a description of the link to further accommodate readers with line-mode browsers.

```
<P><A HREF="kayak.htm#gear"><IMG SRC="gif/kayak.gif"
ALT="[Kayak Icon]"> kayaking gear</A>
<P><A HREF="kayak.htm#seakayak"><IMG SRC="gif/sea.gif"
ALT="[Sea Icon]"> sea kayaking</A>
<P><A HREF="kayak.htm#paddle"><IMG SRC="gif/paddle.gif"
ALT="[Paddle Icon]"> paddle information</A>
<P><A HREF="kayak.htm#resources"><IMG SRC="gif/kayak2.gif"
ALT="[Kayak Icon]"> kayaking resources</A></P>
```

It looks like this in Netscape Navigator:

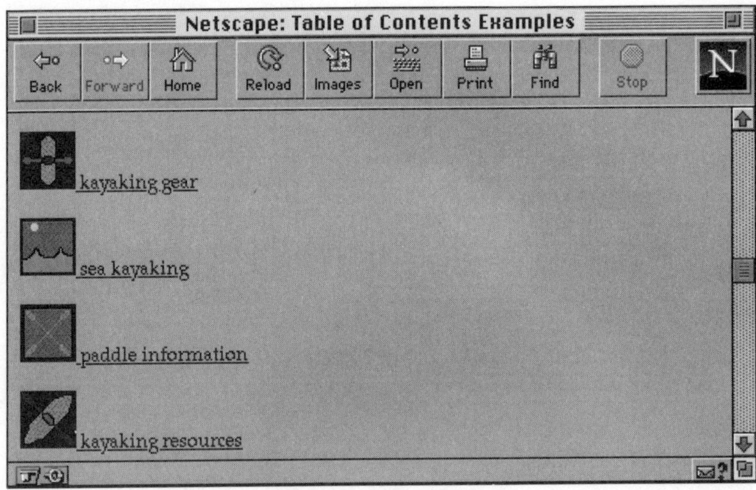

Here it is in the Lynx browser:

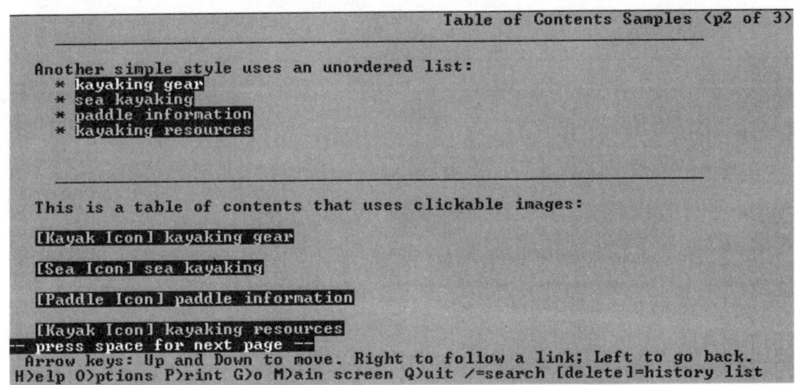

Notice that we placed our text in the ALT attribute in square brackets. Many line-mode browsers do not do anything special to indicate that text comes from an ALT attribute. By putting our text in square brackets, we separate it visually from the rest of the document's text and help to clarify that it is an alternative to an image.

DON'T GO HYPERLINK-WILD.

While hyperlinks allow individual users to locate items of personal interest within large document spaces, they should be used judiciously. Presenting the user with too many options can be overwhelming, and clutters up the document's look. Find a happy medium, based on the content of your document.

DON'T FALL INTO THE "CLICK HERE" TRAP.

When implementing a hyperlink don't say, "If you want to see more, click here." This is redundant. It can also confuse readers, since most browsers try to highlight links in some fashion. If you fall into this trap, your reader will be confronted with a page of "heres." Instead, embed the hyperlink within the referring text.

PROVIDE NAVIGATION BUTTONS.

In a large set of related documents, provide buttons that allow users to move to the "next" document in the series, the "previous" document in the series, and the top-level table of contents. For example, a computer manual stored as a set of Web documents can use the "Next" button to take the user to the subsequent section. Similarly, the "Previous" button will take the user to the preceding section. Finally, a "Top" or "Home" button returns the user to the table of contents. These buttons can be represented as actual graphical buttons with hyperlinks to the appropriate page, or the buttons can simply be text hyperlinks. Supporting such navigation will allow users to effectively and quickly locate information of interest.

PROVIDE A WAY "HOME".

This is actually an extension of the idea of providing navigation buttons, but it is important enough to warrant a separate mention. You should always provide a way to jump back to your top-level document. Remember that links may be made to any document on the Web from any other document—so you may have readers that get to your documents from some starting point over which you have no control. You can help these readers to find all of your documents by providing them with a link to your top-level document.

We have included a number of arrow icons on the CD that can be used as navigation buttons. You can find a catalog of these icons in the document *icon-index.html*. Here is an example of some navigational icons at the end of a document:

```
<TABLE BORDER=5>
<TR><TD ALIGN=CENTER WIDTH=50%><A HREF=index.html><IMG
SRC=gif/larrow4.gif ALIGN=middle ALT="[Home]" BORDER=0><BR>
Home</A>
<TD ALIGN=CENTER WIDTH=50%><A HREF=next.html><IMG
SRC=gif/rarrow4.gif ALIGN=middle ALT="[Next Page]"
BORDER=0><BR>Next</A><BR>
</TABLE>
```

Here is how this looks in Netscape Navigator:

CHECK YOUR DOCUMENT IN DIFFERENT BROWSERS.

Our navigation example makes use of a table and a number of Netscape extensions to create arrows in beveled buttons. But what happens when our document is viewed in a browser that does not support all of the Netscape extensions or in a browser that does not support tables? What happens in a line-mode browser—does our use of images still make sense?

We use a version of the EINet browser that does not support tables to see what happens to the display in the first situation. This is what we find:

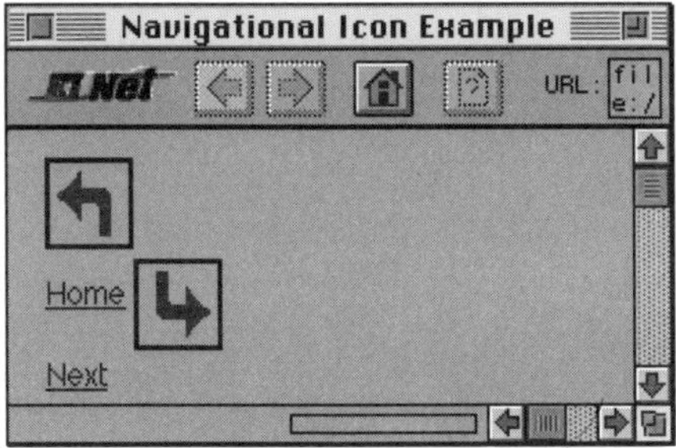

We've lost the beveled-button effect. Even worse, "Home" appears on the same line as the arrow that actually goes with "Next." Fortunately there is an easy fix for this problem. We modify our source to include a BR tag at the end of each cell.

Table-aware browsers should ignore the BR tag at the end of the cell, so this change does not affect the way that it looks in those browsers. Now our document is more understandable:

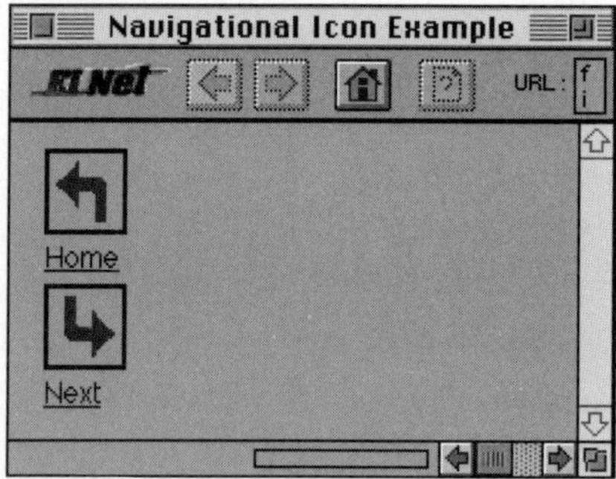

Now let's take a test drive in a line-mode browser. Here it is in Lynx:

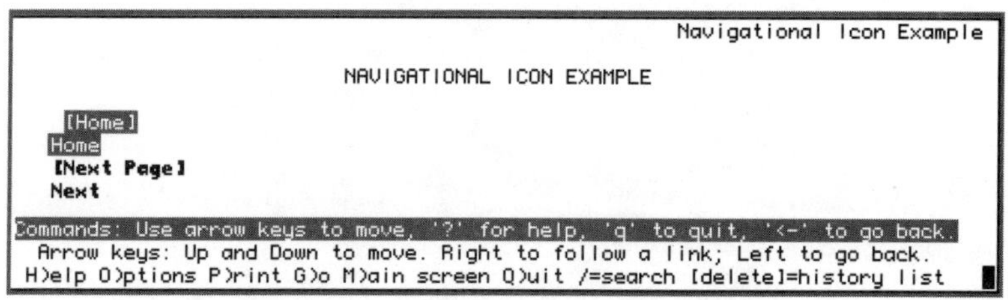

The navigation is still clear, but it looks a little awkward. Since there are actually two links —one image-based, and one text-based—to each destination, we see duplicate text in our line-mode browser. The simplest solution to this problem is to move the text into our images so that we no longer need double links. Here is the HTML source used with our updated images:

```
</TABLE>
<TABLE BORDER=5 CELLPADDING=0>
<TR><TD><A HREF=index.htm><IMG SRC=gif/HomeArrow.gif
ALIGN=middle ALT="[Home]" BORDER=0></A>
<TD> <A HREF=next.htm><IMG SRC=gif/NextArrow.gif ALIGN=middle
ALT="[Next Page]" BORDER=0></A>
</TABLE>
```

As you can see, even the source is simpler. The resulting display in Netscape Navigator is nicer as well:

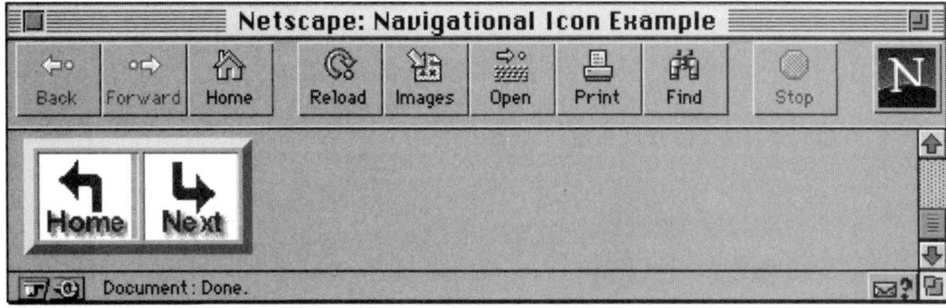

Let's check it with EINet's browser to see how it fares without tables:

Since the buttons are on the same line, it takes up less space. It looks better too. Now the line-mode test:

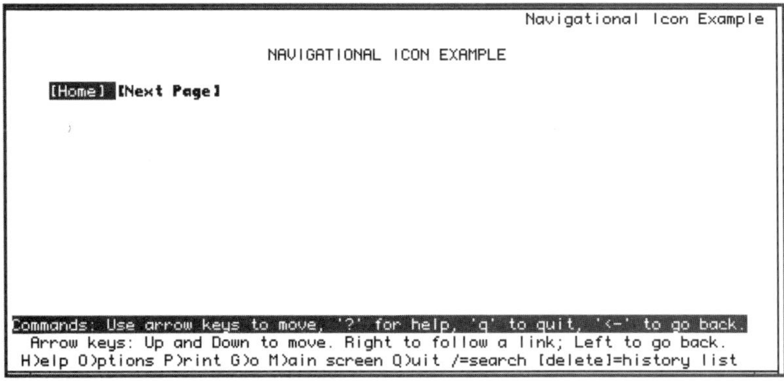

Without the text link, only our ALT attribute is displayed. As you can see, this is an improvement as well.

By viewing our document in three types of browsers, we were able to make changes that improved its appearance in all of the browsers. We also eliminated confusion that might have arisen when the original document was displayed in some of the browsers. While it is not always practical to view every document in multiple browsers, you should always try to review at least the framework you plan to use.

Use of System Resources

Well-designed web pages take into account the impact that different types of elements have on the systems on which the page is viewed. Beautiful pages will be of little use to the majority of readers if they are difficult or time-consuming to load into a browser. Nontext elements should be of particular concern when designing your pages. We have already gone over some of the ramifications of the use of images in the "Using Graphics" section. Now we will go over some of the other system-related issues you need to consider.

Minimize Document Size

Recall that in a networked environment, delays can occur when transferring large documents. Moreover, users throughout the Internet have different amounts of bandwidth in their network connection. The larger the number of bytes in a document, the longer it takes for a browser to load it. Users without high-bandwidth connections will usually not have the patience to wait long periods of time for documents to be loaded.

Although images, video, and audio usually contribute the largest number of bytes to documents, it is possible to create large documents primarily composed of text. If you find yourself with such a document, you should review its structure and see if it can be divided into smaller documents that are linked to one another.

Therefore:

- Minimize the number of multimedia elements within documents in order to minimize byte size.
- If you find that you have a very long document composed primarily of text, examine the document's contents to see if it may be broken into smaller documents connected with links.

Test Your Documents

It can be very frustrating to encounter a poorly or incorrectly formatted document on the Web. Users may form negative opinions about a Web site based on a single substandard document. Therefore:

ALWAYS TEST THE DISPLAY OF YOUR DOCUMENTS BEFORE PUBLISHING THEM.

If possible, test documents using multiple graphical and text-only browsers. Recall that different flavors of browsers may result in subtle variations in document display. If you currently have only one browser, you can use browsers.html on the CD to download Mac and Windows browsers.

DON'T RELY ON THE APPEARANCE OF A PARTICULAR STYLE.

Remember that many browsers allow users to modify the way that logical and physical styles are displayed. Therefore, you cannot be sure how a style will look even if you know which browser your reader uses. Use styles with consistency.

ALWAYS CHECK THE ACCURACY OF THE URLS IN YOUR DOCUMENTS

If your documents contain links, Make sure that you check your links both before and after your documents have been moved to a server. If you used relative paths in your URLs, some links may not work after your documents are moved to a server. There are a number of automated tools that you can use to check your URLs. We were unable to locate any Mac-based checkers, but many are available for UNIX systems.

Checking and Verifying Your Web Documents

Before making your Web pages public, you should check them to ensure that they are using accurate and correct HTML. You could, of course, check everything by hand, but this is painstaking and time consuming. It is also easy to miss errors this way. Fortunately, many tools are available for checking your HTML documents for errors and verifying link accuracy. These validation tools come in two general formats. First, they exist as software that can be downloaded and run on your own computer. Unfortunately, we were not able to find easily installable Mac-specific Web checking software utilities.

Fortunately, if you have Internet access, a second option is available. Validation services exist on Internet Web sites to which you can send the URL of the page you want checked. Typically, you use your Web browser to access the Web checking site. You are then usually presented with a form, which asks you to enter the URL of the document or documents you wish to have checked. You can also specify which version of HTML you are using. You submit the form, and the checker presents you with a new document listing the HTML errors found in your document. You must, of course, have Internet access for this service to work.

There are many such checking and verifying programs available on the Internet. For each of these services, you can use the listed URL and your Web browser in order to access the site. You will find a listing of many validation services at:

`http://www.ccs.org/validate/validate.html`

Weblint:

`Source: http://www.khoral.com/staff/neilb/weblint.html`

Weblint form-based checking service:

`http://www.unipress.com/weblint/`

With these form-based checking services, you are given the option of entering the URL for the document that you wish to check or of typing in the HTML that you wish to check. For example, we used the Unipress form service to check a small HTML document. The form looks like this:

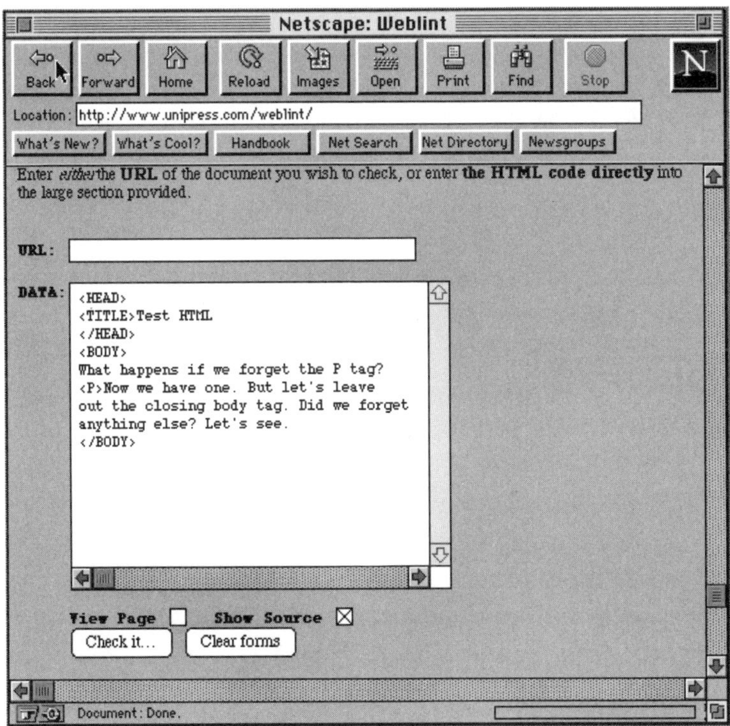

Can you spot the errors in the HTML document that we entered in this form?

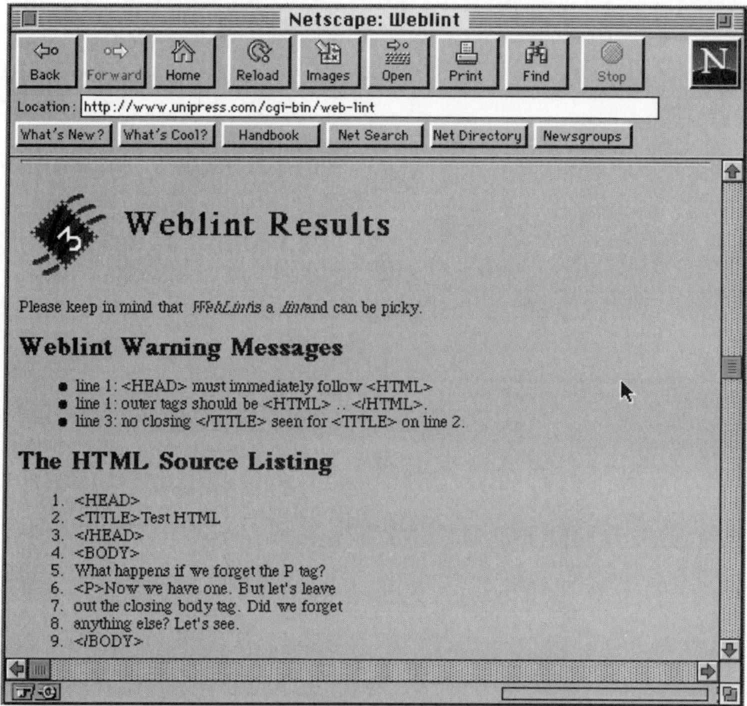

Netscape: Weblint
Back
Forward
Home
Reload
Images
Open
Print
Find
Stop
Location: http://www.unipress.com/cgi-bin/web-lint
What's New?
What's Cool?
Handbook
Net Search
Net Directory
Newsgroups
Weblint Results
Please keep in mind that WebLint is a lint and can be picky.
Weblint Warning Messages
line 1: <HEAD> must immediately follow <HTML>
line 1: outer tags should be <HTML> .. </HTML>.
line 3: no closing </TITLE> seen for <TITLE> on line 2.
The HTML Source Listing
1. <HEAD>
2. <TITLE>Test HTML
3. </HEAD>
4. <BODY>
5. What happens if we forget the P tag?
6. <P>Now we have one. But let's leave
7. out the closing body tag. Did we forget
8. anything else? Let's see.
9. </BODY>

Even in a short document it is possible to make numerous errors. Finding all of the errors by hand can be difficult. As you can see, Weblint had no problems finding them. Try it yourself and see how much easier it is than manual checking.

In Closing

It is easy to write a document that can be displayed by a Web browser. Even a plain ASCII file can be linked into the Web. The difficult part of Web publishing is to make an *inviting* set of documents—ones that your readers will enjoy and be able to use easily. In this chapter we reviewed the guidelines that will help you to create a set of documents that do this. In the next chapter we'll show you how to apply these principles to actual document design.

IN THIS CHAPTER YOU WILL LEARN HOW TO CREATE DIFFERENT TYPES OF HOME PAGES INCLUDING

- PERSONAL HOME PAGES
- BUSINESS HOME PAGES

All of the home pages in this chapter can be found on the CD.

DESIGNING HOME PAGES

What's In This Chapter

This chapter explains how to author a number of types of home pages, including a personal, autobiographical page, an on-line travel guide, and a set of pages for a business. You can find all of the pages in this chapter on the CD.

Personal Home Pages

One of the most popular uses for HTML is the creation of personal home pages. We will present several sample pages to give you some ideas for your own page.

Kelly Kayaker's Home Page

In this example we will create a personal home page for Kelly Kayaker. Kelly is a writer and editor of travel guides for a publishing company, called Ozone Books, Inc., which maintains a Web server on the host ozone.com. Kelly has two children, Ray and Neil. As hobbies, Kelly likes to bicycle, white-water kayak, and play Ultimate Frisbee. Kelly is indeed a busy woman!

We begin by creating the file that will contain our initial document. Since it is an HTML document, we give it the .html extension. We call our document kelly-homepage.html. Following good html practice, we include the following:

```
<HTML>
<HEAD>
<TITLE>Kelly Kayaker Home Page</TITLE>
</HEAD>
<BODY>
</BODY>
</HTML>
```

We include our closing tags so that we don't forget them, even though we are not yet done with the document.

We put Kelly's name in a large heading and include a thumbnail picture of Kelly, which is linked to a full-size picture. We also include a section on Kelly's work. To minimize the size of the document, we use a black-and-white picture of Kelly. Where possible, we add the appropriate hyperlinks. For example, since Kelly works for a publishing company we include a link to the company's catalog. Now our document contains the following:

```
<H1>Kelly Kayaker
<A HREF="gif/kelly.gif"><IMG ALIGN=middle
SRC="gif/kellthum.gif" ALT="My photo"></A>
</H1>
I am a writer and editor of travel books at Ozone Books,
Inc., a small publishing company. I am currently writing a
book on kayaking. My book includes an  <A
HREF=kelkayak.html>HTML document about kayaking</A>.
<HR>
```

```
<H2>Ozone Books</H2> <A
HREF="http://ozone.com/ozone.html">Ozone Books, Inc</A>
is a small publishing company. We specialize in
<EM>travel books</EM>. <P> Our <A
HREF="http://ozone.com/catalogue.html">catalogue of
books</A> is available on the Web. Books can also be <A
HREF="http://ozone.com/order-form.html"> directly ordered
</A> on the Web
<HR>
```

Note that the links to Kelly's publishing company are to a different system, so we have used complete URLs for these files. Here is the first part of Kelly's home page:

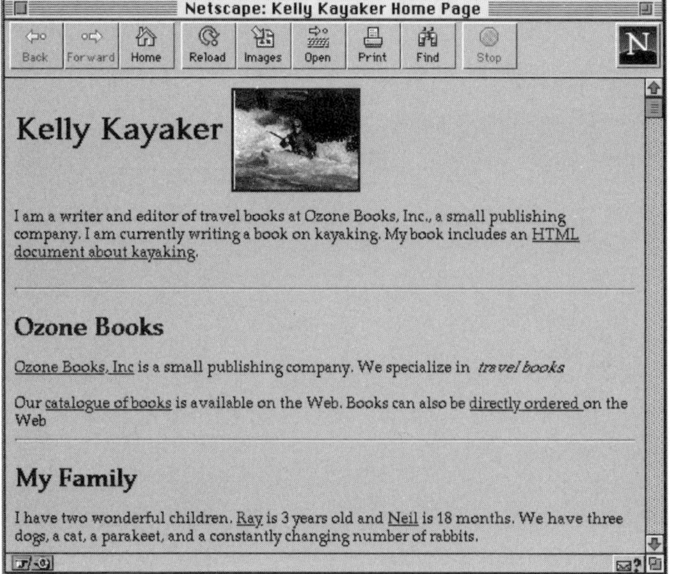

Now we add more personal information about Kelly—we describe her children, pets and hobbies. We have used partial URLs for the links in this section, since they are Kelly's files and are kept on the same system as her personal home page.

Because we wish to keep the file small in order to minimize network transfer time, we have not directly included the GIF files of her children. Instead, users may load the images by clicking on the hyperlinks.

```
<H2>My Family</H2>
I have two wonderful children. <A HREF="ray.gif">Ray</A> is 3
years old and <A HREF="neil.gif">Neil</A> is 18 months. We
have three dogs, a cat, a parakeet, and a constantly changing
number of rabbits.
<HR>
<H2>My Hobbies</H2>
I have several hobbies that keep me very busy. I wish there
were more hours in the day!
<DL>
<DT><B>Bicycling</B>
<DD>I own a tandem bicycle, and my husband and I ride
frequently in the hills near our home.
<DT><B>White-water kayaking</B>
<DD>I have been <A HREF="kayak.htm">kayaking </A> for 5 years
in the rivers and creeks in the mountains near our home.
<DT><B>Ultimate Frisbee</B>
<DD>I play frisbee on a woman's ultimate frisbee team.
</DL>
<HR>
```

We end Kelly's page with an address. We make Kelly's e-mail address a "mailto" link, so that it will be easy for people to contact her over the Net.

```
<ADDRESS>Kelly Kayaker, <A
HREF="mailto:kelly@ozone.com">kelly@ozone.com</A><BR>
Ozone Books, Inc.</ADDRESS>
```

The rest of the file appears as follows:

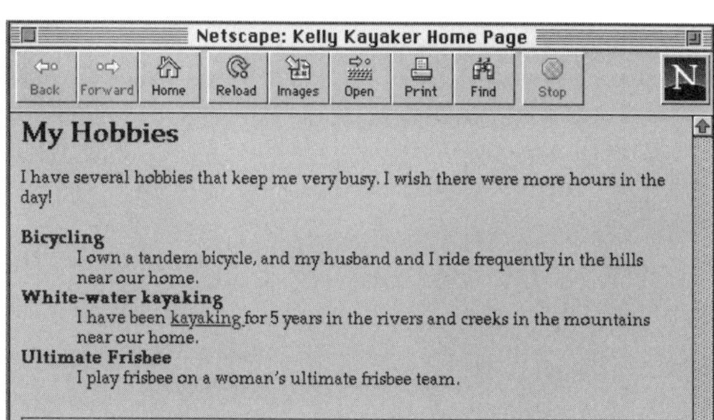
Netscape: Kelly Kayaker Home Page
Back
Forward
Home
Reload
Images
Open
Print
Find
Stop
My Hobbies
I have several hobbies that keep me very busy. I wish there were more hours in the day!
Bicycling
I own a tandem bicycle, and my husband and I ride frequently in the hills near our home.
White-water kayaking
I have been kayaking for 5 years in the rivers and creeks in the mountains near our home.
Ultimate Frisbee
I play frisbee on a woman's ultimate frisbee team.
Kelly Kayaker, kelly@ozone.com
Ozone Books, Inc.
Document: Done.

Kelly's Kayaking Document

On page 3 we described a kayaking document that Kelly was writing. The document consisted of a number of kayaking-related pictures, which were linked to documents about each picture. The descriptions of the pictures were written and maintained by Kelly's kayaking friends. The document ended with a guest book so that readers could leave comments about it. Let's take a look at that document now. Here is the first part:

```
<HTML>
<HEAD>
<TITLE>Kayaking with Kelly Kayaker and Friends</TITLE>
</HEAD>
<BODY BGCOLOR=#FFFFFF>
<H1 ALIGN=CENTER>Kayaking with</H1>
<H1 ALIGN=CENTER>Kelly Kayaker and Friends</H1><HR>
<P><I>Page Under Construction</I></P>
```

```
<P>This is my kayaking hot spot list. I've gotten
together with some of my kayaking buddies to put together
descriptions of some of our favorite kayaking spots. I'm
looking for help with my descriptions of rivers in the US
and New Zealand. If you have an awesome run that you
would like to add to this list, please sign the guest
book at the end of the document or send me <A
HREF="mailto:kayaker@ozone.com">e-mail</A>. I'll be in
touch.<P>
<P>[ <A HREF=#newzealand>New Zealand</A> | <A HREF=#usa>United
States</A> | <A HREF=#guest>Guest Book</A> ]
<HR>
```

Here it is:

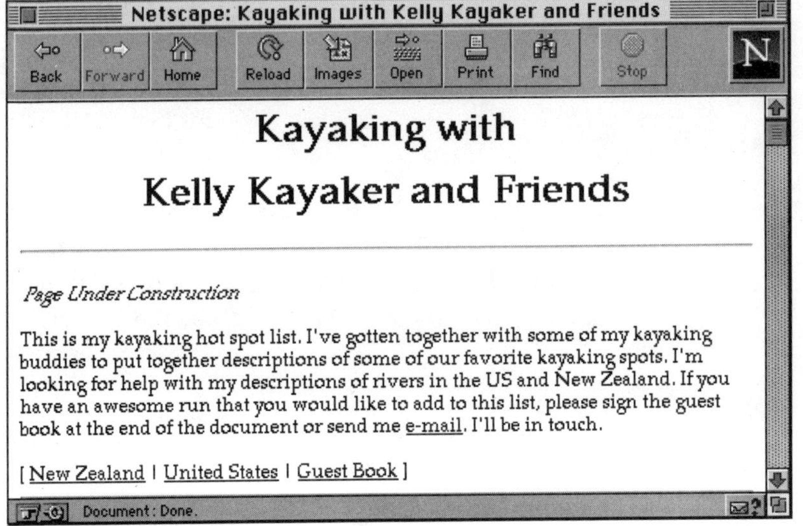

The first thing you should notice about this page is the *Page Under Construction* notice. Kelly is not really done with this page, but she wanted to make it available so that people could begin to use it. By encountering a notice at the beginning of the document that it is a work in progress, people know that it is still evolving, and this provides motivation to revisit the page later.

Right now the document is in one file. However, as more listings are added, the file will grow and may become too large to easily download and navigate. Kelly has planned for growth by dividing the document into sections that may easily be split into separate files later. She includes a table of contents at the beginning of the document to allow easy navigation between these sections. In the current document the links point to locations within the same file. However, it will be easy for her to split sections into separate files as she adds more listings.

The next part of the document is a section on rivers in New Zealand.

```
<H2><A NAME=newzealand></A>New Zealand</H2>
<P>Kayaking and other river sports are very popular
recreational activities in New Zealand. Popular rivers for
these sports are:</P>
<H3><A HREF="http://river.net/funstuff/shot.html"><I>The
Shotover River, South Island</I></A></H3>
<P>A hair-raising tale of a run down the Shotover by Joe
Paddle, Last Updated: Nov. 13, 1995
<P><A HREF="http://river.net/funstuff/picture.gif"><IMG
SRC=images/mimithum.gif ALIGN=middle>Image of the Shotover
River, 65Kb</A></P>
<H3><A HREF="http://kayak.net/descrip/buller.html"><I>The
Buller River, South Island</I></A></H3>
<P>A moving description of a solo journey down the Buller by
Sally Shooter, Last Updated: July 8, 1996</P>
<P><A HREF="http://river.net/funstuff/picture.gif"><IMG
SRC=images/lavathum.gif ALIGN=middle>Image of the Buller
River, 78Kb</A></P>
```

Here it is:

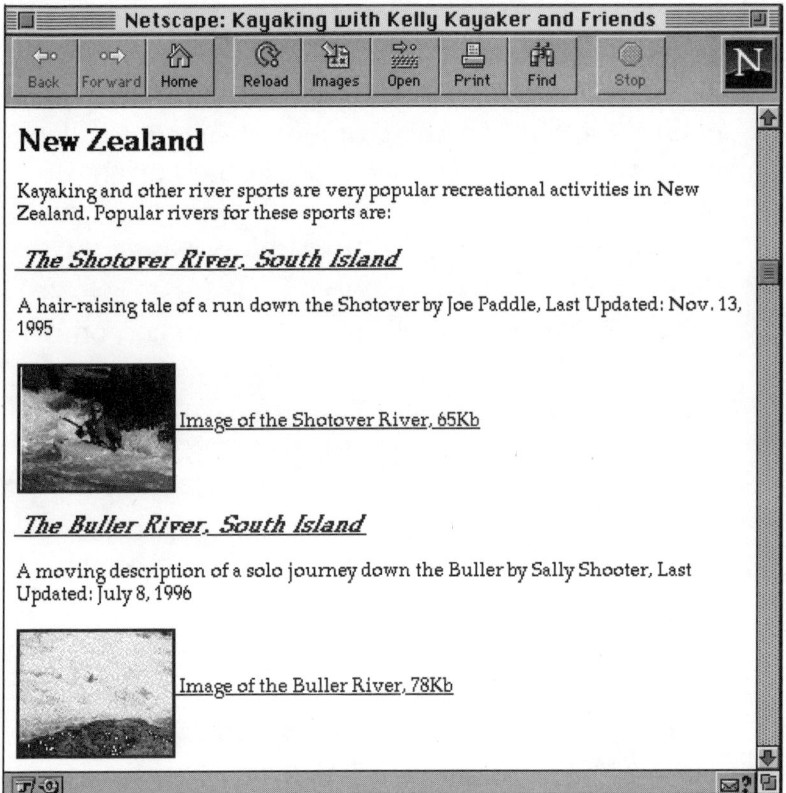

Notice that each link is accompanied by a brief description and the date it was last updated. This makes it easy for people who may revisit the page to determine if anything has changed since their last visit. The thumbnail pictures, which are linked to full-size images, are labeled with the size of the full image to help readers decide if they want to download the picture.

The next section illustrates some useful design ideas for evolving pages.

```
<H3><A HREF="http://kayak.net/descrip/karamea.html"><I>The
Karamea River, South Island</I></A><IMG
SRC=images/newred.gif></H3>
```

```
<P>The exciting saga of a blind kayaker's excursion down the
Karamea River by Darla Daring. Last Updated: April 10,
1995</P>
<P><A HREF="http://river.net/funstuff/picture.gif"><IMG
SRC=images/terrthum.gif ALIGN=middle>Image of the Karamea
River, 56Kb</A></P>
<H3><I>Still Under Construction...</I></H3>
<UL>
<LI>The Rangitikei River, North Island
<LI>The Mohaka River, North Island
</UL>
```

Here it is:

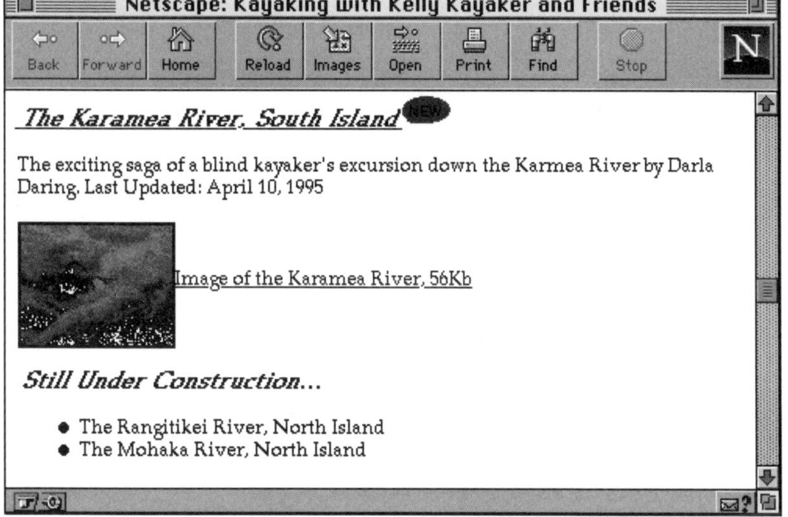

Kelly has only recently added the description for the Karamea River, so she includes an image of the word "new" in a red cloud. This makes it easy for people to notice the addition. Kelly has also left place holders for two other rivers that still need images and stories.

Kelly's Guest Book

Now let's look at the guest book. Kelly has requested that interested readers let her know if they have descriptions that they would like to add to her document. She also wants general comments about her page. She provides two methods for people to give her feedback. They can send her e-mail, or fill out the guest book form at the end of her document. The form is fairly simple, since she only needs a few fields to get the information that she wants.

```
<H2><A NAME=guest></A>Kayaking Guest Book</H2>
<P>Like this page? Hate this page? Want to tell me about your
kayaking experiences? I'd like to hear from you -- please
sign in!</P>
<FORM METHOD=post ACTION="http://ozone.com/cgi/guest">
<P><B>First Name:</B> <INPUT NAME="fname" TYPE=text
MAXLENGTH=30 SIZE=30></P>
<P><B>Last Name:</B> <INPUT NAME="lname" TYPE=text
MAXLENGTH=30 SIZE=30></P>
<P><B>E-mail Address:</B> <INPUT NAME="eaddr" TYPE=text
MAXLENGTH=50></P>
<P><B>Tell me about your favorite kayaking run.</B><BR>
<TEXTAREA NAME="comments" ROWS=4 COLS=60>
</TEXTAREA>
</P>
<P>Thanks for visiting - come again soon.</P>
<P><INPUT TYPE=SUBMIT VALUE=" Finished - Submit ">
<INPUT TYPE=RESET Value=" Restart - Clear "></P>
```

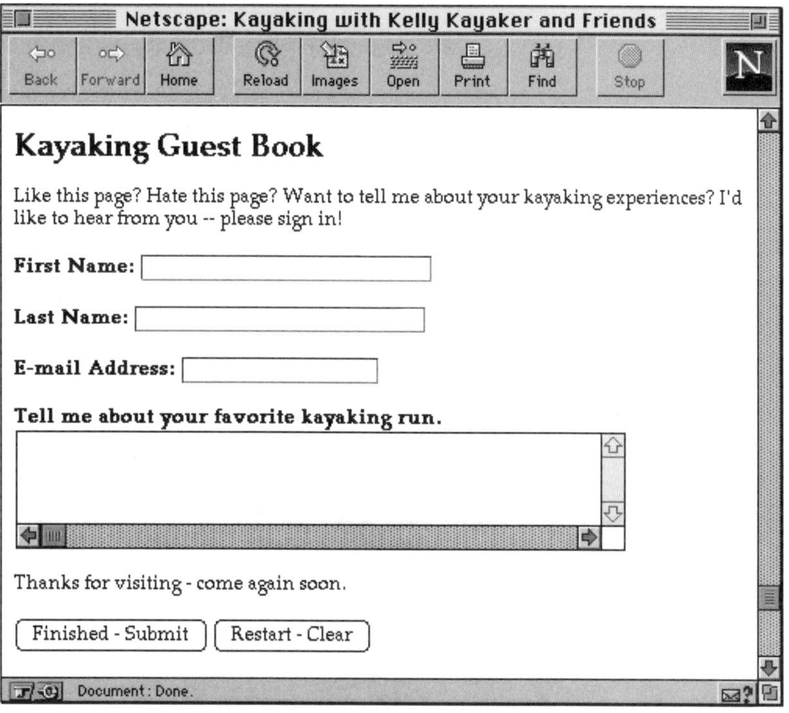

Kelly ends the page with her contact information, a last update date, and a copyright notice:

```
<HR>
<ADDRESS>Kelly Kayaker, <A
HREF="mailto:kelly@ozone.com">kelly@ozone.com</A><BR>
Ozone Books, Inc.<BR>
Last Update: April 15, 1996</ADDRESS>
<P>&#169 1996 Kelly Kayaker</P>
```

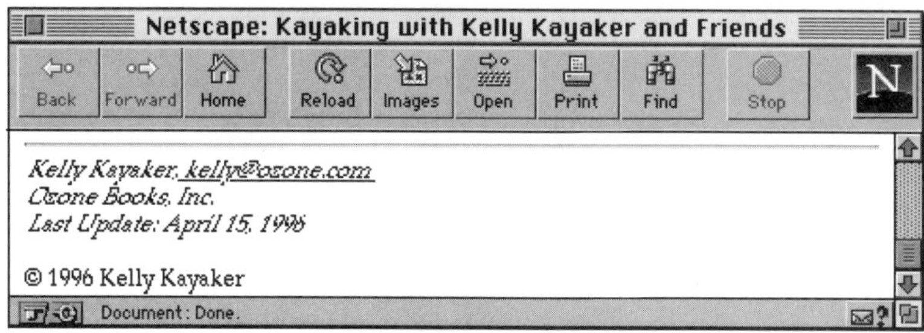

Mimi's Home Page

Now we'll look at a real home page—Mimi's. Mimi is a lecturer at a university in New Zealand. She has made it easy for readers to load her home page by leaving all images out of her top-level page. Instead, there are links to pages with images. In her description of her work history, she has included links to the pages for the places she has worked and studied.

```
<!DOCTYPE HTML PUBLIC "-//W3O//DTD W3 HTML 2.0//EN">
<HTML>
<HEAD>
<TITLE>Mimi Recker</TITLE>
</HEAD>
<BODY>
<H1><A HREF="mimipics.html">Mimi Recker</A></H1>
I am a lecturer affiliated with the University Teaching
Development Centre (UTDC) at  <A
HREF="http://www.vuw.ac.nz">Victoria University</A> in
Wellington, New Zealand.<P>
I received a Ph.D. from the <A
HREF="http://www.berkeley.edu">University of California,
Berkeley</A>, in 1992, and a B.A. from the <A
HREF="http://www.upenn.edu">University of Pennsylvania</A>,
both in the U.S.A.<BR>
More recently, I was employed as a research scientist in the
<A HREF="http://www.cc.gatech.edu">College of Computing</A>,
at  <A HREF="http://www.gatech.edu">Georgia Tech</A>.
<P>
```

Let's see how this looks.

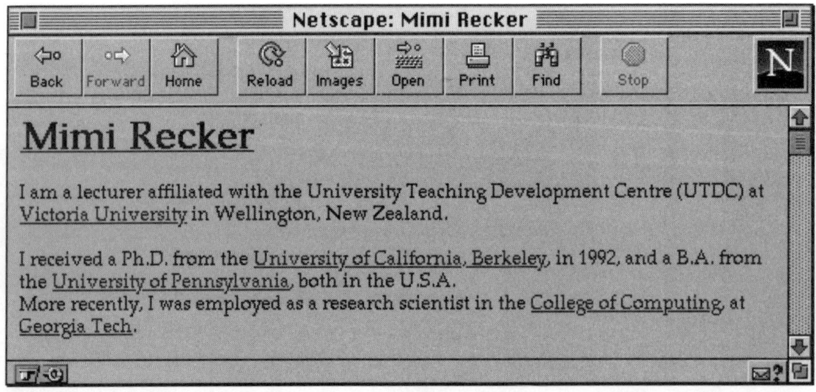

Rather than including her lengthy list of publications in her home page, Mimi keeps a separate document with a list of her publications and makes a link to this page. This keeps the top-level page short so that it loads quickly. It also makes it easy to maintain the list, which she may want to incorporate in other documents. Mimi also provides a way for readers to contact her by including a "mailto" link to her e-mail address.

```
<H2>Some recent papers and publications</H2>
Click to see recent <A HREF="mimipubs.html">papers and
publications</A>. Send <A
HREF="mailto:mimi.recker@vuw.ac.nz">email</A>
if you have trouble downloading a particular paper.
<HR>
<ADDRESS>UTDC<BR>
Victoria University of Wellington<BR>
P.O. Box 600<BR>
Wellington New Zealand<BR>
mimi.recker@vuw.ac.nz<BR>
+64 4-472.1000 x8868 </ADDRESS>
</BODY>
</HTML>
```

Here is the rest of Mimi's page:

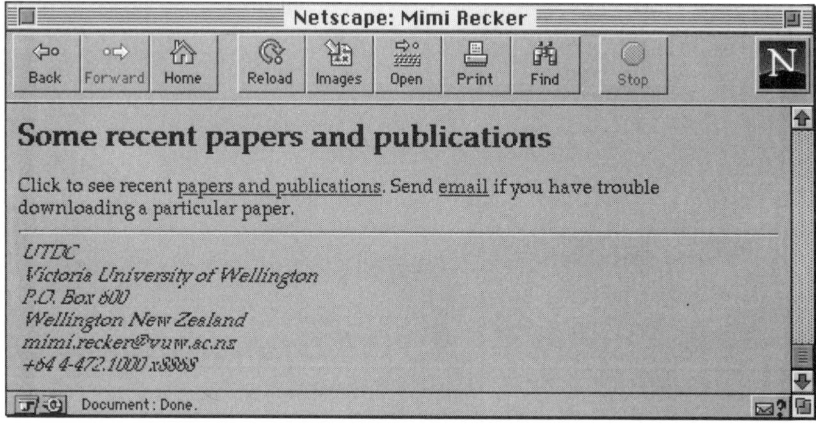

Business Home Pages

In this section we present a couple of examples of how a business might set up their home pages. When you set up home pages for a business, you should first decide what portions of your business are to be presented. Are you advertising the business as a whole? Do you want to give control of various pieces to different departments? Will you allow people to order your products through forms in some of your pages? Do you want customer feedback?

In our first example we will look at a small business. Our first example will be for Kelly Kayaker's publisher, Ozone Books, and its affiliate, Raging Wahine Adventures. Ozone Books is a publisher of travel books, and Raging Wahine Adventures is a travel company specializing in adventure expeditions.

We create a top-level page that includes a logo for each division of the company. We have placed both of the logos into the same image and created a map file for the image. Readers may click on the logo for a division to go to the home page for that division. We also include a short overview of both companies.

```
<HTML>
<HEAD>
<TITLE>Ozone Books and Raging Wahine Travel</TITLE>
</HEAD>
<BODY>
<A HREF="http://ozone.com/cgi/imagemap/obrwa>
<IMG SRC=wahine/obralogo.gif ISMAP ALT="[Ozone Books and
Raging Wahine Logos]"></IMG></A>
<H1 ALIGN=CENTER>Welcome to</H1>
<H1 ALIGN=CENTER>Ozone Books and Raging Wahine Adventures</H1>
<P>Ozone Books and Raging Wahine have teamed together to
provide for all your adventure travel needs. Ozone books is a
publisher of travel books, specializing in adventure travel.
For those of you who prefer
firsthand experience, Raging Wahine Adventures provides
travel expeditions.</P>
```

We displayed this page in Chapter 8 on page 234. Next, we add short summaries for each division. If you have several divisions in your company, you may wish to add a table of contents to make it easier for readers to find the section they want.

However, since this company has only two divisions, we do not use a table of contents. The description for each division includes links to the division's home pages.

```
<HR>
<H2><A HREF=ozone/index.html>Ozone Books</A></H2>
<P>Ozone Books has been publishing and selling travel and
adventure books since 1987. We are based in Alberta, Canada.
We hope that you enjoy our <A
HREF=ozone/catalog.html>catalog</A>. Our books are available
at many bookstores, or you may <A HREF=ozone/order.html>order
them directly</A> from
us.</P>
<HR>
<H2><A HREF=wahine/raging.html>Raging Wahine
Adventures</A></H2>
<P>Raging Wahine Adventures is an adventure travel company,
based in Wellington, New Zealand. We have been offering
adventure travel trips since 1988. We provide all levels of
trips -- from the backcountry novice to the most hardened
thrill-seeker.</P>
```

We store the documents for the two divisions in separate folders. All the pages related to Ozone Books are kept in the Ozone folder, while Raging Wahine Adventures' pages may be found in the Wahine folder. This separation of pages makes it easy to find the pages for the relevant division and provides a consistent structure so that links may be made in a consonant fashion.

Notice that for the Ozone division we have included links to Ozone's order form and catalog. This allows readers who may wish to place an order or look up a specific book to jump directly to the document of interest.

Finally, we end the page with contact information, as well as an e-mail address. The e-mail address is a mailto link, to make it as easy as possible for customers to contact the company:

```
<HR>
For more information, you may send us <A
HREF="mailto:queries@ozwa.com">
electronic mail</A>, or write to us at the address below.<P>
We look forward to hearing from you.
<P>
```

```
<ADDRESS>
Raging Wahine Adventures and Ozone Books<BR>
P.O. Box 600<BR>
Wellington, New Zealand<BR>
<AHREF="mailto:queries@ozwa.com">queries@ozwa.com.nz</A><BR>
</ADDRESS>
</BODY>
</HTML>
```

Here is how this section looks:

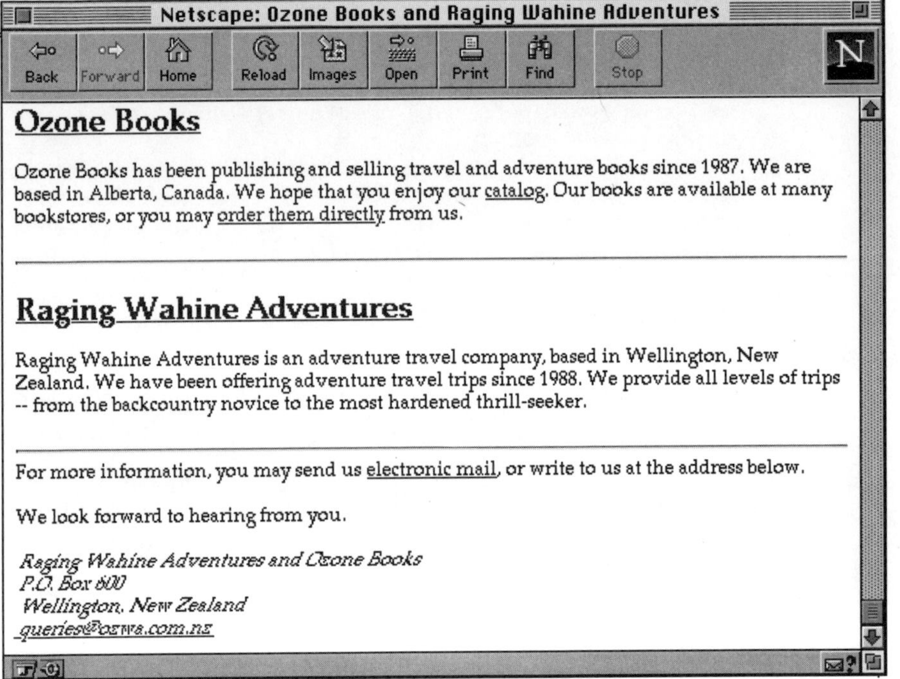

Now let's look at Ozone's pages. We divide Ozone's pages into two sections—one that describes books, and one that allows people to submit orders. Ozone's top-level page is a description of Ozone along with links to the other sections.

We start our top-level page with Ozone's logo. Notice that we have included the logo in a consistent location for all of the pages used in this company. Next, we include a short description of the company:

```
<HTML>
<HEAD>
<TITLE>OZONE BOOKS</TITLE>
</HEAD>
<IMG SRC=images/ozlogo.gif><H1>Welcome to Ozone Books</H1>
<P>Ozone Books publishes travel books. with an emphasis on
adventure travel. You can find a complete listing of our
books in our <A HREF=catalog.html>catalog</A>. Many of our
books are available at bookstores. You can also order books
dirctly from us by filling out this <A HREF=order.html</A>
order form. You can also place orders over the phone.
```

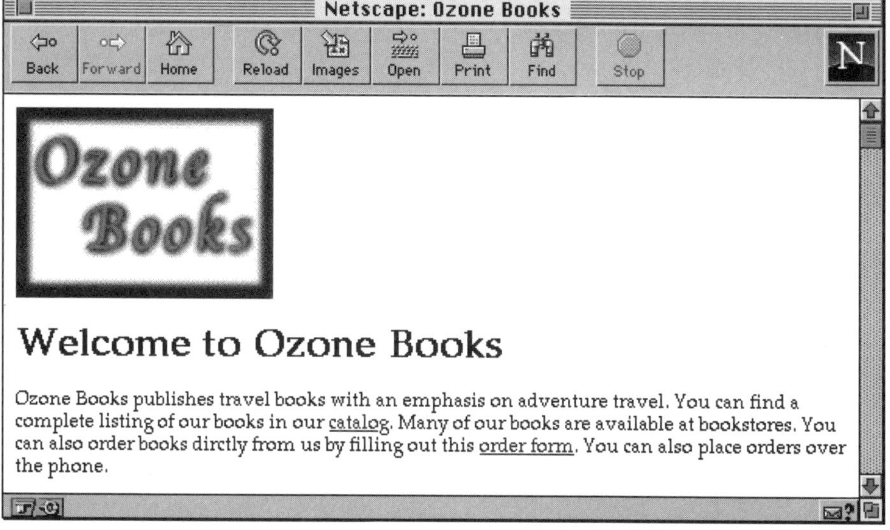

Ozone's Order Form

Ozone Books sells books over the Internet. We will now develop an on-line form for book orders. In keeping with our desire to have a similar look for all of the business's home pages, we include a logo at the top of the form. However, since this is a form, we do not want to use up too much space with a logo, so we use a thumbnail version.

We start the form with some information about Ozone. We include contact numbers for telephone and fax support. It is always a good idea to provide alternate contact information since network problems may prevent people from reaching you via the Internet.

```
<HTML>
<HEAD>
<TITLE>Ozone Book Order Form</TITLE>
</HEAD>
<BODY BGCOLOR=#FFFFFF>
<H1><IMG SRC=../images/ozsmall.gif> Ozone Book Order Form</H1>
Thank you for choosing Ozone for your travel book needs. In
addition to Internet orders, we also accept orders over the
phone and via FAX. Our staff is available Monday through
Friday from 9 a.m. to 5 p.m. Eastern Standard Time to take
your orders and answer your questions. FAX orders may be sent
at any time. Phone Orders: (304) 555-1368. FAX: (304) 555-
3712.
<HR>
```

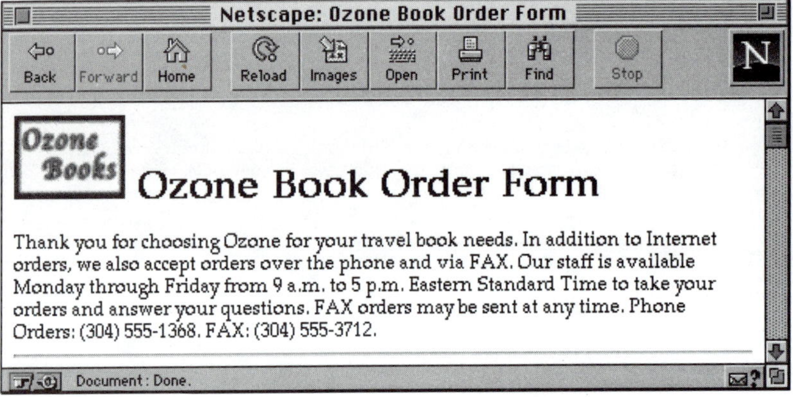

The data input portions of the form make heavy use of the TABLE tag to align input fields. As you may recall from our discussion about navigational buttons in a table, it is important to include the BR tag at the end of each row when you use TABLE. This accommodates readers using line-mode browsers and other browsers that do not understand the TABLE tag.

Next we provide areas for the customer's name and address:

```
<FORM METHOD="POST" ACTION="http://ozone.com/cgi/orderform">
<TABLE>
<TR><TD><B>First Name:</B> <TD><INPUT NAME="fname" TYPE=text
MAXLENGTH=30 SIZE=30><BR>
<TR><TD><B>Last Name:</B> <TD><INPUT NAME="lname" TYPE=text
MAXLENGTH=30 SIZE=30><BR>
<TR><TD><B>Address:</B> <TD><INPUT NAME="add1" TYPE=text
MAXLENGTH=45 SIZE=45><BR>
<TR><TD><B>Address:</B><TD><INPUT NAME="add1" TYPE=text
MAXLENGTH=45 SIZE=45><BR>
<TR><TD><B>City:</B> <TD><INPUT NAME="city" TYPE=text
MAXLENGTH=30 SIZE=20>
<B>State:</B> <INPUT NAME="state" TYPE=text MAXLENGTH=2
SIZE=2>
<B>ZIP:</B> <INPUT NAME="zip" TYPE=text MAXLENGTH=30 SIZE=10>
<BR>
<TR><TD><B>E-mail:</B> <TD><INPUT NAME="E-Mail" TYPE=text
MAXLENGTH=50 SIZE=50><BR>
<TR><TD><B>Daytime Phone:</B> <TD><INPUT NAME="phonenum"
TYPE=text MAXLENGTH=30 SIZE=20><BR>
</TABLE>
```

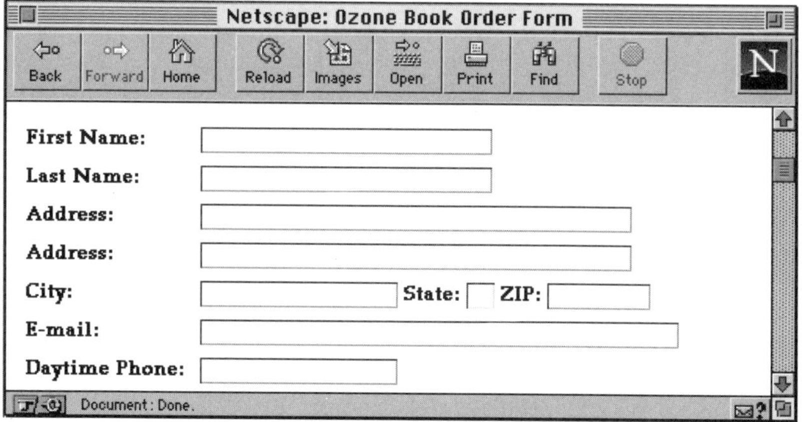

Next, we create the section for placing orders. Since we allow people to order gift certificates, we preload one of the lines with our gift certificate code. Note that customers can overwrite our predefined values in this line.

```
<TABLE>
<TR><TH>Product<BR>
Number<TH>Title<TH>Qty<TH>Price<TH>Total<BR>
<TR><TD><INPUT NAME="PN1" TYPE=text MAXLENGTH=5 SIZE=5>
<TD><INPUT NAME="TITLE1" TYPE=text MAXLENGTH=40 SIZE=40>
<TD><INPUT NAME="QTY1" TYPE=text MAXLENGTH=5
SIZE=5><TD><INPUT NAME="PRICE1" TYPE=text MAXLENGTH=6
SIZE=6><TD><INPUT NAME="TOTAL1" TYPE=text MAXLENGTH=9
SIZE=9><BR>
```

<similar lines removed for brevity>

```
<TR><TD><INPUT NAME="PN6" TYPE=text MAXLENGTH=5 SIZE=5>
<TD><INPUT NAME="TITLE6" TYPE=text MAXLENGTH=40 SIZE=40>
<TD><INPUT NAME="QTY6" TYPE=text MAXLENGTH=5
SIZE=5><TD><INPUT NAME="PRICE6" TYPE=text MAXLENGTH=6
SIZE=6><TD><INPUT NAME="TOTAL6" TYPE=text MAXLENGTH=9
SIZE=9><BR>
<TR><TD><INPUT NAME="GIFT" TYPE=text MAXLENGTH=5 SIZE=5
VALUE="GIFT"> <TD><INPUT NAME="TITLEG" VALUE="Gift
Certificate" TYPE=text MAXLENGTH=40 SIZE=40> <TD><INPUT
NAME="QTYG" VALUE=0 TYPE=text MAXLENGTH=5 SIZE=5><TD><INPUT
NAME="PRICEG" VALUE=0 TYPE=text MAXLENGTH=6 SIZE=6><TD><INPUT
NAME="TOTALG" VALUE=0 TYPE=text MAXLENGTH=9 SIZE=9><BR>
</TABLE>
```

Notice that although the fields from line to line look almost identical, each one has a unique NAME attribute. When setting up forms with multiple lines that are fairly similar, be sure to check that each field has a unique NAME—otherwise you will have problems when you try to sort out the data that is returned by the form!

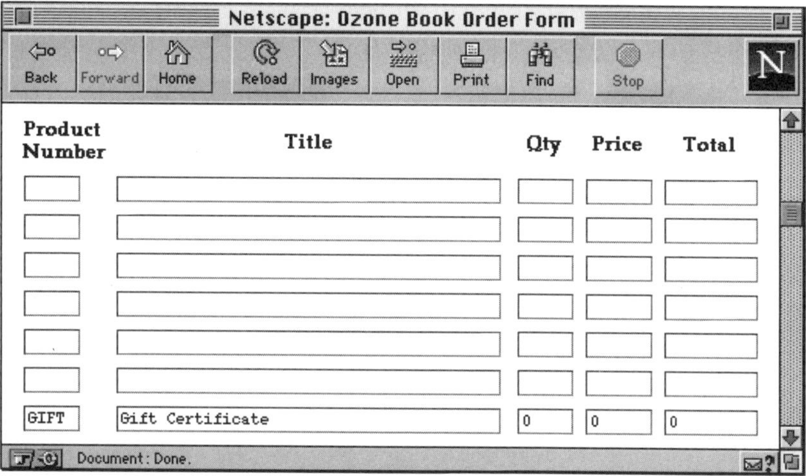

Our next section allows the customer to enter address information for a gift certificate. Since this section is essentially the same as the section for entering customer information, we will not display it here.

Now we include a payment section. We use radio boxes to allow the customer to pick one of four payment options.

```
<STRONG>Method of Payment:</STRONG>
<INPUT NAME="payment" VALUE="check" TYPE=radio>Check or Money
Order
<INPUT NAME="payment" VALUE="VISA" TYPE=radio>VISA
<INPUT NAME="payment" VALUE="Discover" TYPE=radio>Discover
<INPUT NAME="payment" VALUE="MC" TYPE=radio>MasterCard<BR>
```

If you plan to create a form that requests credit card information, you should try to make sure that your pages are placed on a secure server. Secure server technology provides a way for information that is exchanged between the browser and server to be transmitted in an encrypted format. This means that the browser scrambles the information before sending it to the server, so that a casual observer would not be able to understand it. When the browser receives the information, it unscrambles it.

Servers that do not use secure technology make it easy for someone watching network traffic to see the numbers. Since Ozone Books does not use a secure server, they do not allow people to send their credit card information in the form. Instead, they request that customers call to confirm the order and provide a credit card number.

```
<STRONG>Important:</STRONG> We do not accept credit card
numbers over the Internet at this time. To complete your
order please call us within 48 hours to provide us with your
credit card number. At your request, we will retain your
credit card information in our files so that future orders
may be completed without additional calls. Credit card orders
which have not been completed with 48 hours will be
cancelled. Checks must be received within one week of the
order. Books will not be shipped until the check is
received.</P>
```

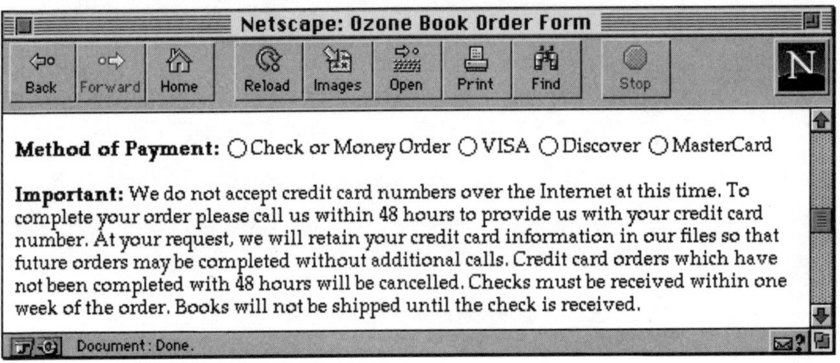

We end the input part of the form with a comment box so that our customers can give us feedback. We also provide submit and reset buttons.

```
<P>Please enter any additional comments here:<BR>
<TEXTAREA NAME="comments" ROWS=2 COLS=60>
</TEXTAREA>
</P>
</PRE>
<P>Thank you for your order!</P>
<P><INPUT TYPE=SUBMIT VALUE="Finished - Submit">
<INPUT TYPE=RESET Value="Restart - Clear All Fields"></P>
</FORM>
```

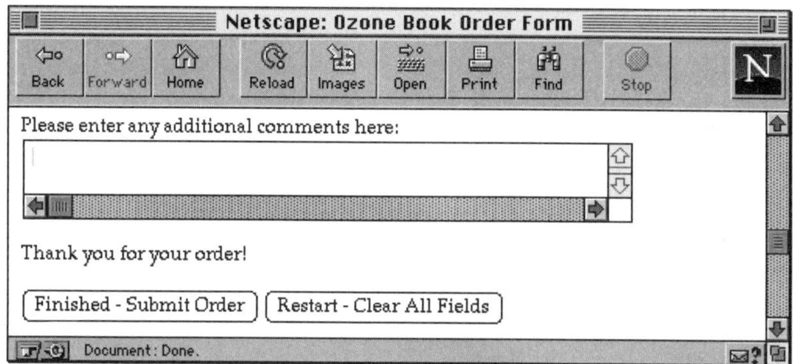

We finish off the form with some detailed information about Ozone's policies. At the very end we put our standard contact information along with some navigational buttons to allow customers to go back to the Ozone/Raging Wahine Home Page or to the Ozone Home Page.

```
For more information, you may send us
<A HREF="mailto:queries@ozwa.com">electronic mail</A>, or
write to us at the address below.<P>
We look forward to hearing from you.<P>
<ADDRESS>
Raging Wahine Adventures and Ozone Books<BR>
P.O. Box 600<BR>
Wellington, New Zealand<BR>
<A HREF="mailto:queries@ozwa.com">queries@ozwa.com.nz</A> <BR>
</ADDRESS>
<HR>
<A HREF="../ozwatop.htm"><IMG SRC="../gif/ozwahome.gif"
ALT="[Ozone/Wahine Home Page]"></A>
<A HREF="../wahine/raging.htm"><IMG SRC="../gif/wahihome.gif"
ALT="[Raging Wahine Home Page]"></A>
<A HREF="index.htm"><IMG SRC="../gif/ozhome.gif" ALT="[Ozone
Books Home Page]"></A>
</BODY>
</HTML>
```

You can see how this looks on page 236 in Chapter 8.

We included ALT values for each of our navigational buttons so that readers with line-mode browsers or who have image loading turned off will still be able to use the links. For example, here it is in Microsoft Internet Explorer with image loading turned off:

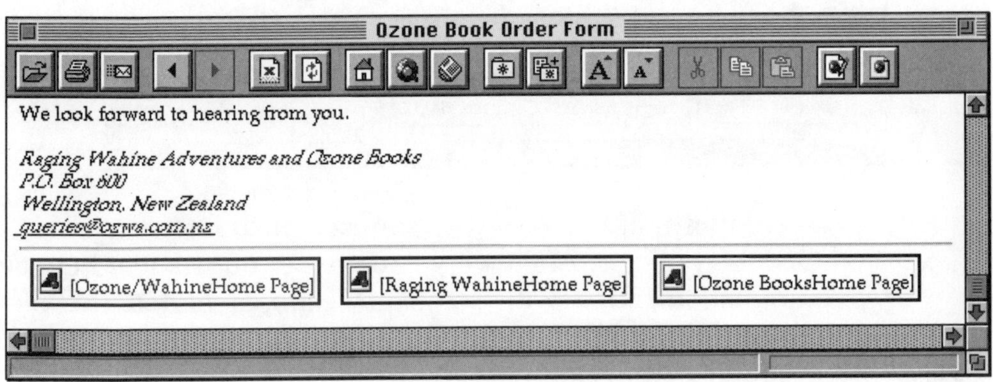

As you can see, the navigational links are usable even without the corresponding images.

Finding More Examples

We've presented a number of examples to illustrate the principles of good Web document design. However, you will find millions of other examples (both good and bad) on the Web itself. You can learn more about document design by looking at the HTML sources for any of these pages. Most Web browsers provide a way to view the source for the HTML document being displayed. Take advantage of this ability! Look at sources for both good and bad pages. This way, you will learn what to avoid as well as what to do.

IN THIS CHAPTER YOU WILL LEARN ESSENTIAL GUIDELINES FOR

- HOW TO INSTALL AND USE MACHTTP
- HOW TO INSTALL AND USE INTERACTION
- HOW TO INSTALL AND USE HTTPD4MAC
- MANAGING A PUBLIC WEB SERVER

MACINTOSH WEB SERVERS

What's In This Chapter

This chapter explains how to install and use the software packages in the HTTP Servers folder on the CD (most of the CGI scripts are covered in Chapter 6). When you open this folder you will see:

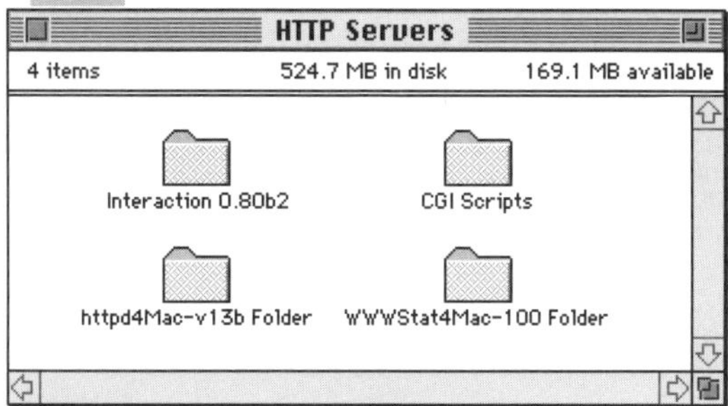

In addition to httpd4Mac, you will find:

- Interaction, a MacHTTP add-on that provides interactive bulletin boards and chat rooms
- Mac-ImageMap, an image map processing application for use with MacHTTP (in the CGI Scripts folder)
- WWWStat4Mac, a log file processing program for use with httpd4Mac
- a number of other CGI scripts that may be used with MacHTTP.

The chapter concludes with some general tips and guidelines for running a Web server.

Choosing the Right Server

We review two HTTP servers in this chapter. The first server, MacHTTP, is a shareware server. Although it is not on the CD, you will find a pointer to it in our utility.html document. The second server, httpd4Mac, is completely free.

Which of these servers should you use? It depends on what you plan to do. httpd4Mac is very simple to set up and requires few system resources. However, it does not have CGI or image map support. If you plan to use it only to share documents among a small group and don't plan to use forms, it is probably the best choice (and certainly the most inexpensive). MacHTTP can support up to 48 simultaneous users and includes CGI support. Since it is shareware, you will have to pay an additional fee if you choose to use it past the evaluation period. It is a good choice for a site with moderate traffic.

If you need a server for heavy-duty, around-the-clock work, we recommend getting MacHTTP's commercial successor, Webstar. You can find more information on Webstar at:

```
http://www.starnine.com/webstar/webstar.html
```

MacHTTP: A Shareware Web Server

In earlier chapters we touched briefly on the role that a server plays in the World Wide Web. There are a number of ways that a HTTP server can be of particular use for you as an HTML/Web author. The MacHTTP server can be used to support a full-blown Web publishing business; it is also perfect for small Web sites and for testing your HTML documents. For example, if you are authoring HTML documents for a large site, you could run a personal server on your system and let your colleagues check your documents before putting them on the primary, public server. Having control of your own server also makes it easy to test your image maps and forms.

Installing MacHTTP

MacHTTP requires System 7 and MacTCP, a networking control panel. If you are running System 7.5, you get MacTCP for free. If you don't have MacTCP, you can purchase it from Apple. Naturally, if you plan to publish on the Internet, you need the appropriate network access. However, the server can be run in stand-alone mode so that you can test your server and the documents that you plan to publish. We describe how to set up your Macintosh so that you can run the server in stand-alone mode below.

If you want to take advantage of advanced interactive features, such as clickable maps and searchable documents, you will need to install Applescript. Applescript is a scripting language that allows you to send commands to your Macintosh and to applications. Macintoshes running System 7.5 will come bundled with this software, but if yours isn't, it is provided on the CD along with the server software. Finally, you'll want to have at least 600k of free memory.

Like most Macintosh software, MacHTTP is easy to install. However, we strongly recommend that you read all of the documentation provided with the server software. Web publishing can rapidly become quite complex!

Setting Up Your Macintosh for Stand-alone Mode

If your Macintosh is connected to a network, you can skip this section. If it is not connected to a network, in order to make MacHTTP work, you need to set up your Mac up so that it thinks that it is connected to a network. Although this will not allow you to display documents on the Internet, it will allow you to test the server locally.

MacTCP must be installed for this to work correctly. If you do not have it already, get it (it can be purchased from Apple) and install it. Once MacTCP is installed, you should turn on AppleTalk (via the Chooser in the Apple menu). Next, configure the MacTCP control panel. In the control panel, set the TCP connection to LocalTalk. You then need to enter a fake IP address, for example, 192.2.2.2:

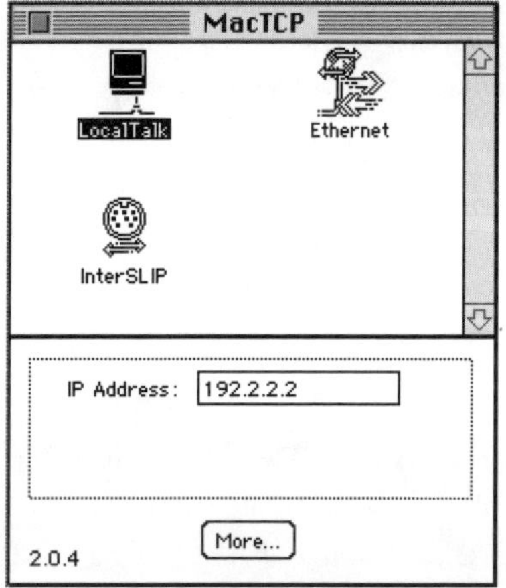

Restart your computer and start MacHTTP.

Starting the Server

After downloading MacHTTP, and expanding the archive you should have a MacHTTP folder that looks like this:

When you open the folder you should see this:

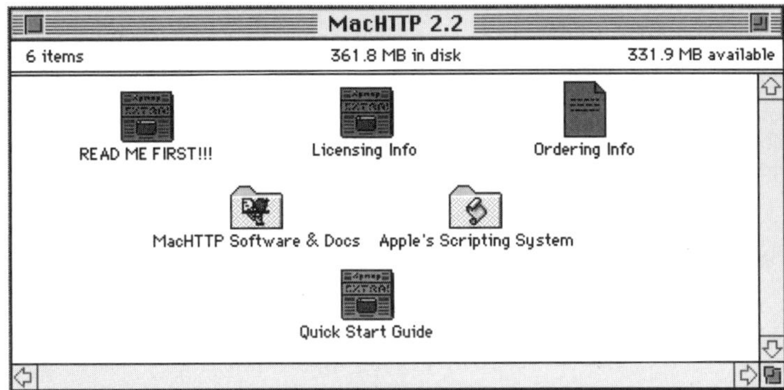

Before proceeding with the server setup, you must read and agree to the licensing terms contained in the file "Licensing Info."

To start the server, open the folder "MacHTTP Software & Docs":

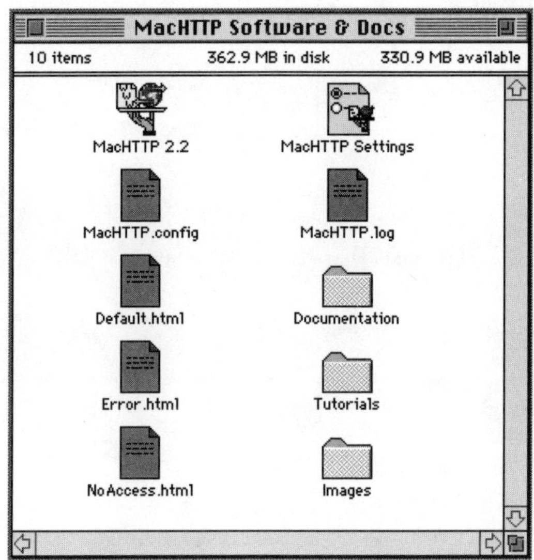

Double click on the MacHTTP application icon. Voila! In just two mouse clicks, you are running a Web server on your Macintosh.

The server comes with a status window that lists at the top of the screen the default settings for your server. If any errors occur while starting the server, they will be listed in this window. The window also logs all connections to your server, including the time, the name of computer connecting to your server, and the name of the document requested.

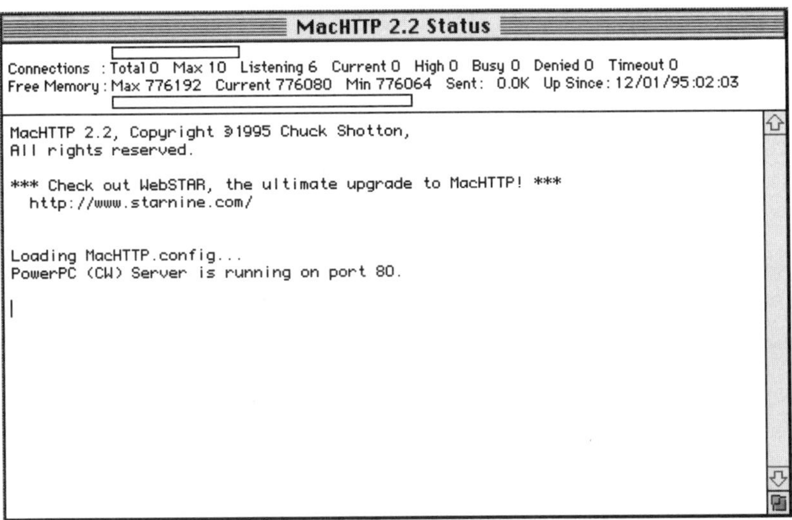
MacHTTP 2.2 Status
Connections : Total 0 Max 10 Listening 6 Current 0 High 0 Busy 0 Denied 0 Timeout 0
Free Memory : Max 776192 Current 776080 Min 776064 Sent: 0.0K Up Since: 12/01/95:02:03
MacHTTP 2.2, Copyright ©1995 Chuck Shotton,
All rights reserved.
*** Check out WebSTAR, the ultimate upgrade to MacHTTP! ***
http://www.starnine.com/
Loading MacHTTP.config...
PowerPC (CW) Server is running on port 80.

Now you are ready to test your server. If your Macintosh is connected to a network, start the browser of your choice (preferably one that handles forms) and give it the URL:

```
http://yourhostname
```

Make sure that you replace "yourhostname" with your Macintosh's network name or IP number.

If you are running your server in stand-alone mode, you should now be able to access your server via a Web browser running on the same machine. From the browser, you will access your server by specifying the fake IP address that you entered in the MacTCP control panel. For example, if you used the fake address 192.2.2.2, you would use the URL:

```
http://192.2.2.2
```

If everything is working correctly, your browser should display a screen that looks something like this:

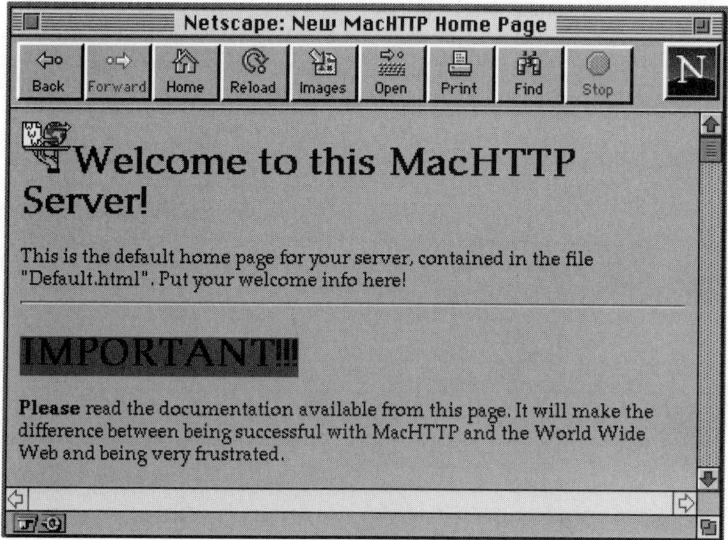

Netscape: New MacHTTP Home Page
Back
Forward
Home
Reload
Images
Open
Print
Find
Stop
Welcome to this MacHTTP Server!
This is the default home page for your server, contained in the file "Default.html". Put your welcome info here!
IMPORTANT!!!
Please read the documentation available from this page. It will make the difference between being successful with MacHTTP and the World Wide Web and being very frustrated.

The browser is now displaying the default document for your server. This document is called Default.html and is located in the same folder as the server. Naturally, you can customize the server to use your own home page. However, before doing that, we recommend that you read the original default page and follow the links provided. These documents contain important information for operating your server. We suggest you make a copy of the original Default.html document, as you may later wish to refer to its many useful links to on-line help and documentation.

After familiarizing yourself with this information, you are now ready to customize the server to use your home pages.

Customizing the Server

Before proceeding, you must already have created a master home page for your server. If you haven't, you will need to do that first. You can find help on setting up your pages in the chapter on designing home pages.

Configuration File: MacHTTP.config

The server uses one configuration file, MacHTTP.config, for customizing your server, which is kept in the same folder as the server application. This file allows you to customize your server by, for example, specifying the name of your top-level server document, the destination file for error messages and server logs, and the security setup of your server. In most cases, you shouldn't have to change anything in this file. Before making changes to this file, it is advisable to make a copy of the original. This way if you make a mistake, you can always start with a fresh copy.

In the configuration file, comment lines begin with #. Lines not beginning with # are directives to the server. The documentation that comes with MacHTTP describes in detail the various settings in the configuration file.

Loading Your Master Home Page

Once you have verified that your server is working correctly, you will probably want to replace the home page that comes with the server with one of your own home pages. MacHTTP requires that the top-level page for your server be located in the same folder as the server application. You can name this file, Default.html, and the server will load it automatically when someone connects to your server. Alternatively, you can copy the file containing your top-level home page to the folder containing the server application, and modify the directive in the configuration file called INDEX to point to this file.

NOTE: The top-level page for your server must be located in the same folder as the server application!

That's it! Now check with your favorite browser to make sure the server is loading the correct home page.

Example: Modifying Configuration Files

We choose to modify the configuration files to set up the master home page for our server. Let's look and see how we did it. We used the index file from the CD as our master home page. This file, called index.html, is on the CD in the folder called HTML Treasure Chest. We copied this file and associated subfolders to the server folder. We then changed the configuration file to tell the server about the location for our top-level home page. The modification is as follows:

```
#The following lines specify where to find HTML files for
#error messages, the default home (or index) page, the name
#of the log file, and the message returned for security
#violations. Any of these three file directives point to a
#HTML document, script, or CGI application.
#
#NOTE!!! INDEX must be a simple file name, not a path like the
#other files.
INDEX    index.html
```

Now, all of our files are in subdirectories, so we don't need to do anything else—we're ready to test our server again and see if it is using the correct files. We double-click on our server icon to start it, and then use a browser to check it. When you do this, if everything went correctly, you should see your top-level page instead of the demo page. In our case we see:

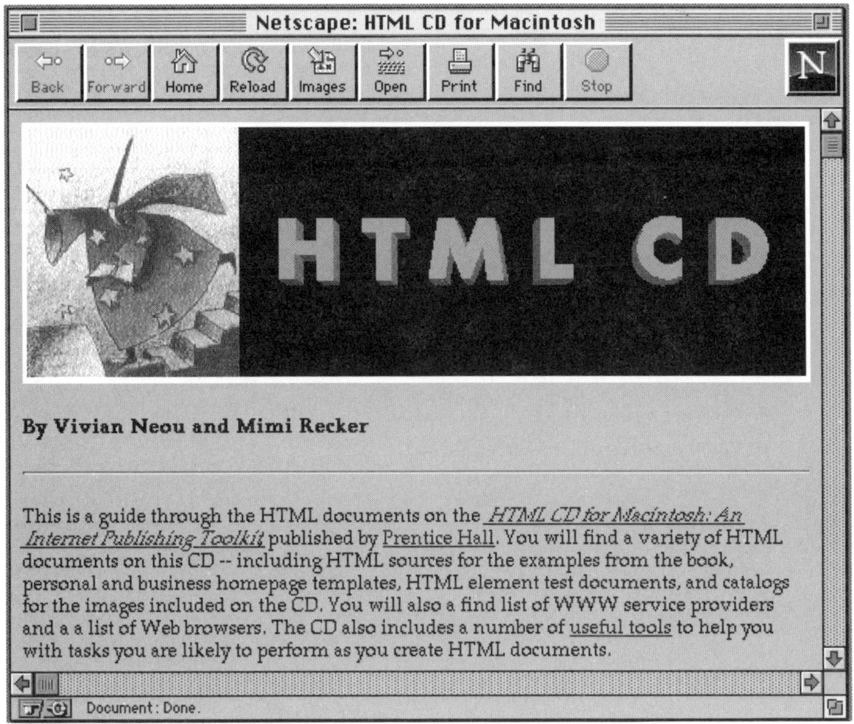

Netscape: HTML CD for Macintosh
Back
Forward
Home
Reload
Images
Open
Print
Find
Stop
N
HTML CD
By Vivian Neou and Mimi Recker
This is a guide through the HTML documents on the HTML CD for Macintosh: An Internet Publishing Toolkit published by Prentice Hall. You will find a variety of HTML documents on this CD -- including HTML sources for the examples from the book, personal and business homepage templates, HTML element test documents, and catalogs for the images included on the CD. You will also a find list of WWW service providers and a a list of Web browsers. The CD also includes a number of useful tools to help you with tasks you are likely to perform as you create HTML documents.
Document: Done.

Log and Error File Locations

You may change the location(s) for the access and error logs by modifying the following lines in the configuration file:

```
ERROR    :Error.html
#If the LOG file directive is missing or commented out, no
#logging will occur.
LOG      :MacHTTP.log
```

Security and Access Control

MacHTTP allows you to control access to files based on host names and users. In the first case, you may specify host names or networks that are allowed or denied access. In the second case, remote users must specify a username and password in order to access specified files. User and host security options are specified in the configuration file, MacHTTP.config. If none are listed, then all files are available to all Web browsers.

Host Filtering

Host filtering is used to limit access to specific computers. For example, you might want to limit access to only your company's machines. MacHTTP looks at the Internet (IP) address or domain name of the client browser requesting a document and matches it to the list of security directives in the configuration file. If a match is found, MacHTTP will either pass on the document or display a message to the user saying access is denied.

For example, if Kelly Kayaker managed a server with documents that she wanted only her associates at Ozone Books to view, she would have the following directive in the configuration file:

```
ALLOW ozone.com
```

A client browser from outside the ozone.com domain requesting a document from Kelly's server would be denied access.

User Authentication

User authentication allows you to require people to enter a username and password before accessing files in a specific directory. The person trying to access the file must be using a browser that supports basic user authentication (most browsers now do).

Basically, documents that you want password-protected are assigned to a "realm." For MacHTTP, a realm is simply a word or string of characters defined by the Web manager. If a user requests a document that contains that string in the name of the document, then the user must supply a username and password. If the user cannot supply this information, an error message is displayed.

In the configuration file, you add a new security realm by using the REALM directive. To add usernames and their passwords to preexisting realms, use the Password command under the Edit Menu in MacHTTP. We illustrate with an example from Kelly's complicated life.

Kelly Kayaker has a directory named "Ongoing Biking Projects," where she has a number of files that she wants to allow only her associate Bob Biker to view. She has set up a realm, called "biking," and named it "biking_work" by adding the following directive in the configuration file:

```
REALM biking biking_work
```

She then starts up her MacHTTP server. She uses the Password command under the Edit menu in MacHTTP to add Bob. Using the dialog box, she enters his name, Bob, and his password, endorphin, and puts him in the "biking_work" realm:

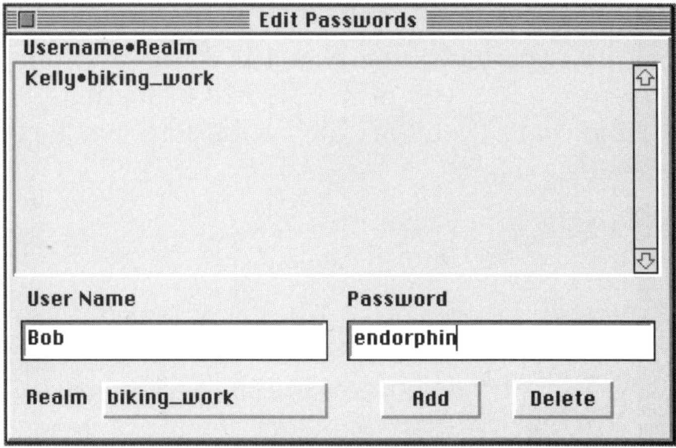

If she wishes, Kelly may add other colleagues by entering their username and password and assigning them to a security realm. For best security, it is advisable that users have different passwords, even if they are in the same realm.

Verifying User Access-Control Setup

After you are done setting up your user authentication files, be sure to check them. If they are working correctly, your browser should display an error when you try to access a restricted area with an invalid username and/or password. You should also find entries in the status window for unsuccessful attempts to access restricted files, for example:

```
09/17/95 17:17:39  PRIV ozone.com. :biking.html 0
```

Serving Files via MacHTTP

Remember, MacHTTP will only serve files that are in the same folder as the MacHTTP application, or within subfolders! While you may find this an inconvenience, it allows for much greater security in your server. Therefore, you must think of the "root" or top level of your server as being the folder that contains the MacHTTP application.

Also remember that MacHTTP uses the filename suffix to determine the type of the file (for example, .gif for graphic in GIF format). Therefore, always be sure to use correct filename suffixes.

Aliasing Files

Files within the MacHTTP folder structure can be aliased to other files, and MacHTTP will follow Mac aliases in the usual way. It uses the suffix of the alias filename to determine the type of file, then serves the document pointed at by the alias.

NOTE: MacHTTP will not understand aliases to folders. Only use aliases to files! If the aliases file contains links to local documents, MacHTTP interprets these URLs relative to where the MacHTTP application resides!

Image Maps: Mac-Imagemap

One of the nice things about having your own server is that it gives you complete control over the interactive part of your documents—including the capability to test your image maps without having to go to anyone else. You will find Lutz Weimann's free image map processing application, Mac-Imagemap, on the CD.

To use image maps with MacHTTP, you will first need to install the Mac-Imagemap application. You will find it in the imagemap folder, which is in the CGI Scripts folder. To install it, simply copy the imagemap folder into the "MacHTTP Software & Docs" folder (or wherever you have installed MacHTTP) on your hard disk. When you open the imagemap folder you should find:

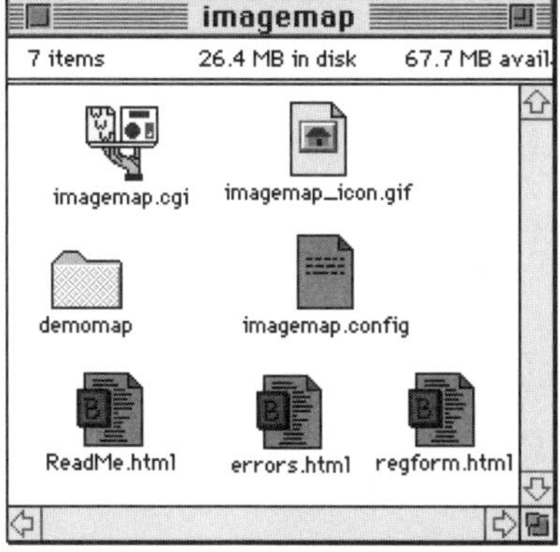

The program is ready to use now. You can check to see if it is working correctly by trying out the demo map that is included with the distribution. Make sure that MacHTTP is running, and then use this URL to access the demo:

```
http://yourhostname/imagemap/demomap/demomap.html
```

Be sure to replace "yourhostname" in this URL with your Mac's host name. If everything is installed correctly you should see this document:

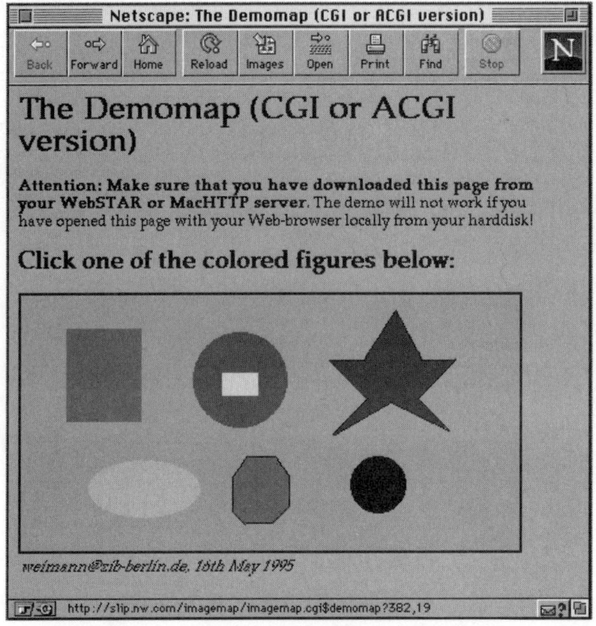

You can verify that imagemap is running by clicking on one of the figures. The figure will then be displayed by itself. Once you have verified that the installation is working correctly, you are ready to add your own image maps to your server.

Mac-Imagemap uses NCSA-style map files. Before adding an image map to your server, make sure that you have an NCSA-style map file for your image. If you don't already have a map file, you must create one before proceeding. You can find information about this process in the section "Images With Clickable Spots: Image Maps" in Chapter 4.

Although you can put map files anywhere within the MacHTTP folder structure, it is usually simpler to place them all in the imagemap folder. Next edit the imagemap.config file in the imagemap folder and add the information for your image. Entries are in the form:

```
mapname : mapfilename
```

The "top" folder is the imagemap folder and is indicated with a leading colon. The filename should include any folder names, using a colon to separate subfolders. For example, if we have a map file named menubar.map which is in a subfolder named "mymaps", we would add the following line to the imagemap configuration file:

```
menumap : :mymaps:menubar.map
```

It is then a simple matter of testing the map from your Web browser.

As you may recall, we had a menu-bar image map for our kayak page in a file called kayakmenubar.gif.map. Note that these files are all on the CD, so that you can try this yourself if you want to practice. First, we create a folder named kayak in the imagemap directory and copy the map file into it. Next we edit the imagemap.config file and add the line:

```
kayakmenu : :kayak:kayakmenubar.gif.map
```

Finally we go back to the HTML document that references this image map and add the link:

```
<A HREF="http://ozone.com/imagemap/kayak/kayakmenu">
<IMG SRC="gif/kayakmenubar.gif" ISMAP></IMG></A>
```

This tells the server that the imagemap program should look for the map named kayakmenu when this link is chosen. The image map is now ready to be used. You should always test your image maps after you have set them up to make sure that your links work correctly.

For more information about Mac-Imagemap, please read the ReadMe.html document included in the imagemap folder.

Scripting for MacHTTP: CGI and Forms

In order to use forms with this server, you will need something behind the server that can process data from a form and return information to the server that the server will in turn pass back to the browser. We have included email.acgi, a general forms-processing program, on the CD. We explained how to install and use this program In Chapter 6. If you have specific needs for forms-processing, you must write a script (or program) that conforms to the CGI (Common Gateway Interface) standard.

MacHTTP requires that CGI scripts have the filename extension .cgi, or .acgi. These filename extensions indicate that both are CGI scripts, but that the "acgi" script can be run in "asynchronous" mode by the server. Therefore, the internals of a .cgi and .acgi script can be identical. However, the server will process the scripts differently.

In the .cgi case, the server will send an event to the script and wait until something is returned. During this wait, it will not handle other connections to the server. In the .acgi case, the server will send an event to the script and then continue handling other connections to the server. When something is returned from the script, the server will pass this on the requesting client. This asynchronous mode adds a bit of overhead to the server.

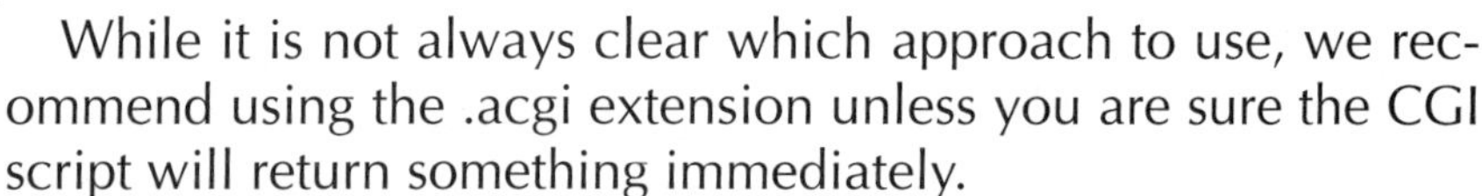

While it is not always clear which approach to use, we recommend using the .acgi extension unless you are sure the CGI script will return something immediately.

CGI scripts can be written in many programming languages. On the Macintosh, the most popular options are:

- Applescript
- Frontier
- MacPerl
- C
- Hypercard

Within the MacHTTP folder structure on the CD, the folders named "Examples" and "Extending MacHTTP" contain more information on writing CGI scripts using these languages.

Using Applescript

MacHTTP will execute AppleScripts and display the results of the script in a new document to clients. The scripts must be placed within the MacHTTP folder structure.

The server documentation comes with several example CGI AppleScripts. In this section we walk you through a short example. We use the Applescript called "test" in the Tutorials/Examples folder.

You may use the Script Editor to view the contents of the script, test.txt. To execute the script, simply use the link:

```
<A href="Tutorials/Examples/test.cgi"> testing the script</a>
```

You should then see the following displayed in your browser:

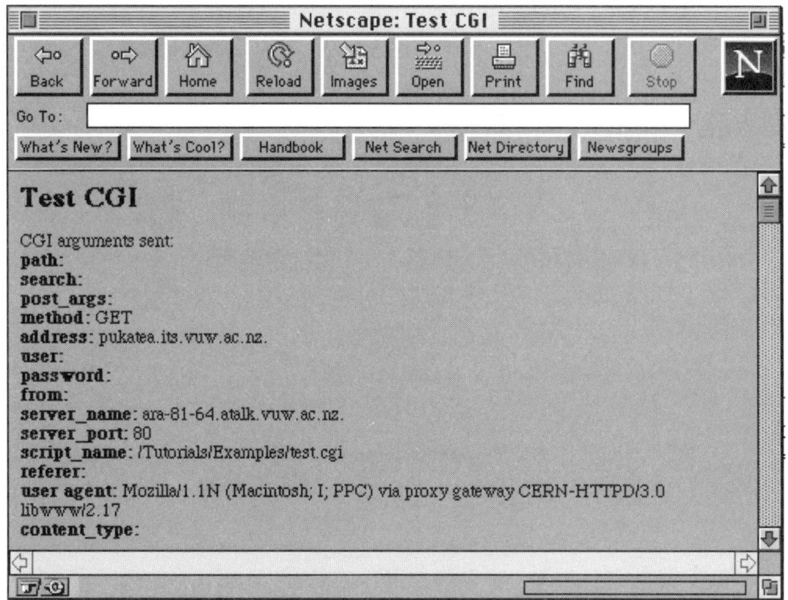

Administering Your MacHTTP Server

The best way to monitor your server is to keep an eye on the status window. This window displays all browser accesses, errors, server load, and other assorted details. Each time you start MacHTTP, it creates a new status window and wipes out the old one.

Log Files

MacHTTP records document access information in two places:

- The status window for MacHTTP
- MacHTTP.log, in the MacHTTP application folder.

The access log contains a list of all queries made to the server. Each entry in the access log includes the name (or IP address) of the system from which the browser query originated, a date and time stamp, and the request that was made. For example:

```
08/09/95 16:54:15  OK   ozone.com. :Default.html 3050
```

This entry indicates that on August 8, 1995, at 4:54 pm, the browser on the host ozone.com requested the document called default.html.

The log also contains a list of all of the failed queries made to the server. You will probably find that most of the entries in this log are from queries for files that do not exist. Each entry includes a date and time stamp and a description of the invalid query.

```
08/09/95 16:54:15  ERR   ozone.com. :foo.html 3050
```

MacHTTP does not automatically cycle the access and error logs—new entries are simply appended to the end of the logs.

Log File Analysis

In utility.html you will find a pointer to Webstat, a useful application that analyzes the contents of the access log file and produces a nice summary report. To run the application, simply put it in the same folder as the access log file and double-click on the application icon. A new file will appear, called Webstat.html, which contains the summary report.

Load this file in your Web browser, and you will be rewarded with a report listing total number of files and bytes transmitted. These data are then presented as daily, weekly, host, and document-name statistics. These data can be very useful in determining the load on your server, the kinds of documents requested, and where requests are coming from.

Interaction/IP

Interaction by Terje Norderhaug is an advanced but inexpensive add-on for MacHTTP and WebStar that allows you to create services such as interactive bulletin boards and chat channels as part of your web site. Interactive message boards allow your readers to post messages, which are instantly made public, available for other visitors.

The visitor enters messages through the use of forms. A typical form looks like this:

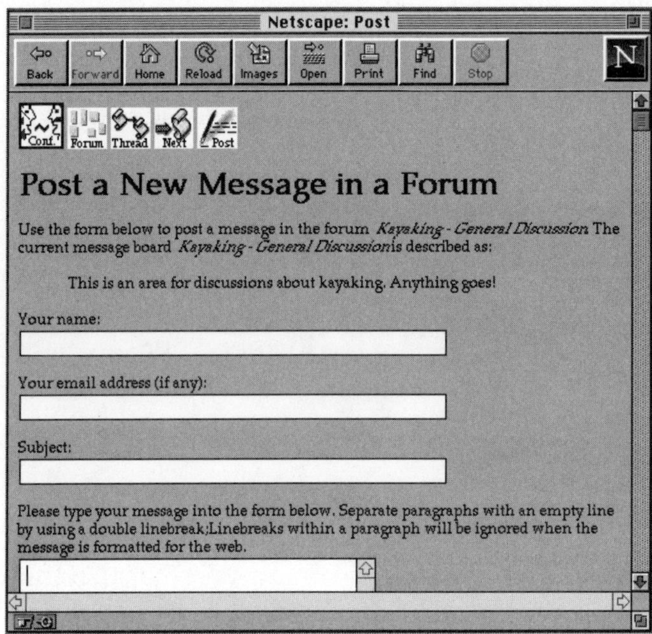

Since the forms are all built into Interaction, you do not need to write any HTML to provide message boards, nor do you have to edit any cryptic files. All you need to do is install Interaction and configure the boards or chat areas that you wish to use.

It also comes with a collaborative calculator and shopping cart feature (these features are still at an early state of development). You'll find Interaction in the Server folder in the "interaction80b2" folder.

Installing Interaction

Interaction requires at least 3 megabytes of memory. If you do not have this much memory, make sure that you have virtual memory turned on. To install it:

1. *Drag the Interaction 0.80b2 folder to some location on your hard drive (to avoid security risks do not place it in your MacHTTP folder).*
2. *Open the folder. You should see:*

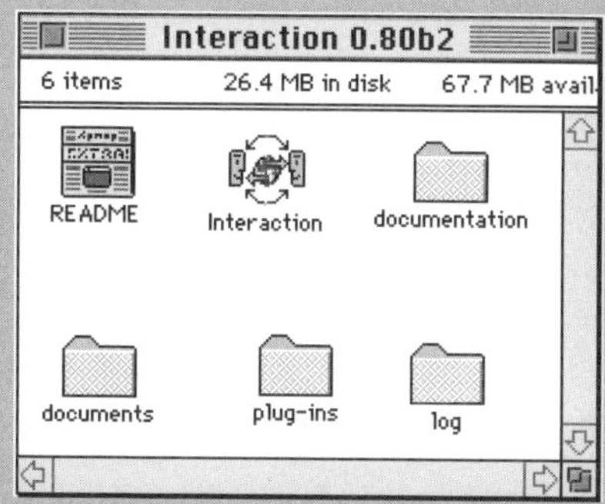

3. *Choose the Interaction icon. Use "Make Alias" from the File menu in Finder to make an alias for the Interaction icon.*
4. *Drag the alias to the MacHTTP folder, and rename it to "Interaction" by removing the "alias" postfix. Make sure that you do not leave any trailing spaces in the name, or the server may not be able to find it.*
5. *Start MacHTTP.*
6. *Start Interaction by double-clicking on the Interaction icon in the MacHTTP folder. Note that it may take a little time to start, so do not be concerned if you need to wait a minute or two before it is ready to use. The Interaction menu looks like this:*

File Edit Monitor Services Windows

7. *You're done! You can access your Interaction directory at the URL:*

```
http://myhost/interaction
```

If you load the URL for Interaction's top-level directory, you will see something like this:

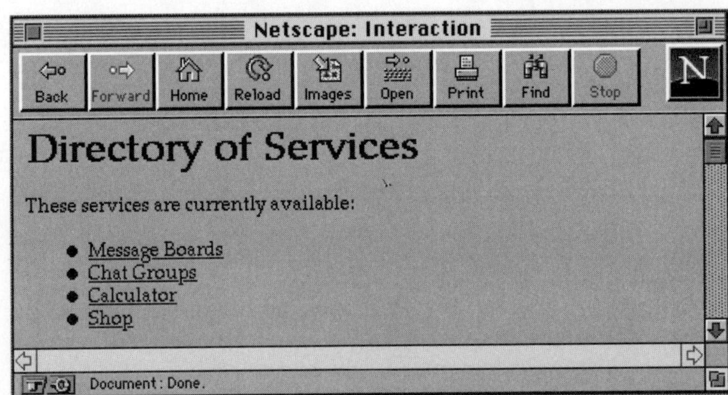

To integrate links to the message-board directory in other documents on your site, you can make a reference to the bulletin board directory directly through the URL:

`http://`*`myhost`*`/interaction$forum`

and to the chat directory at:

`http://`*`myhost`*`/interaction$chat`

Note that these URLs are composed of the general URL to Interaction, then a dollar sign, and then a keyword for the service.

Although there is no way to disable specific features in this version of Interaction, future versions will offer this ability. If you decide to use Interaction, and wish to disable some of the features, you can get the latest version of Interaction on the Internet at:

`http://www.ifi.uio.no/~terjen/interaction/index.html`

Customizing the Directory

You will probably wish to put in custom descriptions for your directories of bulletin boards and chat groups. The default directory for bulletin boards looks like this:

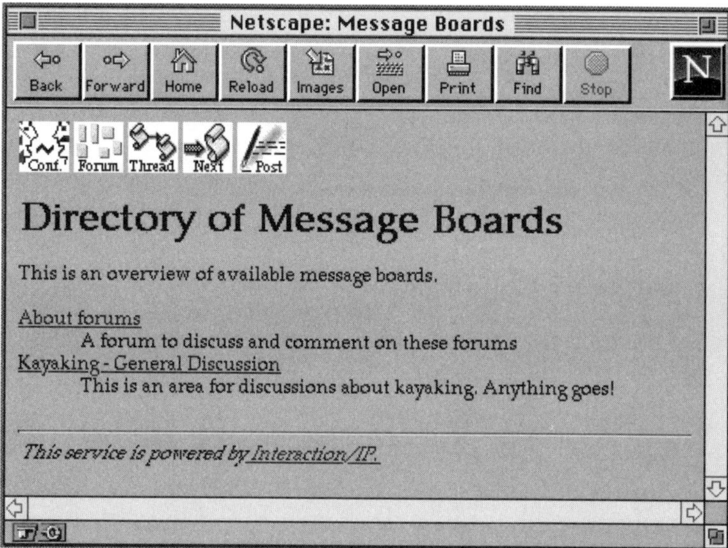

It is easy to tailor the description and heading for your site. To do this for bulletin boards, choose Message Boards and then Customize Directory from the Services menu.

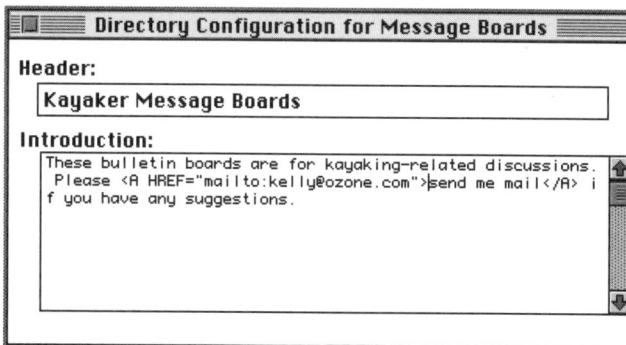

Directory Configuration for Message Boards

Header:

Kayaker Message Boards

Introduction:

These bulletin boards are for kayaking-related discussions. Please <A HREF="mailto:kelly@ozone.com">send me mail</A> if you have any suggestions.

Notice that you can enter HTML tags in the introduction if you wish. Once you have entered the information, you will see it rather than the default displayed when you go to the directory:

Creating Bulletin Boards and Chat Groups

Adding new bulletin board and chat groups is simple. To create a new bulletin board, choose Message Boards and then Define Boards from the Services menu. The following dialog box will be displayed:

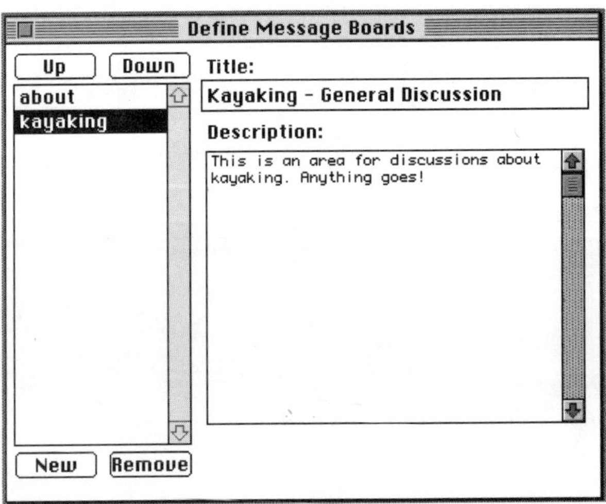

Click on the "New" button, and then add the information for the board that you wish to create. You can now access the forum at the URL:

```
http://myhost/interaction$forum/forum_name
```

In this example, where our host is named "www.ozone.com" and the forum is named "kayaking," we would access it at:

```
http://www.ozone.com/interaction$forum/kayaking
```

You can remove a board at any time simply by choosing it in the "Define Message Boards" dialog box and then clicking on the Remove button.

Note that any changes you make in the Define Message Boards dialog will not take effect until you "save" the dialog. When you close the dialog, you will be given the option of installing the changes or cancelling all of the modifications made.

Creating a new chat group follows a similar procedure to the one for creating bulletin boards. Simply choose Chat Groups and then Define Group from the Services menu. Enter the information for the group you wish to create, close the dialog box, and your chat group is ready for use.

The appearance of the default chat groups is very basic, and you might want to tailor them further. Interaction makes it possible for you to turn any HTML document into a chat group, so you have a high degree of freedom to tailor it as you like. More details about how to do this is in the "documentation" folder that comes with Interaction.

Learning More about Interaction

We have gone over only basic maintenance tasks here. If you want to do more, please refer to the on-line documents that come with the package. You can also get additional help with the package by subscribing to the www-interaction mailing list. Do this by sending a request to:

```
www-interaction-request@math.uio.no
```

or by using the subscription form available from:

```
http://www.ifi.uio.no/~terjen/interaction/
```

Httpd4Mac: A Freeware Web Server

Httpd4Mac by Bill Melloti is a freeware Web server for the Macintosh. Like most freeware, the software comes with no warranty.

The httpd4Mac server is perfect for small Web sites and for testing your HTML documents. The server allows you to serve Web documents with images, and separate images, sound, and movie files. However, it does not support clickable images, forms, or other kinds of interactive pages. It also doesn't allow you to make documents password-protected.

Installing httpd4Mac

You need a Macintosh running at least System 7, with the MacTCP control panel, and preferably 500K available memory (though the server will probably run with less). Of course, if you plan to publish on the Internet, you need the appropriate network access.

Httpd4Mac is easy to install. You will find it in the folder named httpd4Mac in the Server folder on the CD. To install the it, copy the httpd4Mac folder onto your main drive.

Starting the Server

To start the server, open the httpd4Mac folder. The contents should look like this:

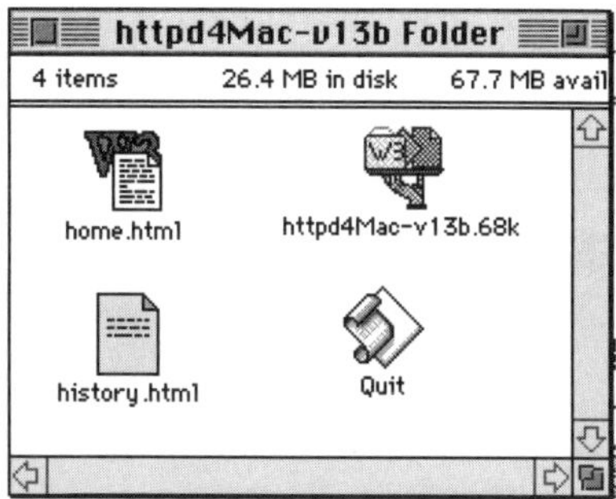

Now double-click on the httpd4Mac icon. The server takes about 10 seconds to get up and running.

The server runs as a "Faceless-Background Application." This means that when you launch the server, the icon will appear greyed-out, but no windows or menu bar will appear. The application will also not show up in the application menu. As we will describe below, you can modify the configuration file (the preferences file) to notify you about major events. Otherwise, the server runs quietly in the background.

Now you are ready to test your server. To do this, start the browser of your choice (preferably one that handles forms) and give it the URL:

`http://`*your.site*

When you try this, make sure that you replace "your.site" with your Macintosh's network name or IP number. If everything is working correctly, your browser should display a screen that looks something like this:

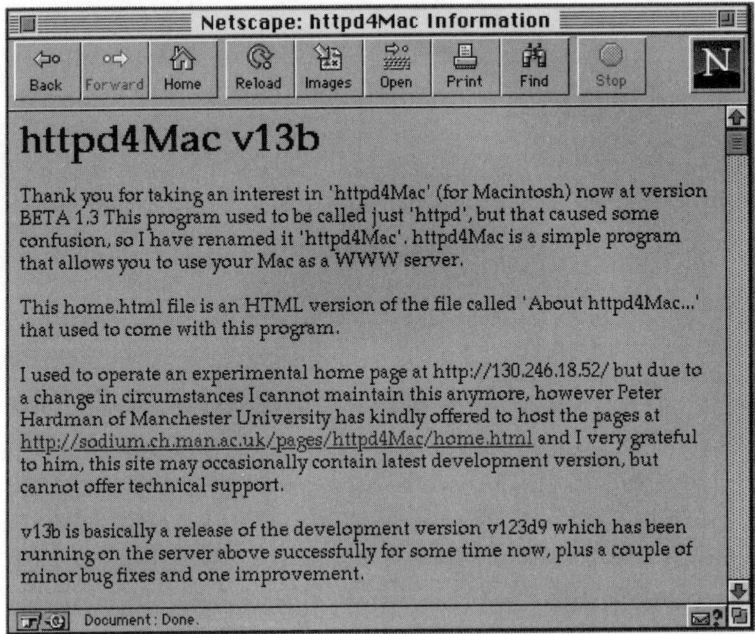

The browser is now displaying the default document for your server. This document is called home.html and is located in the same folder as the server. Naturally, you can customize the server to use your own home page; you simply replace the file home.html with your own top-level page. We suggest you make a copy of the original home.html document, as it contains useful documentation.

Configurating httpd4Mac

The server uses its preference file, httpd_prefs, for customizing the server. On startup, it looks for this file in the same folder as the application. If it is unable to find one there, it looks in your System/Preferences folder. Failing that, one is created by the server in the System/Preferences folder. If the server needs to create a preference file it will put up the following window:

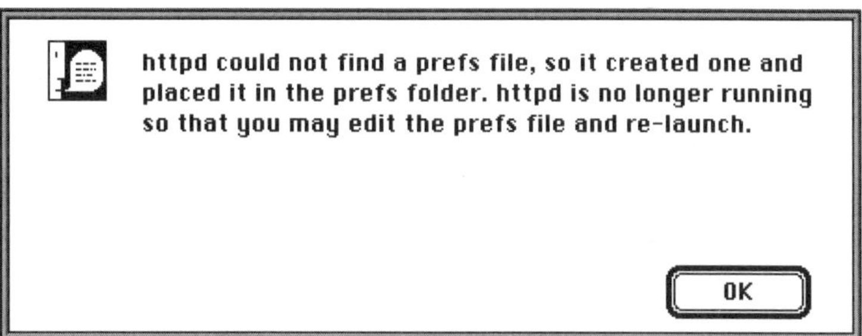

httpd could not find a prefs file, so it created one and placed it in the prefs folder. httpd is no longer running so that you may edit the prefs file and re-launch.
OK

As stated in this window, httpd4Mac will exit after creating the preference file, so you will need to relaunch it if you want to use it right away.

This file can be edited to customize the server. In most cases, the only modifications you will want to make are changing the time zone and enabling an access log file.

To change the time zone to reflect your proper location, locate the following directive in the preferences file:

```
time_zone   +1200
```

and replace it with appropriate offset or recognized letter code for your time zone.

Log Files

If you wish to record all document requests made to your server, locate the following directive in the preference file:

```
log_access  off
```

and change it to:

```
log_access  on
```

You may also want to change the following directive:

```
create_error_log  off
```

to:

```
create_error_log on
```

This last directive tells the server to start a new access log file each time the server is restarted. Unless you change the directive, the access log is saved in a file called httpd_access_log. If an access log file already exists, it is renamed to a file called httpd_access_log.bak.

If you leave the create_error_log directive set to off, then httpd4Mac looks for a file named httpd_access_log and simply appends to it. Thus, when starting fresh, you need to create an empty file with the name httpd_access_log in the server folder.

Double-click on the server icon when you wish to relaunch the server with your new modifications.

The access log contains a list of all queries made to the server. Each entry in the access log includes the name (or IP address) of the system from which the browser query originated, a date and time stamp, and the request that was made. For example:

```
131.195.2.193 - - [04/Oct/1995:15:17:27 +1200] "GET
/home.html HTTP/1.0"  200  23005
```

This entry indicates that on October 4, 1995, at 3:16 PM, the browser on the computer 130.195.2.193 requested the document called home.html.

You can use the WWWStat4Mac application to produce access statistic reports from your log files. You will find the application in the WWStat4Mac folder. There is complete documentation on the use of this package at:

```
http://sodium.ch.man.ac.uk/pages/wwwstat4Mac.html
```

Loading Your Master Home Page

Once you have verified that your server is working correctly, you will probably want to replace the home page that comes with the server with one of your own home pages. httpd4Mac requires that the top-level page for your server be located in the same folder as the server application. You can name this file "home.html," and the server will load it automatically when someone connects to your server.

An easy way to run httpd4Mac without having to do much rearranging is to copy httpd4Mac into the folder where you keep your html pages. Make sure that your top-level page is named home.html, and then start httpd4Mac from that folder. Note that your http_prefs file should be in your system folder if you do this (or copy it into your html folder).

Serving Files via httpd4Mac

Remember, httpd4Mac will only serve files that are in the same folder as the application, or within subfolders, using the "/" delimiter to indicate subfolders. It also does not understand Macintosh aliases. Note that it will serve any and all documents in the same folder and subfolders as the application—including the application itself, log files and the preference file (for this reason you may prefer to keep your preference file in your system Preference folder)!

Also remember that the server uses the filename suffix to determine the type of the file (for example, .gif for graphic in GIF format). Therefore, always be sure to use correct filename suffixes.

Stopping the Server

To quit the server, you must either reboot your machine or run the AppleScript called Quit, which you should find in the httpd4Mac folder. To run Quit, simply click on the Quit icon. You should see this window:

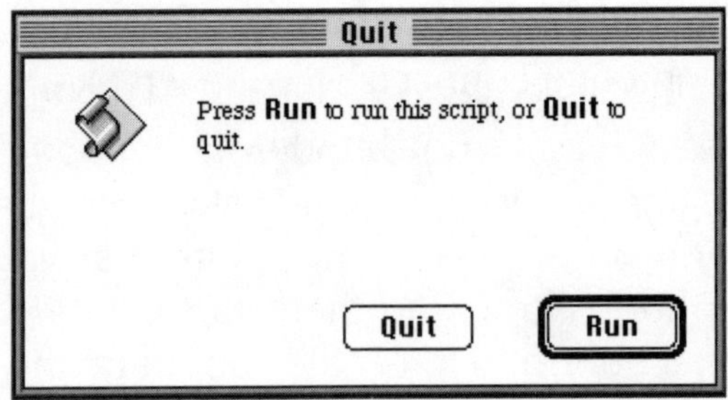

Click the Run button (if you click the Quit button, you will cause the Quit script to quit, not httpd4Mac!), and it will stop httpd4Mac.

More Information

You will find more information about httpd4Mac in the documentation provided with the server software.

Connecting Your Server to the Internet

Almost everything we've described in this chapter can be done whether or not your Mac is actually connected to the Internet. However, if you are serious about publishing on the Web, you will need to either copy your documents to a Web service provider (see Appendix D if you choose this route) or connect your Mac to the Internet. If you have the good fortune to have a Mac that is already connected to the Internet, you can skip this section. If not, here are some guidelines to help you find an Internet Service Provider (ISP) and choose an appropriate level of service. This section makes the assumption that you are looking for a connection to provide around-the-clock Web service rather than casual dial-in.

Communications Equipment

In addition to your Macintosh, you will need to have equipment to connect your home or business to your ISP. You are probably already familiar with simple modems. However, you will need much more for a dedicated connection. A typical list would include:

- Leased line from the telephone company.
- Channel Service Unit/Digital Service Unit (CSU/DSU). This piece of equipment connects your line to your network equipment. It is usually provided by the ISP or telephone company.
- Network router. Routers direct traffic on a network and will guide your data between the line and your network.

Most ISPs will provide all of this equipment, although some may allow you to make your own choices.

Bandwidth

Bandwidth is the amount of data a line can handle. Determining the correct amount of bandwidth to purchase is very important. If you have a low-bandwidth line, and a high-volume site, your customers will have trouble reaching you. If you have a high-bandwidth line, and a low-volume site, you will end up paying extra money for services that you do not use.

It is not easy to determine the exact amount of bandwidth you will need, but there are some general guidelines you can use to estimate your requirements.

- Figure out the size of an average document on your system. Be sure to include the size of any images that may be included in the document.

- Estimate the number of simultaneous connections you expect to have (remember that the connection only stays open as long as it takes for the document to be transferred).

Multiply these figures to see how much data you expect to transfer during busy times. Now calculate how much time it will take your customers to get those documents by dividing the amount of traffic by different bandwidths. For example, if you had an average document size of 200 kb, and expected to have 50 simultaneous connections during busy times, your customers could expect transfer times of:

23 minutes for a 56-kb line

50 seconds for a T1 line (1.5 Mb/sec)

2 seconds for a T3 line (45 Mb/sec)

This example uses a fairly large document size and a high number of simultaneous users. The average small business will probably have much smaller numbers. Since higher-bandwidth lines tend to be very expensive, it is better to start small and upgrade. Check with your provider to see how much they charge for upgrading to a higher level of service.

General Server Guidelines

If you've read this far and followed the examples in this chapter, you're probably a server administrator now. Whether you are using httpd4Mac, MacHTTP, or some other server, if you're planning on making your server public, here are a couple of tips to help make your server user-friendly and easy to manage.

- Define a generic host name for your server. The convention for host names that act as web servers is www.domain-name. For example, if we were to run a web server for ozone.com, we would define a name "www.ozone.com" that would point to the name of the machine running the server. This way, when you build your URLs or publicize them, you use the alias host name. If you need to move your server to another machine, you only need to update the alias to point to the new machine rather than having to change all your URLs.

- Provide a contact address in your documents. The convention for the contact point for a server is the address

  ```
  webmaster@www.domainname
  ```

  If you do not already have an e-mail alias defined, you should add one for this address. You should point the alias to the e-mail address for the person in charge of the server. This is especially important for your master page, since people need a place to report problems.

You will find more hints on designing master home pages in Chapter 8, "Design Guidelines, Styles and Tips."

In this chapter you will learn about

- Criteria for choosing an HTML editor
- The 5 HTML editors on the CD: Alpha, HTML Pro, HTML Editor, Site Writer Pro and Webtor
- HTML converters and other maintenance tools

All of these tools are available on the CD.

Editors and Converters

What's In This Chapter

The number of HTML editors available for Macintosh systems has been increasing rapidly. We've included 5 editors on the CD:

- Alpha
- HTML Editor
- HTML Pro
- Site Writer Pro
- Webtor

If none of these editors is to your liking, we have included an editor document on the CD that you can use to download

some of the other Macintosh HTML editors available on the Internet. You will also learn about HTML converters—applications that turn plain text documents or documents in word processing formats into HTML. We also provide an overview of HTML Grinder, an HTML document maintenance tool.

HTML Editors

You can use just about any application that allows you to save text in an ASCII format to create an HTML document. Even a simple editor like SimpleText can be used to create an HTML document. If you have most of the tags memorized (or just keep the HTML reference card close by), you may find it easier just to keep a browser open in one window, and your favorite ASCII editor open in another (we'll confess—this is what we do). This way you can reload your document in the browser to check on it as you go, and you don't have to learn how to use an additional application.

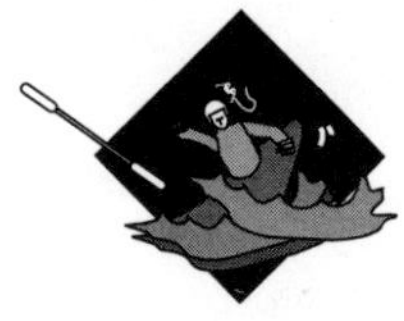

However, when you use an editor that doesn't know anything about HTML, it is up to you to remember all the HTML tags and to verify that you've used them correctly. As HTML becomes more complicated, this becomes more and more difficult to do by hand. Fortunately, there are a wide range of HTML editors, and one is bound to meet your needs.

There are a number of features you should consider when choosing an HTML editor:

WYSIWYG

What You See Is What You Get. Editors used to create HTML documents range from plain ASCII editors, in which you type the tags (and hence see them), to editors that try to display the document as it would be seen in a browser. In between are editors that allow you to configure them with the browser of your choice and will automatically start the browser and display your document for you, and editors that show some tags and hide others

(while showing the text in a formatted manner). Most editors that provide WYSIWYG HTML editing also allow you to set a switch to display the tags if you wish. Keep in mind that documents may look quite different in different browsers, and the editor can only show you its interpretation of the way in which the document will be displayed by a browser.

Add-on vs. stand-alone

Some HTML editors are add-ons for existing word processing applications, such as Microsoft Word. Others are stand-alone editors. If you already use a word processing application, you may find it easier to learn an add-on than to get a stand-alone application.

HTML verification

Some editors do no checking of the HTML tag usage. They will insert the tags for you, but if you use them incorrectly (such as putting text outside the tag or using invalid characters in your text), they will not notice or warn you. Other editors have extensive HTML rule-checking facilities and will always create HTML documents that adhere to the HTML standard (one of them anyway!). The drawback of an HTML-verifier editor is that it may be difficult to load documents that were created by some other source, which do not adhere to the standard.

HTML support level

As we mentioned earlier in the book, HTML is an evolving standard. Some editor maintainers have been aggressively updating their editors to support proposed HTML 3 elements and Netscape additions. Other editors do not offer these features, so you would have to type in extended tags yourself.

Price

HTML editors come in a wide range of prices. The editors on the CD and listed in our editor document are all available on the Internet. Some are freeware, while others are shareware. This is one area where price is not necessarily a good measure of quality. Some of the best editors are free or available for a nominal fee.

System requirements

In general, the more features an editor offers, the more resources your Macintosh must have in order to run the editor. Some editors have fairly extensive memory requirements, which may make it difficult to run any other application while using the editor. This can be frustrating, since many editors provide a link to a browser so that you can preview your document. If your system does not have enough memory, it may not be able to load both a browser and an editor at the same time.

The freeware and shareware HTML editors that you will find on the CD cover a wide range of these features. At the end of the chapter we'll also discuss some commercial HTML editors that are worth a look.

Editor Overview

You will find these editors in the HTML Editor folder:

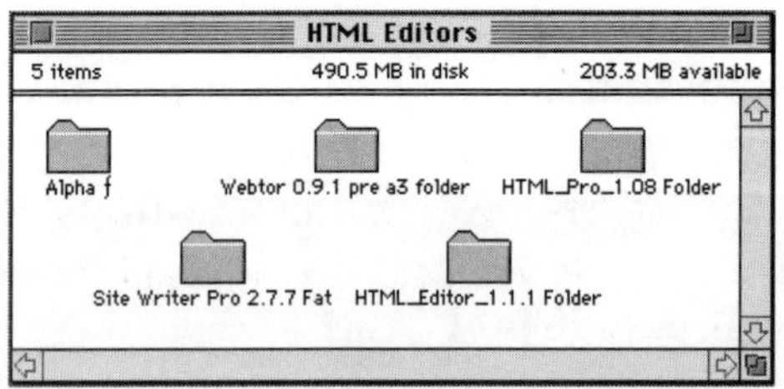

With so many editors on the CD, it is impossible to provide an in-depth description on the use of each editor here. To help you get started with each editor, we will show you how to use each editor to create the following HTML document:

```
<HTML>
<HEAD>
<TITLE>Editor Test Document</TITLE>
</HEAD>
<BODY>
<CENTER><H1>Editor Test Document</H1></CENTER>
<HR>
<P>We will create this document using a number of different
editors.
The elements we include:
<UL>
<LI>A horizontal rule
<LI>An unordered list
<LI>An image map
<LI>The annoying <BLINK>Netscape BLINK tag</BLINK>
<LI>The Netscape CENTER tag.
<LI>A link to <A HREF=index.html>the HTML CD page</A>
<LI>A table
</UL>
<TABLE BORDER>
<CAPTION ALIGN=BOTTOM><STRONG>A Table</STRONG></CAPTION>
<TR><TH ALIGN=CENTER>Column One<TH ALIGN=CENTER>Column Two
<TR><TD>One Cell<TD>Two Cells
<TR><TD COLSPAN=2>Three Cells
</TABLE>
<HR>
<P><A HREF="http://myhost.com/cgi-bin/imagemap/menubar"
BORDER=0>
<IMG SRC="menubar.gif" ISMAP ALT="[Menu Bar]"]>
</A>
</BODY>
</HTML>
```

Although this is a fairly short document, we have included many HTML elements in it—including some Netscape extensions, and new HTML tags.

In addition to the documentation provided in this chapter, you will also find that most of the editors include fairly extensive on-line help. Some of the shareware editors also include a hardcopy manual as part of the registration fee.

HTML Editor

HTML Editor by Rik Giles is a nice semi-WYSIWYG shareware editor written in Prograph. To install it, simply drag its folder to the location on your hard disk where it is to be installed. When you open its folder you should see:

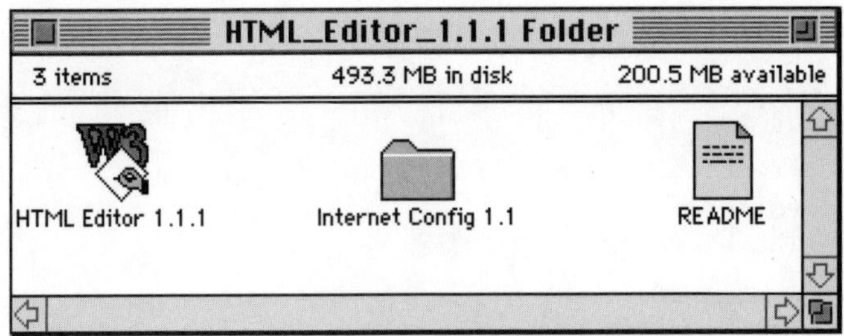

Getting Started

To start HTML Editor, simply click on its icon. It may take a little while to start, so don't be concerned if nothing happens immediately. After it is done loading, it displays a registration window:

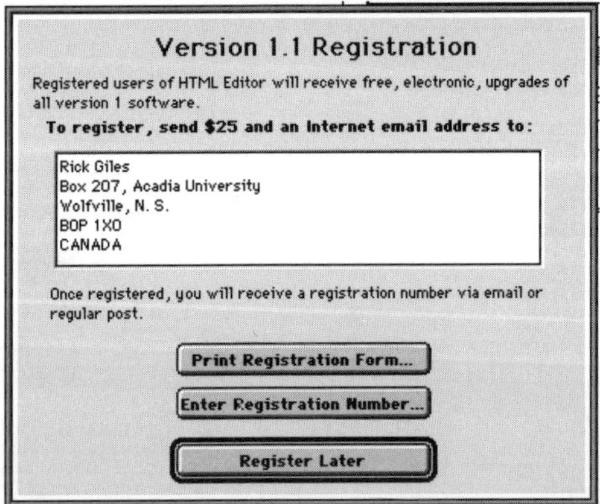

If you are still evaluating the package, click the Register Later button to finish the start-up process. You should then see something like this:

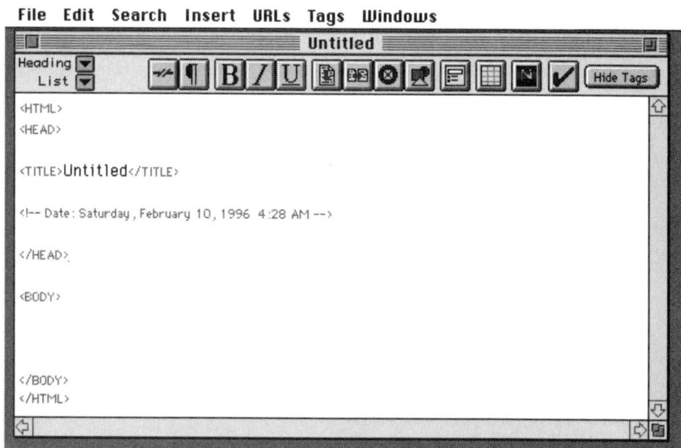

As we mentioned before, HTML Editor is a semi-WYSIWYG editor. In the default mode, it will show the HTML tags in a light grey. At any time you can click on the Hide Tags button at the top of the window to see how the document looks without tags. However, since HTML Editor does not provide browser-like formatting for all elements (most notably the table elements), what you see will not be exactly what a browser would display. Fortunately HTML Editor does allow you to send your document to a browser with a single button click, so it is easy to see exactly how your document will look in the browser of your choice. Now let's get started on our test document.

Entering HTML Tags

HTML Editor provides a number of methods for entering HTML tags: keyboard shortcuts, buttons in the document window, and the pulldown menu. It also opens new documents with the basic HTML tag framework already setup.

The first two elements in our document are a title and a heading. The title tags are already part of the document, so we simply position our cursor in the appropriate location (over the Untitled text) and enter our title.

We decide to use the Heading button in the document window to enter our heading. We simply click on the button (which is in the upper left of the window) and choose the type of heading we want. Alternatively we could have chosen Soft Formatting -> Heading 1 from the Tags menu or used the keyboard shortcut of <CLOVERLEAF>-1.

We also enclosed our heading in the Netscape CENTER tag. To do this, we highlight the heading (text and tags), and then choose Alignment -> Center from the Tags menu.

Our next element is a horizontal rule, which we enter by choosing Divider -> Horizontal Rule from the Tags menu. Although we do not use them, notice that there is also support for the Netscape enhancements to Horizontal Rule. The horizontal rule is followed by a paragraph which we enter by choosing the paragraph button from the menu bar in the document window:

Lists

To create our list, we first enter the text for the list with each list item separated by a carriage return. Then we highlight the list text:

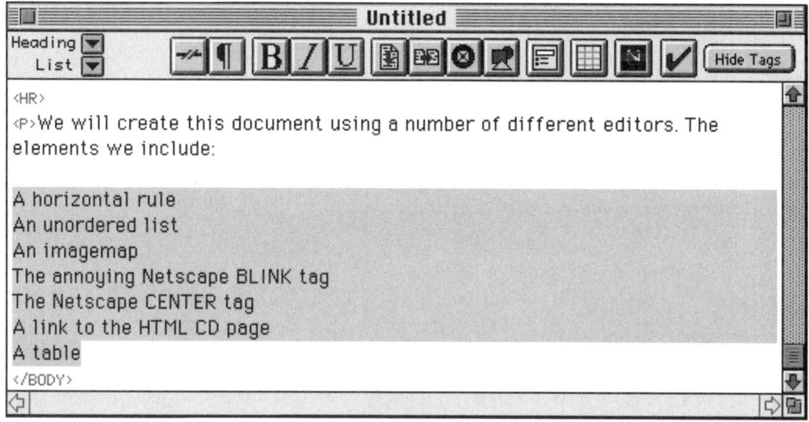

We transform it into an unordered list by choosing Unordered List from the List pulldown menu in the document window menu bar. And with a single click we now have an unordered list:

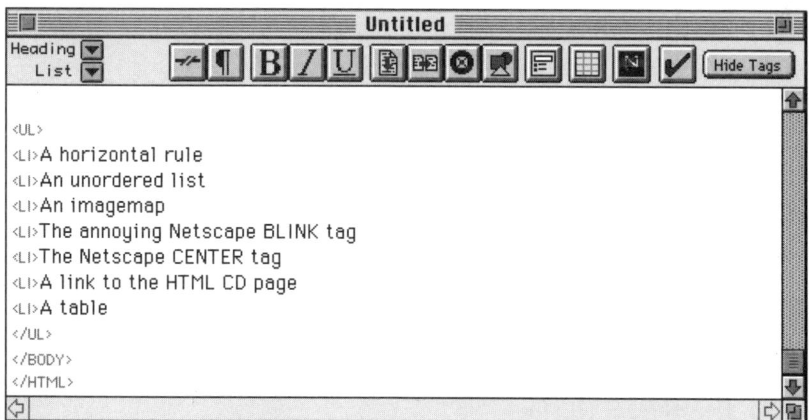

Some of our list items also include other tags such as CENTER and BLINK. We add these tags by highlighting the appropriate text and then choosing them from the applicable Tags submenu.

Links

Our list also includes a link to the HTML CD page. As with any other tag, we first enter the text to be linked. We then click the external link button from the document window menubar:

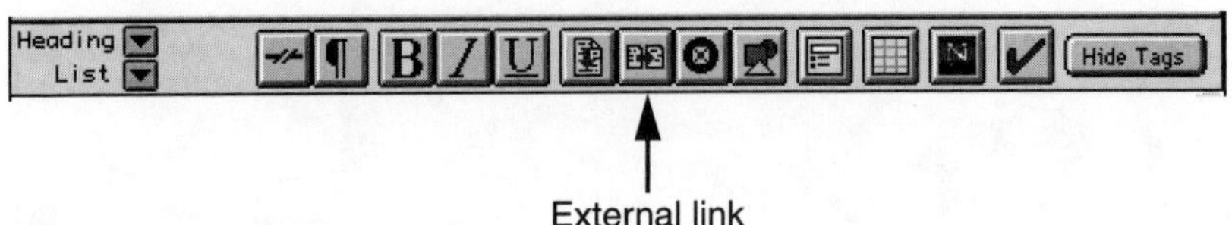

HTML Editor will pop up a window to enter the information for the link:

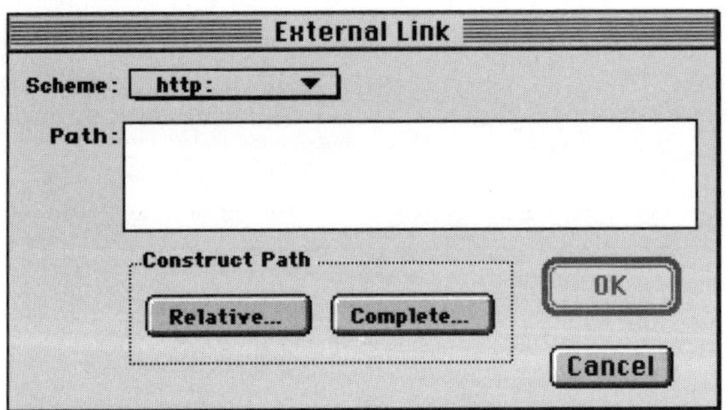

After entering the name of the file in the path box, we click the OK button. Since our link is to a local file, we only need to enter the filename. However, this box can also be used to enter a link to an offsite document by putting in the entire URL minus the protocol portion, which is specified with the Scheme pulldown menu.

Tables

Now we are ready to enter our table. Unlike our list, we set up the tag framework for the table before entering the text. We use the table designer by choosing Table -> Table Designer from the Tag menu:

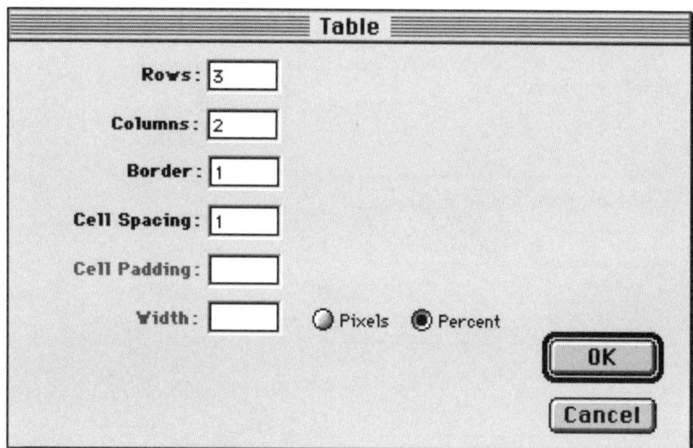

Now we have a framework for our table:

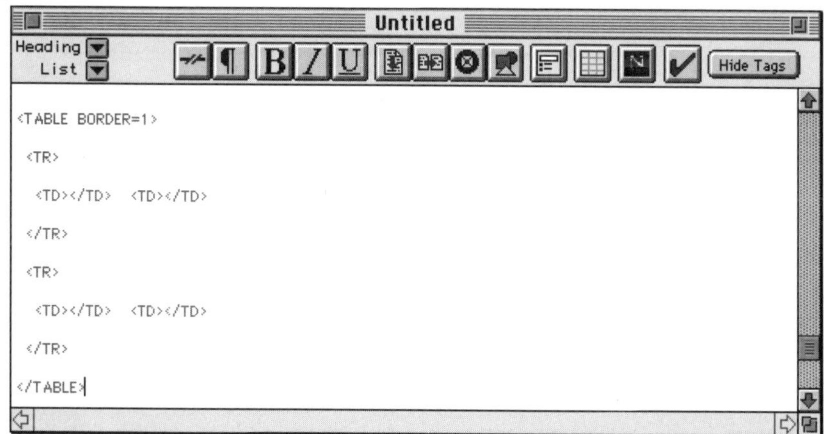

However, this table does not include a caption or a table heading row. Fortunately it is easy to enter these items by first entering the text, highlighting, and then choosing the appropriate tag from the Table submenu.

Images and Image Maps

The last item in our document is an image map. There are two steps to creating an image map: setting up the image, and then linking the image to the appropriate location. First we enter the image by choosing Link -> Image from the Tags menu:

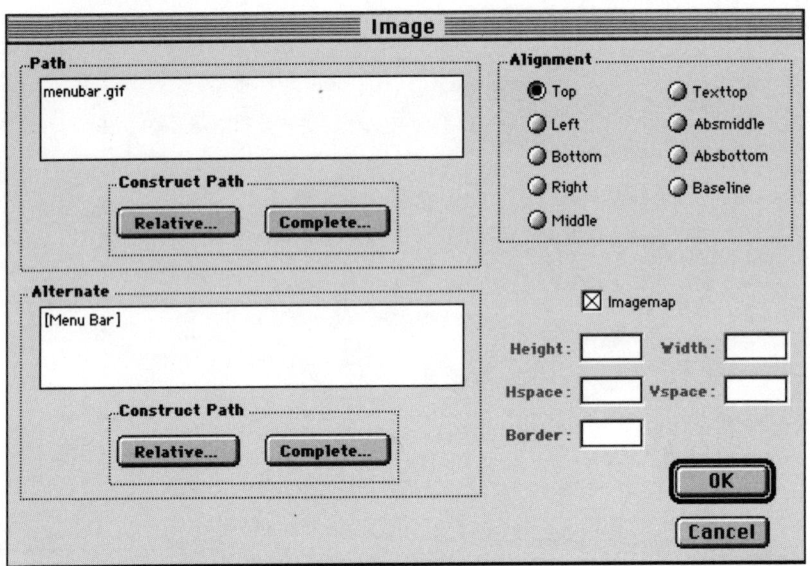

We enter the image's filename in the Path box, the alternate text in the Alternate box, and choose the Imagemap box. Next, we highlight the image tag and enter the link by clicking on the External Link button.

Pros and Cons

HTML Editor has many nice features, such as support for almost all HTML 2.0, 3.0, and Netscape tags. The tags are easily accessible through buttons, menu selections, and keyboard shortcuts. It is semi-WYSIWYG so that you can see tags if you wish, or if you prefer, hide the tags. It also allows you to define tags, so that you can add support for new HTML tags such as FRAME.

On the downside, it is fairly slow (especially starting up), and since it does not do any verification, you can easily jumble up your tags by placing the cursor in the wrong location while inserting new tags.

HTML Pro

HTML Pro is part of the Niklas Frykholm Shareware package. By paying a registration fee of $5 you will become a registered owner of the entire package. Although we do not include the other programs in the package on the CD, they may be downloaded over the Internet. For complete registration information please see the HTML Pro documentation.

To install HTML Pro, drag the HTML Pro folder from the CD to the location on your hard disk where you would like it to be installed. When you open the folder you should see:

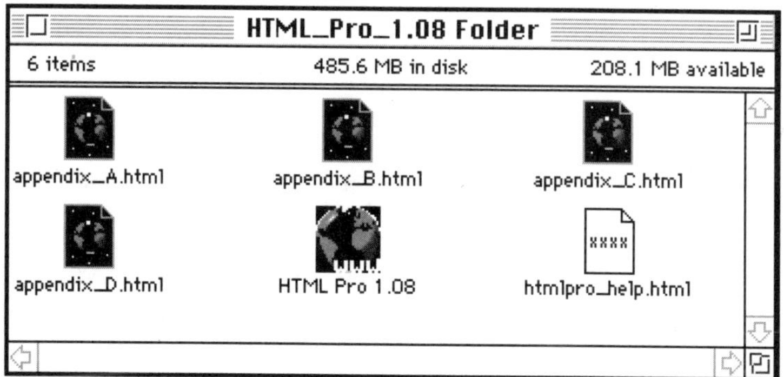

Double click on the HTML Pro icon to start the application:

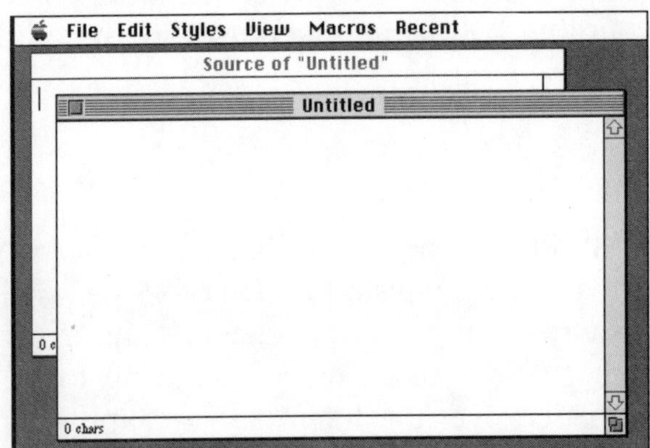

After the application is started, two windows should appear. The top window will show your document in a WYSIWYG fashion while the lower window will display the HTML source.

Title and Headings

The first item we wish to include in our document is the title. To insert a title, we choose Special from the Styles Menu and then pick Title. "[TITLE:]" appears in the upper window, while the actual TITLE tags are displayed in the source window. We choose to enter our title in the WYSIWYG window, although HTML Pro also allows text entry in the Source window.

The next thing in our document is a heading, which we wish to place in an H1 tag along with a CENTER tag. We begin by choosing Headers -> Heading 1 from the Style menu (<COMMAND>-1 is a shortcut for this command) and entering the text for our heading.

Defining Macros

Now we wish to place our heading in a CENTER tag. However, when we look for CENTER in the menu, we do not find it. This is not surprising, since HTML Pro only has built-in support

for HTML 2 tags. Fortunately, HTML Pro also allows us to easily define macros which can be used to insert other tags. To define a macro, we choose New Macro from the Macro menu. It pops up a window, which we use to enter our tags and the name for the macro:

After we are done entering the tags, we click on OK. Now when we look at the Macro menu, we see the Macros that we have defined at the end of the menu. To apply the macro, we highlight the section of text that we wish to tag and then choose the macro. Although macros may be inserted in either the source or WYSIWYG window, we found it to be more reliable to enter them in the source window.

Note that the tag will have no effect on the way that text is displayed in the WYSIWYG window, since HTML Pro has no way of knowing what the tag actually represents from a markup standpoint.

Horizontal Rule and Lists

Now we wish to enter a horizontal rule followed by a list. To enter the HR, we choose Special -> Horizontal Line from the Styles menu.

Creating a list requires three steps

1. *Enter the text that you wish to include in your list*
2. *Highlight the text that is to be converted into a list*
3. *Choose the type of list that you wish to create from Lists in the Styles menu.*

In our case, we wish to create an unordered list. First we enter our text:

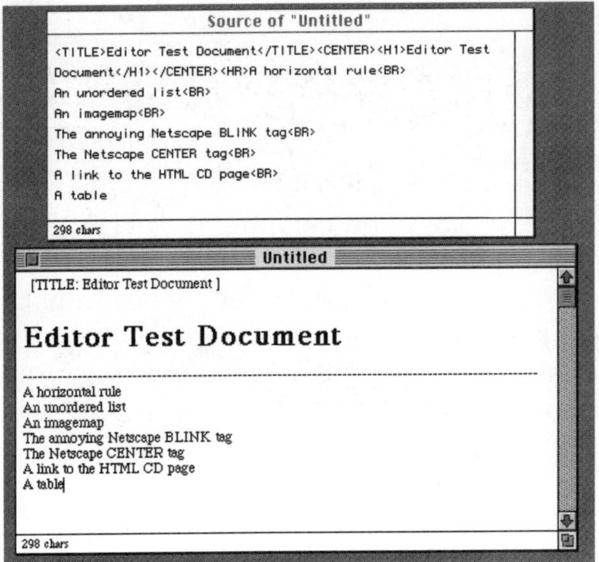

If you look in the source window, you can see that at this point our list items are separated by the <BR> tag. Next we choose the text that we wish to include in our list:

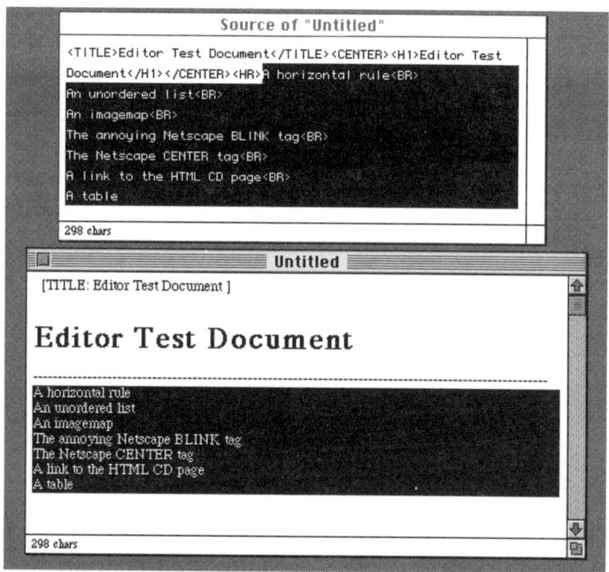

Finally, we choose Lists -> Unordered List from the Style menu. Our text is then converted into an unordered list:

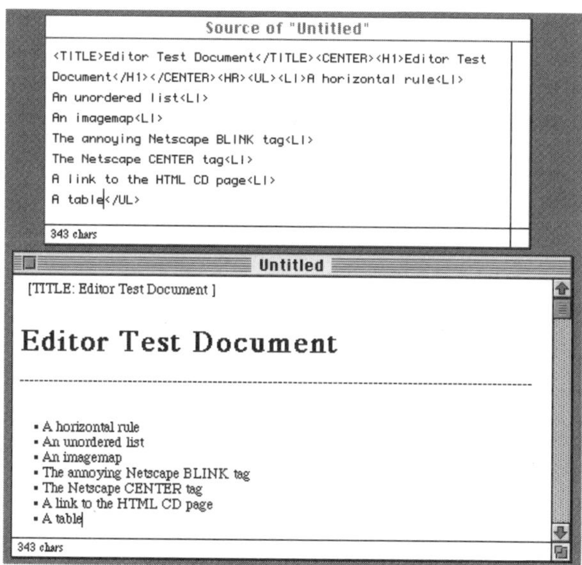

Adding Links

Now we need to go back and add a few tags to our list. We create a macro for BLINK and add it in the appropriate place. Next we need to add a link to the HTML CD document. To do this, we highlight the text that is to be linked, "HTML CD page," and choose Links -> Other Document from the Styles menu. We enter the reference for the link in the window that appears:

Now our document looks like this:

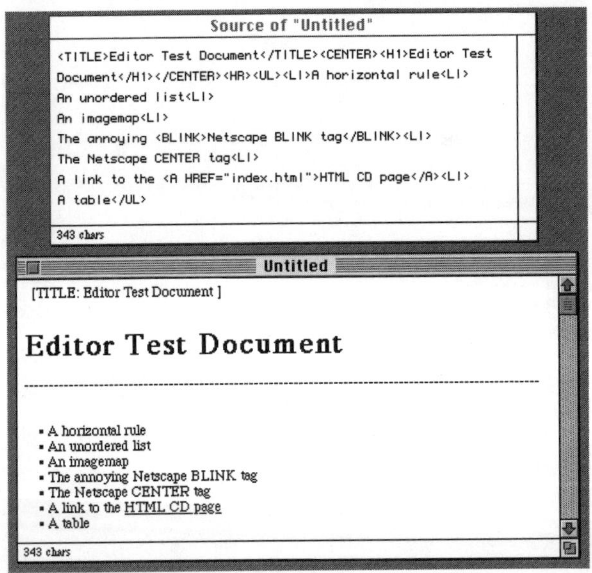

The linked text will show up in blue and underlined in the WYSIWYG window.

Adding Tables

HTML Pro does not have any table support, but thanks to macro definitions it is easy to create commands for the elements we wish to add to our table. We use the new macro command to define macros for Table, Caption, Table Heading, Table Cell, Table Cell (span 2). Note that we made separate macros for a regular table cell and the table cell that spans two columns. We then add our table to the document using these macros. Trying to use the WYSIWYG window to add the table occasionally resulted in tags ending up in the wrong places, so we used the document source window to add the table instead. In general, we found that tag placement with macros was more reliable in the document source window than in the WYSIWYG window.

Images and Image Maps

We end our document with a image map. We insert the image by choosing Links -> Image from the Styles menu and entering the appropriate information in the Image window:

Unfortunately there is no automated way to add an ISMAP attribute to the tag, so we simply go to the source window and add it ourselves. The next step is to link the image to the appropriate location. This is done in the same way as any other link, by choosing Links -> Other File from the Styles menu.

Previewing the Document

Now we are done with our document:

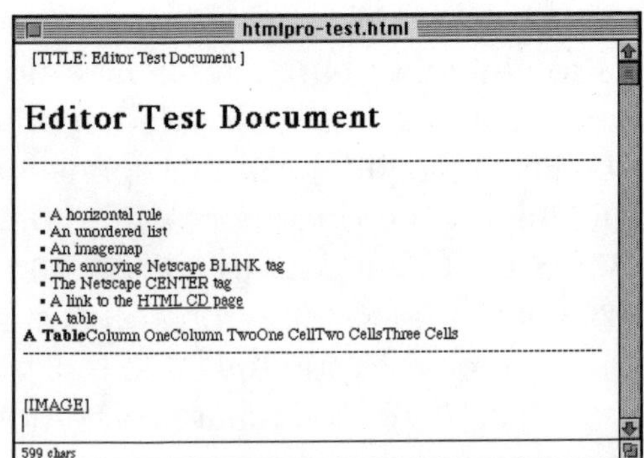

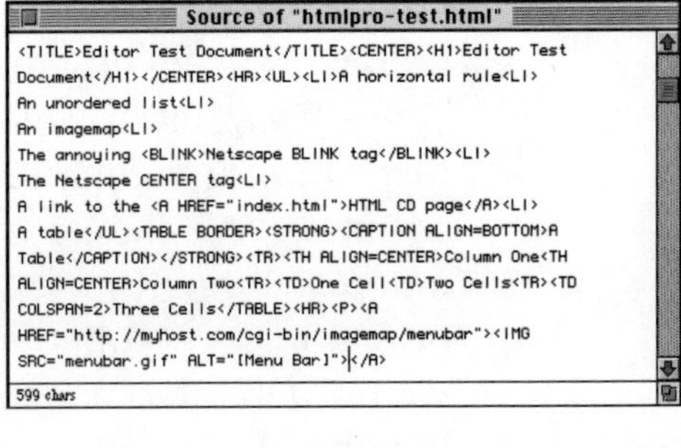

To check how the document looks in a browser, we first go to Preferences in the File menu, choose Helpers, and set a browser:

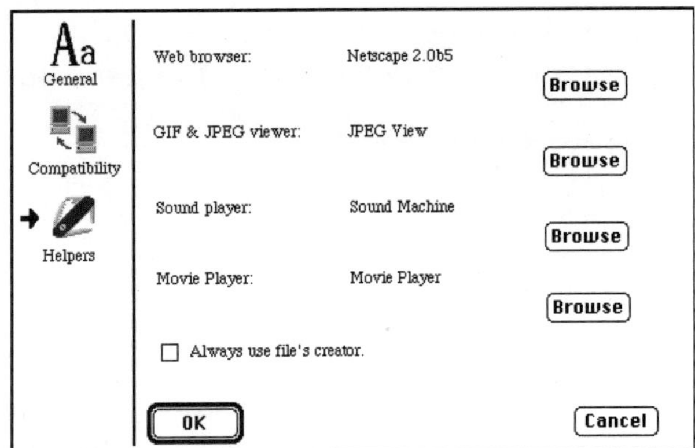

Then, to view the document, we choose Launch Browser under the View menu.

Pros and Cons

HTML Pro isn't perfect. It doesn't do any validation on the HTML, so you can tangle up your tags pretty badly. At times we found that it also placed tags in odd places, even though our cursor appeared to be in the correct location in the WYSIWYG window. It also has built-in support only for HTML 2. But even with these drawbacks, it is still a pretty nice editor. The dual window display makes it easy to see what is going on as you create your document. The ease with which macros can be defined compensates for the lack of built-in support for tags that are not in HTML 2. And finally, the price, $5, is tough to beat!

SiteWriter Pro

SiteWriter Pro is a hypercard-based shareware editor by Rik Jones. There is a $20 registration fee should you decide to use it on an extended basis. When you open the SiteWriter Pro folder, you should see something like this:

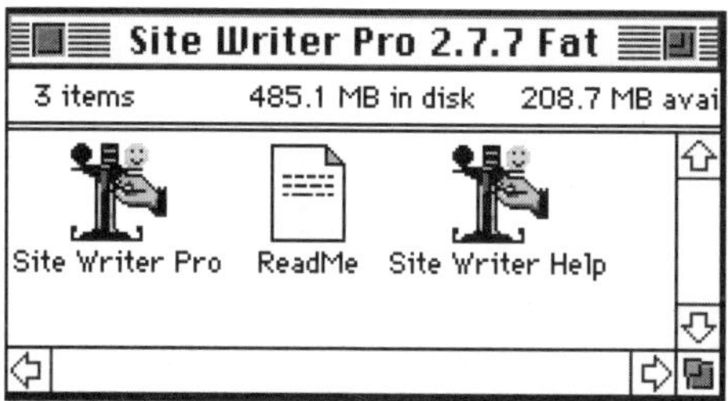

Getting Started

To start Site Writer, simply click on the Site Writer icon. A window that looks like this should appear:

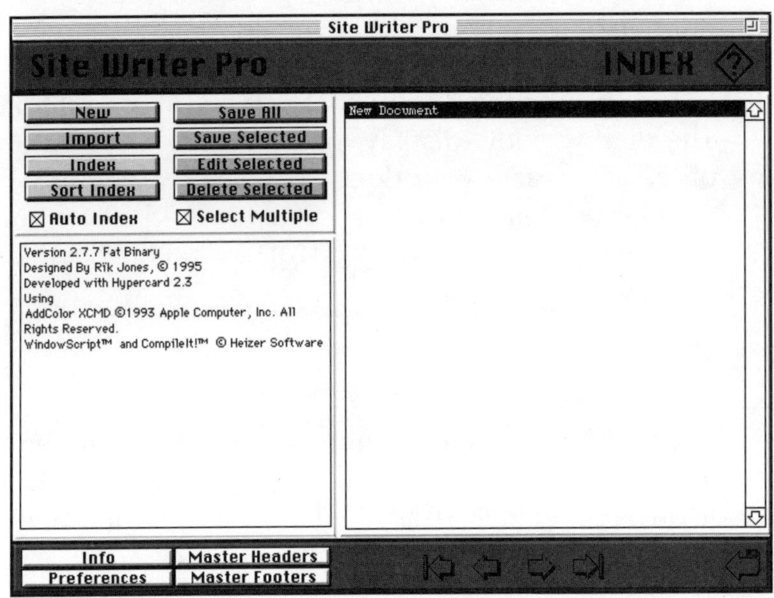

Site Writer provides a number of methods for you to enter commands. In addition to the main window, you can also enter commands from the menu bar:

File Edit Go Basics Anchor List Heading Form Format Palette

and from "Palettes." We'll explain more about Palettes later.

We start our document by clicking on the New button in the main Site Writer window and entering the filename we wish to use for our document. Note that you can also start the document by choosing "New" from the File menu. After getting the filename, Site Writer switches the main window to a document entry mode:

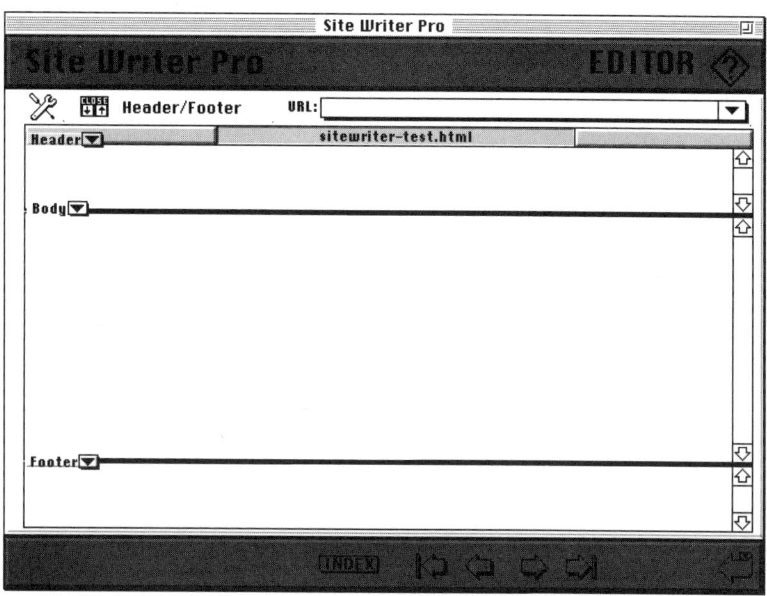

Entering a Title

Now we are ready to enter our title. We click on the arrow next to "Header" in the main window and choose "Title for HTML Document." A window for the title appears, and we enter our title:

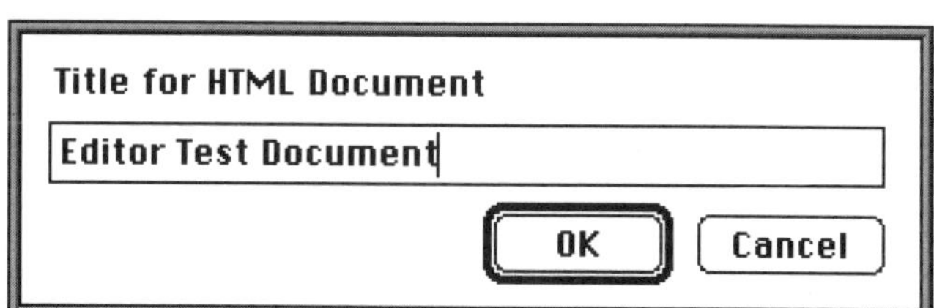

Headings, Paragraphs and Palettes

We enter our heading by choosing Heading 1 from the Heading menu. This adds the H1 tags to the document, and we simply type our text between the tags. The next elements in our

document are a horizontal rule and a paragraph. Rather than using one of the pulldown menus to add them, we decide to use a palette.

Palettes in Site Writer Pro are sets of buttons that allow you to insert tags for various HTML elements. There is a palette for each pulldown menu selection. You add a palette by going to the palette menu and choosing the palette that you want to display. You can put up as many or as few palettes as you wish. However, your screen can get fairly cluttered if you try to put all the palettes up at once. We recommend choosing a few with the tags that you use most frequently. In our case, we want to add a horizontal rule and a paragraph, so we choose the "HTML Basics" palette:

We add a horizontal rule simply by clicking on the Horizontal Rule button. The second Horizontal Rule button allows you to include some of the Netscape horizontal rule attributes such as SIZE and ALIGN.

There are two paragraph buttons on the HTML Basics palette. The first button simply adds a <P> tag at your insertion point. The second button allows you to use the container version of the P tag and to specify an alignment attribute. In our case we are using a plain P, so we simply click on the Paragraph button.

Creating a List

Next, we add an unordered list. To do this, we first type in our list elements separated by carriage returns. We then choose the section that we wish to convert into a list and pick the type of list we want from the List menu. Since we chose Unordered List, Site Writer Pro pops up a window to see which type of bullet we wish to use. After we choose, it converts each line in our selection into a list item and encloses the whole list in UL tags.

One of our list items includes the Netscape BLINK tag. To add it, we simply choose the text and then choose Blink from the Format menu.

Adding a Link

We also have a link to one of the items in our list. We choose the text and then choose HREF from the Anchor menu. It presents us with:

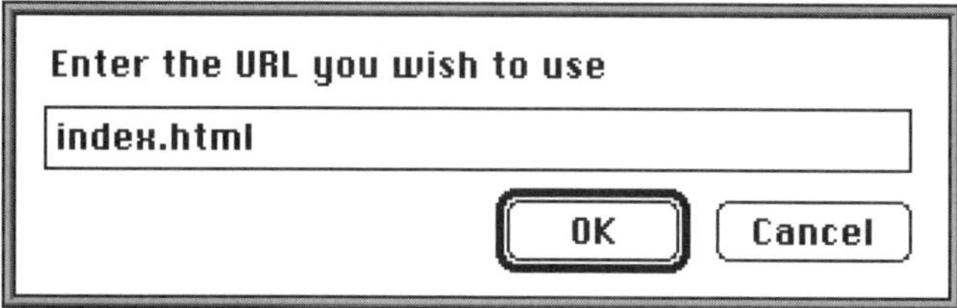

Since we are linking to a file in the same directory, we enter the name of the file rather than a fully qualified URL.

Tables

The next thing in our document is a table. As with our list, we first enter the text that we wish to include in the table, separating each element in the table by a carriage return:

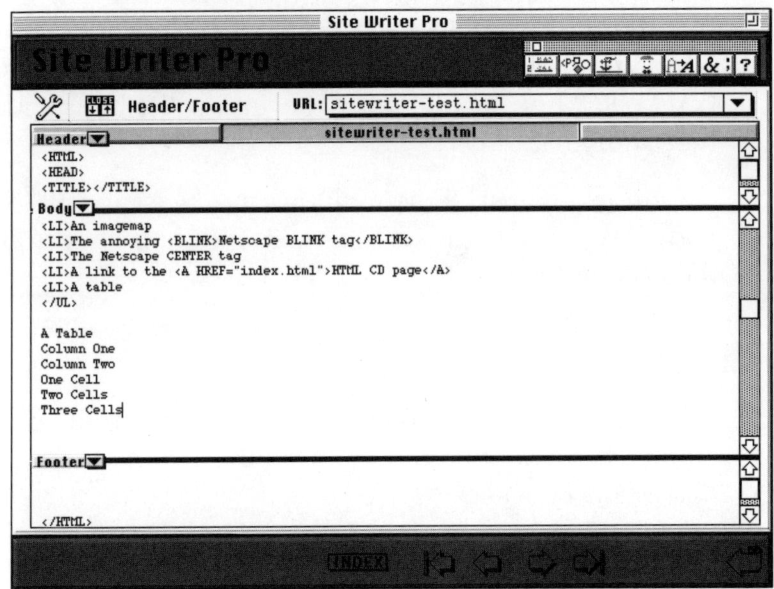

The next step is to add tags to our text. To do this, rather than repeatedly having to go to the pulldown menu, we decide to use the Table palette, so we go to the Palette menu and choose Table:

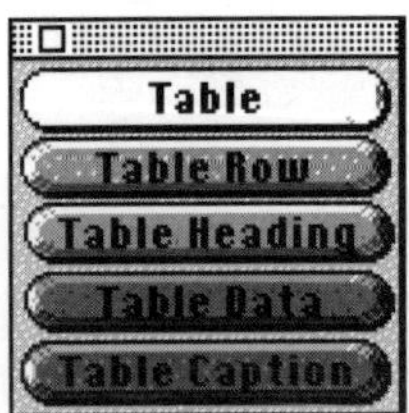

As we did when we created our list, we choose the text that we wish to tag and then click on the tag in the palette. We first add the table tag:

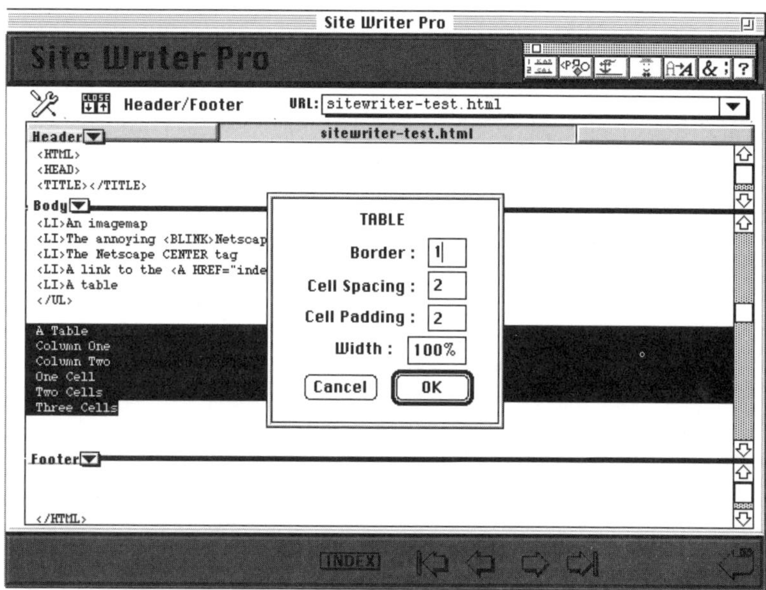

As you can see in this example, choosing the table tag causes a dialog box to appear that allows you to specify how you wish your table to look. If you do not wish to set any parameters, simply clear the boxes for the items that you do not wish to use. In our case, we do not use the Width parameter, so we clear it and then click OK.

We repeat this procedure for each element we wish to add to our table:

- Highlight the text that is to be tagged
- Click the appropriate tag in the palette

For example, the second row in our table spans two columns. We use the Table Data dialog box to specify this:

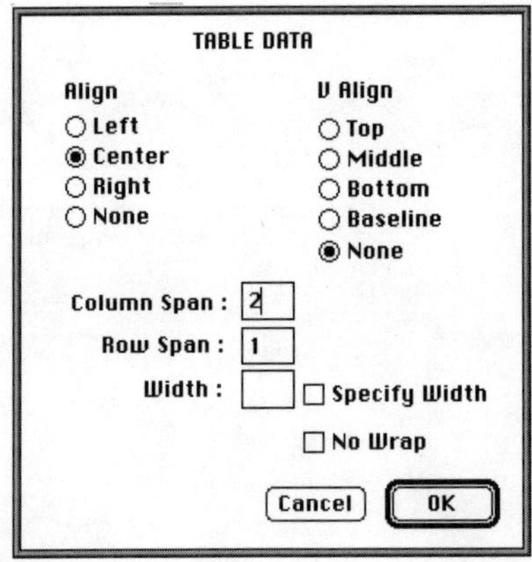

Images and Image Maps

The last element in our document is an image map. Site Writer makes it easy to enter image maps by providing a single dialog box for both the link reference and the image source. We open the dialog box by choosing Complex Image from the Basics menu:

Rather than having to add the image and then create a link to the map program, Site Writer uses the information from this box to create the link and the image tags in one step.

Testing Your Document

After finishing the document, we want to view it in a browser. Since Site Writer is not a WYSIWYG editor, this is an especially important step.

To do this, we first need to make an alias to our browser and place it in the same folder with our document. Although this is not strictly necessary, it make it much easier to use the browser check mode in Site Writer. Once the alias is in place, we choose "Test Document" from the File menu.

Pros and Cons

Site Writer Pro has built-in support for many Netscape extensions, HTML 3 enhancements as well as HTML 2. It provides multiple methods for entering tags—including pulldown menus, palettes with buttons for tags (and allows you to decide which sets of buttons will be displayed), and keyboard shortcuts. The dialog boxes appear when you choose a tag that has attributes, making it easy to select the attributes that you wish to use.

However, owing to its hypercard base, this editor is unable to create documents that are longer than 32K. It does no validation and is not WYSIWYG.

Webtor

Webtor was written by Jochen Schales as part of his Diploma Thesis. It is a free WYSIWYG editor and supports HTML 2. To use it, you will need a system with System 7.1 or higher and 4 megabytes of memory.

Webtor is probably not going to meet your needs if you plan to do extensive HTML work. However, it has a number of features that can help you to learn the basics of HTML while creating simple documents. Since; it validates HTML, the documents that it produces conform to the HTML 2 specification. We recommend it more as a learning tool than as a full-fledged HTML editor.

Starting Webtor

When you open the Webtor folder, you will see the application and a documentation folder:

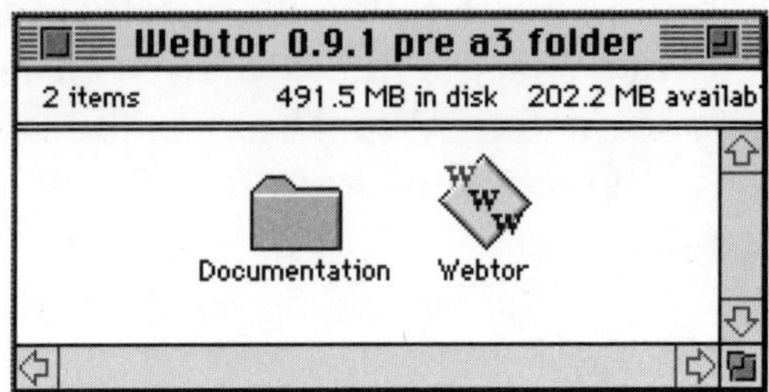

Click on the Webtor icon to start the application. It will start with a new document:

Titles and Headings

We start our document by entering the title. To do this, go to the Windows menu and choose Document Header. You should then see a window that looks something like this:

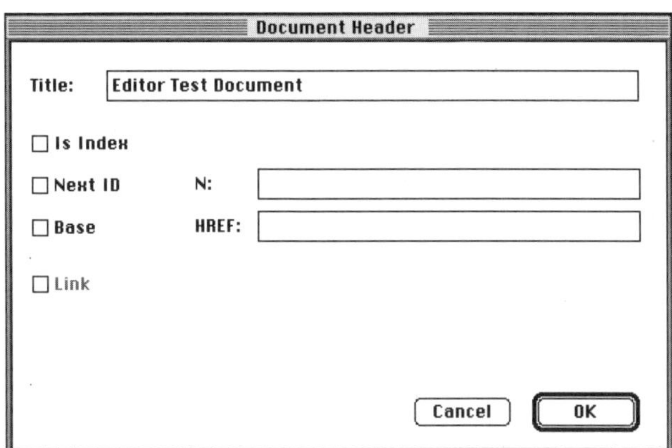

We're not doing anything fancy with the header of this document, so we simply enter the title in the Title box and click on OK. However, you may also use this box to add a number of additional options such as ISINDEX, BASE or NEXTID to your header.

Next, we wish to add a heading to our document, so we choose Headline 1 from the HTML Elements menu. Note that you can use a keyboard shortcut of <CLOVERLEAF>-1 to do this. This command is the equivalent of entering an H1 tag with an ASCII editor, but Webtor does it invisibly—only changing the font so that we can tell it is a heading:

We enter our heading. Now we run into our first problem. In our master document, we placed the heading in a CENTER tag. However, Webtor does not provide a way to enter the Netscape CENTER tags. If you try to type them in, Webtor will simply convert the angle brackets to their HTML special-character equivalents of < and >. So we skip the CENTER tag and move on to the next element, a horizontal rule. We add it by choosing horizontal rule from the HTML Elements menu.

The next element in our document is a paragraph. You can start new paragraphs either by choosing Paragraph from the HTML Element menu or by using the <CLOVER-LEAF><RETURN> shortcut. Do not try to start a paragraph by typing a plain <RETURN> as this will cause Webtor to insert a <BR> tag in your document.

Lists

An unordered list follows our paragraph. We start our list by choosing Unordered List from the HTML Elements menu. Webtor automatically inserts a list element as well when we do this, so we can start entering our list. Our next problem arises when we get to the list element that includes a BLINK tag. Since this tag is not part of HTML 2, there is no way to enter it. So far, our document looks like this in Webtor:

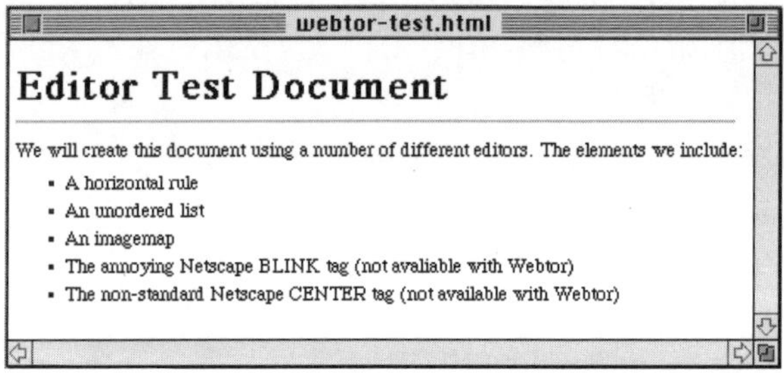

webtor-test.html
Editor Test Document
We will create this document using a number of different editors. The elements we include:
A horizontal rule
An unordered list
An imagemap
The annoying Netscape BLINK tag (not avaliable with Webtor)
The non-standard Netscape CENTER tag (not available with Webtor)

Links

The next element in our list includes a link. To enter a link in Webtor, we choose Inlines->Anchor from the HTML Elements menu. When we enter text after making this choice, it is displayed underlined and in blue to indicate that it is in an anchor element. To enter the link references we must first save the file (it will not work correctly if you skip this step). Then we place the cursor in our anchor text and double-click while holding down the option key. The following window then appears:

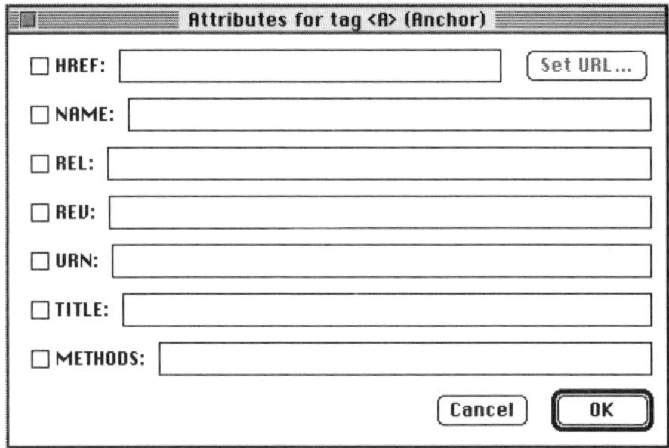

We check the HREF box, enter the URL for our link, and click OK.

Now we're done with our list. The next element in our document was supposed to be a table, but Webtor does not have table support, so we skip it. We enter another horizontal rule.

Images and Image Maps

A clickable image is the next item in our list.To create a clickable image, an image with an ISMAP attribute is placed in an anchor tag. We start the anchor tag just as we did in our previous example. Next, we add our image by choosing

Images from the HTML Elements menu. Webtor inserts a little picture with a "?" in it to indicate that an image is to be placed in this location:

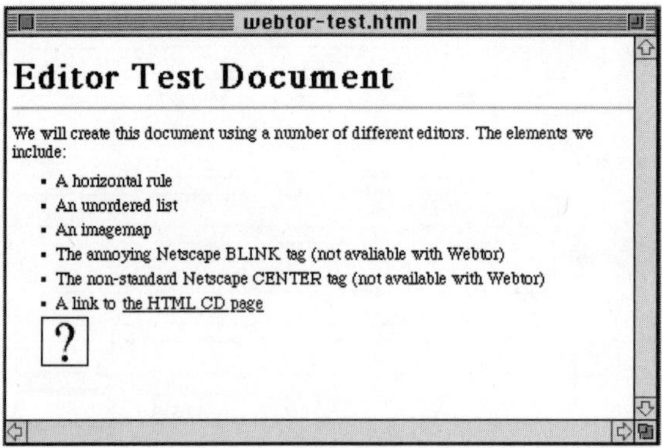

webtor-test.html
Editor Test Document
We will create this document using a number of different editors. The elements we include:
A horizontal rule
An unordered list
An imagemap
The annoying Netscape BLINK tag (not avaliable with Webtor)
The non-standard Netscape CENTER tag (not available with Webtor)
A link to the HTML CD page
?

To enter the information for the image, doubleclick on it while holding down the option key. Webtor should then display a window that looks like this:

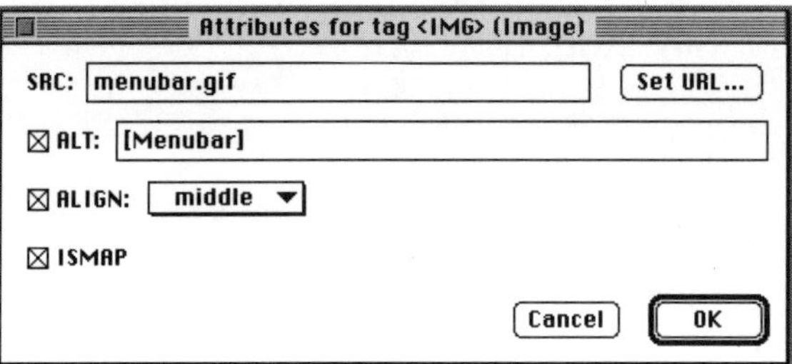

We still need to enter the information for the link, but unfortunately we discovered that double-clicking with option on displayed only the image tag window regardless of where we placed the cursor.

Finally, we tell Webtor to display our document in Netscape by choosing "Test Document" from the Extras menu:

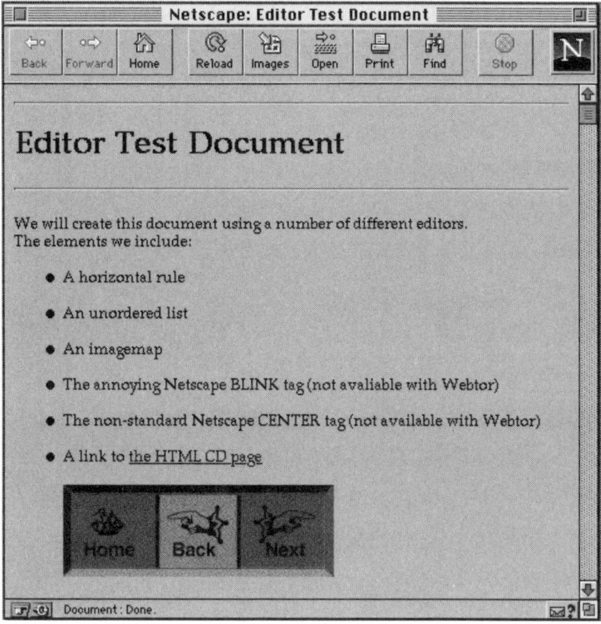

Webtor Features

Webtor has two additional information windows that can help you to learn HTML. Choosing "Document Structure" from the Windows menu displays a window with an outline of the document:

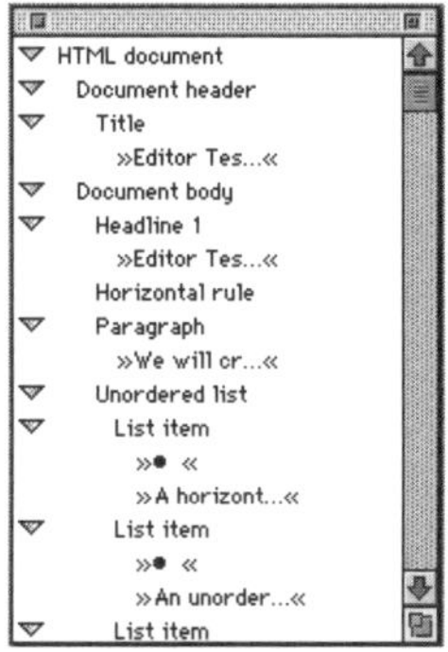

while "Inspector" shows a list of the tags in use:

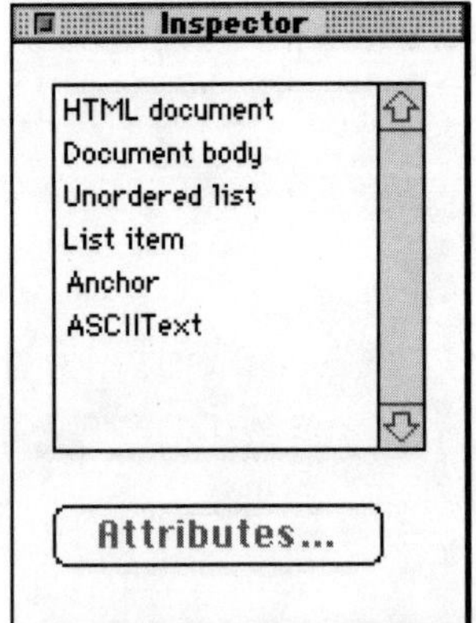

You can also view the document source itself by choosing "View Source" from the Extras menu. This will cause the document to be displayed in SimpleText (or whatever editor you specified in the Preferences window).

Pros and Cons

There are many good things about Webtor:

- Free.
- WYSIWYG.
- HTML syntax checking.
- Setting of local links via a file selector box.
- Previewing of inline images.

Unfortunately it has problems too:

- No support for Netscape or HTML elements (including forms and tables).
- No way to enter HTML tags directly (so there is no way to enter forms and tables) with this editor.

- Has occasional problems importing HTML 2-compliant documents.
- Tries to be overly WYSIWYG by entering <BR> tags in inappropriate places in the document source.

As we mentioned at the beginning of the section on Webtor, it is a good tool for learning to write HTML documents that conform to the HTML standard. However, as your skills develop you are likely to find that the very thing that makes it a good training aid—its validation of HTML code—is too limiting for regular use.

Alpha

Alpha is a a shareware editor by Pete Kelher. It has an HTML mode that was created by Scott Brim. We like Alpha because it is much more than a plain HTML editor. It includes modes for many different types of environments. If you are a programmer, you will probably find other uses for Alpha in addition to its HTML abilities.

Getting Started

To install Alpha, drag the folder to the location on your hard disk where you wish to keep it. When you open the Alpha folder you will see something like this:

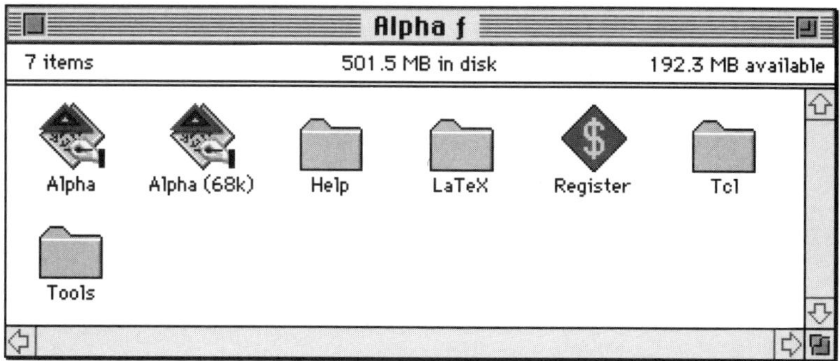

To start Alpha click on either the Alpha or Alpha (68k) icon depending on the type of Mac you are using. After Alpha starts, your screen will look something like this:

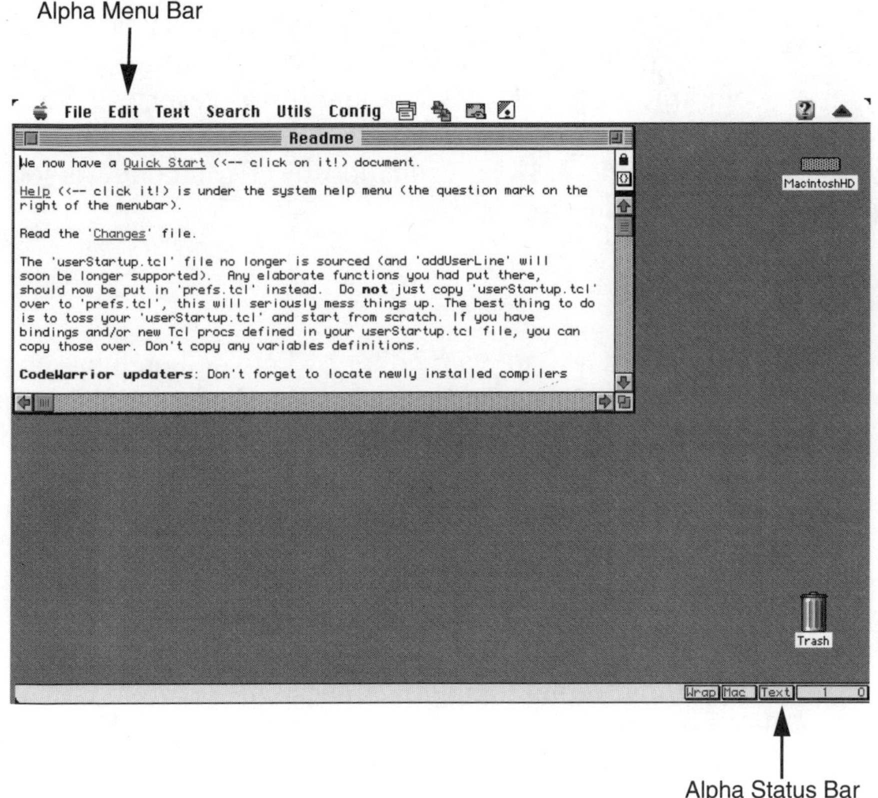

To start a new file, choose "New" from the File menu. An "Untitled "window should then open. Next, you will need to switch Alpha into HTML mode. At the bottom of your screen (note that we mean, screen, not window here!) you should see a status bar. One of the buttons on the right side of the status bar should show "Text". When you push this button, a pop-up menu of the various modes that Alpha supports should appear. Choose HTML. Now you should see something like this:

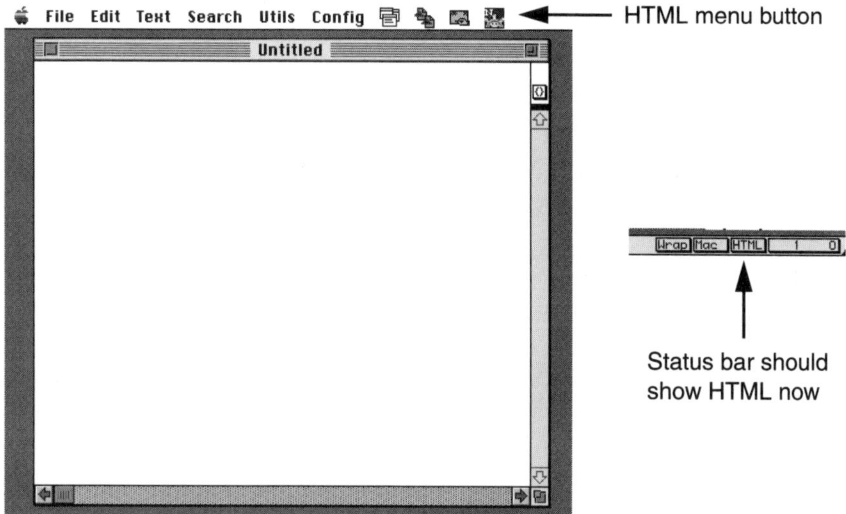

Notice that there is a new icon in the menu bar, which should look like the icon for a browser. When you click on this icon, you will see the menu for the HTML commands that Alpha supports.

The first thing you should do is to have Alpha set up your document template. Choose "New doc template" from the HTML menu, or use the keyboard shortcut: control-option-0 (zero, not "oh").

Title, Headings and Paragraphs

When you tell Alpha to create your document template, it includes TITLE tags in addition to the basic HEAD, BODY and HTML tags. The cursor is placed in the appropriate position to enter the title:

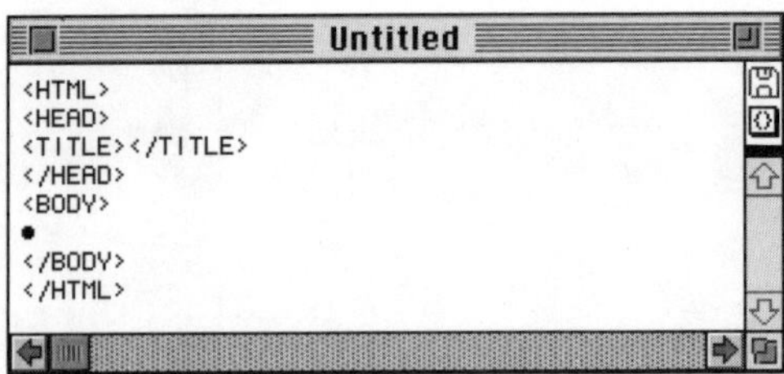

We enter our document title and then type a tab to get to the next location. Alpha places a marker at the next location where it expects a tag to be entered. You can see the marker as a "•". To enter our heading, we tab to the bullet and then choose Headers->Header1 from the HTML menu. After entering our heading, we want to place it in a CENTER tag, so we highlight it and then choose Text Blocks->Center.

We enter our introductory paragraph by choosing Text Blocks->paragraph followed by the text of the paragraph. There is also a keyboard shortcut for paragraph: <ctrl-option-return>.

Creating a List

We set our list up by choosing Lists->bulleted from the HTML menu. We enter our first list element and then tab over to the next spot. We could use the menu to enter each list item by choosing Lists->new list entry but found it simpler to use the keyboard shortcut of <ctrl-option-n>.

Tables and Setting Attributes

The next element in our document is a table. We start our table by choosing Tables->table, which causes Alpha to ask if we want to use the border attribute with our table.

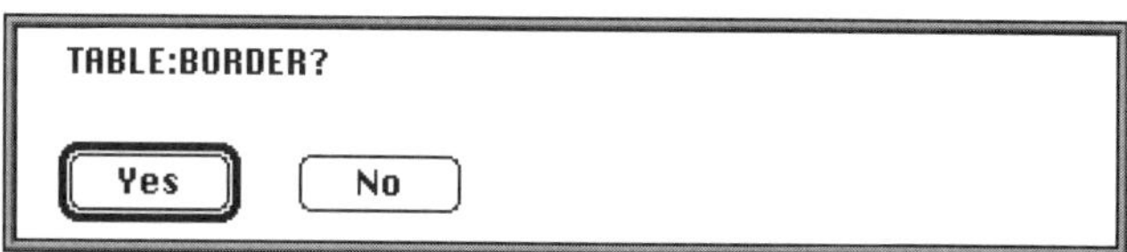

You will probably find it annoying to have Alpha ask this if you make lots of tables that do not include borders. Fortunately, it is easy to choose which attributes you wish to have Alpha ask you about. To do this, choose Use Attributes followed by the tag that you wish to customize. For example, here is what you get if you choose tables:

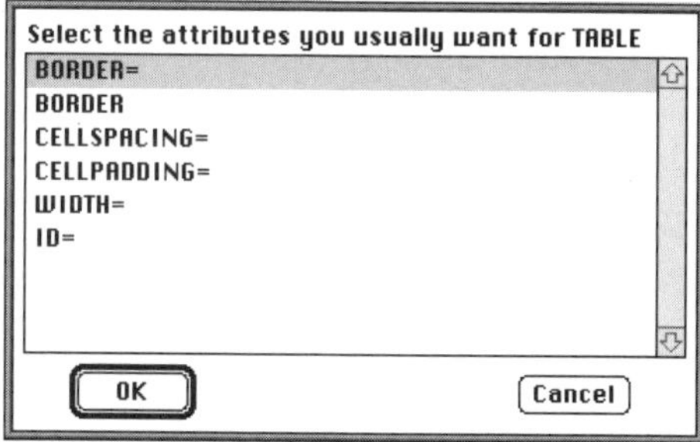

Choose the attributes that you want by clicking on them while holding down your shift key.

The next element in our table is a caption. We start our caption by choosing Tables -> caption. Alpha asks where we would like to place our caption:

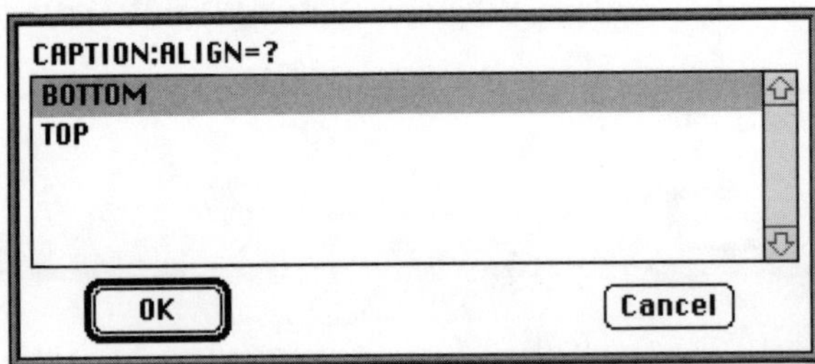

We enter our table heading and table rows in a similar fashion—choose the element to be entered from Table, and select the attributes and their settings.

Images and Image Maps

The last element in our document is an image map. We first enter the image by choosing Links->image. This will cause a number of dialog boxes to appear. Remember that you can customize the boxes that show up through Use Attributes ->IMG. We chose SRC, ALT and ISMAP which include the following boxes:

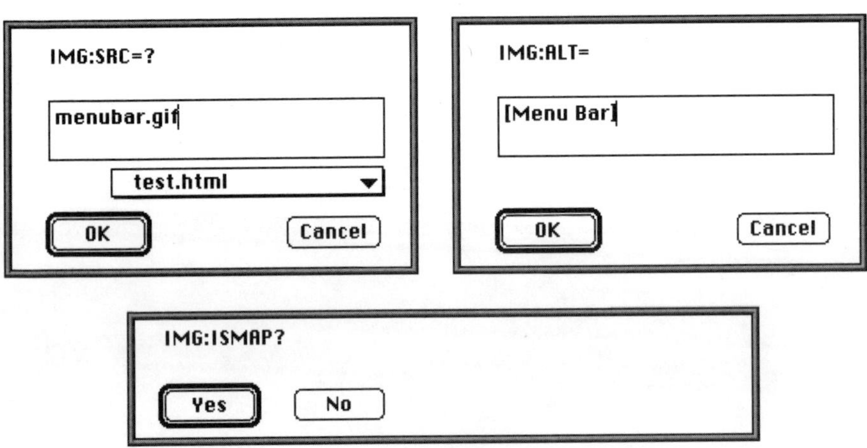

Once our image has been entered, we need to link it to the image map. We do this by choosing the image in the HTML document and then adding an anchor tag through Links->HREF. This allows us to enter the path to our image map:

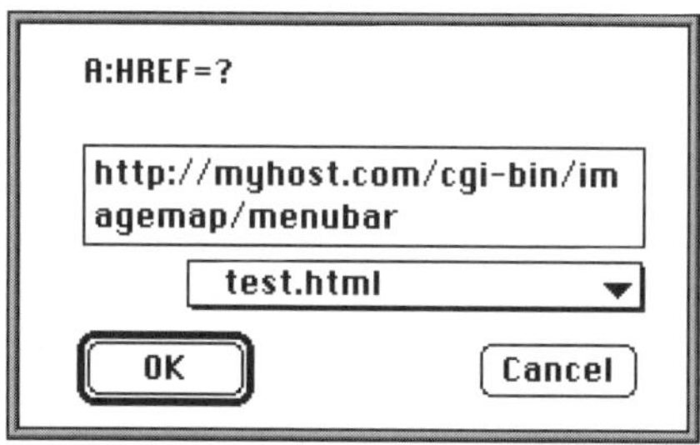

Viewing the Document in a Browser

Now our document is done:

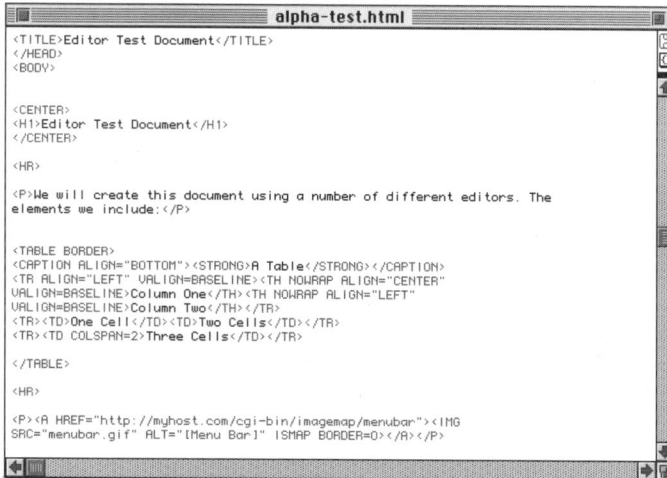

alpha-test.html

```
<TITLE>Editor Test Document</TITLE>
</HEAD>
<BODY>


<CENTER>
<H1>Editor Test Document</H1>
</CENTER>

<HR>

<P>We will create this document using a number of different editors. The
elements we include:</P>


<TABLE BORDER>
<CAPTION ALIGN="BOTTOM"><STRONG>A Table</STRONG></CAPTION>
<TR ALIGN="LEFT" VALIGN=BASELINE><TH NOWRAP ALIGN="CENTER"
VALIGN=BASELINE>Column One</TH><TH NOWRAP ALIGN="LEFT"
VALIGN=BASELINE>Column Two</TH></TR>
<TR><TD>One Cell</TD><TD>Two Cells</TD></TR>
<TR><TD COLSPAN=2>Three Cells</TD></TR>

</TABLE>

<HR>

<P><A HREF="http://myhost.com/cgi-bin/imagemap/menubar"><IMG
SRC="menubar.gif" ALT="[Menu Bar]" ISMAP BORDER=0></A></P>
```

We wish to see how it would look in a browser. To do this we must first configure Alpha with the location of browser we wish to use. This is done through Config->App Paths->Web Browser. A dialog box will appear:

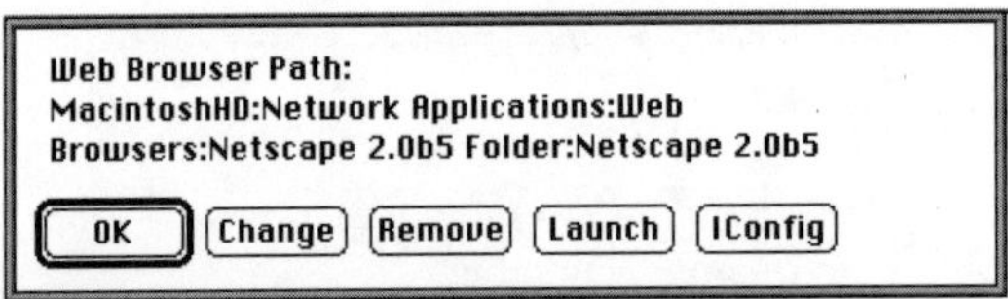

To set a new browser, click the Change button and then enter the path to the browser that you wish to use. Then click OK to enter it in Alpha's configuration file. Once the browser is set, you can easily send your document to it for review by choosing "HTML Helpers -> send to browser" or by using the shortcut key: <cloverleaf-s>. Here is our test document:

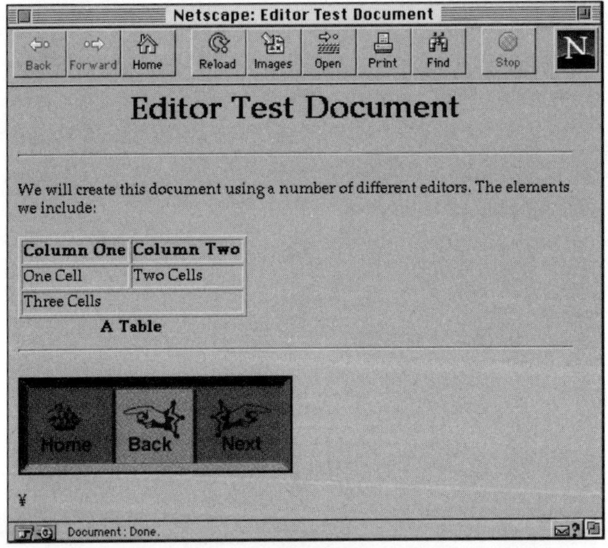

Notice the odd character at the bottom of the document? This is the marker that Alpha places where it expects the next tag to be entered (so that it knows where to go when you hit the tab key). When you are done with your document, you should remove any remaining markers by choosing "Remove marks" or <cloverleaf-tab>.

Pros and Cons

Alpha is a programmer's editor that has been extended to support HTML. As a result it has many powerful features that are not available in the HTML-only editors we included on the CD. On the down side, it doesn't have a fancy button interface or a WYSIWYG display.

Other Editors

If you haven't been able to find an editor on the CD that meets your needs, you can find more references on the mac-htmleditors.html document. This document also includes links to commercial HTML editors such as Adobe's Pagemill.

Converters

Converters take text in one format and translate it into another. For example, if you have a set of documents in Microsoft Word that you wish to offer on the Web, you could use a converter to translate your documents into HTML.

On the CD you will find two text-to-HTML converters, and one HTML-to-plain-text converter. One of the markup packages, TextToHTML can also convert documents in Rich Text Format (RTF) into HTML as well. All of the converters can be found in the HTML Converter folder on the CD:

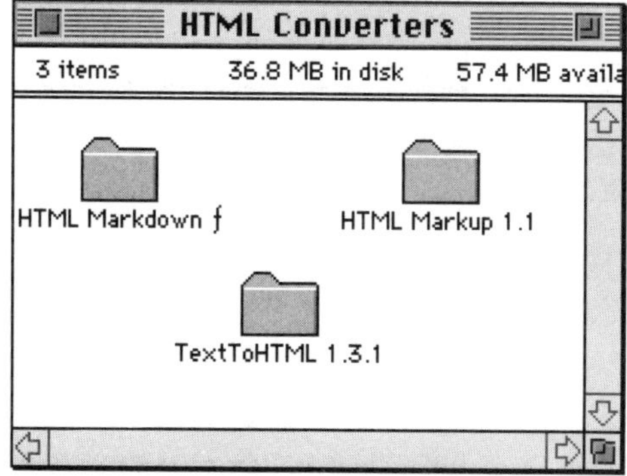

HTML Markdown and HTML Markup by Scott Kleper are shareware packages that can be used to add (HTML Markup) or remove (HTML Markdown) HTML tags to your documents. TextToHTML is a freeware converter that can convert both plain text files and RTF into HTML. Its ability to convert RTF files is particularly handy, since many word processing packages (most notably Microsoft Word) are able to output documents in this format. All three of these packages come with complete on-line documentation.

If you do not want to use HTML Markdown to remove the HTML tags in your documents, there is another fairly simple way to do this. Some browsers, including Netscape and NCSA Mosaic, allow you to save documents in a number of formats. All you have to do to get a plain-text version of your HTML document is to load it into one such browser and then save it as plain text.

HTML Grinder

The last tool we describe in this chapter is HTML Grinder by Michael Herrick of Matterform Media. Grinder is a shareware package that provides many useful maintenance tools for HTML documents. As the number of HTML documents that you author grows, performing basic maintenance tasks (such as updating address information) becomes more and more difficult.

HTML Grinder automates many of the tasks that you may wish to perform on all of your documents. All you have to do is to choose the documents that you wish to update, and drag and drop them on Grinder.

Some of the functions available with Grinder include:

- *Find and replace* words or phrases in one or multiple documents.
- *Glossary.* This is a multiple find and replace function. It allows you to build lists of phrases and replacements for them. You can then use it to replace occurrences of all of the phrases in one pass.

- *Replacing Tagged Text.* This allows you to specify a starting and ending tag. The text between the tags is replaced with whatever new text you specify.
- *Appender.* Appender allows you to insert text and specified locations in your documents, such as at the beginning, end, and before or after text. This is very useful for adding copyright or contact information to a set of documents.
- *Index Builder.* This function will go through a set of HTML documents and build an alphabetical table-of-contents document that includes the title of each document linked to the document itself.
- *Date Stamp.* This adds a "last-modified" stamp to the document. It uses the system modification date for the document to create this stamp.
- *Insert Image Size.* As you may recall, Netscape allows you to include an image-size reference in your IMG tags that helps the browser to display your document more quickly. However, it is painful to do this if you have many images since you have to remember (or find) the size of the image. This function finds and adds the size in one simple pass over your documents.

These are just some of the functions available with Grinder. You will find a complete list in the on-line documentation included in the Grinder folder:

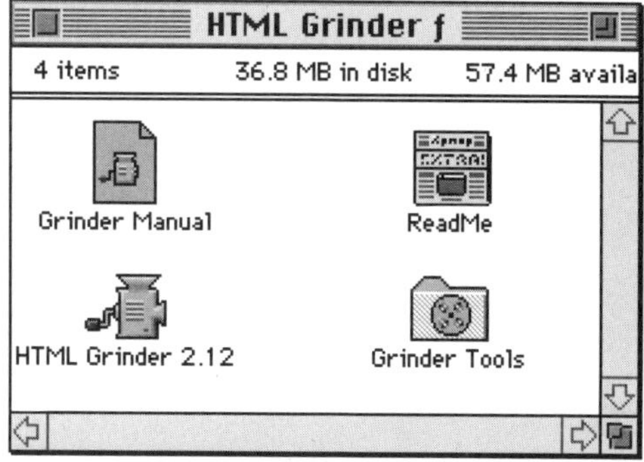

Each of these functions is contained in what Grinder calls a "wheel." You can use any of the functions for 30 days. The basic search-and-replace function is free. If you decide that you want to continue to use any of the other functions, you must register that function—if you don't, it will cease to work.

We think you will find Grinder an invaluable aid in building and maintaining your HTML documents.

IN THIS CHAPTER YOU WILL LEARN

- HOW TO GET PEOPLE TO VISIT YOUR SITE
- WHERE TO GO FOR MORE HELP

PUBLICIZING YOUR WEB PAGES

What's In This Chapter

Once you have finished authoring documents for your Web site, you naturally want to encourage people to visit them. This chapter provides some ideas to help you to get people to visit your pages.

HTML is constantly changing. We've done our best to explain how things work at the time this book was written. However, there are a number of places on the Internet that you can go for more help. Toward this end we've listed a number of HTML-related mailing lists and newsgroups at the end of this chapter. Finally, we provide the URL for this book's Web page.

Generating Traffic

Once you are done setting up your piece of the Web you will undoubtedly want people to visit. The best method for encouraging people to visit your Web pages depends, of course, on their contents. Before announcing new pages, consider who the best and most appropriate audience might be. Don't announce your pages in an unsolicited way to groups and people who haven't requested the information because, just like unsolicited advertising, you are likely to quickly antagonize them. With this caveat in mind, we mention here some of the most common means for announcing new Web pages and sites.

Personal Home Pages

For personal pages, people are increasingly including the URLs of their home pages in their "signatures" attached to electronic mail. In addition, many people are listing their URLs on their business cards.

Announcing to Newsgroups

A common approach is to advertise your new Web pages in a relevant USENET newsgroup or mailing list. If you choose to do this, you must make sure that the group or list you target is appropriate and that your announcement is directly related to it. Otherwise, your announcement might be treated as "spam," and you risk receiving angry complaints.

In addition, there is a moderated newsgroup for announcing generally interesting and useful Web sites, called comp.infosystems.announce. Before submitting to this group, please read the charter posting and several of the group's postings to get an idea of what is considered appropriate.

Announcing to the Web

Naturally, you can use the Web to announce your new pages or Web server. You can submit your URL to the "What's New Page" at NCSA:

```
http://www.ncsa.uiuc.edu/SDG/Software/Mosaic/Docs/whats-new.html
```

This page will provide you with information on how to send in your listing. However, because of the Web's popularity, it might be a while before your submission appears.

You can also register your pages with sites that are building Web catalogs. These sites collect submitted URLs (and also search the Web itself) in order to generate catalogs of Web documents. These catalogs can then be searched by Web users in order to find documents of interest.

There are many such catalogs, and we provide only the URLs of a few of them here. You can use the listed URLs in order to access the site of each of these catalogs. This will enable you to both search their databases and submit the URLs of your Web pages for inclusion in the catalogs.

The Lycos Database

```
http://www.lycos.com/
```

Yahoo

```
http://www.yahoo.com
```

WWW Virtual Library

```
http://info.cern.ch/hypertext/DataSources/bySubject/Overview.
html
```

EINet Galaxy

```
http://www.einet.net/
```

ALIWEB index

```
http://web.nexor.co.uk/aliweb/doc/aliweb.html
```

Submit It!

http://www.cen.uiuc.edu/~banister/submit-it/

This is actually a form that allows you to submit an announcement to many indices at one time.

Australia Announce Archive (AAA)

http://www.com.au/aaa/

Announcing a Server

If you are adding a server rather than just a single page or set of pages, you can also register in the WWW list of servers maintained by the World Wide Web Consortium. The URL for this resource is:

http://www.w3.org/hypertext/DataSources/WWW/Geographical_generation/new-servers.html

Making an Even Bigger Splash

So far, we've described only standard Internet locations for announcing Web pages. However, the Web is attracting a wider audience every day. If you're developing pages that you wish the general public to visit—for example, if you're developing an on-line store—you'll need to advertise your site in other ways. Depending on the audience you want to reach, and your advertising budget, here are some places you should consider including your URL:

- Business cards
- Print advertisements
- Radio and television advertisements
- Billboards

Many popular Web sites take advertisements in the form of a banner with a link to the advertised site that pops up before displaying the rest of their pages. Placing an advertisement on one of these sites (such as Yahoo) is a good way to increase the traffic to your site.

Places To Go For More Help

We've presented some ideas on ways to get people to visit your site. If you're interested in getting more help in this area, or simply want to find other people with similar interests, there are a number of Internet e-mail lists that address this topic:

Resources for All Levels

HTML Writer's Guild

URL: http://www.mindspring.com/guild/

The Charter of the HTML Writers Guild: To build awareness within and beyond the Internet community of Web page authoring and related services as a skilled pursuit; to assist members in developing and enhancing their capabilities; to communicate to prospective users of Web services what they should expect from a Guild member and demand from others offering these services; and to contribute to the development of the Web and Web technical standards and guidelines.

Intermediate Level Resources

The resources listed in this section require familiarity with HTML. If you have gone through this book you should be able to participate in the forums listed in this section. First we list a number of e-mail lists.

List Name: web-support@mailbase.ac.uk

Subscription Address: mailbase@mailbase.ac.uk

Subscription Instructions: Send a message to the subscription address with:

`JOIN web-support` *FirstName LastName*

in the body of the message.

Description: This list is based in the United Kingdom and has a European orientation.

List Name: Internet Marketing Discussion list

Subscription Address: IM-SUB@I-M.COM

Subscription Instructions: Send a message to the subscription address with anything (or nothing) in the body of the message.

Description: This list is devoted to the discussion of marketing goods and services in an appropriate way on the Internet. You can find more information at http://www.i-m.com/.

Advanced Resources

List Name: ADV-HTML

Subscription address: LISTSERV@UA1VM.UA.EDU

Subscription Instructions: Send a message to the subscription address with:

`SUBSCRIBE ADV-HTML` *FirstName LastName*

in the body of the message.

Description: A moderated discussion list for the discussion of both advanced hypertext markup language and other advanced Web topics.

List Name: WWW-MANAGERS

Subscription Address: majordomo@lists.stanford.edu

Subscription Instructions: Send a message to the subscription address with:

```
sub www-managers
```

in the body of the message.

Description: This list is for managers of WWW servers and sites to get answers to specific questions about the setup and maintenance of HTTP servers and clients. It is not for discussions—answers are to be mailed back to the person who asked the question, who then has responsibility for summarizing the relevant answers and posting back to the mailing list.

The Latest Book News

You can find the Web page for this book at:

```
http://catalog.com/vivian/machtml.html
```

We'll put up errata sheets there as well as a list of sites that used this book to get started. If you've found this book instrumental in getting your site up and would like to be listed, drop us a line (you'll find a link on the book's page) with the URL for your site. While we can't promise to list everyone, we'll try to put up links to our favorite sites.

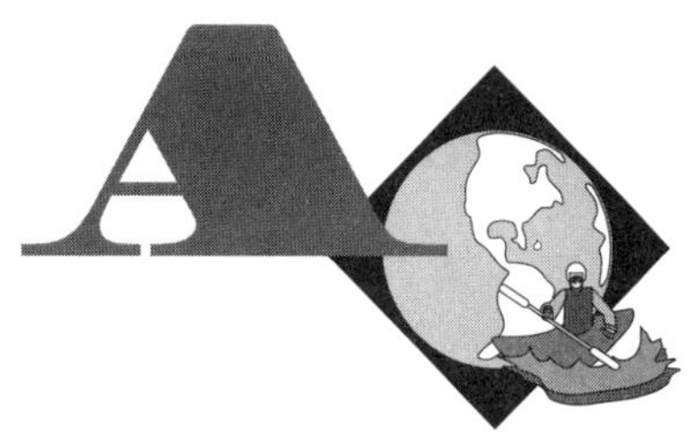

ISO Latin 1 Entities in HTML

HTML Tag	Character	Description
Æ	Æ	capital AE diphthong (ligature)
Á	Á	capital A, acute accent
Â	Â	capital A, circumflex accent
À	À	capital A, grave accent
Å	Å	capital A, ring
Ã	Ã	capital A, tilde
Ä	Ä	capital A, dieresis or umlaut mark
Ç	Ç	capital C, cedilla
Ð	Ð	capital Eth, Icelandic
É	É	capital E, acute accent

HTML Tag	Character	Description
Ê	Ê	capital E, circumflex accent
È	È	capital E, grave accent
Ë	Ë	capital E, dieresis or umlaut mark
Í	Í	capital I, acute accent
Î	Î	capital I, circumflex accent
Ì	Ì	capital I, grave accent
Ï	Ï	capital I, dieresis or umlaut mark
Ñ	Ñ	capital N, tilde
Ó	Ó	capital O, acute accent
Ô	Ô	capital O, circumflex accent
Ò	Ò	capital O, grave accent
Ø	Ø	capital O, slash
Õ	Õ	capital O, tilde
Ö	Ö	capital O, dieresis or umlaut mark
Þ	Þ	capital THORN, Icelandic
Ú	Ú	capital U, acute accent
Û	Û	capital U, circumflex accent
Ù	Ù	capital U, grave accent
Ü	Ü	capital U, dieresis or umlaut mark
Ý	Ý	capital Y, acute accent
á	á	small a, acute accent
â	â	small a, circumflex accent
æ	æ	small ae diphthong (ligature)
à	à	small a, grave accent
å	å	small a, ring
ã	ã	small a, tilde
ä	ä	small a, dieresis or umlaut mark
ç	ç	small c, cedilla
é	é	small e, acute accent

HTML Tag	Character	Description
ê	ê	small e, circumflex accent
è	è	small e, grave accent
ð	ð	small eth, Icelandic
ë	ë	small e, dieresis or umlaut mark
í	í	small i, acute accent
î	î	small i, circumflex accent
ì	ì	small i, grave accent
ï	ï	small i, dieresis or umlaut mark
ñ	ñ	small n, tilde
ó	ó	small o, acute accent
ô	ô	small o, circumflex accent
ò	ò	small o, grave accent
ø	ø	small o, slash
õ	õ	small o, tilde
ö	ö	small o, dieresis or umlaut mark
ß	ß	small sharp s, German (sz ligature)
þ	þ	small thorn, Icelandic
ú	ú	small u, acute accent
û	û	small u, circumflex accent
ù	ù	small u, grave accent
ü	ü	small u, dieresis or umlaut mark
ý	ý	small y, acute accent
ÿ	ÿ	small y, dieresis or umlaut mark

ASCII Table

00	nul	16	syn	2c	,	42	B	58	X	6e	n
01	soh	17	etb	2d	-	43	C	59	Y	6f	o
02	stx	18	can	2e	.	44	D	5a	Z	70	p
03	etx	19	em	2f	/	45	E	5b	[	71	q
04	eot	1a	sub	30	0	46	F	5c	\	72	r
05	enq	1b	esc	31	1	47	G	5d	]	73	s
06	ack	1c	fs	32	2	48	H	5e	^	74	t
07	bel	1d	gs	33	3	49	I	5f	_	75	u
08	bs	1e	rs	34	4	4a	J	60	‘	76	v
09	ht	1f	us	35	5	4b	K	61	a	77	w
0a	nl	20	sp	36	6	4c	L	62	b	78	x
0b	vt	21	!	37	7	4d	M	63	c	79	y
0c	np	22	“	38	8	4e	N	64	d	7a	z
0d	cr	23	#	39	9	4f	O	65	e	7b	{
0e	so	24	$	3a	:	50	P	66	f	7c	|
0f	si	25	%	3b	;	51	Q	67	g	7d	}
10	dle	26	&	3c	<	52	R	68	h	7e	~
11	dc1	27	‘	3d	=	53	S	69	i	7f	del
12	dc2	28	(	3e	>	54	T	6a	j		
13	dc3	29	)	3f	?	55	U	6b	k		
14	dc4	2a	*	40	@	56	V	6c	l		
15	nak	2b	+	41	A	57	W	6d	m		

JavaScript Summary

Netscape's JavaScript is an object-based scripting language that can be embedded in HTML documents. As an object-based language, JavaScript contains *objects* in a hierarchy that is based on the structure of the HTML page. These objects have properties and associated methods. In addition, scripts can be run in response to events triggered by the user.

This appendix describes the most useful built-in JavaScript objects, together with their properties, their methods, and event handlers. Remember, this is not an exhaustive list. In addition, JavaScript development is in its infancy, so language specifications are likely to change.

Using the Tables

The tables that follow contain the most useful JavaScript objects. Each object is listed with the properties, methods and event-handlers that may be used with that particular object. To determine what a particular property, method or event handler does, simply check the table in the appropriate section.

Remember that unlike HTML, JavaScript is case sensitive, so you must use the correct capitalization for the interpreter to recognize your commands. For example, onLoad is not the same as Onload.

Objects

In JavaScript, the topmost object is the window. Every window always has the following subobjects: *location* (the current URL), *history*, and *document*. These objects have the following properties, methods, and event handlers.

Object	Properties	Methods	Event handler
window	defaultStatus, status, window, frames	alert, close, confirm, open, prompt, setTimeout	onLoad, onUnload
location	hostname, href, pathname, protocol		
history	length	back, forward, go	
document	alinkColor, bgColor, fgColor, forms, lastModified, links, location, title	clear, close, open, write	

Depending on the actual loaded document, the document object has many subobjects, including the document's forms and links:

Object	Properties	Methods	Event handler
link	target		onClick, onMouseOver
form	action, method, name, target	submit	onSubmit

The form object may have its many subobjects, including text fields, text areas, and checkbox, radio, submit, and reset buttons.

Object	Properties	Methods	Event handler
text fields	defaultValue, name, value	focus, blur, select	onBlur, onChange, onFocus, onSelect
textarea	defaultValue, name, value	focus, blur, select	onBlur, onChange, onFocus, onSelect
checkbox	checked, defaultChecked, name, value	click	onClick
radio	checked, defaultChecked, length, name, value	click	onClick
button	name, value	click	onClick
submit	name, value	click	onClick
reset	name, value	click	onClick

The Math object provides a way to manipulate mathematical expressions. There are no event handlers associated with this object. Note that we do not describe the properties and methods associated with this object, since they are common mathematical functions.

Object	Properties	Methods
Math	E, LN2, LN10, LOG2E, LOG10E, PI, SQRT1_2, SQRT2	abs, acos, asin, atan, ceil, cos, exp, floor, log, max, min, pow, random, round, sin, sqrt, tan

You may find it convenient to use the "with" statement in functions that utilize many Math objects, since this removes the need to type "Math." at the beginning of every math object. For example:

```
with (Math){
x = round(i);
y = abs(x);
i = PI * y;
}
```

Properties

Objects have *properties* that describe their attributes.

Property	Applies to	Description	Syntax
defaultStatus	window	default message in status bar	window.defaultStatus
frames	window	array of objects containing frame windows	window.frames[*]
status	window	message in status bar	window.status
hostname	location	hostname of URL	location.host
href	location	entire URL	location.href
pathname	location	file path portion of URL	location.pathname
protocol	location	protocol portion of URL	location.protocol
alinkColor	document	color of anchor link on mouse-down	document.alinkColor
bgColor	document	color of document background	document.bgColor
fgColor	document	color of document foreground text	document.fgColor
forms	document	array of objects containing document forms	document.forms[*]
lastModified	document	last modification date	document.lastModified

Property	Applies to	Description	Syntax
linkColor	document	color of hyperlink	document.linkColor
location	document	complete URL of document	document.location
title	document	title of document	document.title
vlinkColor	document	color of visited links	document.vlinkColor
action	form	destination URL for form being submitted	formname.action
method	form	method for sending form input to user	formname.method
target	form, link	destination of completed form or clicked-on link	document.*.target
checked	checkbox, radio	selection state of checkbox or radio element (true or false)	name.checked
name	form, text, textarea, radio, checkbox, button	a string containing name of element	*.name
value	form, text, textarea, radio, checkbox, button	a string containing value of element	*.value

Methods

Objects can have associated *methods* (or procedures). These methods describe actions that the object can take, such as opening or closing a window.

Method	Applies to	Description	Syntax
alert	window	display an Alert dialog box	alert("message")
confirm	window	display a Confirm dialog box	confirm("message")
close	window	close window	window.close()
open	window	open new window	window.open("URL", "window name")
prompt	window	display a Prompt dialog box	prompt("message")
setTimeout	window	evaluate an expression after a certain amount of time	timeoutID=setTimeout(expression, msec)
back	history	load previous URL in history	history.back()
forward	history	load next URL in history list	history.forward()
go	history	load a URL in history list	history.go()
close	document	close output stream	document.close()
open	document	open output stream	document.open()
write	document	write expression	write(...)
writeln	document	write expression followed by a newline character	writeln(...)
submit	form	submit form	formname.submit()
blur	password, text, textarea	remove focus	*.blur()
focus	password, text, textarea	give focus to current object	*.focus()
select	password, text, textarea	select input area of object	*.select()
click	button, checkbox, radio, reset, submit	simulate mouse click	*.click()

Event Handlers

JavaScript is mostly event driven. This means that script execution is triggered by user events on the client. These user events apply to specific elements in the browser environment. Events include loading a document, clicking the mouse, or submitting a form. A script can use *event handlers* to cause specific JavaScript functions to be run in response to recognized user events.

User Event	User action	Event handler	Applies to
blur	removes focus from form element (opposite of focus)	onBlur	text fields, text areas, selections
click	clicks on button or link	onClick	buttons, links
change	changes value of form element	onChange	text fields, text areas, selections
focus	selects element for input (opposite of blur)	onFocus	text fields, text areas, selections
load	loads page	onLoad	documents
mouseover	moves mouse over link	onMouseOver	links
select	selects input field	onSelect	text fields, text areas
submit	submits form	onSubmit	form submit buttons
unload	leaves page	onUnload	documents

Statements

JavaScript statements provide a method for connecting and using objects and functions in your script. A statement is composed of keywords and may span multiple lines. This section contains a list of the keywords that may be used in a statement.

You may include multiple statements on a single line by separating them with semicolons.

break

For use in a while or for loop. It terminates the current loop and transfers program control to the statement following the terminated loop.

Syntax

```
break
```

Example

This function decrements the variable *i* in a while loop. Since the condition for this loop is always true, the loop would never end were it not for the break. The if statement in the loop checks to see if *i* equals 7, and if it does, break will terminate the loop, and *i*'s value will be printed.

```
function breaktest(){
    var i = 10
    while (true){
        i--
        if (i==7) {
            break
        }
    document.write(i)
    }
}
```

continue

To be used in a while or for loop. It causes statement execution to jump from the current to the next iteration of the loop. In a while loop, this will cause it to go to the condition check; in a for loop it will go to the update expression.

Syntax

```
continue
```

Examples

This function decrements the variable *i* in a while loop and prints the value of *i* on each iteration of the loop. The if statement in the loop checks to see if *i* equals 7, and if it does, continue will cause the loop to jump to the next iteration. Since the print command comes after the if statement, it will not be executed if continue is called. Thus, this function will print all the numbers except 7 between 9 and 1.

```
function continuetest(){
    var i = 10
    while (i>0){
        i--
        if (i==7) {
           continue
        document.write(i)
        }
    }
}
```

for

Creates a loop based on three expressions:

1. *An expression used to initialize a counter variable*
2. *A condition that is evaluated on each pass*
3. *An expression used to update the counter variable*

All of these expressions are optional and should be enclosed in parentheses and separated by semicolons. They are followed by the block of statements to be executed in the loop.

Syntax

```
for ([expression1]; [condition]; [expression]) {
   [statements in the loop]
}
```

expression1 can be a statement or variable declaration.

Example

This loop will print out the numbers from 1 to 5.

```
for (var x=1; x <=5; x++) {
    document.write{x}
}
```

for...in

Iterates a variable over all the properties of an object obj. For each distinct property, it executes the statements in the loop.

Syntax

```
for (var in obj) {
    [statements in the loop]
}
```

Example

The following function prints all the members in the telephone-extension example from the JavaScript chapter.

```
function printbook(){
   for (counter in lastname) {
      document.write("<P>"+ lastname[counter])
      document.write(" " +extension[counter])
   }
   document.close()
}
```

function

This is used to create a JavaScript function name. It may include parameters, which can be strings, numbers, and objects. Parameters are passed by value, so any changes made to them are not reflected globally.

Functions can be set to return a value by including a *return* statement specifying the value to return.

Syntax

```
function functionname([parameter1] [, parameter2][...,parametern])
{
   [statements] }
```

Examples

This function compares two input strings and returns true if they are equal.

```
function compstring(InString1, InString2) {
    if (InString1 == InString2) {
         return true;
    } else {
        return false;
    }
}
```

if...else

Executes statements if the condition is true. The else clause is optional and is executed if the condition is false.

Syntax

```
if (condition) {
   [statements]
} [else {
   [statements]
}]
```

Example

If MyString equals "Hello", "World" is appended to it. If not, the string is set to "Go away".

```
if ( MyString == "Hello" ) {
   MyString = MyString + "World"
} else {
   MyString = "Go away"
}
```

return

Specifies the value to be returned by a function.

Syntax

```
return expression
```

Example

The following function returns its argument, InStr, appended to the string "Hello ".

```
function AddHello(InStr) {
   return "Hello " + InStr
}
```

this

A keyword used to refer to the current object.

Syntax

`this[.propertyName]`

Example

We use "this" in our phone-book makeArray function:

```
function makeArray(n) {
this.length = n
for (var i=1; i <= n; i++)
        this[i] = null
        return this
}
```

var

Creates a variable and may initialize it to a value. Variable names can be any legal identifier, and the value can be any legal expression. The scope of a variable is the current function or, for variables declared outside a function, the current application.

To create a variable outside a function, you can simply assign a value to a variable name. However, it is good style to use var. It is required in functions when there is a global variable with the same name.

Syntax

```
var varname [= value] [..., varname [= value] ]
```

Examples

Create a variable named myvar:

```
var myvar
```

Create a variable named myvar and initialize it to 1:

```
var myvar = 1
```

Create variables named i and j and initialize them to 10:

```
var i,j = 10
```

while

Creates a loop that evaluates the expression condition, and if it is true, executes statements. The loop terminates when the condition is false.

Syntax

```
while (condition) {
   [statements]
}
```

Examples

This will print the numbers from 1 through 5. It is functionally equivalent to the example we used for the for loop.

```
var x=1
while (x <=5) {
    document.write{x}
    x++
}
```

with

Establishes a default object for the statements. Any property references without an object are assumed to be for the object. Note that the parentheses are required around object.

Syntax

```
with (object){
    statements
}
```

Examples

```
with (Math){
    x = round(i);
    y = abs(x);
    i = PI * y;
}
```

Conditional Expressions

A conditional expression can have one of two values based on a condition. The syntax is

```
(condition) ? value1 : val2
```

If condition is true, the expression has the value of value1, otherwise it has the value of value2. You can use a conditional expression anywhere you would use a standard expression.

For example, here is a use of a conditional expression in our phone-book database:

```
form.result.value = (foundMatch) ? ext[i] : "No match found"
```

This statement assigns the value in the variable ext[i] to the variable form.result.value if foundMatch is true. Otherwise it assigns "No match found" to the variable.

Useful URLs

There are many HTML resources for authors available on the Web. Here are some useful links.

General HTML and WWW Information

The World Wide Web Consortium

http://www.w3.org

RFC 1866: Hypertext Markup Language Specification Version 2.0

ftp://ds.internic.net/rfc/rfc1866.txt

WWW Frequently Asked Questions

http://www.boutell.com/faq/index.htm

Introductions to HTML

http://www.ncsa.uiuc.edu/demoweb/html-primer.html

HTML Style Guides

http://www.w3.org/hypertext/WWW/Provider/Style/Overview.html

http://info.med.yale.edu/caim/StyleManual_Top.HTML

HTML Working Group Mailing List Archive

http://www.ics.uci.edu/pub/ietf/html/

HTML Bibliographies

http://www.utirc.utoronto.ca/HTMLdocs/NewHTML/bibliography.html

http://info.med.yale.edu/caim/M_Resources.HTML

HTML Elements

Image Map Information

http://hoohoo.ncsa.uiuc.edu/docs/setup/admin/Imagemap.html

Forms Information

http://www.ncsa.uiuc.edu/SDG/Software/Mosaic/Docs/fill-out-forms/overview.html

Table Information

http://www.hpl.hp.co.uk/people/dsr/html/tables.html

CGI Information

Documentation

http://hoohoo.ncsa.uiuc.edu/docs/

http://hoohoo.ncsa.uiuc.edu/cgi/overview.html

Scripts for NCSA httpd: C Routines

ftp://ftp.ncsa.uiuc.edu/Web/httpd/Unix/ncsa_httpd/cgi/ncsa-default.tar.Z

Scripts for NCSA httpd: Perl Routines

ftp://ftp.ncsa.uiuc.edu/Web/httpd/Unix/ncsa_httpd/cgi/cgi-lib.pl.Z

CGI Standard

http://hoohoo.ncsa.uiuc.edu/cgi/overview.html

HTML Validation

Webtechs HTML Validation Service

http://www.webtechs.com/html-val-svc/

Weblint

http://www.khoros.unm.edu/staff/neilb

GIF Animation

Royal E. Frazier's GIF89a Document

http://members.aol.com/royalef/

Netscape Extensions

Extensions to the BODY Tag

http://home.netscape.com/assist/net_sites/bg/index.html

Netscape offers a number of GIF-format images suitable for backgrounds on their server. You can find these images at the URL:

http://home.netscape.com/assist/net_sites/bg/backgrounds.html

JavaScript

JavaScript FAQ

http://www.freqgrafx.com/411/jsfaq.html

JavaScript Examples

http://www.c2.org/~andreww/javascript/

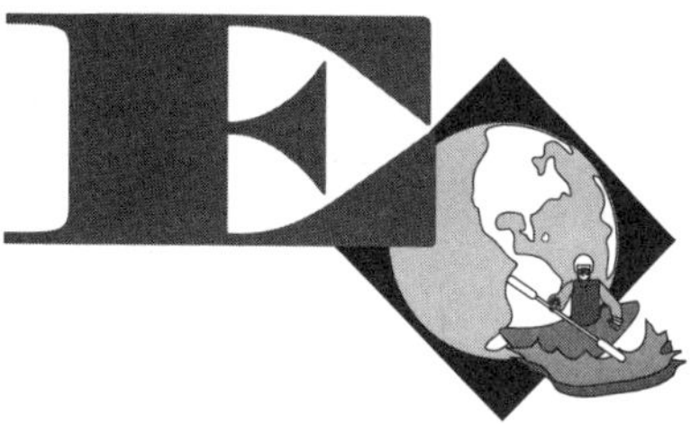

WWW Service Providers

This appendix contains a list of Web service providers. New service providers seem to pop up every day, so if you do not find a service provider that suits your needs listed here, there are a number of places you can check for additional listings on the Internet.

Criteria for Choosing a Provider

There are an overwhelming number of Web service providers around. Choosing the right one is important, since your provider will be an integral part of your business. Switching providers can also be painful, so getting it right the first time can make your life much simpler. To help you find a match, we've provided a list of questions to consider when choosing a

provider. Not all of the questions may apply to your situation, since the requirements for a site to host a personal home page are very different than the requirements for a business.

- What type of bandwidth does the provider have? If your customers can't reach you, you will lose business. A provider with connections to multiple sources and a high-speed connection is a must.
- Does the provider allow access to the CGI directory? If not, does the provider have generic CGI programs that can be tailored to meet your needs?
- Support. Does the provider have 24-hour support? What are its procedures for dealing with outages?
- Price. There are many methods for charging for services. In general, you can expect to receive a fixed amount of disk space for your monthly service charge. Some providers allow an unlimited amount of transmission as part of the basic service, while others may place a surcharge on transmissions in excess of a base amount. If you anticipate building a high-volume site, you will probably find it more economical to choose a service provider with no limit on transmission. On the other hand, providers that do not charge for transmission may also have difficulty maintaining enough bandwidth to service all of their customers.
- Availability of a secure server. If you plan on conducting financial transactions as part of your site, you should make sure that your provider has a server that uses secure service technology.

When choosing a Web provider, keep in mind that the Web is a global entity. Your audience may be located anywhere in the world; so as long as *you* have a way to get onto the Internet, your Web provider does not need to be close to you (as opposed to a general Internet service provider, for which you would probably want to have a local access point).

Each provider is listed in the following format:

Provider name
Surface mail address (if available)
Phone number
Fax number
Internet e-mail address
URL

If you are a provider and would like to be added to this list in future editions of this book, please send your update to Vivian@catalog.com.

World Wide Web Service Providers

a2i communications
1211 Park Avenue #202
San Jose, CA 95126–2924
408–293–8078
Fax: 408–263–0461
support@rahul.net
http://www.rahul.net/

Able Technical Services
ABLECOM.NET
P.O. Box 26530
San Jose, CA 95159
408–441–6000
howard@ablecom.net
http://www.ablecom.net/

Access Nevada, Inc.
702–294–0480
Fax: 702–293–3278
info@accessnv.com
http://www.accessnv.com/

Achilles Internet Limited
613–723–6624
Fax: 613–723–8583
office@achilles.net
http://www.achilles.net/

Advanced Network Solutions
http@adnetsol.com
http://www.adnetsol.com/

Berbee Information Networks Corp.
455 Science Drive
Madison, WI 53711–1058
608–233–5222
Fax: 608–233–9795
info@binc.net
http://www.binc.net/

Best Internet Communications, Inc.

421 Castro Street
Mountain View, CA 94041
415–964–2378
Fax: 415–691–4195
info@best.com
http://www.best.com/

BlueMarble

Bloomington, IN
support@bluemarble.net
http://www.bluemarble.net/

BBN Planet Corporation

150 Cambridge Park Drive
Cambridge, MA 02140
800–472–4565
Fax: 617–873–5620
net-info@bbnplanet.com
http://www.bbnplanet.com/

Board of Directors Internet Service

303-571-5271 voice
303-571-5273 FAX
lc@bod.net
http://www.bod.net/

Canada Connect Corporation

201 1039 17 Avenue SW
Calgary, Alberta T2T 0B2
Canada
403–777–2025
Fax: 403–777–2026
info@canuck.com
http://www.canuck.com/

Charm.Net

2228 E. Lombard St.
Baltimore, MD 21231
410–558–3900
Fax: 410–558–3901
admin@Charm.Net
http://www.charm.net/

CERFnet

California Education and Research
Federation Network
P.O. Box 85608
San Diego, CA 92186–9784
800–876–2373
619–455–3900
Fax: 619–455–3990
sales@cerf.net
http://www.cerf.net/

CHANNEL 1 Communications

1030 Massachusetts Avenue
Cambridge, MA 02138
617–864–0100
Fax: 617–354–3100
support@channel1.com
http://www.channel1.com/

CICNet

Committee on Institutional Cooperation
Network
ITI Building
2901 Hubbard Drive
Ann Arbor, MI 48105
313–998–6703
800–947–4754
info@cic.net
http://www.cic.net/

CityNet
P.O. Box 3235
Charleston, WV 25332
304–342–5700
http://www.citynet.net/

Clarknet
Clark Internet Services, Inc.
10600 Route 108
Ellicott City, MD 21042
800–735–2258
410–254–3900
Fax: 410–730–9765
info@clark.net
http://www.clark.net/

Colorado SuperNet (CSN)
SuperNet Inc.
One Denver Place
999 18th Street
Denver, CO 80202
303–296–8202
Fax: 303–296–8224
help@csn.net
http://www.csn.net/csn/

Computer Service Langenbach GmbH
Germany
http://www.csl-gmbh.net/csl/

Connect.com.au pty ltd
129 Hawthorn Road
Caulfield
Victoria 3161 Australia
61–3–528–2239
1–800–818–262 (Australia-wide)
Fax: 61–3–528–5887
connect@connect.connect.com.au
http://www.connect.com.au/

Crossroads Communications
P.O. Box 30250
Mesa, AZ 85275
602–813–9040
800–892–7040
Fax: 602–545–7470
http://xroads.xroads.com/home.html/

CTS Network Services (CTSNET)
Division of Datel Systems Inc.
4444 Convoy Street, Suite 300
San Diego, CA 92111–3761
619–637–3637
Fax: 619–637–3630
info@crash.cts.com (server)
support@crash.cts.com (human)
http://www.cts.com/

CyberGate, Inc.
305–428–4283
Fax: 305–428–7977
info@gate.net
http://www.gate.net/services.html/

Data Basix
Ray Harwood
P.O. Box 18324
Tucson, AZ 85731
602–721–1988
Fax: 602–721–7240
info@data.basix.com (server)
sales@data.basix.com (human)
http://data.basix.com/

Dayton Internet Services

Dayton Internet Services
3131 South Dixie Drive
Suite 103
Dayton, OH 45439
513–643–0188
Fax: 513–643–0190
http://www.firstnet.net/About.html/

Demon

Demon Internet Systems (DIS)
44–081–349–0063
internet@demon.co.uk
http://www.demon.co.uk/

Direct Network Access

2039 Shattuck Avenue, Suite 206
Berkeley, CA 94704
510–649–6110
Fax: 510–649–7130
info@dnai.com (Automated response)
support@dnai.com (User technical support)
http://www.dnai.com/

Dreamscape Online

315–446–2626
Fax: 315–446–2626
http://www.dreamscape.com/

EmeraldNet

1718 East Speedway
Suite #315
Tucson, AZ 85719
520–670–1994
Fax: 520–670–1922
INFO@Emerald.NET
http://www.emerald.net/

EUnet Communications Services BV

Singel 540
1017 AZ Amsterdam
The Netherlands
31–20–623–3803
Fax: 31–20–622–4657
info@EU.net
http://www.eu.net/

Frontier Internet

303–385–4177
jbd@frontier.net
http://www.frontier.net/

Frontier Internet Services

London, UK
01–71–242–3383
Fax: 01–71–242–3384
support@ftech.co.uk
http://www.ftech.co.uk/frontier/frontier.htm/

GetNet International, Inc.

7325 North 16th Street, Suite #140
Phoenix, AZ 85020
602–943–3119
info@getnet.com
http://www.getnet.com/

Global Enterprise Service, Inc.

3 Independence Way
Princeton, NJ 08540
800–358–4437
609–258–2400
Fax: 609–897–7310
market@jvnc.net
http://www.jvnc.net/

Helix Internet
#902–900 West Hastings
Vancouver, B.C., V6C–1E6
Canada
604–689–8544
Fax: 604–685–2554
accounts@helix.net
http://www.helix.net/sub/about.html/

HoloNet
Information Access Technologies, Inc.
46 Shattuck Square, Suite 11
Berkeley, CA 94704–1152
510–704–0160
Fax: 510–704–8019
info@holonet.net
http://www.holonet.net/holonet/

HookUp
HookUp Communication Corporation
519–747–4110
Fax: 519–746–3521
info@hookup.net
http://www.hookup.net/

IDS World Network
InteleCom Data Systems
5835 Post Rd., Suite 214
East Greenwich, RI 02818
800–IDS–1680
Fax: 401–886–4050
info@ids.net
http://www.ids.net/idstext.html/

IndyNet
5348 N. Tacoma Ave.
Indianapolis, IN 46220
317–251–5208
http://gopher.indy.net/index.html/

InfoCom Networks
P.O. Box 590343
Houston, TX 77259–0343
helpdesk@infocom.net
http://www.infocom.net/

Inter'Acces
Montreal, Quebec
Canada
514–367–0002
sales@Interax.net
http://www.interax.net/

InterAccess
3345 Commercial Avenue
Northbrook, IL 60062
800–967–1580
708–498–2542
Fax: 708–671–0113
http://www.interaccess.com/

Internet Direct, Inc.
800–879–3624
602–274–0100 (Phoenix)
602–324–0100 (Tucson)
Fax: 602–274–8518
sales@direct.net
http://www.indirect.com/

Internet Express
800–592–1240
info@usa.net
http://www.usa.net/

The Internet MainStreet
334 State Street, Suite 106
Los Altos, CA 94022
415–941–1068
info@mainstreet.net
http://www.mainstreet.net/

KAIWAN

Knowledge Added Information Wide Area Network Corporation
18001 Sky Park Circle, Suite J
Irvine, CA 92714
714–638–2139
Fax: 714–638–0455
info@kaiwan.com
http://www.kaiwan.com/

Klink Net Communications

Gloversville, NY
518–725–3000
800–KLINK–123
admin@klink.net
http://www.klink.net/

Lanka Internet Services, Ltd (LISL)

5th Floor, IBM Building
48 Nawam Mawatha
Colombo 2, Sri Lanka
94–1–342974
Fax: 94–1–343056
info@lanka.net
http://www.lanka.net/lisl.html/

LinkAGE Online

webmaster@hk.linkage.net
http://www.hk.linkage.net/

LinkNet

318–442–LINK
Fax: 318–449–9750
support@linknet.net
http://www.linknet.net/

The Little Garden

3004 16th St., #204
San Francisco, CA 94103
415–487–1902
Fax: 415–552–6088
sales@tlg.net
http://tlg.org/

Maestro

Maestro Technologies, Inc.
29 John Street, Suite 1601
New York, NY 10038
212–240–9600
Fax: 212–566–0315
info@maestro.com (server)
staff@maestro.com (human)
http://www.maestro.com/

Magic Online Services

1483 Pembina Hwy. #150
Winnipeg, Manitoba R2T 2C6
Canada
204–949–7777
Fax: 204–949–7790
sbrooker@magic.mb.ca
http://www.magic.mb.ca/

MCSNet

1300 West Belmont, Suite 405
Chicago, IL 60657
312–248–8649
Fax: 312–248–8649
support@mcs.com
http://www.mcs.net/

Michigan BizServe

Online Technologies Corporation
staff@BizServe.com
http://bizserve.com/

Milwaukee Internet X

Mix Communications
P.O. Box 17166
Milwaukee, WI 53217
414–962–8172
wwwinfo@mixcom.com
http://www.mixcom.com/

MindVOX

Phantom Access Technologies, Inc.
175 Fifth Avenue, Suite 2614
New York, NY 10010
800–MindVox
212–989–2418
Fax: 212–989–8648
info@phantom.com
http://www.phantom.com/

MSEN, Inc.

320 Miller Avenue
Ann Arbor, MI 48103
313–998–4562
Fax: 313–998–4563
info@msen.com
http://www.msen.com/

MUC.DE e.V.

Muenchner Technologiezentrum
Frankfurter Ring 193 a
80807 Muenchen
Germany
089–324683–0
vorstand@muc.de
http://www/muc.de/

Mundo Internet

Centro de Investigación y de Estudios Avanzados del IPN
Unidad Mérida
Sección de Telemática
km 6 Antigua Carretera a Progreso
Apdo. Postal 73 Cordemex Mérida, Yuc. CP 97310
99–812960, ext. 265
Fax: 99–812923
http://w3mint.cieamer.conacyt.mx/

NeoSoft, Inc.

1770 St. James Place
Suite 500
Houston, TX 77056
800–GET–NEOSOFT
713–968–5800
sales@neosoft.com
http://www.neosoft.com/

Netcom Online Communication Services

P.O. Box 20774
San Jose, CA 95160
408–554–8649
info@netcom.com
http://www.netcom.com/

NETConnect

Cedar City, UT
801–865–7032
http://www.tcd.net/

NetHeaven

518–885–1295
800–910–6671
stpeters@NetHeaven.com
http://www.netheaven.com/

Netrail, Inc.

2007 N. 15 St., Suite 5
Arlington, VA 22201
703–524–4800
Fax: 703–524–5510
sales@netrail.net
http://www.netrail.net/

Network Wizards
PO Box 343
Menlo Park, CA 94026
415–326–2060
Fax: 415–326–4672
info@nw.com
http://catalog.com/

North Shore Access
Eco Software, Inc.
145 Munroe Street, Suite 405
Lynn, MA 01901
617–593–3110
info@northshore.ecosoft.com
http://northshore.ecosoft.com/

NovaLink
Inner Circle Technologies, Inc.
79 Boston Turnpike, Suite 409
Shrewsbury, MA 01545
800–274–2814
508–754–9910
info@novalink.com
http://www.novalink.com/

Nuance Network Services
904 Bob Wallace Avenue, Suite 119
Huntsville, AL 35801
205–533–4296
info@nuance.com
http://www.nuance.com/

OnRamp
1950 Stemmons Freeway
Suite 5061 – INFOMART
Dallas, TX 75207
214–746–4710
Fax: 214–713–5400
Faxback: 214–746–4852
info@onramp.net
http://www.onramp.net/

Open Door Networks, Inc.
110 S. Laurel St.
Ashland, OR 97520
503–488–4127
help@opendoor.com
http://www.opendoor.com/

OuterNet Connections
8235 Shoal Creek, #105
Austin, TX 78758
512–345–3573
info@outer.net
http://www.outer.net/

Panix Public Access Unix
110 Riverside Drive
New York, NY 10024
212–741–4400
infobot@panix.com
http://www.panix.com/

Pavilion Internet
Brighton, Sussex
44–0–1273–607072
Fax: 44–0–1273–607073
info@pavilion.co.uk
http://www.pavilion.co.uk/

Performance Systems International, Inc. (PSI)
510 Huntmar Park Drive
Herndon, VA 22070
800–827–7482
Fax: 800–329–7741
info@psi.com
http://www.psi.net/

Pacific Information eXchange, Inc. NETwork (PIXINET)

1142 Auahi Street, Suite 2788
Honolulu, HI 96814
info@pixi.com
http://www.pixi.com/

Pegasus Networks

PO Box 284
Broadway Q 4006
Australia
61–7–257–1111
Fax: 61–7–257–1087
pegasus@peg.apc.org
http://www.peg.apc.org/

PIPEX

Unipalm Ltd.
44–223–424616
Fax: 44–223–426868
pipex@unipalm.co.uk
http://www.pipex.net/

Planet Access Networks

55 Rt. 206 – Suite E
Stanhope, NJ 07874
201–691–4704
info@planet.net
http://www.planet.net/

Portal Communications, Inc.

20863 Stevens Creek Boulevard
Suite 200
Cupertino, CA 95014
408–973–9111
http://www.portal.com/

Power Net

Los Angeles, CA
310–643–4908
sales@power.net
http://www.power.net/

QuakeNet Internet Services

830 Wilmington Road
San Mateo, CA 94402
415–655–6607
Fax: 415–377–0635
info@quake.net
http://www.quake.net/

RainDrop Laboratories

5627 SW 45th
Portland, OR 97221–3505
info@agora.rain.com
http://www.rdrop.com/agora/

Real/Time Communications

6721 N. Lamar, Suite 103
Austin, TX 78752
512–451–0046
Fax: 512–459–3858
sales@realtime.net
http://www.realtime.net/

RedIRIS

Secretaria RedIRIS
Fundesco
Alcala 61
28014 Madrid
Spain
34–1–435–1214
Fax: 34–1–578–1773
secretaria@rediris.es
http://www.rediris.es/

Renaissance Internet Services

Phase IV Systems, Inc.
Huntsville, AL
custsrv@ro.com
http://www.ro.com/

Seanet

OSD, Inc.
Columbia Seafirst Center
701 Fifth Avenue, Suite 6801
Seattle, WA 98104
206–343–7828
Fax: 206–628–0722
seanet@seanet.com
http://www.seanet.com/

Sierra-Net

Lake Tahoe/Northern Nevada
702–832–6911
Fax: 702–831–3970
info@sierra.net
http://www.sierra.net/

South Coast Computing Services, Inc.

713–661–3301
Fax: 713–917–5005
info@sccsi.com
http://www.sccsi.com/

SSNet

302–378–1386
800–331–1386
info@ssnet.com
http://ssnet.com/

Structured Network Systems, Inc.

503–656–3530
800–881–0962
Fax: 503–656–3235
sales@structured.net
http://www.structured.net/

Suburbia PAN

P.O. Box 2031
Barker 3122
Australia
helpdesk@suburbia.apana.org.au
http://suburbia.apana.org.au/

Supernet

800–746–0777
info@supernet.net
http://www.supernet.net/

SWITCH

SWITCH Head Office
Limmatquai 138
CH–8001 Zurich
Switzerland
41–1–268–1515
Fax: 41–1–268–1568
info@switch.ch
http://www.switch.ch/

Systems Solutions Inc.

2108 East Thomas Road, Suite 200
Phoenix, AZ 85016–7758
602–955–5566
Fax: 602–955–0085
webmaster@syspac.com
http://www.syspac.com/

Tachyon Communications Corporation

100 Rialto Place, Suite 747
Melbourne, FL 32901
407–728–8081
Fax: 407–725–6315
sales@tach.net
http://www.tach.net/

TANet

Computer Center, Ministry of Education
12th Floor, Number 106
Sec. 2, Hoping East Road
Taipei, Taiwan
Attn: Chen Wen-Sung
886–2–7377010
Fax: 886–2–7377043
nisc@twnmoe10.edu.tw
http://www.edu.tw/

Teleport

Beaverton, OR
503–223–4245
info@teleport.com
http://www.teleport.com/

TerraNet, Inc.

729 Boylston Street, Floor 5
Boston, MA 02116
617–450–9000
sales@terra.net
http://www.terra.net/

Texas Metronet

1701 W. Euless Blvd.
Metro Center, Suites 130, 131b
Euless, TX 76040–6819
214–705–2900
Fax: 817–267–2400
info@metronet.com
http://www.metronet.com/

UltraNet Communications, Inc.

910 Boston Post Road, Suite 220
Marlboro, MA 01752
508–229–8400
info@ultranet.com
http://www.ultranet.com/

UniComp Technologies International Corporation

15851 Dallas Parkway, Suite 946
Dallas, TX 75248
214–663–3155
Fax: 214–663–3170
info@unicomp.net
http://www.unicomp.net/

UUNET Canada Inc.

1 Yonge Street
Suite 1801
Toronto, Ontario, M5E 1W7
Canada
416–368–6621
Fax: 416–369–0515
info@uunet.ca
http://www.uunet.ca/

UUNET Technologies, Inc.

3060 Williams Drive
Fairfax, VA 22031–4648
800–488–6383
703–206–5600
Fax: 703–206–5601
info@uu.net
http://www.alter.net/

Vector Internet Services

12 South 6th Street
Minneapolis, MN 55402
612–288–0880
Fax: 612–288–0889
info@visi.com
http://www.visi.com/

Vnet Internet Access, Inc.

PO Box 31474
Charlotte, NC 28231
800–377–3282
info@vnet.net
http://www.vnet.net/

WestNet Internet Services

Westchester County, NY
914–967–7816
chris@WestNet.com
http://www.westnet.com/

Water Wheel Systems

Marlton, NJ
609–596–0032
info@waterw.com
http://www.waterw.com/

Whole Earth 'Lectronic Link (WELL)

27 Gate Five Road
Sausalito, CA 94965
415–332–4335
info@well.sf.ca.us
http://www.well.sf.ca.us/

WIDE

c/o Prof. Jun Murai
KEIO University
5322 Endo, Fujisawa, 252
Japan
81–466–47–5111 ext. 3330
jun@wide.ad.jp
http://www.wide.ad.jp/

Wimsey Information Services Inc.

8523 Commerce Court
Burnaby, BC V5N 4A3
Canada
604–257–1111
Fax: 604–257–1110
info@wimsey.com
http://www.wimsey.com/wimsey/

@wizard.com

Las Vegas, NV
702–871–4461
Fax: 702–871–4249
gajake@wizard.com
http://www.wizard.com/

WombatNet

236 Hamilton Avenue
Palo Alto, CA 94301
415–462–8800
Fax: 415–462–8804
info@batnet.com
http://www.batnet.com/

The World

Software Tool & Die
1330 Beacon Street
Brookline, MA 02146
617–739–0202
office@world.std.com
http://world.std.com/

World Web Limited

906 King Street
Alexandria, VA 22314
support@worldweb.net
http://www.worldweb.net/

WorldWide Access

P.O. Box 285
Vernon Hills, IL 60061–0285
708–367–1870
Fax: 708–367–1872
http://www.wwa.com/

The Xensei Corporation

Boston South Shore area
617–376–6342
info@xensei.com
http://www.xensei.com/

XNet Information Systems

3080 E. Ogden Ave. , #202
Lisle, IL 60532
708–983–6064
Fax: 708–983–6879
info@xnet.com
http://www.xnet.com/

Zilker Internet Park

1106 Clayton Lane, Suite 500W
Austin, TX 78723
512–206–3850
Fax: 512–206–3852
support@zilker.net
http://www.zilker.net/

zNET

777 South Pacific Coast Highway
Suite 204
Solana Beach, CA 92075
619–755–7772
Fax: 619–755–8149
info@znet.com
http://www.znet.com/

Glossary

ACK

Acknowledgment. A message sent to indicate that data has been received.

anchor

One of the ends of a hypertext link.

anonymous FTP

A mechanism that allows public files to be copied from systems on the Internet without having a login account on the system. It uses the login name “anonymous” with a password of “guest” or the e-mail address of the person using anonymous login. Browsers use anonymous FTP when an FTP URL is chosen.

ASCII

American Standard Code for Information Interchange. It is a 7-bit code that can represent up to 128 characters. Appendix B contains a list of ASCII characters.

attribute

An optional indicator that can be added to markup tags in order to specify a variation in the way the tag is displayed.

browser

An application used to display HTML documents. Browsers may be used to display local HTML documents or to retrieve documents across the Internet. Some popular browsers are Netscape Navigator and NCSA Mosaic.

cache

Hold information in memory. Many browsers temporarily keep copies of documents in a cache directory on the local hard disk so that they do not have to be reloaded over the network each time they are referenced.

cello

Along with NCSA Mosaic, one of the first graphical browsers available for Windows. It was created at the Cornell Legal Information Institute (LII).

CERN

European Center for Particle Physics, located in Geneva, Switzerland. Birthplace of the Web.

CGI

Common Gateway Interface. An interface for running external programs or scripts under an information server, such as a Web server. A common use of a CGI script is handling data from HTML forms.

clickable image

See Image map.

client

A general term for a computer or application that can access and retrieve information from a server computer. A Web client is usually called a Web browser.

container

See Markup Tag.

CSLIP

Compressed SLIP. See the entry for SLIP.

dial-up

A connection made between machines using phone lines and modems.

DTD

Data Type Definition for the HyperText Markup Language; provides a formal description of HTML with respect to SGML.

element

A portion of an HTML document delineated by markup tags.

entity

An HTML symbol representing a special character. A list of ISO character entities may be found in Appendix B.

e-mail address

The address that is used to send electronic mail to a specified destination. For example, Vivian's e-mail address is "vivian@catalog.com".

FAQ

Frequently Asked Questions. List of frequently asked questions and their answers.

finger

An application that shows information about all of the users logged on to a system. It can also display information about a particular user. It typically shows full name, last login time, idle time, terminal line, and terminal location (where applicable). It may also display plan and project files left by the user.

form

Fill-out forms are HTML tags that were added to HTML 2.0, which enable documents to display interactive elements used on forms, such as radio buttons, checkboxes, and text-entry boxes.

FTP

File Transfer Protocol. The protocol that defines the way in which files are exchanged around the Internet. FTP also refers to the name of the application that uses the FTP protocol.

FYI

For Your Information. FYI also represents a series of informational documents about the Internet published by the Internet Engineering Task Force (IETF).

gateway

A program or device that passes information between networks or applications.

GIF

Graphic Interchange Format. An image storage format developed by Compuserve. It is the most widely supported image format on the Web.

Gopher

A menu-driven information service developed at the University of Minnesota that makes information across the Internet available through a single application. Gopher clients can get information from any accessible Gopher server, providing the user with a single "Gopher space" of information.

head

The beginning of an HTML document. The head portion of an HTML document should contain the document's title.

host

A computer; usually one that is connected to a network.

home page

A browser's home page refers to the first document that is loaded when the browser is started up. A user's personal home page refers to a Web page that describes and introduces that individual. A company or organization home page is its top-level or starting Web page.

hostname

The name given to a computer.

HTML

HyperText Markup Language. The language in which Web documents are written; what this book is about.

HTTP

HyperText Transfer Protocol. The protocol used to transfer HTML documents on the Web.

hotlist

The term used in Mosaic to describe the list of URLs that it remembers; also known as a bookmark list.

hypermedia

Hypermedia is hypertext which may include nontext elements such as images, video and sound. The Web is a hypermedia system.

hypertext

A hypertext document contains links to other parts of the document or to other documents. Users can select hypertext links in order to view documents in a nonlinear and individual way. The term was coined by Ted Nelson in 1965.

IETF

Internet Engineering Task Force. The technical group that works on protocol standards used on the Internet.

image map

An image map is a graphical image containing "hot spots." When a hot spot is clicked on by a user, the browser loads the corresponding document.

Interlaced GIF

The scanlines in an interlaced GIF have been rearranged so that when it is viewed in a browser with appropriate support, it first appears with poor resolution and then, over time, improves in resolution until the entire image is loaded. This is a useful technique for giving users a quick impression of the image, without having to wait for it to be entirely loaded.

inline image

Inline images in HTML documents are images that appear as part of the document rather than shown by an external viewer.

internet

While an internet is a network, the term "internet" is usually used to refer to a collection of networks interconnected with routers.

Internet

(Note the capital "I.") The Internet is the largest internet in the world.

internet address

An IP address that uniquely identifies a node on an internet. An Internet address (capital "I") uniquely identifies a node on the Internet.

Internet Relay Chat (IRC)

A worldwide "party line" protocol that allows one to converse with other people on the Internet in real time via typed comments.

IP address

The 32-bit address defined by the Internet Protocol in STD 5, RFC 791. It is usually represented in dotted decimal notation; for example, 10.0.0.51.

ISO

International Organization for Standardization. An international standards body that defines many technical standards.

JPEG

Joint Photographic Experts Group. A standard format for image storage created by this group. It is a popular image storage format on the Web.

knowbot

Knowbots (or softbots) are programs that wander the Web collecting document titles and URLs. These are then indexed and can be searched by users.

line-mode browser

A nongraphical Web browser. These browsers may be used on dumb terminals. Although they cannot display graphics, most of the other features in a graphics-based browser may still be accessed with such browsers. Lynx is one of the most popular browsers of this type.

link

A link (or hyperlink) is the pointer in a hypertext document that points to another location or another document.

Lynx

A line-mode browser developed at the University of Kansas. Versions are available for many platforms, including DOS.

mail gateway

A computer that connects two or more electronic mail systems (including dissimilar mail systems) and transfers messages between them.

mail server

A software program that distributes files or information in response to requests sent via e-mail. Internet examples include Almanac and netlib. Mail servers have also been used in Bitnet to provide FTP-like services.

mailing list

A list of e-mail addresses used to send e-mail messages to groups of people. Generally, a special-interest group mailing list is used to discuss a specific topic.

markup language

A language that is used to specify document formats by embedding tags within the document. These tags are then interpreted by browsers in order to properly display the document.

MIME

Multipurpose Internet Mail Extension. An extension to Internet e-mail which provides the ability to transfer nontextual data, such as graphics, audio and fax. It is defined in RFC 1341.

Mosaic

One of the most popular Web browsers. The first widely used graphical browser. See also NCSA.

MPEG

Motion Picture Experts Group. One of the most widely used formats for storing video on the Internet.

NCSA

National Center for Supercomputing Applications based at the University of Illinois. This is where NCSA Mosaic was developed.

netiquette

A pun on "etiquette" referring to proper behavior on a network.

Netnews

A bulletin board system.

NNTP

Network News Transfer Protocol. The protocol used to transfer network news. It is defined in RFC 977.

OS

Operating System. The program that controls a computer's hardware. Operating systems typically control the use of the CPU (through a scheduler), memory, and peripheral devices (through device drivers). User applications send requests to the operating system to access the computer.

Perl

Practical Extraction and Report Language. It is an interpreted language created by Larry Wall. Originally based on UNIX systems, it is now available on other platforms, including DOS. A number of useful HTML filters have been written in Perl.

PPP

Point-to-Point Protocol—defined in RFC 1171. It provides a method for transmitting packets over serial point-to-point links.

POP

Post Office Protocol. A protocol designed to allow single-user hosts to read mail from a server. There are three versions: POP, POP2 and POP3. Later versions are not compatible with earlier versions.

post

To send a message to a newsgroup or e-mail list. Also, a method for accessing a CGI application.

protocol

A standard communication format allowing networked computers to exchange information. Protocols are developed for each kind of information exchange; for example, electronic mail uses the SMTP protocol, and the Web uses, among others, the HTTP protocol.

proxy server

A proxy server acts by keeping local copies of documents requested by users. When a local user requests a document, the proxy server is first consulted to see if a copy is held there. If it is, the user receives the document much more quickly than were it remotely retrieved.

Quicktime

A digital video and audio standard developed by Apple Computer.

RFC

Request For Comments. A document series, begun in 1969, which describes the Internet suite of protocols and related experiments. Not all (in fact, very few) RFCs describe Internet standards, but all Internet standards are written up as RFCs.

RFC 822

The Internet standard format for electronic-mail message headers. Mail experts often refer to "822 messages." The name comes from "RFC 822," which contains the specification (STD 11, RFC 822). 822 format was previously known as 733 format.

RFC 1392

Internet Glossary. If you run across an Internet-related term that isn't defined here, check the Internet Glossary. It is available at ftp://ds.internic.net/rfc/rfc1392.txt

RFC 1866

Hypertext Markup Language Specification Version 2.0. It is available at ftp://ds.internic.net/rfc/rfc1866.txt.

robot

See knowbot.

server

A program that handles certain types of requests on a continuous basis. For example, a mailing list server handles requests for list subscriptions and may also handle archive file requests from list members.

SGML

Standard Generalized Markup Language. SGML is a broad language used to define specific markup languages. HTML is a particular application of SGML.

signature

The three- or four-line message at the bottom of a piece of e-mail or a Usenet article which identifies the sender. Many mail programs allow you to set up a signature and automatically attach it to all the messages that you send. Long signatures (over five lines) are generally frowned upon.

SLIP

Serial Line IP. A protocol used to run IP over serial lines, such as telephone circuits or RS-232 cables, interconnecting two systems. SLIP is defined in RFC 1055.

SMTP

Simple Mail Transfer Protocol. A protocol defined in STD 10, RFC 821, used to transfer electronic mail between computers. It is a server-to-server protocol, so other protocols are used to access the messages.

spider

See knowbot.

tag

See markup language.

TCP/IP Protocol Suite

Transmission Control Protocol over Internet Protocol. This is a common shorthand which refers to the suite of transport and application protocols which runs over IP.

Telnet

Telnet is the Internet standard protocol for remote terminal connection service. It is defined in STD 8, RFC 854, and extended with options by many other RFCs.

UNIX

One of the most popular operating systems in use on the Internet today.

URL

Uniform Resource Locator. The address for a document on the Web. The format for a URL is

```
protocol://pathname
```

URN

Uniform Resource Name.

Usenet

A collection of thousands of topically named newsgroups, the computers which run the protocols, and the people who read and submit Usenet news. Not all Internet hosts subscribe to Usenet, and not all Usenet hosts are on the Internet.

viewer

A special-purpose application program for displaying data in specific formats. For example, a GIF viewer is used to display GIF images.

WAIS

Wide Area Information Servers. A distributed information service which offers simple natural-language input, indexed searching for fast retrieval, and a "relevance feedback" mechanism which allows the results of initial searches to influence future searches.

whois

An Internet program which allows users to query databases of people and other Internet entities, such as domains, networks, and hosts. The original whois databases are kept at the Internet Network Information Center (NIC) or Data Defense Network (NIC), depending on what you need, but many companies and educational institutions also make whois databases available now. The information for people shows a person's company name, address, phone number and e-mail address.

WWW

World Wide Web (W3). A hypertext-based, distributed information system created by researchers at CERN in Switzerland. Users may create, edit or browse hypertext documents.

Zine

On-line magazine.

INDEX

A

B

C

G

I

J

K

L

M

N

O

P

T

U

V

W

Y